How Economics Professors Can Stop Failing Us

How Economics Professors Can Stop Failing Us

The Discipline at a Crossroads

Steven Payson

LEXINGTON BOOKS
Lanham • Boulder • New York • London

Published by Lexington Books
An imprint of The Rowman & Littlefield Publishing Group, Inc.
4501 Forbes Boulevard, Suite 200, Lanham, Maryland 20706
www.rowman.com

Unit A, Whitacre Mews, 26-34 Stannary Street, London SE11 4AB

British Library Cataloguing in Publication Information Available

Library of Congress Cataloging-in-Publication Data Available

ISBN 978-0-7391-9833-9 (cloth : alk. paper)
ISBN 978-0-7391-9834-6 (electronic)

∞™ The paper used in this publication meets the minimum requirements of American National Standard for Information Sciences—Permanence of Paper for Printed Library Materials, ANSI/NISO Z39.48-1992.

Printed in the United States of America

In memory of
Professor Kelvin John Lancaster,
one of the greatest economics professors who ever lived.

Regardless of this book's title, professors like
Kelvin Lancaster could never fail us!

Contents

Preface

There seem to be three general types of "economics books" these days: First, you have your hardcore technical books that only economists, or graduate students in economics, could understand and truly love (and often only libraries can actually afford). Then you have your "economics made easy" books for everyone to understand, that usually go into recent economic history, such as how the economic crisis of 2008–2009 happened, often from the perspective of an author with some inside information about the events that took place. And finally, you have your economic policy books on particular heated debates involving economic issues, such as arguments for or against "economic globalization," where the author takes a position on the debate and uses their book to support it. Well, for whatever it's worth, this book does not fall under *any* of these categories. In fact, it does not seem to fall under *any category* that I could think of, but I suppose this does not say very much. So I will try again:

This book is an exposé on what is terribly wrong with economics professors these days, which many people do not realize, including many economics professors themselves. There you have it. So it *is* an economics book of sorts as well, but it is written for anyone in the general public who might like to know, in fact, how economics professors have been failing us, and how they can stop doing it.

If you, yourself, happen to know something about economics professors—or if you happen to be one yourself—or have had the experience of being a student in an economics class, then you might already have some opinions on this topic. Perhaps, from whatever experience you might have had, you might not believe that there are things that are terribly wrong with economics professors. That is fine—you just didn't know any better—and that is what this book is for; you will begin to know soon enough.

I do more than complain about economics professors, however. I offer solutions for how the profession can and should greatly improve. For readers to understand my critiques, and my proposed solutions, I do have to explain some things about economics; otherwise, none of it will make any sense. But again, readers do not need to be experts on economics or even economics students, to understand this book.

If you do happen to be an economics professor, though, you had *better* read this book! After all, I *am* talking about *you.* So, wouldn't you rather at least hear this conversation than to have it take place behind your back? Likewise, if you are a graduate student in economics, you too really need to read this book, especially if you aspire to become an economics professor someday. After reading this book, you might want to give that aspiration a bit more thought.

Now let us get more serious: This is an exposé that, in actuality, takes on the academic economics profession *on its own terms*, and *in its own language*. It provides, in fact, a detailed analysis of how the incentive system within the academic economics profession is obdurate, counterproductive, and in many ways unethical and lacking in scientific integrity. It explains how there are many economics professors who are hypocritical in the ways they teach economics and in the methodological principles they espouse. It demonstrates how there are many economics professors who cause more harm than good, not only in terms of deceiving their students and the public, but in behaviors that ultimately lead to incorrect policy advice and bad economics in general. In turn, such behavior ultimately causes economic hardship in our society. I contrast these economic professors with highly distinguished professors, like my former dissertation advisor, for example, Kelvin Lancaster, who have stood out for upholding the highest virtues of the profession. It is so unfortunate for the profession that these model professors represent a small minority, and that the majority has largely ignored their virtues.

This book demonstrates that many of our leading economics professors—some Nobel laureates, in fact—have made and expressed many of the *same concerns* about the profession that I express in this book, and they have stated these concerns for several decades. The book then goes on to explain how and why the profession, in spite of all this feedback, has still managed to ignore its own leaders' warnings. In short, the book explains a bitter truth about the academic economics profession that is indisputable, and confirmed substantially by the profession's own members as well as by many outside observers.

Unlike other critical economics books, this book will not explain the problem as something wrong with any particular economic *theory*, or particular group of economic theories, or particular school of economic thought. No—this discussion is much more personal. It is about ethics, scientific integrity, and responsible leadership, and how economics professors need much more of these qualities in order for economics and economic policies to improve. It is in these areas that economics professors, as a whole (with some notable exceptions), have *failed us.*

To some readers, perhaps, this may all seem like sensationalized journalism of sorts, especially among those who are not very familiar with this topic. I assure you, however, that it is not—I provide factual analysis, and in some respects, an *economic* analysis of these concerns. I dare say that my analysis of the concerns I raise about the profession meets the same level, if not a higher level, of analytical and scientific rigor than the economic studies that economics professors perform themselves.

In this book I am thus *calling out* the academic economics profession for a debate on their overall *lack* of ethics, integrity, and responsible leadership! As I just suggested, it is a debate on their own terms, in their own language, and using their own concepts. There are surely many critiques of the profession that cannot even penetrate the castle gates—but this is *not* one of them. As you will find in the very first chapter alone, this book is *already inside the castle gates, and facing the king in his own chambers!*

The profession is at a crossroads, where its failure has, as I have just stated, been recognized by many of its members of the profession, including many of its most prominent ones. Unfortunately, as I will also argue, even its most prominent critical members have done essentially nothing about the problem, apparently refusing to use their influence to improve the situation, often for the wrong, political reasons. I wanted to write this book, not to belittle or embarrass economics professors, but to ensure that the profession does take the right path at these crossroads. Now that I have written this book, I am more hopeful that it will.

Acknowledgments

I am most indebted to my family, and especially my wife Rong, for supporting me while I worked on this book. It took about four years to complete, and I am so grateful to my family's patience during those many hours that I spent working on the project. I therefore want to thank all my children as well, in increasing order of age: Albert, Faith, Emanuel, Shirley, and Mikhail.

Most of the chapters in the book evolved from conference papers or presentations that I had written (though never published), and so I want to thank many of the colleagues who had commented on those papers and had given me incredibly valuable advice on them, especially: David Colander, Mark Costa, George DeMartino, Deirdre McCloskey, William Charles Sawyer, and the late Thomas Mayer (who passed on in 2015). Finally, I want to thank the anonymous reviewers of the work for their valuable comments.

Disclaimer: The views expressed in the book are those of the author only, and they do not necessarily reflect views held of any organization to which that author is affiliated.

Chapter 1

No, This Is Not a Joke

I would expect many people, especially economics professors, to assume that this book, from its title alone, cannot be taken seriously. Some of the harshest critics of the field of economics have argued that it legitimizes and outwardly promotes greed and selfishness. So I wonder if some people might then guess that this book's author must be one of those critics—a philosopher, sociologist, anthropologist, historian, or some other ponderer at 50,000 feet, dictating some ideological argument about what he personally believes is ultimately best for humanity. Along the same lines, some might speculate that the author is simply hostile to the economics profession for its promotion of capitalism, perhaps because the author is one of those elderly individuals who lived on a commune in the late 1960s and never changed since. Under this last hypothesis, the author must have come up with the book's title under some altered state of consciousness. Yes—that must be it! Given this book's title, the author must be one of those obsolete, stoned, elderly hippies from the 1960s, who is simply too spaced out to have anything important or useful to write about economics professors, or probably about anything else for that matter.

OTHER REASONS TO DISMISS THIS BOOK

If this suspicion, alone, is not enough for people to dismiss this book as a joke, then there are plenty of others, at many levels. Some might suspect that the author of this book feels so much hostility that he must accuse economics professors of "failing," instead of offering a nicer title like "How Economics Professors Should Improve." Such a more civil approach would offer economics professors a chance to openly consider whatever arguments the book might present, without being instantly put on the defensive. Indeed, no one else (with rare exceptions) has appeared to offer such a harsh assessment. So how can any idea that is so different from the public's view of economics and economics professors be anything but a joke?

Let us further consider that there are some people who do have the authority to evaluate the performance of economics professors, such as the chairs of economics departments or the deans of universities. None of them have proposed an idea of this kind, and have generally praised the work of economics professors. On the other hand, the author of this book himself has never held a position of such authority at any institution of higher learning. So he must then be completely unqualified even to write about the topic. Similarly, people will frankly ask, "Who does this author think he is?" Does he not recognize that there are *brilliant*, world-renowned economics professors who would be much better able to address any problems that exist in the profession? If he is so interested in recognizing these problems, why has he not consulted with those leaders in an effort to find a solution based on *their* guidance?

Finally, we all know that standard rules of etiquette surely preclude any expression of hostility or belittlement of any legitimate group of scholars, such as those who teach economics. By such standards the title of this book is surely "unprofessional," suggesting that the author must have "an axe to grind" far beyond the rules of proper decorum and professional demeanor. If the author is thus so inappropriate in his style of communication, how can he hope to persuade any audience with whatever arguments he presents?

BURYING MYSELF EVEN DEEPER

Not only will I indulge these obvious criticisms but I will throw more fuel on the fire by momentary feeding these critiques even further. Thus, I will momentarily mimic an even more exaggerated image of myself as a troubled, juvenile-minded person with a chip on my shoulder. I will, in this way, "bury myself even deeper" into the compounding evidence of the supposed illegitimacy of this book. I will do this only to demonstrate that it does not matter how apparently foolish this book may appear on the surface. By the end of this chapter alone, readers will realize none of it is foolish at all. I will crawl out of the hole rather easily, in fact, and proceed to explain how most economics professors have failed us, and how they can stop it.

Now, burying myself even deeper, I will share with readers my own adolescent disdain I have toward the arrogance that I have seen among the economics professors whom I have encountered in my life. What I have detested the most, in this regard, were the snide smirks and condescending laughter that some economics professors have shown in response to two interrelated subject areas that I have personally always taken very seriously: scientific integrity and professional ethics.

A Question I Once Raised During a Conference Session

Many years ago, when I was attending a session at an economics conference, I heard a presentation by a professor about the relationship between economic growth and technological change. In his presentation he purported to show a high correlation between the number of new patents (registered with the US Patent and Trademark Office) and economic growth. This enabled him to conclude that there was a causal relationship between technological change (as reflected by patent counts) and economic growth. This finding, by the way, is the kind that is very often hailed by organizations that offer research grants to economics professors and to other scientists. This is because such findings serve as evidence for the "social benefits of R&D" which these organizations can, and often do, use to drum up political support for their organizations. It is also highly appealing to many people—admittedly, myself included—who love science and love thinking about how beneficial scientific and technological advancement can be when it is properly and responsibly managed. So I realized that the paper being presented would be music to many people's ears, and that it would help him receive praise, perhaps a publication, and perhaps even grant money, for his research.

Given my own background on the topic (which I will discuss later in the book), I had a question about his stated findings, which I politely asked during the question-and-answer session. In asking my question I mentioned that I was familiar with a well-known change in patent laws that occurred at the beginning the time span that he was analyzing. As many who are familiar with patents know, the vast majority of patents that are issued have no real value and are not in fact used by the company that holds the patent. What generally occurs is that a company acquires a very valuable patent and also creates dozens of other patents that are "close" (in their subject matter) to that valuable one. The reason for their doing this is to protect their valuable patent so that no other company can produce a similar patent that competes with theirs. The change in patent laws, which I just referred to, had made it easier for companies to acquire similar patents to ones that already existed, which essentially created a need for companies issuing important patents to "surround" their main patent by more of these other unused "protective patents."

So, in my question to the presenter, I asked whether it might simply be possible that the increase in registered patents that his study observed was attributable to that change in patent laws, which was apparently occurring at the same time that GDP was growing fairly well. GDP was growing at that time due to a general upturn in the economy in which employment was on the rise and inflation had been brought under control. In other words, perhaps it was simply coincidental that both patent counts and real GDP were rising during the same period, but that there was no causal relationship between the two. I asked him, essentially, if he thought that such a coincidence might be an alternative explanation for why patents and GDP were rising at the same time.

The presenter's reaction, especially in terms of his facial expression, reflected a typical response that I must have seen hundreds of times in my 35 years as an economist. Upon hearing my question he condescendingly smiled from ear-to-ear, while constraining himself from laughing, and he replied in an artificially diplomatic and sarcastic tone, "Oh I know all that [about the patent law change.] But . . . that's not *my story*!" In other words, he was there using data and econometric analysis "to tell a story"—the story that he *wanted* to tell—and he was thoroughly amused that someone in the audience would be naïve enough to actually think about whether his findings were scientifically valid. Scientific validity of one's findings is not only rarely discussed during paper presentations at economics conferences, but when it is, it is, more often than not, a source of amusement by the presenters of the papers and their audiences than an actual concern that might lead to improving people's work.

The Profession's Genuine Arrogance toward Concerns about Scientific Integrity

I will demonstrate in this book, though only as an aside, that many academic economists respond with smug, arrogant dismissal or laughter when the topic of scientific integrity or professional ethics is brought before them. It might be surprising to those who are less familiar with the profession that such arrogance and frivolity is as observable as much among some of the most prominent economics professors as among those who are not prominent. In the documentary *Inside Job*, one can observe this kind of arrogance directly among high-ranking professors as they were being interviewed.

As another example, Deirdre McCloskey, a former member of the board of directors of the American Economic Association (AEA) (which consists only of highly ranked professors), has told of how she was there when the board broke into laughter when a letter was read aloud at one of their meetings. The letter was by someone who was simply asking whether the AEA would consider adopting a code of ethics for economists.[1]

Many economics professors do not laugh or make arrogant statements, but express conceit in an entirely different way, such as feeling sorry for those who are even thinking about scientific integrity or professional ethics—thinking to themselves how pathetically stupid, naïve, or childishly innocent those people must be. There is, in fact, quite a substantial literature on the problem of arrogance in the academic economics profession. This literature was written entirely by "insiders"—highly prominent professors themselves, some even Nobel laureates, and some of this literature will be referenced in this book (though most of this book will be on other topics).

Back to Burying Myself!

I promised a few pages back that I will momentarily "bury myself even deeper," which I will now do by revealing my own adolescence in coping with the arrogant, school-yard laughter of many economics professors that I just described. I can see in my mind such laughter as occurring when some economics professors chance upon the title of this book. Their anticipated reaction, in my mind, reminds me of a story told to me about forty years ago by my college roommate at Wesleyan University. He later received an MBA from Harvard Business School, though he hailed from a rough neighborhood in the New York City area. My roommate was a fairly short man, who told me that during the summers when he was in high school he received special training in boxing, at a highly advanced level. He was thus trained to use boxer's footwork, that is, lightly jumping back and forth as boxers do in the ring. In contrast, the much larger and older gang-member kids in the rough neighborhood where he attended high school did not fight that way. One of the largest leaders of one of the gangs at first did not know my roommate, and only saw him as a short, young kid and an easy target. So the boy started a fight, and in the first few seconds the boy was thoroughly amused to see my roommate jumping around, using boxer's footwork. In front of the crowd of kids in the school yard who were gathered around for the event, the bully pointed at my roommate's moving feet and laughingly shouted, "look at that!" followed by the crowd joining in the laughter. But, as my roommate explained the story to me, his opponent's laughter, and that of the audience, completely vanished as the next few seconds unfolded. I will leave the explanation of why that silence occurred to the readers' power of imagination.

I am now willing to admit own human inclination toward adolescent immaturity by saying that I see analogies between this story that I just described and the knee-jerk reaction that I expect many economics professors will have toward the title of this book. As I mentioned already, I fully anticipate that those who started laughing will surely cease their laughter by the end of this chapter.

NOW TIME TO CRAWL OUT OF THE HOLE I CREATED

Now that I have buried myself, and embarrassed myself sufficiently, I will proceed to crawl out of the hole. I will begin by addressing the issue of the profession's arrogance. Arrogance by people with authority naturally evokes anger from those who are offended by it. It would surely be dishonest on my part to claim that the arrogance that exists in the economics profession does not anger me, and, by the way, I am hardly alone in this regard. However, I will say right now, as emphatically as I can write the idea, that any such anger is *irrelevant*—irrelevant to my motivation for writing this book (if readers might hopefully believe this) and irrelevant to the conclusions I derive in this book. The profession's arrogance, however, is relevant for a very different reason than for the anger it evokes among sensible economists who are critical of the profession. What the profession's arrogance also does, which makes that arrogance relevant, is that it blinds most academic economists from being able to see what is so fundamentally wrong with what they do. Most academic economists, and especially most of the elite, highly recognized, and acclaimed academic economists, are simply too proud of themselves to entertain and explore arguments that they are *not* "doing the right thing." Perhaps some academic economists need their arrogance in order to delude themselves into thinking they are doing valuable work, in spite of the fact (which I will prove in this book) that most are not.

On a more general note, I recognize the simple fact that anyone could write a book about how prominent members of *any* profession are often arrogant. This can be done by simply compiling enough piecemeal, anecdotal evidence to support such an argument. In my view, any book that offers such an analysis, in actuality, contributes nothing. Furthermore, I would think it fair to assume that no publisher would want to publish such a pointless book—and certainly not the publisher of this book.

Allow me to speak for the moment as an economist (as I happen to do throughout this book): Economics professors draw resources from society, not only with regard to their own compensation, but with regard to the use of their students' time, and governmental spending decisions made upon the advice of economics professors. Similarly, economics professors provide a service to their students and another service as economic advisers to the society. They also provide a service "to each other" which is peripheral to the question of at hand. That question is simply this: Do most economics professors contribute *positively*, that is, do the benefits of what they do exceed the costs of what they do? Ultimately, this is the economic question that this book will address.

Just What Is "Useful Knowledge"?

The real problem, which many great economists over the past hundred years have identified in their writing, is the lack of commitment within the profession toward *honestly advancing useful knowledge*. Many economists are confused here about the word "useful," thinking that it must mean "having a direct application" as opposed to developing a better understanding of the world. This confusion then gets contorted, where an economist might think: I am more interested in *understanding* than direct application—therefore, why should I concern myself over what is "useful"? In turn, that alleged better understanding is confused with an interest in esoteric theory, which, more often than not, offers no better understanding. Rather, all that such esoteric theory really offers, in most cases, is a self-contained and self-serving exercise of mental self-gratification. This is where many theoretical economists are so impressed with the mathematics involved, and so proud of themselves for having the gray matter to handle that math, that they lose sight of the fact that their theory offers nothing valuable for anyone (beyond self-amusement), regardless of whether the work results in a technical journal article.

Most academic economists need to realize that it is not about any contrast between direct, practical application and higher understanding or theory. One's "understanding" of phenomena, independent of direct practical application, can be useful or it cannot be useful. That is, by "useful" here I do not mean "applied" in contrast to "theoretical" knowledge—*theoretical knowledge that is not applied can be extremely useful because anything that advances our true understanding of how the world actually works is inherently useful*, even if the only immediate benefit is to grant us the satisfaction that we understand the universe better. In economics, knowledge that is *not* useful (if we go even as far as calling it "knowledge") is typically literature that shows how certain published mathematical models, which usually have virtually no relevance to the real world, can be related to another newly created mathematical model which also has no relevance. Such useless "knowledge" is analogous to "knowledge" about what the next move should be in a particular chess game, after thirty moves have already been played, in a chess game that will never be repeated again by anyone in the world for the next hundred years.

Do Economics Professors Even Know What They Should Care About?

Consider the excerpt below from a chapter that an economics professor wrote recently (with my own emphasis):

> Most academic economists will *care little or not at all* about the benefits of their research to those financing the research. Working at a university rather than a research organization is often valued because of the autonomy that a university is *supposed to give*. . . . Even so, is it right for university economists to do their own work *without regard to its consequences to others?* What is the economist's defense for professional autonomy when taxpayers demand

> accountability for the research money spent? . . . Would the neglect of taxpayers have been the right thing to do—or had academic economists shirked their social responsibility by neglecting to consider these duties to society?
>
> To deal with these moral questions, economists need to practice phronesis; the practical wisdom that involves the weighting of values and the assessing of varied circumstances. . . . This requires self-knowledge and knowledge of the social contests in which they operate. *Most important is the continuous feedback of colleagues that is needed to stay focused, to evaluate past actions, and to correct bad or inappropriate judgments.*[2]

This was written by the highly distinguished professor (by publications and job standards), Arjo Klamer, in a chapter he coauthored, entitled "About Doing the Right Thing as an Academic Economist," which Deirdre McCloskey and George DeMartino (the editors) included in the *Oxford Handbook of Professional Economic Ethics*.

Upon reading this passage we easily see that Klamer is not taking the specific position that academic economists are wrong when they "care little or not at all about the benefits of their research"—he is, in fact, legitimizing it. By saying that "most" academic economists do this, he is indicating that they are "in good company" and are in the majority if they, too, decide not to care at all whether their research is beneficial. What is most telling here is that Klamer offers this position, or perspective, as a defensible option, "because of the autonomy that a university is supposed to give its researchers."[3]

One might ask where this policy of the university is ever stated. It does not appear to be something that would be formally expressed in writing. There is certainly no citation or reference to such a policy, but merely an assertion by Klamer that this is what universities are supposed to do. In turn, this begs the additional question of why universities are supposed to do this. Is there any reason to assume any more to this than the simple wishful thinking that economics professors want universities to have this policy, so that is why they should?

I have been promoting DeMartino and McCloskey's *Handbook of Professional Economic Ethics*, through several sessions and seminars that I have organized at economics conferences. In one of them, in November 2015, in a session I organized on professional ethics and scientific integrity in economics, at the annual meetings of the Southern Economic Association, I had openly discussed this chapter by Klamer after it had been presented by its coauthor, Erwin Dekker, who flew to New Orleans from The Netherlands to give the presentation. At that session, when I criticized the above passage of the chapter (in the same way as I had just done above, though more politely), Dekker was quick to say that he agreed with my criticisms and that his coauthor (Klamer) was the one who had written those words in the chapter. Dekker also expressed the idea that from his knowing Klamer personally, he truly believes that Klamer really does care about ethics and social responsibility in economics and so, as Dekker expressed to me and the audience at the session, Klamer himself would agree with the criticisms that I expressed of what he wrote. Also attending the session was Professor Stephen Ziliak (whom I had invited to deliver a presentation on another chapter he wrote in the same volume), who spoke up after my criticisms. Ziliak defended Klamer personally, saying that he (Ziliak) also knew Klamer very well. Ziliak said that he had just coauthored a book with Klamer, and that he can vouch for Klamer as being essentially a "good guy" who, again, really does care about ethics in economics.

Let us step back and fully take in the fact that the above-quoted passage by Klamer was written, essentially, as the last and final word of his chapter entitled "About Doing the Right Thing as an Academic Economist," in a volume entitled the *Oxford Handbook of Professional Economic Ethics*. As such, people who know nothing about Klamer as a person will be reading that chapter to seek expert guidance on "doing the right thing." If Klamer agrees that what he said is actually wrong, and that it is not good guidance to be offering to fellow academic economists, then why did he write it?

Another way of assessing the situation, however, is that it is quite likely that the chapter will be read by people who are already fans of Klamer, and who have decided to read it primarily because they simply saw that he wrote it. To some of the economists in the session in which I criticized the chapter, this to them was the heart of the issue. People were not focusing on whether Klamer's writing was wrong or even harmful—they were focusing on the effect of my criticism at the level of sociology—particularly whether I was indirectly undermining Klamer's "fan base" in the comments I was expressing.

Though Klamer mentions societal benefit as an optional motivation (again in the above passage), what he identifies as "most important" is not societal benefits, or even advancement of fundamental knowledge (though that would be a societal benefit as well), but "continuous feedback of colleagues." Why should this be "most important"—above and beyond the advancement of knowledge or the benefits to society? My guess is that there is no real reason, except that it was ultimately most important to Klamer himself, and that this utterance of "what is most important" was merely a passing thought of Klamer's own wishful thinking that he quickly slapped into the end of his written chapter before sending it off for publication, so that he could begin work on another project.

In spite of what may appear on the surface, the discussion here is not at all about Klamer himself. My point is simply that many academic economists (like Klamer) often freely, and even proudly, acknowledge that, in their minds, they believe they have the right to pursue any area of research they wish without having any commitment to serving the purpose of advancing useful knowledge, or to serving the purpose of benefiting society. For many of them what is more important is the social approval of their immediate colleagues (as Klamer expressed), the mental self-gratification that they enjoy from their work, and, in some cases, the credentials in publications they feel they need to acquire in order to advance in their careers. It is quite sad that when many economics professors are given the "perfect opportunity" (such as writing a chapter on "doing the right thing" for an *Oxford Handbook*) to encourage their colleagues to pursue a legitimate purpose, they simply blow it. It is simply that the entire topic of what is ultimately right or wrong in what they do is too remote from their mindset.

In the absence of a commitment to contributing to useful knowledge, the behavior and the work of academic economists have been dominated by two other major forces: (1) the mathematical games that are played for the sake of getting published and acquiring grant money, and (2) cronyism within the profession, which, in combination with the mathematical game playing, has dominated the reward system and incentive system of the profession. These forces will be examined quite extensively in this book.

I am not, and have never been, a practicing full-time professor. I have worked instead primarily as a federal government economist for over twenty-five years, as a private-sector economic consultant for three years, and as an economic analyst at the Inter-American Development Bank for four years. I have also been an adjunct professor, and have taught economics courses at Columbia University, American University, Georgetown University, Virginia Tech, Marymount University, and Trinity College in Washington, DC. I have also taught training courses in economics to federal employees. As one might guess from my experience, I happen to be as strong a believer in economics as it gets, having devoted my life to the field.

Most importantly, as an economist, I am writing this book as an *economic analysis* in part, so that all economics professors may evaluate my arguments for their credibility *within the science of economics itself*. To be more precise, I will be analyzing the "output" of "economics teaching services," and will focus on one of the "factors of production" that are used for producing that output—the labor of economics professors. I am thus coming to challenge the academic economics profession very much on its own terms, and very much in its own language, though without the esoteric mathematical modeling that so many economics professors enjoy.

Given the book's title, we already know that my findings will demonstrate that most economics professors, and the profession as a whole, have failed us. As I see it, the greatest challenge for my fellow economists will not be any lack of ability to understand or acknowledge the economic arguments that I will present here. The real challenge will be whether they can even approach the topic seriously, for reasons that I have already alluded to, and for additional reasons that I will explain in subsequent chapters.

On the Topic of Loyalty

Criticism of the economics profession generally comes from two completely different sources: One source is people who inherently object to the field of economics itself, and what it purports to accomplish; the other source is people who have studied economics and who recognize why the field is vitally important, but have criticisms nevertheless. I would call the first group of people "those who do *not* believe in economics" and the second "those who *do* believe in economics." In this book I focus only on criticisms from those who, like myself, *do* believe in economics.

Within the profession, however, there will be those who regard any criticism of the profession, from others within the profession, as a form of disloyalty. For example, this perspective might be common among leaders in the profession who often praise the work of economics professors in making public appeals for grant money. For these leaders, the last thing they would want to admit publically is that economics professors are doing anything wrong, and of course anyone else who does say they are doing something wrong is ruining their sales pitch. Nevertheless, to all individuals who would view such criticism as disloyalty, I would pose to them, and to everyone, the exact opposite perspective: I would argue that their perspective, that any criticism of the profession as a form of disloyalty to the profession, *is, itself, a form of disloyalty to the profession!* They should realize that people who truly believe in economics (which may not even include them), and who have come to criticize the profession, are doing so precisely because such critics truly care about making the profession better. Those who would censor the critics for the short-sighted objective of better public relations reveals a disinterest, on their part, in how the profession could be improved. In this sense, those who would censor the critics are betraying not only the profession, but our society overall for denying our society the best economic policies, and knowledge of economics, that it could otherwise be achieved if the critiques are heard and acted upon.

For this very reason, in fact, some of the sharpest criticisms of the economics profession have come from the most distinguished members of the profession—from the chairs of economics departments at universities, from the presidents of economic associations and research institutes, and from Nobel laureates in economics, as I will demonstrate throughout this book. To start off with a sample to demonstrate that I am far from alone in this regard, I will provide a quotation below from Professor David Colander, a highly distinguished professor who, among other things, has been a leading author of standard textbooks used in thousands of economics classes throughout the world. In an essay on "Creating Humble Economists," Colander notes the following (of all economists—not just economics professors), in which he quotes from another prominent professor expressing a similar idea nearly a century earlier:

> The more serious ethical problem of economics . . . has to do with lack of humility. . . . Too many economists are willing to make seemingly defensive scientific statements about policy based on models, that they know, or should know, are highly imperfect. . . . Back in 1927, Lionel Robbins . . . argued that "what precision economists can claim at this stage is largely a sham precision. . . . [T]he man who can claim for economic science much exactitude is a quack." Despite the advances economic science has made, that remains true today. Yet, all too often economists allow lay people and policymakers to believe that our policy suggestions have far more scientific foundation than a neutral objective observer would give them.[4]

Who Is Qualified to Discuss Their Failure?

Most people may not realize that decisions about the hiring, firing, or promotion of economics professors are based on elaborate rules that are, at best, peripheral to what most people would consider the "right reasons" for hiring or firing a professor, and at worst contradictory to such basic expectations. For example, many professors, themselves, at the "top-ranked" schools, will say that displaying a devotion to teaching is often discouraged by their superiors, because it suggests that in doing so, they are weakening their productivity in the production of articles in technical journals (which is what their department cares about more).

Overall, the career success of economics professors is based primarily on publication counts of professors, and to some extent on the following other factors: student-teacher evaluations, participation in community service, and the department's financial capabilities to hire and retain its professors. A department's policies with regard to these standards enables the department to appear to be objective in its hiring decisions, which in turn helps it promote better relations with its faculty (and with the students who might have issues with the university's removal of a popular professor). *Thus, the people who generally possess the power to fire the professors approach the topic in the context of applying existing policy, rather than in the context of considering the establishment of any new policy.*

As this book will argue, the establishment of new policy in this regard is not something to be left only to those with the current authority to carry out such policy—it is too big a topic for that. A new policy should be established, in part, on the basis of public opinion, and on the basis of economic analysis, rather than administrative procedures (and public relations, which many administrators would view as important). Therefore, the fact that the author of this book has not been a department chair or dean is irrelevant, since the basis for decision-making in this area resides at a much broader level.

What I Have Learned from the Profession's Leaders

Let us move on now to the other question some people might ask, which is why I have not consulted with the brightest leaders of the profession to get their guidance on the profession's problems, and to hear and think about what their solutions would be, which would surely not lead to the conclusion that most economics professors have failed us!

Actually, for about twenty-five years, I have been discussing the problems I have observed in academic economics with key figures in the profession, many of whom have agreed with most of the arguments I present in this book. In fact, many of them had suggested to me that there was no point in my even writing down many of my arguments, because these arguments were already common knowledge within the profession, even though most academic economists are too shy to admit it publicly. In this book I will reference several of their supporting arguments.

Among the individuals with whom I have discussed some of the issues I raise in this book was Professor Robert Solow, who had won the Nobel Prize in Economics in 1987 and had mentored several other Nobel laureates. From about 30 years ago to around 10 years ago, he was arguably the most prominent, or most widely recognized, leader of the academic economics profession in United States. As a case in point, in 2010 he had been called upon to testify before the US House of Representatives Committee on Science and Technology, Subcommittee on Investigations and Oversight, to address the obvious failure of academic economists to identify the warnings and to prevent the Great Recession of 2008–2009. This was a failure that other Nobel laureates, academic economists, like Joseph Stiglitz and Paul Krugman, would recognize as well, which I will discuss later on this book. In that testimony before Congress, Professor Solow mentioned the following (with my emphasis shown in italics):

> Especially when it comes to matters as important as macroeconomics, a mainstream economist like me insists that every proposition must *pass the smell test*: does this really make sense? I do not think that the currently popular DSGE [dynamic stochastic general equilibrium] models pass the smell test. They take it for granted that the whole economy can be thought about as if it were a single, consistent person or dynasty carrying out a rationally designed, long-term plan, occasionally disturbed by unexpected shocks, but adapting to them in a rational, consistent way. I do not think that this picture passes the smell test. The

> protagonists of this idea make a claim to respectability by asserting that it is founded on what we know about microeconomic behavior, *but I think that this claim is generally phony*. The advocates no doubt believe what they say, but *they seem to have stopped sniffing or to have lost their sense of smell altogether*. . . . The point I am making is that the DSGE model has nothing useful to say about antirecession policy because *it has built into its essentially implausible assumptions the "conclusion" that there is nothing for macroeconomic policy to do*. I think we have just seen how untrue this is for an economy attached to a highly-leveraged, weakly-regulated financial system.[5]

I personally agree with most of what Solow says here, with the important exception of my strong disagreement with his remark "the advocates no doubt believe what they say." In my view, ultimately, most do not believe what they say, and I am expressing this view, in part, as a compliment to their intelligence. That is, I think that most of them are, indeed, smart enough to not believe in what they say. This is a topic area that I cannot even attempt to explain in the next few paragraphs—it will take most of the rest of this book to explain it.

In 2007, I had founded a nonprofit organization for "Integrity and Responsible Leadership in Economics" which received support from various notable academic economists such as David Colander and Deirdre McCloskey. In the next year, I had contacted Professor Robert Solow to get his feedback, whom I knew from our working together at the National Science Foundation. My question to Solow, and more generally to all of the most prominent leaders of the academic economics community, is simply this: If the macroeconomists' understanding of the world was so blatantly wrong, so as not being able to "pass the smell test" (in Solow's words), then where were Solow and all the other leaders of the community when all this wrong behavior was going on, prior to the crisis?

Part of the answer to this question is revealed in the letter that Solow had written to me on August 14, 2008, after I invited him to join the Board of the Association for Integrity and Responsible Leadership in Economics. In his letter, Solow displayed his basic stance on this issue in a remark where he agreed with our opposition to excessive theoretical abstraction and esoteric theory that had no apparent usefulness with regard to solving particular problems. He added that he had even expressed such agreement with this opposition in some of his published work.

I am glad that he did express opposition in his writing prior to the financial crisis, but I then need to ask, with due respect to Professor Solow: *What GOOD did it actually do?* Unfortunately, the answer is remarkably obvious—*absolutely nothing*. In his letter to me in 2008, he is clear that the only resistance that he believes should be offered to the fundamental problems in the profession is, essentially, nothing more than *scholarly discussion*. In this book I will devote a chapter to explaining the futility of expecting scholarly discourse to solve any of the fundamental problems in academic economics, though many of the points in this explanation, I expect, readers will find obvious.

I dare offer the simplistic explanation that, the main reason prominent leaders in academic economics resort to scholarly discussion as the means toward solving the problems of the profession is because, essentially, *it is all that they know.* These leaders effectively control the profession, in deciding who is hired and promoted within it, who is published in the most prestigious outlets, and even, through their recommendations, who becomes prominent economic leaders in other sectors—especially in government and NGOs, and to some extent in industry as well. Yet, these leaders are often the last to recognize and acknowledge their own power and ability to influence the academic economics profession, or they refuse to exercise that power as, in their mind perhaps, an honorable expression of modesty and humility. I must state, however, that what might be interpreted as *humility* in certain respects might, in more relevant respects, be interpreted as *irresponsibility.*

Over many years I have found Solow's letter to be extremely typical of the perspective shared by the vast majority of the prominent leaders in academic economics. This commonality should not be surprising—there is a great deal of imitation that exists within the community, in which aspiring leaders often greatly admire and imitate existing leaders until they become one themselves. The perspective I am referring to was exemplified in Solow's letter when he explicitly wrote that he *did not approve of the idea that there should be any kind of organized effort to help guide the work of young and bright economics professors* (as he described them).

My question, in my own mind, in response to his position is, "*Why the heck not?*" I, and many others, would argue (and *have* argued) that, if only such a campaign to improve the profession had actually existed, and had been effective, in the years prior to the Great Recession, then perhaps the Great Recession, as implied by Solow's and others' own testimonies to Congress after the fact, could have been avoided. That recession cost the world some $20 trillion in losses, and with the economic hardships that it created was, in effect, responsible for many thousands of lives that were lost unnecessarily. It was easy for Solow to say, in retrospect, that this work *smells*, and yet imply in a different conversation about guiding the profession that there was nothing that we should have done to stop it, because young, bright economics professors should be free to do as they please. Imagine the reaction he would have received from the public if he would have included this complete perspective—that the work smells, but who are *we* to ask them to fix it?—in his testimony at the congressional hearing that was investigating whether economics professors had been responsible for the great recession. It would have clearly made the congressional committee *even more inclined* to hold the academic economics profession accountable for the great recession as well as it should.

How important is it, then, for leaders to express humility, or for them to honor the scholarly independence of young and bright economics professors, in comparison to the greater goal of reducing the risk of a major economic crisis with all its real-world catastrophic effects? In contrast to the perspective suggested by Klamer in the earlier discussion, academic economics is not a scholarly pastime that exists for the self-amusement of people lucky enough in life to have become economics professors. Rather, academic economics is an extremely important causal factor in the well-being, or lack thereof, of people in the world. *Academic economists have a great responsibility in this regard—a responsibility that most of them, in general, simply do not recognize, and this lack of recognition is as easy to find among the most prominent academic economists, who are generally assumed to be brilliant, as it is to find among the most junior members of the profession.*

One aside I feel I should express with regard to Solow's above-mentioned remark is my disagreement with his focus on the sanctity of what young, intelligent economics professors decide to do. The perpetuation of literature that Solow himself has described in his congressional testimony as "not passing the smell test" has been continually generated by academic economists of absolutely all ages—his reference to young economics professors in his letter I do not understand at all. It is as if there is some sort of appeal to letting the young enjoy their youth while they can, as a paternal characteristic that might be expressed by a university professor sharing their affinity for the young people they see on campus. I am also confused by the reference to the term "intelligent," or "bright," in this context. Is there an allusion to the idea that, as bright young economics professors they may know better than we, and then who are we to redirect what they do? Moreover, what is meant by a term like "bright" or "intelligent" in this context? All that we do know, with certainty, is that these young professors are very good in math and in having memorized economic models. If this makes them "bright" by definition, then I am fine with that, as I should be fine for any semantic convention. However, if that is the *reason* we call them "bright," then this calls into question how important it is for economists to be "bright" as opposed to being *wise* and to being *responsible* to their students and to society overall.

But Does This Book Have to Be So Critical, When It Could Be Nice Instead?

Some people will surely regard the tone of this book's title to be very wrong. Nevertheless, many will argue that it is nonsensical that anyone should withhold the observation that something is horribly wrong, only in order to avoid insulting the people who were responsible for what is horribly wrong. Yet, I have seen this nonsensical philosophy for several years in certain cultures where I have worked. I have seen newspapers articles, for example, where the headline was that the leader of a nation was "insulted" by a leader of another nation, where the only issue discussed was the insult itself, under the assumption that the person who was insulted is necessarily a victim and the person who expressed the insult is the perpetrator, regardless of why the insult was made. In my own inability to comprehend this, I am inclined to ask the question: Should a police officer not arrest a suspected murderer, because in doing so, and saying in the process "you are under arrest for murder," he or she will have insulted the murderer?

Politicians, unlike most economics professors, get hate mail (or even hate threats) and face the fear of public embarrassment and disgrace when they make bad decisions. Of course I am completely against expressions of hatred, and in chapter 8 of this book I condemn how academic economists often express forms of hatred. In any case, the hate mail that politicians sometimes receive has helped them realize the importance of making the right decisions, even though they should realize that importance without it. Unlike politicians, doctors tend not to receive hate mail, nor face the prospect of public embarrassment, but many of them see human pain, misery, and death occurring before their eyes, and this of course helps to motivate them to make the right decisions. As Professor George DeMartino and so many other economics professors have pointed out, and as many economics professors should already know, the consequences of decisions by many economics professors can, in the end, be as dramatic as the consequences of the decisions by politicians and doctors.[6] Many economics professors do not realize this at all, and remain complacent about their decisions within their own independent, alternative worlds, which I also discuss throughout this book.

In the history of human beings on Earth, it should be obvious that human beings fail the most whenever ignorance, arrogance, and authority coincide. Arrogance and complacency provide the barriers that have enabled economics professors to avoid changing for the better and have even helped many of them laugh at any suggestion that they must, indeed, change for the betterment of society. In this environment, polite, scholarly critiques of economic discourse, in the most cordial of manners, and in the most proper etiquette, have dramatically failed to break these barriers. Sometimes it is simply that the "medium is the message"—politeness, whether for the right reasons or the wrong reasons, implies less urgency and less demand for change than rudeness does. In my view, if impolite criticism of economics professors can somehow reduce the level of complacency in the profession by only 1 percent, and it is at a cost of my being perceived as "unprofessional" in having been so impolite, then to me it would a worthwhile trade-off. In my view the bottom line is how much change for the good I can induce, not how much popularity within the profession I might acquire from a less critical approach.

Some may repeat the adage, "You get better results with sugar than with vinegar." I am all too familiar with that adage, and I agree that it works great in many situations like asking a spouse to please make a fresh pot of coffee. When it comes to asking economics professors to think differently about the research they perform, and to be more responsible to their students and to economic science, I have not seen sugar work very well at all, and trust me, there is an awful lot of such sugary literature about this topic that has been written over many generations—again, with no real effect.

But Why Is This Only About Economics?

Implicit in arguments that I have already made, and will continue to make throughout this book, is the idea that academic economists are uniquely different from academic natural scientists, most of whom, in contrast, have not failed us, by any means. I can understand how many would find this perspective to be flawed. Those who do, I suspect, might reason as follows: Human behavior is primarily reactive to the conditions under which human beings are exposed. Therefore, the ultimate cause of differences between fields of study (e.g., economics and the natural sciences) must be inherent aspects of what makes those fields different to begin with, which is their subject matter, as opposed to any inherent differences in the individuals who happen to occupy those fields. By this reasoning, it is not the behavior of the professionals that cause the problems, but simply the subject matter of their fields itself. It would then follow from this logic that the field of economics itself is the underlying cause of the problems described in this, not the people involved.

This simplistic perspective, however, ignores the fact that the subject matter of any field of study is, for better or worse, influenced greatly by the behavior of the professionals within that field. What we actually have, then, is a circular situation: Fundamental problems in the subject matter of academic economics create problems in the behavior of academic economists, and those behavioral problems, in turn, prevent needed corrections in the field's subject matter. Attempting to attribute the overall problem to either the initial subject matter, or to the initial behavior of economics professors (e.g., which came first, the chicken or the egg?), would be both futile and meaningless. The important take from this, however, is that it would be completely invalid for economics professors to claim that no aspects of their behavior is "their fault" and that it is all because of their chosen field.

For those who may be disappointed or perhaps even offended by my somewhat plebian, informal approach to this topic, let me provide something a bit more scholarly. A noted sociologist, Stephen Fuchs, conveyed the following similar ideas in a broader comparison between social science and natural science:

> There can be little doubt . . . that the social sciences . . . differ from more mature fields. The dominant philosophical explanation for this is that there are some deep ontological differences between things natural and things social, and that two different methodologies are required to study them. Silent natural objects and their immutable laws can be explained by strong and nomothetic natural sciences, while interpreting people who interpret themselves requires a softer and idiographic approach. From a sociological perspective, however, the difference is not in the nature of the things studied, but in the structures of the groups and organizations doing the studying.[7]

Many economics professors who read this book may feel that they are being unfairly accused of wrongdoing when they are simply doing what the leaders in their profession require them to do. I address this issue of "we are just following orders" (an expression made famous, of course, by the Nuremberg trials of the Nazis after World War II) in the next chapter.

Let us also bear in mind that some economics professors, even though they may have reached a ripe old age, may never have batted around in their lives any hard decision making about what profession they should choose to pursue. Many studious kids in college become naturally attracted to scholarly pursuits, and so they may easily fall into wanting to become the professors that they encounter when they are in college, without ever struggling with all of the career options they have, but simply accepting academia as the default option for scholarly people like themselves. Many will then go straight to graduate school after their bachelor's degree, and their first "real job" (permanent, as opposed to a part-time or summer job) will be that of an assistant professor upon completing their doctorate. There may thus be a dimension of maturity that they may not have ever fully reached. That is, they were led by their parents when they first entered college, and were led by their professors ever since. They were led by professors when they were first impressionable students, and then impressionable new employees, answering to other professors who hired them on the basis of their original professors' recommendations. Thus, for many economics professors, the university economics departments have been *taking care of them* ever since their own parents stopped *taking care of them*. Under these circumstances it is indeed easier for many economics professors to have never questioned the work they do in their lives in the same way that other adults may have questioned the work they do after having struggled to consider and find alternative jobs. Of course, this is generally true for all academic fields, and perhaps even more so for certain other professions outside of academia, such as carrying on family businesses where the transition from childhood to early adulthood is even more seamless. However, the fact that this factor could be generalized to other academic fields and to some other professions does not make it any less relevant in our developing an understanding of the behavior and perspectives of economics professors.

The bottom line is that, yes, we can acknowledge the existence of a wide variety of causal factors that might explain how economics professors do simply what they have been told (or encouraged) to do, and how, in this sense, what they do is "not their fault." Nevertheless, whether any of what economics professors do is ultimately their fault, in my view, is entirely irrelevant with regard to this book, and is irrelevant all together.

And Now for the Final Step Out of the Hole

Despite all of this, let me now truly mix things around by speaking in phrase of some of the economics professors whom I have greatly admired. One of the best professors who I ever had in economics was the first one I ever had—Professor Richard Adelstein at Wesleyan University. His class was so inspiring that I seriously considered pursuing economics as a career after taking it, which had never before entered my mind.

In 2014, I edited the three-volume set *Public Economics in the United States: How the Federal Government Analyzes and Influences the Economy*. The set contained forty-eight chapters, written by sixty authors (and coauthors), including myself. Of these sixty authors, twenty-eight were full-time professors at the time they wrote chapters for my set, and another fourteen had been professors at some earlier time in their life, either full- or part-time. I was honored to have worked with them and was especially appreciative of their contributions to the volumes. The vast majority of them had nothing to gain financially, either directly or indirectly, from the chapters they wrote for the volumes. They contributed chapters which were designed to be useful to the public, on their own time, simply because they wanted to make that contribution.

Among the chapter authors was the highly distinguished professor Murray Weidenbaum, former chairman of the President's Council for Economic Advisors under Ronald Reagan. When Professor Weidenbaum passed on at the age of eighty-seven, he had just completed the final version of his chapter, and was never able to see it in print. In my mind his writing it in his mid-80s showed his incredible devotion to the field, and his commitment to making economics useful to the public, which is something that I think all of us should greatly admire. Thus, if any of those economists who are associated with the Weidenbaum Center (which was named after him) in St. Louis come across this book, and are wondering if I might be including Professor

Weidenbaum among those economics professors who have "failed us," they should know that I most certainly am not. Indeed, if all economics professors were only half as committed to economics serving a useful purpose as Murray Weidenbaum, then I would have had no motivation to write this book.

From 2006 up to the present, I have continued to serve as the executive director of the Association for Integrity and Responsible Leadership in Economics and Associated Professions (AIRLEAP). In all of these years I have been extremely grateful to the professors who have served on the organization's board of directors, especially the chair of our board, distinguished professor Deirdre McCloskey, whose work on integrity in economics I have cited on several occasions in this book, along with the work of several other professors who have served on the board, including, for example, George DeMartino, Gary Hoover, Thomas Mayer, and W. Charles Sawyer. Several other economics professors have been part of our organization and have worked hard to promote integrity and responsible leadership in economics, on their own initiative. Many others have been members and have supported the principle of promoting integrity and responsible leadership in the profession. Indeed, AIRLEAP works hard to appeal to economics professors to join us, precisely because many economics professors stand with us in our efforts to improve the profession. AIRLEAP's leaders and members, however, generally do not say that most economics professors have failed us, and I fear that many of them will be disappointed in my taking this hard-line position, because many of them may have more faith in, and perhaps tolerance of, the economics professors who I criticize in this book. In any case, the many professors who genuinely care about integrity and leadership responsibility in economics, and who show it directly in what they do (as opposed to paying lip service to it), are not professors who I would say have failed us, regardless of whether or not they belong to AIRLEAP (or even heard of it for that matter).

More generally, however, I could discuss a "great divide" that exists in academic economics which ties directly to the question of whether economics professors have failed us. I experienced this great divide at one of most pivotal points in my career, which occurred around the year 1986 during a one-minute conversation that I had when I was a graduate student at Columbia University. The conversation was with a highly admirable professor, who I knew from having been a student of his class on international trade—Professor Ronald Findlay. At that time I had begun to develop ideas for a dissertation, and was excited about the topic I had in mind. (Five years later I would successfully defend it, and three years after that see it published as my first book, on *Quality Measurement in Economics*.) However, when I had that one-minute conversation with Professor Findlay, I had not yet been appointed a dissertation advisor, and that was what the conversation was about.

Professor Findlay was responsible in the department for ensuring that students were finding dissertation advisors. So he asked me if I were talking to anyone about a dissertation topic and if I were trying to find an advisor. He was also asking me about my future, and at the time I was interested in teaching after I received my doctorate. Findlay advised me to find someone to work with who was active in publishing theoretical work that was receiving attention. I mentioned to him that I was kind of interested in speaking with Professor Kelvin Lancaster (Figure 1.1 below), whose work I will describe later in this book. Lancaster was a very famous professor for work he had done many years before, but he was no longer very "active" at that time. I explained to Findlay that I was interested in research that would expand upon Lancaster's work on the "characteristics of goods." Findlay, in choosing his words carefully to me, said that Professor Lancaster is a great guy (which indeed he was—an incredibly nice person), who would surely be willing to advise me if I asked him to, but that he is no longer active in publishing research and that this could hurt my chances of acquiring a teaching position at a good school after I graduate. I was naively confused by all this, thinking that I had a chance to produce a dissertation that would be recognized on its merits, independent of how active my adviser happened to be. I then replied, with a bit of confused naiveté on the whole topic, that I still wanted Lancaster to be my sponsor, because my interests

Figure 1.1 Professor Kelvin John Lancaster. Photo courtesy Gilead Lancaster.

were closest to his area of expertise among the professors who could be my sponsor.

Findlay paused for a couple seconds because it was clear that he did not know what to tell me. He knew that he could not tell me that I should regard my personal research interests as secondary to the objective of working with a professor who could get me in the limelight of new publications in top journals, thereby securing a good teaching position for me. He guessed correctly that I would probably not agree to it anyway, and that I might only think less of him for having suggesting it. But also, I believe Findlay was a man of integrity, who respected my right to pursue the research topic of my choice, and he wanted to wish me the best in doing it. And so, with a bit of a disappointed expression on his face, he simply replied something like, "Alright . . . I understand . . . then I guess you'll be speaking to Lancaster about your dissertation topic." He knew at that time that, from my choice, I would face a much more difficult time in entering academic economics by my not tapping into one of the "hot publishing topics" that the Economics Department at Columbia was offering to its graduate students.

It would take me a couple years to realize this myself after that, but I have never regretted the decision, for many reasons. In fact, in retrospect, I could have never asked for a better dissertation advisor than Kelvin Lancaster for all the right reasons—that he helped me greatly in understanding the subject matter of my dissertation, and helped me believe enormously in economics and in the importance of advancing knowledge in economics. Because my research overlapped between microeconomic theory and technological change, I also relied heavily on another great professor, who was my "reader" for the dissertation—Professor Richard R. Nelson, a leading expert on the economics of technological change. Another professor who I was close to was Professor Phoebus Dhrymes, who was well known in econometrics and was on my dissertation committee, and whom I worked under briefly as a teaching assistant.

The myth about economics professors that purveys the profession is that the more brilliant they are in theoretical economic modeling, and thus the more they are able to publish, the more important they are, and the "better" they are as economics professors. As I will discuss in greater detail in the chapters that follow, this research-based criterion for professors is precisely what hurts the profession the most. Moreover, it makes little sense, in that, if research is the criterion, then why are they "professors," at all, instead of professionals who are simply being paid to do their research?

The "really good" professors are, of course, the ones who are good at *being professors!* They are good at caring about their students and at showing true leadership in the profession to help students learn how to become good scientists in the field of economics, whether those students decide to teach or not.

Good economics professors help produce economists who believe in doing what is right, and valid, in economics. It is these professors who should carry the way forward for an improved profession.

BELIEVE IT OR NOT—THERE IS *HOPE* FOR ECONOMICS PROFESSORS!

Although I am highly critical of the profession throughout this book, I have actually developed a glimmer of hope that the profession may, in fact, be at a crossroads, where it can greatly improve. This will largely depend on its ability to find new leaders with the motivation to implement such changes. At present, there is an obvious divide within the profession between a small minority of elite professors, primarily in the top-ranked universities, and a majority of professors, and graduate students, who find themselves struggling under great pressure to survive in a "publication contest" that has been largely "rigged" by the elite group, which has enabled them to retain their prominence in the profession.

Over recent years, two interesting developments have been happening: The first development is that the publication contest has intensified, to the point of the profession as a whole becoming obsessed with it, and where people no longer speak of articles being "good" for what they actually contained. Instead, the mindset is that an article is as good as the rank of the journal in which it appears, and in terms of the number of citations the article receives. Accordingly, economics professors have come to define their very existence, in terms of the simple "counts" they have "scored" for their publications. The second development is that resistance has begun to emerge, where the intense competition to acquire publications has led many economics professors to question the degree of fairness that exists in the competition for publications. It has led them to question as well whether the "publication game" truly supports the honest pursuit of advancing useful knowledge in economics.

As further evidence of how bad the situation has become, professors who have achieved a full professorship (and have thus achieved their highest rank) have expressed to me that they feel a sense of social responsibility, of sorts, to slow down, or even discontinue altogether, their efforts to publish in top-ranked journals. The same economics professors have likewise sometimes expressed disdain for those full professors who have 22 continued to publish extensively in top-ranked journals. The reason for this, as they themselves would explain, is that they "do not *need* any more publications," and since there is generally a fixed sum of articles that top journals publish each year, their getting another article published will likely prevent someone else from getting that publication, who really does *need* the publication to get tenure, or to be hired for a new position. For some foreign students and professors, the stakes are even higher, where the publications are needed for teaching positions that would enable them to stay in the United States. In many professors' minds, the publications are like food, available for both the starving and the obese, where it is unconscionable for those who have plenty to take food away from those who are starving.

Let us now explore the true implications of this perspective, and how incredibly contrary it is to basic concepts in how knowledge is generally advanced in fields of study. Full professors are, by definition, recognized as the leading experts in their field. This means that they are regarded as the most knowledgeable, and they should thus be expected to contribute the most to the development of new knowledge in the field. Since publications represent the main forum for new knowledge to be disseminated, we should therefore expect most journal articles, and especially those in the top journals, to be written by the profession's most honorary and wisest members, who would be full professors. Now, either full professors truly deserve their status as the most knowledgeable members of the profession or they do not. If they do, then it follows that articles in top-ranked journals would be highest in quality if they are predominantly written by those professors, and those articles would otherwise be lower in quality.

The argument, then, that full professors should abstain from producing more articles, in order to increase the publications available to the profession's junior members, implies that either the status of full professors is illegitimate or the journal articles themselves have essentially no value in terms of advancing knowledge so that it does not matter who writes them. Either way, there is an incredible contradiction of basic principles here, reflected by the policy recommendation that the most recognized professors should restrain from writing journal articles.

How stable this publishing frenzy is, is hard to say. It is clear now that top leadership within the profession have been finding a need to defend the profession's current practices. Is this recent recognition of such problems enough to carry the profession forward toward great improvement? Or, is this apparent interest in addressing the profession's failures primarily a public relations ploy on the part of the profession's leadership to quell the criticisms? Unfortunately, for now I believe it is more of a ploy than a solution, but it does not have to be, and this is why I have written this book.

NOTES

1. Deirdre McCloskey, "Rhetoric Matters: The Case for Standards of Ethical Conduct in Economics," (paper presented at a session on "Examining the Practice of

Ethical Economics" organized by the Association for Integrity and Responsible Leadership in Economics and Associated Professions, San Francisco, January 4, 2009).

2. Erwin Dekker and Arjo Klamer, "About Doing the Right Thing as an Academic Economist," in The Oxford Handbook of Professional Economic Ethics, ed. George DeMartino and Deirdre McCloskey, (New York: Oxford University Press, 2015), 113.

3. Dekker and Klamer, "About Doing the Right Thing as an Academic Economist," 113.

4. David Colander, "Creating Humble Economists: A Code of Ethics for Economists," in The Oxford Handbook of Professional Economic Ethics, ed. George DeMartino and Deirdre McCloskey, (New York: Oxford University Press, 2015), 737–38.

5. Robert Solow, "Building a Science of Economics for the Real World," (Prepared Statement to the House of Representatives, Committee on Science and Technology, Subcommittee on Investigation and Oversight, Washington, DC, July 20, 2010), 2–3. http://tinyurl.com/j7tpxfo.

6. George DeMartino, The Economist's Oath: On the Need for and Content of Professional Economic Ethics (New York: Oxford University Press 2011).

7. Stephen Fuchs, "A Sociological Theory of Scientific Change," Social Forces 71(4) (1993): 945–46.

Chapter 2

Why Does Theoretical Economic Literature Exist?

The beauty, the pride, and the pleasure of advancing knowledge, and the valuable benefits it offers to humanity—these are surely the reasons for human inquiry and scholarship. Thus, there is no good reason why economic thought and economic theory should defer from this purpose. Furthermore, under the same perspective, most of us would be inclined to assume that theoretical economic literature is simply a consequence of this admirable effort to advance human knowledge through path-breaking mathematical and scientific research. It is for this reason that many theoretical economics papers proclaim to be "contributing to the literature" an end in itself, as doing so were synonymous with "contributing to knowledge and understanding." Let us start by questioning this, by first realizing that literature is published words; and understanding is understanding; and therefore, the two need not be the same. This realization then begs the question: If theoretical economic literature does not necessarily contribute to knowledge or understanding, then what *does* it do, and *why* does it even exist?

EXPLORING BASIC CONCEPTS

Semantics Can be Important

When we consider something that is produced by human beings, and we ask what it is, we generally ask three things about it: its description as a physical object, the reason it exists, and how it is made. We may ask, for example, "What is a car?" As a physical object, it is a complex machine made of a wide variety of substances. It exists for the purpose of providing transport, and it is manufactured in a highly automated automotive industrial plant. Of all these three dimensions of meaning, it is the meaning with regard to purpose that is often the trickiest to address. For example, defining a car as a means of transportation would apply in the vast majority of cases, and it would initially appear to capture the most essential aspect of a car.

Now consider, for instance, the situation in which someone owns a Ferrari that they do not race, but use it to go to work, or to the grocery store, etc. On the surface, their Ferrari is still used for the purpose of transport. From an economic perspective, however, this begs the question of why they would be willing to pay $300,000 for a transportation vehicle, when the same transport function, even with luxury features, can be easily acquired at one-fifth the price. I would argue, as would many economists, that the other 80 percent of the car's value does not actually serve the purpose of transport, but of artistic pleasure (in the same sense that owning the Ferrari is like owning a piece of art), and for the prestige that it bestows upon its owners. In short, from an economic perspective, the Ferrari (when it is not used in a race) is best described, not as mode of transportation, but as an artistic symbol of wealth and prestige.

All scholarly works in economics exist, at least in part, to serve the purpose of advancing knowledge in the field of economics, just like all cars that are driven to the grocery store are, quite obviously, used to transport people and groceries to and from the grocery store. But, for reasons that will be explained shortly, in many respects, the theoretical economics article in a top-ranked journal is much more a *symbol* of advanced knowledge than it is a *provider* of advanced knowledge. This is an important distinction that will be made clearer throughout this book, and making this distinction is, in fact, one of the main objectives of this book.

Those articles that are in the top-ranked journals are symbols of the very best and most highly acclaimed pieces of economic research. One may regard their being the most highly acclaimed by definition—that is, by virtue of the fact that they are in the most cited journals, whose rankings are high because of their high citation rates. As for whether they are truly the best research, I believe this should be treated as an open question that can only be answered by looking at precisely what these articles truly provide.

Mathematical Fairy Tales Dressed Up Like Advanced Knowledge

My grandfather used to tell us a story of how he was once desperately looking for a job as a tailor, when he was a young man in New York City in the 1910s. Job hunting in those days involved simply walking down the street and stopping at each establishment and asking if any of them had any openings. After much unsuccessful searching, he finally arrived at one establishment where the owner said he had an opening for a tailor, but he apologetically explained to my grandfather that he was only looking for a *French* tailor. When my grandfather asked why, the owner explained that French fashion in clothing was the latest, most popular style, and so this is why he wanted his shop to make only French-style clothing. Although my grandfather was not French, in his desperation for a job, he replied that he was very glad to hear it because, he, himself, was a French tailor! The owner, however, was quite suspicious at this response, saying that my grandfather did not look French to him at all.

Nevertheless, after my grandfather kept insisting that he *was* French, the shop owner said that we will need to verify that. Although the shop owner did not speak French himself, he said that he would test my grandfather by having him speak French to another French tailor whom he had just hired. He thus called his French tailor over, and he asked the two men to start speaking in French to each other, in front of him.

My grandfather, who could speak only Yiddish, and some English and Polish, began the conversation by speaking in Yiddish to other tailor, but with a French accent. The other tailor then replied in kind—speaking in Yiddish with a French accent back to my grandfather. Their conversation continued, until the shop owner, who obviously did not speak Yiddish either, ended their conversation with a smile of approval. He hired my grandfather on the spot, happily believing that his shop now had two French tailors!

Economic theory has its own, highly complex, esoteric, mathematical language that to many audiences (including economics students) looks and sounds like physics or advanced engineering. It is by design that the language is as complex as possible, because it enables the producers of economic theory to appear to be as intellectually accomplished as possible, usually much more than is necessary to understand the ideas, or even the economic model, that the literature is presenting. Likewise, this show of intellectual prowess (at a superficial level) better enables economic writing to be published and enables economics professors to appear to be brilliant (especially to naïve audiences). From the standpoint of economics professors, they have no choice but to speak the language fluently, as this is required for publication—and thus required for the promotion of their careers—regardless of how much the esoteric mathematics actually adds to anyone's understanding of the phenomena being studied. Theoretical economists, who are primarily academic economists, are, in this respect, similar to the "French" tailors in my grandfather's shop, whose use of their own language to imply a level of knowledge or understanding greatly exaggerates (at best) what they truly know or understand. Moreover, their use of extremely technical language for concepts that are, in truth, not extremely complicated at all in most cases, does much more to obscure people's understanding of the phenomena being studied than it does to promote and enhance that understanding.

Leaving economics aside for the moment, and just talking about mathematics, consider, for example, the response one might offer to the question of "what is meant by a 'sphere'?" There are three types of answers that one might be provide:

1. A sphere refers to anything that is shaped just like a ball.
2. Consider any point in space and call it the "center." All of the points in three-dimension space that are the same exact distance from the center make up a sphere, which is shaped like a ball.
3. (Readers need not understand this one to follow the remainder of the discussion.) In reference to Cartesian coordinates in three-dimensional space, a sphere is the loci of points (x, y, z) such that $r^2 = (x—x_0)^2 + (y—y_0)^2 + (z—z_0)^2$ for some scalar r and some fixed reference point (x_0, y_0, z_0).

For a lay audience, the first definition is clearly the most appropriate. For a technical audience who want a good understanding of what a sphere is, the second explanation is the best because the most fundamental principle of a sphere is that it is the set of points that are the same distance from a center. The third definition, which has many useful qualities for scientists, engineers, and mathematicians, offers little understanding of what a sphere is. It contains this information about a sphere (expressed in #2) for those who can see the equation and instantly know that it is referring to "equidistance in space." Yet, this third definition is esoteric and obscure for most audiences. If someone were asked what a sphere is, and that person wanted to convey the idea that only someone with advanced knowledge can understand what a sphere is, then that person might provide this third definition. This is what advanced economic theory essentially does—its main purpose is the *impress*, not to *explain*, and this is, indeed, common knowledge within the profession, and common knowledge outside the profession among professionals who often collaborate with academic economists (such as policy analysts).

A Noneconomic Example with Risk, Hazard, and Outrage

When the topic of mathematical show business arises, I am reminded of a lecture I heard on "risk" as it is analyzed by social scientists, especially as it relates to the establishment of environmental and safety regulations. The lecturer, Peter Sandman, is a noted expert in the field. In the beginning of the lecture he expressed an amusing quip about the use of equations to interrelate three concepts: risk, hazard, and outrage. I had first heard that quip around 1993 or 1994 in a video recording that was available at that time. I was then amused to hear him express it in essentially the same way in a lecture he delivered in 2016, entitled an "Introduction to Risk Communication (2016)."[1] I believe this quip could serve as a seed for me to present a metaphor of how mathematics is often used in economic theory to create an enormous amount of, essentially, useless mathematical fluff, to create a façade of understanding, when in actuality there is absolutely no understanding (or at best very little understanding).

Sandman describes "risk" as being related to two factors: hazard and outrage. He defines hazard as the severity of any risk. For example, if it is the risk of car accidents due to drunk driving, then "hazard" would include the average number of fatalities, injuries, and property damage from accidents caused by drunk drivers each year. Outrage, on the other hand, reflects the level of anger and unacceptability of a particular risk. As an example of how outrage can be different for the same level of risk, let us consider the risk of a person being severely bitten by a dog, to the point of requiring some hospitalization but where a full recovery within a few weeks is still expected. Consider two scenarios: (1) An intruder tries to break into a family's house in the late evening, but is bitten by a guard dog in the family's home, precluding his efforts and leading to his arrest, and (2) a small child is bitten by a dog, in the child's own backyard, after the dog's owner who lives down the street simply released the dog without a leash. Although the level of hazard might be the same in both cases, the level of outrage is extremely different, with there being essentially no outrage in the first scenario and a great deal of outrage in the second, explaining why there are substantial laws to protect us from the second type of scenario, and no laws to protect us from the first.

Sandman begins his lecture by explaining the simple relationship: "Risk = Hazard + Outrage." He then introduces the quip that I referred to earlier. He explains that he often encounters people in his audience who are very disappointed and critical of the above-mentioned simple, additive relationship among risk, hazard, and outrage. He, therefore, says, "For the techies in the room I have an alternative definition that you will like better," and he writes on the board (underneath the previous expression): "Risk = F (Hazard, Outrage)." In other words, he is writing the mathematical expression that risk *is a function* of hazard and outrage. He then exclaims, "If you don't know what that means, it's 'risk equals hazard plus outrage' in techy code." Technically, this affirmation of the equivalence of the two expressions is not 100 percent accurate but is reasonably accurate for all practical purposes because we have not defined the units for risk, hazard, and outrage, and can use the leverage of alternative units of measure to make the expressions equivalent in many cases.[2]

Following Sandman's lead, I will take it from here to develop what looks just like "economic theory." For this exercise to work for most readers, though, we need to see, and think of, economic equations *simply as pictures* as opposed to specific mathematical ideas that we might be expected to understand. To emphasize this point, Figure 2.1 displays three pictures. All

爱是你所需要的。

$$dR = \frac{\partial F}{\partial H} dH + \frac{\partial F}{\partial U} dU$$

Figure 2.1 Examples of Pictures that Can Be Seen Without Necessarily Being Understood. Created by the author.

we need to do is to see and understand these figures as a beautiful coastal city, a sentence written in Chinese, and an equation in calculus. You need not know what the city is, what the sentence in Chinese means, or what the equation means. The three pictures are displayed inside frames to emphasize that they are simply pictures and require nothing more to think about.[3]

Figure 2.2 now presents an "Economic Theory Style Show" built on a single, very simple, piece of knowledge, which is Sandman's proposition that risk is based on hazard and outrage. Please look at each framed picture in it as only as a picture to see what an economic theory style show looks like.

I proposed in Figure 2.2 two assumptions which could be reasonably argued but are still rather arbitrary. The second assumption, in particular, uses a very arbitrary functional form—one of many that could have been chosen. With the initial equation, and equations for the two arbitrary assumptions I created, an incredibly complex mathematical solution could be derived for an economic paper or journal article. Virtually no thought might be given to these assumptions, while a great deal of mathematical derivation would be conducted and the vast majority of the work would be involved in this "research" (if one would optimistically call it research). Indeed, more thought might be given to the assumptions in terms of crafting assumptions that could more easily be used to derive the final mathematical solution (i.e., a situation in which the "cart would pull the horse").

The mathematics however does nothing useful other than to show that the author is good in math, and that is all. Otherwise, as is commonly known and understood in the profession, assuming the author's proficiency in mathematics, the "findings" of the study are determined precisely on the basis of the assumptions. It is no different in structure from a paper saying, I assume that X + Y = 5, and that Y = 3, and I have derived the finding that X in this case must equal 2. The only difference is the level of mathematical complexity. Using a common expression in the field, we often say that "the findings rediscover the assumptions."

Framework: We begin the model by defining R as Risk, H as Hazard, U as outrage (not "O" since "O" can be confused with zero). Examining R as a function of H and U, based on Sandman (2016) we find changes in risk over time as: (Here we essentially have fancy math that is applicable to just about anything that is a function of any two other things.)

$$\frac{dR}{dt} = \frac{\partial F}{\partial H}\frac{dH}{dt} + \frac{\partial F}{\partial U}\frac{dU}{dt}$$

Arbitrary Assumption #1. Since outrage is based on newsworthiness, an observed rise in hazard from one period to the next would be expected to raise outrage, all else being equal, while other independent factors (I) would influence outrage separately. Thus, for some constants k and m we have:

$$\frac{dU}{dt} = k\frac{dH}{dt} + m\frac{dI}{dt}$$

Arbitrary Assumption #2. When there are large levels of outrage, there will be more social pressure to reduce hazard each year, while other independent factors (J) will also reduce hazard. Thus, we have the following equation, in which we squared U, as an approximation, to capture the idea that only large values of outrage will tend to reduce hazard.

$$\frac{dH}{dt} = z\frac{dJ}{dt} - aU^2$$

Combining all these equations, we can solve for R, H, and U as follows:

A complex mathematical exercise that serves only the purpose of getting all this published.

Figure 2.2 An Economic Theory Show: Analyzing Risk Determination as a Function of Bio-Medical Hazard and Societal Outrage. Remember to see each framed picture as a picture only, and do not worry about understanding any of the written text either–it is all just a show. Created by the author.

In this hypothetical example, the journal article would be "sold" to the public as if it had achieved advanced, scientific knowledge on the all-important topics of "bio-medical hazard" and "societal outrage" when it would have, in fact, done nothing other than illustrate mathematical "muscle-flexing" on the part of its author. Furthermore, although its two assumptions might be reasonable at first glance, many other equally plausible, and even contradictory assumptions could have been made. For example, we might envision these sets of equations each applying to different types of risks, and we might think that there is only so much outrage to go around (in terms of people's attention, or relative media coverage, etc.). Thus, one could argue that there is, perhaps, a fixed sum of outrage, so that when outrage over one issue goes up, it may reduce outrage over another. (For example, according to the 2015 film *Spotlight*, breaking news about pedophiles among church leaders in Boston in the year 2001 had been postponed because of the events of 9/11.)

We could envision, as well, one article utilizing the first two assumptions I made and another article after that revising the last assumption with a slightly different formulation. The second article could then cite the first article, and purport to be "an expansion of the literature" in this direction. This simple scenario illustrates how theoretical literature can so easily build on itself.

Unfortunately, this is the nature of most theoretical economic research, which begs three easily answerable questions:

1. What do we really learn from it? The answer is: "not much if anything at all."
2. Why is this all done? Most of the remainder of this book will answer this question, though the short answer is that it is done only for the sake of generating a publication, which will in turn promote the author's career.
3. If the assumptions are so arbitrary, how are they even decided upon? Answer: They are determined by combination of logic, appeal, precedent already set in the literature, and, as already suggested, the need to establish fancy mathematical problems that are difficult to understand but can still be impressively solved by the author.

Another Example, Using Economic Theory to "Explain" Drug Addiction

In 2014, at the annual conference of the Southern Economic Association meetings, I saw the presentation of a research paper which provided a theoretical model for the behavior of drug addicts. It addressed the question of whether a drug addict would choose to purchase drugs as a function of their income, the price of drugs, and their perceived probability of getting arrested. In the model, drug addicts are assumed to be methodical and analytical enough to base their decisions on *maximizing a predetermined utility function* whose parameters are already known to the drug addict.

The presentation went through many mathematical formulations following from standard, heroic assumptions, some of which had been established by prior theoretical economists like Nobel laureate, Gary Becker. The author, in giving the presentation, was quite enthusiastic about his work, as were many of the people in the audience, who engaged in a lively, mutually supportive discussion of the sophisticated mathematical model. The top panel of Figure 2.3 provides an illustration of part the same model in published work by the same author (shown here simply to reveal, in the form of a visual image only, its esoteric complexity—it is by no means presented here to be understood by most readers). The bottom panel of Figure 2.3 presents how actual science, rather than mathematical showmanship, approaches the same general topic.

I wondered, however, how relevant the model was at explaining the real world behavior of drug addicts. For example, no one seemed to wonder how drug addicts become much better than most PhD economists at utilizing multivariate calculus to solve their own optimization problem in their decision-making. There was no apparent concern over the assumption that all drug addicts are identical in their preferences so that they all solve the same exact

Theoretical Economics Fantasizing ("Asserting") about the Behavior of Drug Addicts → This discourse is based on whatever assumptions might lead the analysis to use impressive mathematical formulations to support a publication and to *look smart*, regardless of its disconnect to reality.	It is asserted that an agent behaves as if solving the ensuing optimal control problem from the point of view of base period t: $V(a_t, s_t, \boldsymbol{\theta}) \overset{\text{def}}{=} \max_{c_1(\cdot), c_2(\cdot), e(\cdot)} \int_t^{+\infty} U(S(\tau), c_1(\tau), c_2(\tau)) \exp(-\rho[\tau - t]) d\tau$ s.t. $\int_t^{+\infty} [p_1 c_1(\tau) + p_2 c_2(\tau) + e(\tau)] \exp(-r[\tau - t]) d\tau = a_t + \int_t^{+\infty} w(S(\tau)) \exp(-r[\tau - t]) d\tau$, (1) $\dot{S}(\tau) = c_2(\tau) - \delta S(\tau) - h(e(\tau))$, $S(\tau)\vert_{\tau=t} = s_t$, where $\boldsymbol{\theta} \overset{\text{def}}{=} (p_1, p_2, \rho, r) \in \mathbb{R}^4_{++}$, ρ (as opposed to σ) is the rate of time preference, $s_t \in \mathbb{R}_+$ is the given base period habit stock, and $V(\cdot)$ is the current value ***intertemporal indirect utility function***, which by Theorem 14.7 of Caputo (2005), is independent of base period t.
Neuroscience Actually Studying and Understanding the Behavior of Drug Addicts → This discourse is based, first and foremost, on a commitment to understanding causality as it truly occurs.	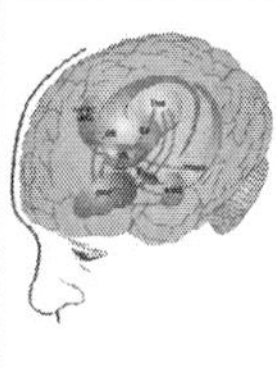 Figure. Neurocircuitry schematic illustrating the combination of neuroadaptations in the brain circuitry for the three stages of the addiction cycle that drive drug-seeking behavior in the addicted state. Note the activation of the ventral striatum/dorsal striatum in the binge intoxication stage. During the withdrawal–negative-affect stage, the dopamine systems are compromised and brain stress systems such as CRF are activated to reset further the salience of drugs and drug-related stimuli in the context of an aversive dysphoric state. During the preoccupation–anticipation stage, contextual cues via the hippocampus and stimuli cues via the basolateral amygdala converge with frontal cortex activity to drive drug seeking. Other components in the frontal cortex are compromised, producing deficits in executive function.

Figure 2.3 Theoretical Economics Pretending to Explain the Behavior of Drug Addicts, in Comparison to True Explanations Offered in Neuroscience. Created by the author with reference to: George F Koob, "The Potential of Neuroscience to Inform Treatment," National Institute on Alcohol Abuse and Alcoholism, Accessed May 5, 2017. http://tinyurl.com/mc6edo4; Michael R. Caputo, "The Intrinsic Refutable Implications of Rational Addiction Theory are not Observable, while the Comparative Dynamics that are, are not Refutable," Accessed April 3, 2015. http://tinyurl.com/mc6edo4.

model. Perhaps most interesting, however, is that no one seemed to wonder whether a drug addict's behavior itself is guided by the mathematical logic of utility maximization, when deciding whether to purchase drugs to which they are pathologically addicted. I could go on and on about the model's ridiculous assumptions, but for the sake of both the readers and myself, I will stop it here.

While hearing the presentation, and the audience's responses to it, it was clear to me that, for the producers and consumers of this discourse, the model's true ability *to explain anything in the real world was neither relevant nor interesting*. Everyone involved in the discussion was apparently interested in the research for the self-gratification they get from staring at "beautiful models" and also for the pride and prestige of understanding the math, and getting it published.

Salaries Being a Factor

In chapter 4, I explain how there is wide dispersion in the salary levels of economics professors. The official explanation that would be offered by economics departments for these huge salary differentials is that they basically separate levels of knowledge among the professors, as reflected by their levels of contributions to top-ranked literature. As an indicator of knowledge, publication counts in top-ranked journals might then be justifiably used to determine promotions and hiring within the profession.

An alternative hypothesis, however, might be that knowledge itself is not the driver, but is merely the by-product of top-ranked literature, and even then, only if we are lucky. That is, economics professors' main objective is not knowledge acquisition, but it is to produce as much top-ranked literature as they can to support their career advancement. The question then becomes, to what extend does this incentive system truly promote the earnest pursuit of valuable knowledge, as opposed to whatever else may be called upon by professors to increase their levels of top-ranked literature. Examples of how more can be produced without a corresponding increase in valuable knowledge include: (1) recycling ideas that have already been published, but with enough cosmetic changes, new data, and a few alterations here or there to make it look like new research, (2) using the graduate students that the professor is advising to perform most (or all) of the research while the work still lists the professor as a coauthor (or sole author in the most abusive cases), and (3) bathing the research in theoretical esoterica and obscurity for which the author is highly proficient and which will easily fly past the reviewers with ease as they are impressed with its complexity, complemented by the author's already-achieved prominence.

It is important to note that the incentive system referred to above for professors' advancement in rank is entirely internal to the single institution in which a professor resides, and that system is incredibly simple in the way it operates. For example, when a full professor retires, a full-professor vacancy is open, and the most likely candidate to replace them is the person with the most impressive publication record. There is no analysis behind this system—it is simply the way it has always been, and it is the way the existing full professors who will make the selection acquired their own positions. Thus, this selection method can be used to rationalize the next promotion with little resistance and a minimum of questions. Moreover, there may be a bit of an adolescent reluctance to change or even question the system among those who have the power to change it, precisely because they themselves had already "paid their dues," in the same way, to get to "where they are now," so why should the younger people have it any better than they had it, by any changes in the rules?

Identifying the "Party Line"

I use the concept "party line" here by its common definition of the principles or policies that are stated publically by a political party. Leadership in academic economics is not a political party, of course. However, it often acts like one in its defense of its practices, and especially in defense of its proliferation of theoretical economic literature which is often supported by research grants. (In other words, like so many other things, when money is involved, politics is often involved as well.)

At an institutional level, the National Science Foundation (NSF), for example, has grant programs for mathematics and for all of the sciences, in order to finance the advancement of basic human knowledge. NSF is a rather unique institution that is a federal agency, an academic institution (in many respects), and a financial institution, especially in terms of its ultimate function as a financing "foundation." The programs are run generally by academics who were temporarily borrowed by the government for a year or two to administer the academically oriented selection process for the issuance of grants, all in support of "basic research." For their economics program, "basic research" usually translates to "theoretical research" as we more commonly know it within the economics profession.

NSF's program office in economics, for example, describes their financial support for basic knowledge as follows:

> The Economics program supports research designed to improve the understanding of the processes and institutions of the U.S. economy and of the world system of which it is a part. This program also strengthens both empirical and theoretical economic analysis as well as the methods for rigorous research on economic behavior.[4]

Let us call this rationale for economic research as the philosophical and spiritual justification for why top-ranked literature exists. It is also the one justification that all institutions offer that are involved in producing top-ranked literature. In this sense, one might also refer to it as the profession's "party line." However, as many economists and noneconomists alike have argued for centuries, this explanation for the profession's proliferation of theoretical literature is, for the most part, a falsehood.

Rules Cannot Be Based on the Exceptions

Analogous to the earlier discussion of the Ferrari, it is important to maintain the belief that "the tail does not wag the dog." Put another way, if a very small fraction of a set exists for one reason, but the vast majority of that set exists for another reason, then the generalization that the entire set exists for the first reason is, indeed, an untruth. One could look, for example, at the population of the United States and say that people in the United States exist because they are the direct descendants of the Native Americans who have lived in the same geographic area for millennia. That would, in fact, be absolutely true for about 1 percent of the US population, and indeed, one could provide as many as three million examples (in the names of existing individuals) as evidence for it.

Nevertheless, the fact that 99 percent of all US residents are either immigrants to the United States or the descendants of immigrants means that the statement would be a lie in 99 percent of the cases, and would thus be a lie in general.

There are, indeed, thousands of examples of how theoretical economic literature does greatly contribute, in very important ways, to scientific knowledge. One of these thousands of examples is the pioneering work by Professor Kelvin Lancaster at Columbia University (before he passed on in 1999) in his theoretical formulation of the "characteristics of goods." In a nutshell, he posed that demand for goods and services was a function of quantities of measureable characteristics of those goods and services, rather than simply a function of the quantities of those goods and services alone. On the surface, perhaps, this might appear somewhat obvious to some observers, but Lancaster developed the theoretical and mathematical foundations that have since enabled economists to analyze demand, and analyze market prices, on the basis of the measured characteristics of products. Lancaster's theory of characteristics, in particular, laid the foundation for "hedonic price analysis" that Zvi Griliches and many other pioneering economists developed soon thereafter. What hedonic price analysis did, in turn, was allow economists to properly measure price changes in products with changing, or viable characteristics—in particular, motor vehicles, housing units, and, most importantly, computers. Without this foundation, economists would be unable to measure inflation correctly, and in turn, would be unable to measure real economic growth in any useful and reliable manner. Without measuring economic growth accurately, economists would have no ability to assess changes in the economy or assess the positive or negative effects of policies to improve the economy. In short, Lancaster's theoretical contribution had become one of the main pillars of economics itself, at both theoretical and applied levels.

Indeed, in much simpler terms, the entire field of study of economics ultimately relies on the development of theoretical economic literature. That small fraction that does exist for the reasons espoused in the "party line" is thus absolutely essential for the very existence of the field. To debar top-ranked literature would thus be tantamount to destroying the discipline of economics itself. Needless to say, this is not at all what is being proposed in this chapter. I wrote this chapter for the benefit of economics, consistent, in fact, with the same party line that I have been discussing.

WHAT IS ACTUALLY BEING CRITICIZED HERE

To help clarify the discussion, let me distinguish between (1) theoretical economic literature and the highly admirable objectives on which it is allegedly based, and (2) the dominance of theoretical economic literature that actually exists within the economics profession. For the reasons just espoused, this chapter does not present a critique of top-ranked literature *per se*, but a critique of its dominance.

In a simplistic sense, the problem with the dominance of theoretical economic literature may be viewed as a "matter of degree." Consider, by analogy, the scientific fact that sodium chloride (table salt) is a necessary ingredient for human life, that is, without it we would be dead, juxtaposed to the other scientific fact that the excess consumption of salt in the human diet is unhealthy. In fact, many people consume salt in their diet in quantities that are far above the recommended levels by heath experts, and ultimately this overconsumption could be identified as the cause of death each year, in an epidemiological and statistical sense, for a significant number of people. The companies that sell salt, as one might hope and expect, are sensible enough not to promote greater consumption of their product with advertising slogans that use, or allude to, the fact that salt "is necessary for life." They, and the consuming public, would be smart enough not to fall for that level of marketing. Whether the same sensibility can be found among economists and the public in distinguishing between theoretical economic literature and the dominance of theoretical economic literature is, unfortunately, highly questionable.

Many economists and others would defend the great proliferation and prowess of theoretical economic literature in the economics profession for two general reasons (or a combination thereof): They may truly believe that most theoretical literature is valuable to humanity, or they have a vested interest in espousing the party line, as producers, publishers, teachers of theoretical literature, or as grant issuers in support for it (or as grant receivers). Many may likewise view that criticism of the dominance of theoretical economic literature at a personal level, seeing such criticism as reflecting unprofessional or disloyal hostility toward theoretical economic literature. Nevertheless, as argued in the previous chapter, the highest level of professional and loyal commitment to economic discourse, as well as the most scientific approach that could be taken, would support the idea that we must maintain an open mind in this discussion and allow such criticism to have its day in court.

Do We Need a Large Pool from Which to Draw Good Literature?

Another thread that enters into this discussion is the defending argument that the tiny fraction of highly valuable theoretical literature is made possible only through a selection process among the greater pool of theoretical economic literature, and consequently the best theoretical literature would not exist were it not for the existence of the larger pool from which it can draw the effective "winners." This argument is analogous to the selection of star performers in theater and sports, where only a tiny fraction of those who actively pursue acting or sports careers become famous. Of course, there is certainly an element of truth in this. It must be the case that superior theoretical literature cannot be planned or easily identified, but rather, that there is some sort of "survival of the fittest" involved with it.

This Darwinist defense of the dominance of theoretical economic literature suffers, however, from a major flaw. To identify this flaw, it may be helpful for us to draw upon the same analogies of the performing arts and athletics. In reality, the vast majority of participants in the theater and in sports, in "not-for-primetime" events, like community theater or athletics in small colleges, are not, by any means, seriously seeing their involvement in these activities as a stepping stone to super-stardom. Most have other central goals and interests in their lives, and are participating in these activities as ends in themselves, that is, simply as pastimes that enrich their lives but hardly define their lives. In other words, they may realize that they have neither the interest nor the ability for stardom, but enjoy what they are doing, and enjoy the limited pleasure they themselves receive from their work.

The same is most certainly true for the vast majority of writers of theoretical economic literature, who are writing to an extremely small audience. Those majority-producers of theoretical literature generally aspire to receiving a few compliments or citations from their miniscule readership, to justify a grant they may have received to perform the underlying research, and to add a few more lines of accomplishments in the publications section of their curricula vitae that will help them advance in their careers. Thus, only a small fraction of theoretical literature is "destined for stardom" *from the beginning*, while the rest exists entirely for other reasons.

It follows that the most acclaimed theoretical literature is drawn from only a small fraction of the pool, and this is a fraction that, for the most part, can be identified from the outset. The rest of the pool, which is the vast majority of the pool, is irrelevant to the selection of "primetime" theoretical economic literature. Therefore, the massive pool of theoretical literature is not justified by any Darwinist process for selecting the "star players" who will significantly affect the advancement of economic thought.

The Properties of Important Advances in Knowledge

Let us step back again to consider all advances in the theories of science, under the temporary assumption (which I will soon relax) that advances in economic theory is a proper subset of this set. I would argue that there are two broad features that can be said about recognized, important advances in scientific theory:

1. They have been extremely valuable for improving human life, or they promise to be valuable in the future when the advanced knowledge can be put into practice, or
2. They are intellectually satisfying and intriguing for those who developed them, and for those who learn and understand them.

With regard to the second feature, I would identify two general reasons that scientific advances may be intellectually satisfying and intriguing:

2a. The scientific advances reveal counterintuitive, profound, and highly interesting discoveries about the universe that may be hard to believe, but where evidence is so overwhelming that they may be essentially accepted as fact. Such discoveries are profound, in part, because of their lack of complexity, that is, many people can easily understand them. Examples include, for example, in mathematics, Euler's Formula ($e^{i\theta} = \cos\theta + i\sin\theta$), and in biology, the encoding of all life (in the DNA of organisms) in terms of sequences of only four nucleobases.[5]

2b. In contrast to the above, some very important scientific advances are indeed highly complex and therefore cannot be well understood by anyone who is not an expert in the field. Or, the scientific advance may be "understandable" in a broad sense, but still incomprehensible to most in terms of its finer details. An example would include Einstein's General Theory of Relativity (the one that explains gravitation as acceleration, not the much simpler Special Theory that finds $E=mc^2$). Another example might be molecular biology that underlies the most recent approaches to understand and disable the AIDS virus.

Reason 2b is most widely applicable to nearly all of theoretical economic literature. Nevertheless, there are exceptions that fit under reason 2a, such as Milton Friedman's "Quantity Theory of Money" ($M^dV=PY$) or the Slutsky Equation in microeconomic theory. Whether such discoveries under 2a are as notable or as valuable as Euler's formula or the discovery of DNA, or whether they are true "discoveries" as opposed to suppositions about how the world should work in the eyes of economists, of course, remains to be seen. Nevertheless, giving credit where credit is due, and the benefit of the doubt in this regard as well, we can certainly say that economics does develop some scientific advances that are in terms of reason 2a.

In contrast, discoveries that fall under 2b have difficulty being as intriguing as they are intellectually satisfying to very small groups of people, because of the "heavy lifting" required to understand them. In fact, within the economics profession, the heavy lifting of economic theory that is so complex as to be incomprehensible to most Ph.D. economists, more often than not, is the deciding factor for the claim of "scientific merit" in the economics profession. This will be discussed in greater detail in the sections that follow.

Useful Discovery versus Impressive Mathematical Exercises

Reason 2b is clearly where there is a weakness in the system if literature meets this criterion only and is not motivated by reasons 1 or 2a. When this occurs, the value of top-ranked literature is highly suspect. As an example for the sake of clarity, Einstein's General Theory of Relativity may, indeed, be incomprehensible to anyone who does not have at least a master's degree in physics. But one of the General Theory's core ideas, that gravity is equivalent to acceleration in curved space, fits squarely into criterion 2a, and given its great pertinence to how the universe works in general, the General Theory also fulfills criterion 1 for its relevance to a variety of practical issues in space travel and space exploration. What many economists who are interested in theoretical economic literature should understand about the pursuit of knowledge in general is that it is not the incomprehensibility of the General Theory that makes it a great scientific discovery—incomprehensibility in itself has no value at best, and a case could be made for it having negative value. That is, if the incomprehensibility of a theory is attributable to the presence of a large number of equations and variables, then this situation would be directly opposed to Occam's razor—a heuristic used in the sciences that favors simpler explanations, all else being equal. There is, indeed, a great difference between mathematical heavy lifting and the acquisition of valuable knowledge—something that is probably blatantly obvious to natural scientists, because of their training, while *not* being obvious to many economists because of *their* training.

Bright-eyed and naïve graduate students in economics, as well as many junior economists, may not realize that this concern regarding the dominance of theoretical economic literature has been with the profession for many decades if not for centuries (depending on how we define it). It is a concern that, in general, has not been expressed by economists "with an axe to grind" or by those who might be supposedly jealous for not being famous for their own efforts to contribute to theoretical economic literature. Rather, as already mentioned, it is a concern that has been raised often by the most prominent economists in the profession, for example, Nobel laureates, who are quite famous for their own contributions to theoretical economic literature. Below are some examples.

What Some Nobel Laureates Have Said

In the wake of the Great Recession of 2008–2009, two highly recognized American Nobel laureates in economics—Joseph Stiglitz and Paul

Krugman—had made fault-finding statements about economists' interests in, and production of, theoretical economic literature. Krugman (2009, 36) wrote:

> [T]he economics profession went astray because economists, as a group, mistook beauty, clad in impressive-looking mathematics, for truth. . . . That vision wasn't sustainable in the face of mass unemployment, but as memories of the Depression faded, economists fell back in love with the old, idealized vision of an economy in which rational individuals interact in perfect markets, this time gussied up with fancy equations. . . . [T]he central cause of the profession's failure was the desire for an all-encompassing, intellectually elegant approach that also gave economists a chance to show off their mathematical prowess. . . . [T]his romanticized and sanitized vision of the economy led most economists to ignore all the things that can go wrong.[6]

Stiglitz wrote:

> The blame game continues over who is responsible for the worst recession since the Great Depression—the economics profession bears more than a little culpability. . . . It is hard for non-economists to understand how peculiar the predominant macroeconomic models were. Many assumed demand had to equal supply—and that meant there could be no unemployment. (Right now a lot of people are just enjoying an extra dose of leisure; why they are unhappy is a matter for psychiatry, not economics.) Many used "representative agent models"—all individuals were assumed to be identical, and this meant there could be no meaningful financial markets (who would be lending money to whom?).[7]

Now flashback about forty years earlier to Wallisy Leontief's presidential address before the American Economic Association in 1970, in which he accused the profession of a continued preoccupation with an "imaginary and hypothetical reality" as opposed to an "observable" reality.[8] Aside from his being the president of the AEA, founder of Input-Output Analysis, Robert Solow's dissertation advisor, and the recipient of the Nobel Prize in Economics three years later, Leontief, like Stiglitz and Krugman today, was certainly not a disgruntled economist who was jealous for not having received recognition in theoretical economic literature. He was simply conveying the same criticism, to as wide an audience as he could, as a responsible and highly recognized leader of the profession, for the sake of making top-ranked literature more applicable to the real world. Perhaps his warning, if the profession had taken it much more seriously, would have prevented the kinds of criticisms that would be expressed forty years later by Krugman and Stiglitz. Indeed, by Krugman's and Stiglitz's own assessments, had economists not been obsessed with the practice of self-gratification while looking at the beautiful models, perhaps the great recession might have been avoided entirely!

The Theory Need Not Rely on Data, and Data Need Not be Accurate

In top-ranked literature authors certainly make use of existing data to support and estimate the parameters of the theoretical models that they present. However, in general, and as is commonly known and admitted, little or no attention is paid by the theoretician to how reliable or robust the data are. Rather, it is enough to have properly documented the source of the data, and this constitutes due diligence for the model tester, as far as the author and the publishing journal (including the peer reviewers it uses) are concerned. I am reminded of a colleague of mine in a statistical agency where I once worked, who always used to say, right after a new set of economic statistics were published, "Well, they may *not* be *right*, but they *are . . . official!*" (To him that was simply a silly joke because he actually did believe the data were accurate, but the alternative interpretation is what would be applicable in this discussion.)

Theory of the Strongest Link

Thomas Mayer covered this topic extensively in his 1993 book, *Truth Versus Precision in Economics*, in which he describes a two-tier level of professional status in economics: Individuals in the lower tier produce economic data and are responsible for ensuring their accuracy to the extent that they can. Those in the higher tier—that is, higher up on "the food chain" within the economics profession—focus their efforts on economic theories and utilize those data in their exploration and testing of those theories.[9]

Mayer pinpoints, in this regard, a more general flaw in the way economic theory is constructed, which he terms the "theory of the strongest link."[10] The idea is that economists who approach the study of a particular issue may often delude themselves into thinking that their approach to the topic is as strong as the most sophisticated aspect of their modeling exercises. At the same time, the weakest links in their analysis, like the arbitrary assumptions that their model is based on, or the unreliability of the data they used, is irrelevant to the strength of their work—hence the theory of the strongest link. This can be seen easily throughout economic discourse; all one needs to do is look for it.

As an example, I once attended a presentation that was given by a leading economist from a very large chemical corporation, which produced and sold a particular pesticide. The pesticide was being considered for stronger regulation because of its adverse environmental and health effects, but the hope for his corporation was that, if it could be shown that the pesticide is highly valued by farmers, those benefits might outweigh the costs of the adverse effects, and in a cost-benefit framework, the regulation might not be imposed. During the presentation, the economist from the pesticide manufacturer explained the methodology of his advanced study, which utilized highly sophisticated econometric techniques to explore the question of whether the pesticide was preferred by farmers over a competing pesticide that is used for the same purpose but manufactured by a different corporation.

The data had been acquired from a survey that his firm conducted of farmers in an area, who were asked to score their preferences for the two pesticides. Nearly all of the presentation, and the paper itself, discussed the econometric techniques that were applied, except for the conclusion, which was that farmers greatly preferred the pesticide that just happens to be manufactured by the presenter's employer. During the question and answer period of the presentation, the economists in the room, who themselves were well versed in advanced econometric techniques, asked the presenter detailed questions about his estimation methodology.

When it was my turn to ask a question, I had a different type of question; I asked, "I was just wondering . . . how did you construct your survey sample?"

The presenter smiled and quickly replied, "Oh . . . we just used our client list."

In other words, the survey of farmers' preferences for one pesticide or another was conducted using a sample of those farmers who have already decided to purchase the pesticide that was produced by the researcher's employer. Thus, the survey was ridiculously biased, and from the standpoint of the most basic science and basic logical reasoning, the study's findings were essentially worthless, regardless of how impressive its mathematics was. While the mathematics provided a link in the chain made of thick steel, the data that was used provided a link made of a thin strand of tissue paper.

At that meeting I simply replied "OK-thanks" in my response to his answer, and there were no follow-up questions or further discussion about the survey sample, which no one else in the room (of about fifteen economists) appeared to find interesting.

McCloskey's "A-Prime, C-Prime Theorem"

In Deirdre McCloskey's 1993 article on the "A-Prime, C-Prime Theorem," she argues that theoretical economists often play the following game: They study a model that was already published which showed specific results, and they join in the discourse by publishing another article that shows how a small and simple tweak in the assumptions of the earlier model can dramatically change the results.[11] The ultimate practical conclusion of such exercises, in most cases, is that neither model is useful, because in most cases little or no attention is paid to which assumptions are truly more reliable. Some might argue that the theoretical exercise, in itself, is valuable, as a lesson in mathematical deduction. I would argue to the contrary that mathematics is best taught in the field of mathematics.

It's Publish or Perish!

Academic economists seeking to advance in their careers (or even to maintain their status, such as in a tenure-track position) are essentially ordered to contribute to the literature, and most often to the theoretical literature. Although this is commonly known and understood in the academic world, an example might be useful for readers who may not be familiar with the process. Thus, as an example, I will refer to my work in editing a three-volume set which was published in 2014, entitled *Public Economics in the United States: How the Federal Government Analyzes and Influences the Economy*.[12] In this effort I invited many professors to write the forty-four chapters that would appear in the three-volume set. One of the professors whom I invited was an assistant professor in a tenure track position. That professor agreed, by signing a contract to write the chapter on "Regulation of the Financial Industry." The chapter invitation provided the author with considerable latitude (subject to a peer review process) to write on issues that the author feels are most relevant and important.

The professor first reacted to the invitation very positively, writing, "That looks like a great project. Please send me the invitation." After that, he signed and returned the contract. Four months later I received an email message from the professor in which he wrote: "I am sorry to say that I must now decline to write this chapter. My tenure committee reviewed my 2 year file and strongly suggested that I stop writing for edited books (even peer reviewed) and instead focus on writing papers for journals, so all my effort is now going to be devoted to publishing there." I was sympathetic to his situation, of course, and told him "no problem" and then found someone else to write the chapter. (The contract was not an issue.)

For professors seeking tenure, publications of top-ranked literature in technical journals are, indeed, ends in themselves, regardless of their value in truly advancing or disseminating human knowledge. The assessed value of their contributions by their tenure committees is based, instead, on the quantity of publications weighted by citation counts, and weighted by some measure of the prestige of the particular journals that publish the articles. (This topic will be discussed in much greater detail in several of the forthcoming chapters.) The top-ranked literature they produce must certainly recognize, pay homage to, and be consistent with the existing body of literature. Furthermore, this classic "publish or perish" pressure prevails in which a professor's existing status and the characteristics of their institution set the standard for what is expected of them in terms of the production of theoretical economic literature.

Are We Infected by a Virus?

Pleading for the reader's indulgence, I will now like to step into the realm of biology, where I will borrow the very important concept of a *virus*. By its standard definition, a virus has the following:

1. A set of instructions that orders a cell to build more viruses, overriding what the cell is otherwise normally supposed to do for the best interests of the "host" organism to which it belongs (like a human being, for example); and
2. A structure that can penetrate the cell to successfully deliver these instructions.

Now consider the process by which academic economists are compelled to produce and publish theoretical economic literature. Whatever one might believe about extraterrestrial intelligence, let us ask, at least, the theoretical question of what aliens from another plant might conclude if they observed the top-ranked theoretical economic literature on the planet Earth, in its published hardcopy and electronic forms, and also observed how top-ranked literature was being produced.

If observed by aliens from another world, it might initially appear that the theoretical economic literature were a type of *virus*—growing year after year, and evolving as it grew—by *effectively ordering humans to produce it continuously*.

SPOKES IN THE WHEEL, AND THE CIRCULAR FLOW

A more earthly interpretation of the problem, however, would be that no one who is part of the system has any control over it, or any ability to change it, but the system tells each person what to do. The newly hired, tenure-track assistant professor has to spend the next few years of his or her life grinding away to publish top-ranked literature upon the command of the leaders of their department. Those leaders consider that command necessary for all new assistant professor hires in order for the status of the department to be maintained, which will have bearing on the grants their department receives, the quality of new students it attracts, etc. In the simplest of terms, everyone is "just following orders." Like the plant in the play and movie *The Little Shop of Horrors*, the literature screams "feed me!" and professors are forced to comply for the sake of their careers. If they are lucky, perhaps, they may still be able to reconcile, at least partially, what they are forced to do with their own personal interests and beliefs in advancing valuable knowledge.

The Circular Flow

Theoretical economic literature is produced within a complex system. As shown in Figure 2.4, its production is integrated within the culture and tradition of literature building on the same previous literature, the establishment of major topic areas, the identification of the individuals who are recognized experts to serve as referees, the issuance of research grants, the policies and practices of the journals (which are managed by the same authors of economic literature), the universities (and other institutions) and their leaders, the authors (professors and graduate students who are incentivized by their institutions to publish), and last, and *often least*, important real world issues and new ideas to address them. (Note that the rectangles in the figure refer to factors that are controlled directly by people; the factors in the ovals are not, at least not directly.)

People naturally think of theoretical economic thought as being produced by a much smaller subset of these factors: the authors, the real world issues, and the new ideas to address them. This simplification is incredibly wrong for many of the reasons already explicated earlier in this chapter, and for many other reasons that will be provided throughout this book. That simpler view is based on a very naïve perspective in which it is the benevolence of the authors that causes the theoretical economic literature to be created. Of course, if we take an economic perspective, then benevolence is not the

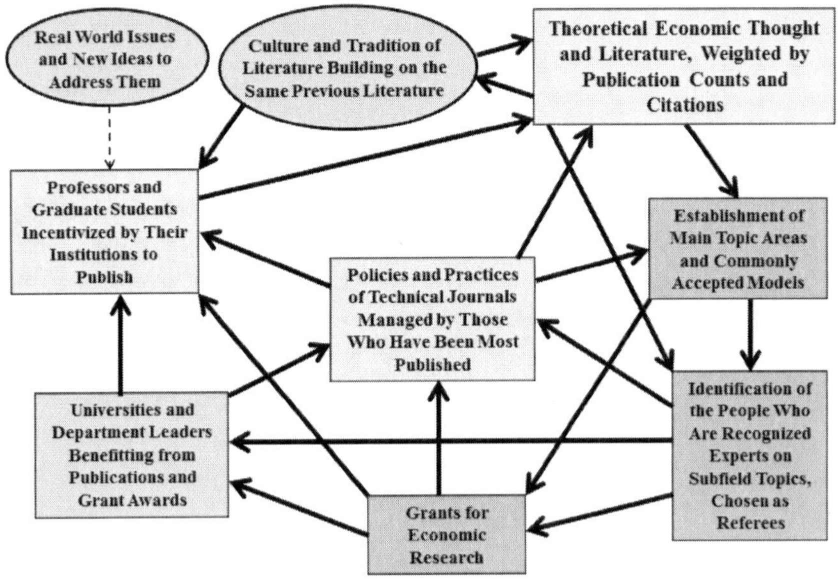

Figure 2.4 The Circular Flow that Determines Theoretical Economic Thought and Literature. Created by the author.

underlying motivational force, but as Adam Smith's *Wealth of Nations* would suggest, authorship is motivated by "self-love."[13] Each element of the "circular flow" in Figure 2.4, with the exception of "real world issues and new ideas to address them," are "spokes in the wheel," basically being controlled by other elements in the system. For example, authors cannot produce theoretical literature that is not consistent with the culture and tradition of how new literature builds on the same previous literature. Those who are recognized as experts on subfield topics have enormous influence over what studies get published and which professors receive research grants, etc.

As shown in the figure, the theoretical economic thought and literature, shown in the top right, are responsible for establishing "main topic areas and commonly accepted models." These are also quite high "barriers to entry" (a common term in economics) to anyone wishing to contribute to theoretical literature. This is because the first part of each theoretical paper requires not only the sufficient mathematics and basic economic theory to understand the topic at hand, but also familiarity with a standard model, or set of models, that have already been published on the same topic. In other words, each theoretical paper starts with a boilerplate that instantly places it within a very small world where there are few high-level experts and few journals that might publish the paper given its topic. As also discussed elsewhere in this book, this small group may be limited, as well, to only those people who are privileged enough to have access to special databases that is relevant to that set of theories. If the researcher wants the paper to actually discover something important about the world, it may be constrained by its own initial assumptions (greatly determined by the previous literature) if that starting point is not very consistent with reality. The paper may also be greatly constrained if it uses variables like "knowledge capital" that may be virtually impossible to measure unambiguously.

Overall, the system favors papers that do not challenge the major initial assumptions of their subfields, because, in most cases, by not making waves the authors have a better chance of allying themselves with the in-crowd of their respective subfields. As most economists know, much of this depends on the flexibility of the subfield, which in turn, could depend on extremely circumstantial factors such as the idiosyncrasies and personalities of the few most prominent leaders of the subfield, the tendency for the in-crowd to want to keep the publications, grants, and limelight in general contained within a small group of prestigious institutions, etc.

Much also depends on the size of the pie. If the subfield is "rich" in terms of grants received, teaching positions offered with expertise in that subfield, several journals offering publication outlets, and a growing interest in the topic by the public, then the leaders within that subfield will be less restrictive of new papers that might challenge the standard assumptions by new entrants into the subfield. Conversely, the leaders within those subfields that are struggling for grants, publications, teaching positions, etc., may want to keep their publications *in the family* by restricting new entrants into the published subfield to the compadres who are already in their club, and to the graduate students who are working on dissertations with them.

The bottom line in all of this is that the incentive system to publish economic theory has very important components that are independent of what this chapter first began to discuss—the beauty, the pride, and the pleasure of advancing knowledge, and the valuable benefits it offers to humanity. At the other extreme is simply a game (in fact, an adolescent or *ruthless* game at times) that is sometimes based, in part, on arrogance, cronyism, and other bad things that have nothing at all to do with the honest pursuit of valuable knowledge. How this game is played is the very subject of chapter 4.

NOTES

1. Peter Sandman, "Introduction to Risk Communication (2016)" (video recorded lecture), accessed February 3, 2017, https://vimeo.com/166620414.
2. For example, suppose one initially had defined units where it was believed that Risk = Hazard x Outrage, rather than Risk = Hazard + Outrage. One could then redefine each of the variables as being the logarithm of their original value, and this would change the product to a sum.
3. For those who might be interested, the seaport is Brisbane in Australia. (The picture is in the public domain.) http://tinyurl.com/zaupaec.
4. National Science Foundation, "Economics," accessed February 11, 2017, http://tinyurl.com/ju7r2dl.
5. In the old days, such references to standard ideas in general mathematics and science might need a reference for a better explanation, while today Wikipedia and Google would be sufficient for any further explanations of these concepts.
6. Paul Krugman, "How Did Economists Get It So Wrong?" New York Times, September 2, 2009.
7. Joseph Stiglitz, "Needed: A New Economic Paradigm," Financial Times, August 19, 2010.
8. Wassily Leontief, "Theoretical Assumptions and Nonobserved Facts." Presidential Address to the American Economic Association. American Economic Review 61 (1971): 1–7.
9. Thomas Mayer, Truth Versus Precision in Economics (Aldershot; Hants; UK: Edward Elgar Publishing; 1993).
10. Thomas Mayer, Truth Versus Precision in Economics.
11. Deirdre McCloskey, "The A-Prime C-Prime Theorem," Eastern Economic Journal, 19(2) (1993): 235–38.
12. Steven Payson, Public Economics in the United States: How the Federal Government Analyzes and Influences the Economy (Santa Barbara, CA: ABC-Clio, 2014).
13. Adam Smith (1776), An Inquiry into the Nature and Causes of the Wealth of Nations (London: William Strahan).

Chapter 3

What Allows "Literature-Only" Theoretical Discourse to Exist?

Regardless of all the various arguments made against most theoretical economics, "defenders of the faith" will continue to espouse the party line. That is, they will say that, regardless of the bad and unproductive habits of theoretical economics, good things—namely, genuine and extremely valuable discoveries in economic theory—do fall out of the chaos. They will continue to argue that these valuable discoveries, even though they may be rare, ultimately justify the chaos and the inefficiencies of the system. To get past this convenient, blind faith, I will argue that it is possible for us to identify what characteristics of most top-ranked, theoretical literature actually do prevent it from contributing to valuable knowledge. In this way, we may be able to filter it out from this point on, without removing any of the top-ranked literature that is truly valuable.

DEFINING A FILTER

Let us consider a subset of all published papers in economics that meet *all* of the following three criteria. If it meets *any one* of the criteria, the paper may still be considered as an acceptable contribution to useful knowledge.

Criterion 1: The paper uses a model that has no "real application." Along these lines, if the paper presents a model for the purpose of being persuasive on a particular policy position, but presents no real evidence in support of that position (and is only a model that essentially "rediscovers its assumptions") then it would still meet this criterion of having no real application.

Criterion 2: The paper relies on assumptions or data that cannot be verified, or the situation exists in which alternative assumptions or data can be reasonably found that would yield entirely different, conflicting results (as in the McCloskey's A-Prime, C-Prime Theorem).

Criterion 3: The methodology of the paper would only be understood, valued, and genuinely studied by a very small group of other economists with advanced expertise in that highly specific topic.

Let us call a paper that meets all of these criteria a "literature-only paper"—its purpose is only for the career advancement of the author and for the production of literature to be read and actually understood by a very small audience. Similarly, let us call the work done by economists to produce literature-only papers "literature-only work" or "literature-only discourse." *To be clear, this chapter does not discuss top-ranked literature in general—only literature-only papers that meet all (every one) of the above-mentioned criteria.*

THE CAUSES OF LITERATURE-ONLY DISCOURSE

I would now like to ask the general question: "What allows such literature-only discourse to exist?" Some of the reasons have already been expressed in the previous chapter, but in answering this question I will be more comprehensive. I will identify and describe eighteen reasons for the existence of literature-only papers in economics in the sections that follow.

The Pretense of Scientific Merit

The only thing that truly constitutes "scientific merit"—indeed, the only thing that really matters in science—is an honest and successful effort to learn how the world actually works—not an effort to create impressive systems of mathematical equations that only very smart and very educated people can proudly decipher. Many graduate students in economics, especially those with little or no interest or experience in natural science, are ignorant of this. They then go on to become economics professors where they remain ignorant, and pass on their ignorance to their graduate students, the cycle repeats with each generation.

In response to this accusation, many theoretical economists will argue that, from looking at the work itself, we have no basis for distinguishing between valid, scientific economic theory, and invalid, unscientific economic theory. Nevertheless, I would like to propose a very simple test that could enable us to make this distinction: We look at the assumptions made in the analysis, and ask, "Can an alternative set of equally defensible assumptions be made that will lead to very different conclusions?" If the answer is "Yes," then the conclusions of the research in question *have no degree of certainty*—implying that the research has not contributed to our understanding of how the real world works. If those conclusions are then used to provide a false understanding of how the real world works, then this is simply a deception, which may be harmful in various respects.

Let us call economic theory that falls under this category "unscientific economic theory" to bring home the point that science plays no role in justifying the existence of such self-serving conceptual games. Of course, I am not the first to make this argument—it has been made one way or another for, perhaps, nearly two centuries, by hundreds of scholars, as will be discussed in greater detail in subsequent chapters.

So why has the problem not been solved? The answer is that this solution, or anything like it, cannot be heard by unscientific theoretical economists—it falls on deaf ears, for three reasons:

1. The arguments are uninteresting to unscientific theoretical economists, who are motivated primarily by what they find interesting.
2. They will automatically dismiss the idea that they could be doing anything wrong, because of all the positive support they receive for what they do from well-respected members of the profession, and from their superiors in their work environment.
3. There is confusion as to what is right or wrong from the diversity of opinion that often exists among the critics.

With regard to the last of these, such critiques come from many different perspectives, and in many cases, even opposite perspectives. Neo-Marxist economists, for example, will argue against unscientific theoretical economics and in the same breadth describe how it fails to capture an important need for more government involvement in the economy. Libertarians will criticize unscientific theoretical economics and in the same breadth argue that it fails to acknowledge the importance of "liberty." I would like to call such critiques of unscientific theoretical economics "combo-critics"—criticizing this aspect of the profession while bringing up other issues that are also important to the critics. Below is a list of the different types of critics (of unscientific, theoretical economic literature), many of which are combo-critics:

Protesters and Shock Jocks: Examples of these critics (in terms of the organizations to which they belong) are the Occupy Movement and the Kick It Over Campaign, which have protested at various events, including at the annual meetings of the American Economic Association. These are combo critics who have offered extremely vague and ambiguous positions against unscientific theoretical economics that coincide with their criticisms of economic thought in general as it relates to corporate greed, economic inequality, and alleged financial instability. These critics actually do more to promote unscientific theoretical economics than to discourage it, by indirectly discrediting all critics of unscientific theoretical economics.

Bloggers and Op-Ed Writers: These individuals often espouse snippets of criticism in blogs and op-eds. Their writings fail to have any effect because they are presumed by readers to exist primarily for the readers' instant entertainment on a daily basis. So, by the next day, the arguments in yesterday's blogs and op-eds become obsolete, old news. This forum absorbs many of the critics' time and efforts, after which they may naively feel that they have done their part to address the issue, and they can then sit back and leave it to others to follow their lead (though the others will be passive readers who will do nothing). Another reason this category of criticism fails to be effective is that it is counterbalanced by the blogs and op-eds of the proponents of unscientific theoretical economics, many of whom are prominent economists who are echoing the party line that all theoretical economics is good.

Authors of Unscholarly Books and Articles for the General Public: These books go way back—I remember, for instance, books by John Kenneth Galbraith in the 1960s and 1970s, such as *Economics and the Public Purpose*,[1] and by Lester Thurow in the 1980s, such as *Dangerous Currents*.[2] These writings, as well, are generally combined with other criticisms of economics, thereby diluting the criticism of unscientific theoretical economics with other issues. But in any case, they are largely ignored by the economics community because they are not advanced or difficult to understand, and so unscientific theoretical economists simply dismiss them as being too simple and thus not worthy of their attention or recognition.

Scholarly Treatises of Unscientific Theoretical Economics: These treatises come in a variety of flavors, some linked to protest movements on the left, like essays by the Network for Post-Autistic Economics, and others, on the other extreme, reflect libertarian perspectives, like articles in the Internet forum *Econ Journal Watch*. Other examples include work published in formal scholarly journals like *Economic Methodology* published by the International Network for Economic Methodology. Also included are scholarly books and journal articles which often combine criticism of unscientific theoretical economics with additional perspectives, especially pluralist perspectives on economics. This topic is discussed extensively in chapter 7.

The Façade of Statistically Significant Results

If a paper presents a theoretical model, and then tests that model using real data, some might believe that this empirical side of the paper negates its classification as a "theoretical" paper. Moreover, they may believe that the statistical tests which were performed, and their success at acquiring "statistically significant results," demonstrate that the model is truly applicable to the real world. In many cases this is true, and in many other cases it is not. The reasons for this ambiguity can be as complex as one might imagine, and indeed many books have been written on this very subject from a wide range of subfields, from econometrics to the history and philosophy of economic thought.

In public debates over political issues we often see latitude in terms of proposed ideas being "both right and wrong" as they are expressed verbally. In contrast to political arguments, however, economic theory is presented in economic literature in a highly mathematical context that, like all mathematical discourse, does not allow for ideas being both right and wrong. For most cases of conflicting empirical evidence in economics, however, there is typically a much greater level of complacency among theoretical economists in contrast to natural scientists. In my view this is because economists generally recognize that, what they have discovered as empirical evidence for a theory can often be dismissed as insufficient or invalid evidence.

One of the most obvious and well-known problems in the empirical testing of economic theory is the "Fallacy that Association is Causation," which is so elementary that many readers might be disappointed (though hopefully only initially) that I even mention it here. I am not suggesting that theoretical economists are unaware of it. Indeed, I would suspect that nearly all of them, at some point in their careers, delivered lectures on it to their students. The fallacy has been referred to by different names, my personal favorite being "The Scotch Effect." "The Scotch Effect" is explained by the statistical tendency for poor people to drink beer, and for rich people to drink Scotch whiskey, thereby implying (through twisted logic) that, if you are poor and would prefer to be rich, you just need to give up beer and drink whiskey instead.

The greatest and most obvious problem with this fallacy in the econometric testing (and supposed verification) of economic models relates again to the economic theoretician's "strongest link perspective." That is, it is often ignored or given minimal consideration, because all the focus is being devoted to the derivation of the theoretical model. The empirical testing performed thereafter is in many cases what economists see as the extra busy work, or icing on the cake, that is needed to get their theoretical article published.

As a simple example, I have seen and summarized a great many studies with theoretical models that "showed" how R&D expenditures by firms "cause" those firms to grow, thus implying that R&D promotes economic growth. This is often (perhaps not coincidentally) music to the ears of foundations that provide R&D grants and at the same time provide grants to economics professors to explore the benefits of R&D to society. Most of these studies have either ignored completely or paid almost no attention to the possibility of a reverse causal effect for some firms, in spite of substantial, well-known evidence that such reverse effects do, in fact, occur. For example, firms that are already experiencing considerable growth have a much easier time expanding their R&D expenditures as a form of retaining their earnings (and not paying taxes on them either) than firms that are struggling to stay in the black for which greater expenditures on R&D would be a luxury they cannot afford. Moreover, it is also the case that firms that are in industries that happen to be growing, like those in the information technology industries, require considerable R&D as a standard requirement for their survival, while firms in very different industries that happen not to be growing, such as domestic cleaning services, would have little to gain from R&D.

Many of us could write thousands of pages, and spend the rest of their lives listing and explaining incidences of the this fallacy in the published economic literature—all one needs to do is peruse through journal articles and, with a little common sense, find one example after another. As just one other example, I saw a paper presented recently about immigration, where the author purported to demonstrate the politically correct, positive correlation between the percentage of immigrants in a metropolitan area and the economic output (gross domestic product, or GDP) of that area per worker. From this the paper concluded that immigrants are beneficial to the economy, all else being equal.

The analysis had two fundamental flaws: First, a worker's contribution to GDP can be much different from the GDP per worker ratio because of the contribution to GDP of capital. For example, if a large parking lot requires only one attendant who gets $10 per hour, the output (of the parking lot) per worker is huge because the revenue of parking services is paying almost entirely for renting the "capital service" of an available parking spot, and not paying for anyone's labor. In contrast, a barber is a much higher-paid employee because of the skills required and might receive a wage of, say, $30 per hour, but the output per worker for the barber is much less because there is so little capital services involved. The barber, as reflected by their higher salary in this scenario, contributes three times as much per hour to the economy than the parking lot attendant, but if we were to base our analysis (incorrectly) on output per worker, then the parking lot attendant would look like a much better worker (since we would be effectively attributing the capital services of the parking lot to them).

The other fundamental flaw in that analysis is the implicit assumption that the first flaw (of ignoring the capital services component) is uncorrelated (unrelated) with the proportion of immigrants in a metropolitan area. However, historically, and very much so still today, populations of immigrants are higher in metropolitan areas that are on coasts or borders, for various obvious reasons, some of which involve the history of the area and others involve current circumstances. If we consider a coastal city that is large and has a significant tourist industry in particular, then there are many jobs that immigrants can easily take, such as being a waiter in a restaurant or a maid in a hotel. Furthermore, resort coastal areas can easily attract wealthy homeowners, who like to live near beaches (or have major offices in Manhattan) and who do not mow their own lawns or clean their own houses, but hire domestic help to do those things, which also creates jobs for immigrants. It makes a great deal of sense, therefore, that metropolitan coastal cities like New York, Miami, Los Angeles, and San Francisco would have a great many immigrants to begin with, a strong demand to hire their labor as well, and have a high GDP per capita. Indeed, the paper's author explained that one great outlier in their analysis was El Paso, Texas, which they dropped out of the analysis because of it being such an outlier. El Paso had a very high proportion of immigrants, but for some reason, which the author could not explain, El Paso happened to have a low GDP per immigrant. Of course, El Paso is not anything like a rich resort, coastal area like Miami—its being an outlier in the regression analysis serves as evidence for the likely fallacy that I just identified.

Yet, this dissertation in economics will surely be accepted, with its politically correct (and perhaps highly publicized) findings, which will be presented as a result of the highly sophisticated model it contains combined with advanced econometric techniques to "test that model." Parts of the dissertation will be published in technical journal articles, and will probably enable the "job market candidate" to land safely into a tenure-track teaching position. This will happen in spite of the fact that the research findings were apparently based on the fallacy that association is causation. Yet, if it passed the scrutiny of the dissertation committee, what example does this set for the new assistant professor who must continue to contribute to the literature in the same way, over the next three years, in order to become a tenured professor?

If confronted with the criticism that there might be this causal-relation fallacy in their econometric conclusions, theoretical economists will often easily admit to that possibility (and they may well be already doing this in their own minds). Some may even mention this possibility as a qualifying remark in the conclusions of their theoretical papers. Nevertheless, as if none of this matters, if the same theoretical economists were accused of producing merely a purely theoretical exercise, without any connection to the real world, they would be dumbfounded by the accusation and wonder how they could possibly be accused of that when they clearly connected their theory to reality on the basis of the econometric testing that they performed. Indeed, the statistical work that typically is presented in the latter third of a theoretical literature-only paper exists expressly for this general purpose—to uphold the idea that the work is legitimately connected to the real world. This is in spite of the fact that its connection might well be seen as illegitimate if readers took the time to study it in any detail. The vast majority of the readers of literature-only papers, however, like the authors themselves, are truly interested only in the theoretical model presented in the paper. As just mentioned, the empirical work is more like administrative busywork in most cases, similar to work required to ensure that the author has used the same citation style for each entry in the paper's reference section.

A very important aspect of the fallacy that association is causation is that when it is considered, it is almost always considered in terms of the relationship between two variables only, as in the above examples of type of alcohol and income. Statisticians and econometricians, however, are thoroughly aware that this fallacy can exist in much more complex forms through, what are often called, "confounding effects" across variables. Table 3.1 below displays a simple example of this, based on what is known as "Simpson's Paradox."[3] The table presents a purely hypothetical example in which an experimental drug was tested to see if it could cure a fatal disease. The test was performed on a total of 164 people, of which 82 were elderly and 82 were non-elderly. All the participants in the study had the disease and were given the option of whether they wanted to try the drug or not. The results of the study, in terms of the numbers of people taking the drug, and whether they recovered, are shown in the table.

As demonstrated in the table, if all of the participants in the study are considered as a single group, then the data imply that the drug has a statistically significant effect (by a "chi-squared test") on curing the disease. But

Table 3.1 Example of the Fallacy that Association is Causation with Three Confounded Variables: Patients Recovering or Not Recovering from a Disease on the Basis of Age and Taking a Drug

	Recovery	*No Recovery*	*Recovery Rate (%)*	*Whether the Drug's Effect was Statistically Significant*
All Participants				
Not Willing to Try Drug	32	48	40%	
Tried Taking the Drug	44	40	**52%**	significant at $p < 0.05$
Non-Elderly (<65)				
Not Willing to Try Drug	14	6	70%	
Tried Taking the Drug	38	24	61%	not significant
Elderly (>64)				
Not Willing to Try Drug	18	42	30%	
Tried Taking the Drug	6	16	27%	not significant

Source: Compiled and created by the author

this result is spurious, and thus the conclusion that the drug helps to cure the disease would be a fallacy. The drug works less effectively on both non-elderly patients and elderly patients, so the drug cannot possibly be beneficial. This paradoxical result is a consequence of the following links that are implied by the numbers in the table: If you recover from the drug, you are much more likely to be non-elderly than elderly; and if you are non-elderly, you were much more likely to have tried the drug than if you were elderly (by the data shown). Thus, age may be a causal factor in whether one recovers, but taking or not taking the drug is not a causal factor. In this example, the fallacy that association is causation is manifested in three, not two, variables: taking the drug, age category, and whether the patient recovers.

As just mentioned, economists as a group are very knowledgeable on the fallacy that association is causation, but they do not regularly consider, nor test for, incidences of the fallacy beyond the level of two variables (and those who do are generally specialized in the field of econometrics, while the vast majority of economic theoreticians are not). Given this additional challenge to the validity of statistical findings in theoretical papers, it is even less likely that the papers adequately address the fallacy that association is causation.

Besides this causality problem, three other, interrelated problems are equally as wrong in terms of often invalidating the statistical findings of literature-only papers. These are: (1) the great imprecision, and arbitrariness, that frequently exists is the use of proxies for variables in the model, (2) the ability through modern techniques to experiment with hundreds of possible model specifications and alternative data sources to find, through exhaustive search, the luckiest results, and (3) the great preoccupation with searching for "statistically significant" coefficients of regression analyses, at the cost of learning what effects are truly most important for understanding the phenomena being studied. These factors will be discussed again in greater detail in other chapters, especially chapter 9 in a discussion on scientific integrity.

These additional problems, as well as the aforementioned fallacy that association is causation, are problems that extend well beyond literature-only research into the all forms of economic literature, including the literature that is often most studied and most influential for public policy and business operations. For example, with regard to the third problem mentioned—the preoccupation with statistical significance—Ziliak and McCloskey have noted: "Statistical significance is . . . a diversion from the proper objects of scientific study. . . . And yet in daily use it produces unchecked a large net loss for science and society. Its arbitrary, mechanical illogic, though currently sanctioned by science and its bureaucracies of reproduction, is causing a loss of jobs, justice, profit, and even life."[4]

The first problem mentioned, regarding proxies or indicators, relates to issues of measurement, and it is quite simple to understand. Economic models are based on ideal concepts, some of which can be highly abstract, such as "the level of knowledge in society" or the "depreciation rate of knowledge capital." Of course, for concepts as abstract as these, there are no real data—even the collection of such data would be futile without much more precise definitions, which simply do not exist and may be impossible to create. Thus, in international comparisons, for example, the knowledge base of each nation might be "measured" by a proxy like the average years of schooling of the population. The depreciation of knowledge capital, which from the outset is conceptually highly problematic, might be measured by something as questionable as the average rate of decay of annual citation counts for scientific articles. As a result, there is often enormous flexibility at the theoretician's disposal to find whatever data they can throw into statistical tests that have been designed on the basis of the theoretical model proposed in the paper.

The second problem mentioned is commonly associated with the practice of "data mining," which is one of the most commonly known problems in the economics profession and quite often the brunt of jokes among economists. It is often described by the adage that most economists have already heard: "If you 'beat-up' the data long enough, the data will eventually throw up their hands and say 'We surrender—we will tell you whatever you want to know!'" This topic is discussed in more detail in chapter 9.

Selling New Terminology and Supposedly New Concepts

In many cases new terminology is offered in literature-only discourse as the basis for a new theoretical model that appears to capture an important concept. In general, the important concept is already known and understood under different names. Nevertheless, when a prominent theoretical economist presents a new term that they promote as a "new concept," and at the same time present a very elaborate and sophisticated model to supposedly "explain" the concept in mathematical terms, it may appear, especially to naïve observers, that their research has truly discovered something important. Many may have trouble distinguishing in their own minds the value of the new terminology from the value of the arbitrary assumptions that were used to create a sophisticated model to explain it.

To illustrate examples of this, I will refer to the subfield of economics that focuses on innovation and technological change. As I mentioned in my book on *Economics, Science and Technology*,[5] examples of new concepts in this subfield include, "'technological trajectory,' 'technological discontinuity,' 'knowledge as a form of capital,' 'national innovation systems,' 'general purpose technologies,' and the 'internationalization of R&D'". Let us now consider just one of these terms. In their book *General Purpose Technologies and Economic Growth* (and in journal articles before the book was published),

Helpman and Trajtenberg define a term that Bresnahan and Trajtenberg originally created, called the "general purpose technology" (GPT):

> In any given "era" there typically exists a handful of technologies that plays a far-reaching role. . . . The steam engine . . . electricity . . . and microelectronics. . . . Breshnahan and Trajtenberg (1995) refer to them as general purpose technologies (GPTs hereafter). GPTs are characterized by the following features: (1) They are extremely pervasive; that is, they are used as input by a wide range of sectors in the economy. (2) Their potential for continual technological advances manifests itself ex post as sustained improvements in performance. (3) Complementarities with their user sectors arise in manufacturing or in R&D technology.[6]

As I discussed in *Economics, Science and Technology*, the concept of the GPT has a broad appeal, and might easily fall into the category of "basic common sense" to most observers. That is, it describes the general nature of what people might expect from a technological breakthrough and subsequent generation of all of the inventions that will follow from it. Let us first step back and realize, and then accept, that this commonsense understanding of how technological advancement occurs is something that we would hope most reasonably intelligent adults would already know. Beyond that, the above quotation by Bresnahan and Trajtenberg reflects a somewhat amateurish perspective on science and technology. For example, the steam engine is only one particular type of machine, while "electricity" is a form of energy that was discovered not invented, and its effects are pervasive across the vast majority of all technological advances in the past century, including "microelectronics" which they list as a separate item. In this sense the authors are not consistent in any scientific manner in terms of what they are calling a "technology." Perhaps this reflects their backgrounds in mathematics and social science as opposed to the natural sciences or engineering, or simply that they were not interested in giving more thought to the examples that they mentioned when they wrote them into the paper.

The text quoted above was at the beginning of Helpman and Trajtenberg's 1998 chapter, after which they devote another two pages of similar discussion. On the third page of the chapter a new section is abruptly introduced on "building blocks," which now begins to explain the GPTs in terms of a mathematical model which becomes the centerpiece of their thesis. The beginning of that model is shown below in Figure 3.1, where I deliberately display their text and equations in a figure, as opposed to a long quotation, so that readers, again, need only see what it looks like, without going through, or even thinking about, the tedious mathematics involved. As I have done earlier in this book, I simply want to illustrate what it looks like and how remarkable (in terms of complexity and restrictiveness) its assumptions are.

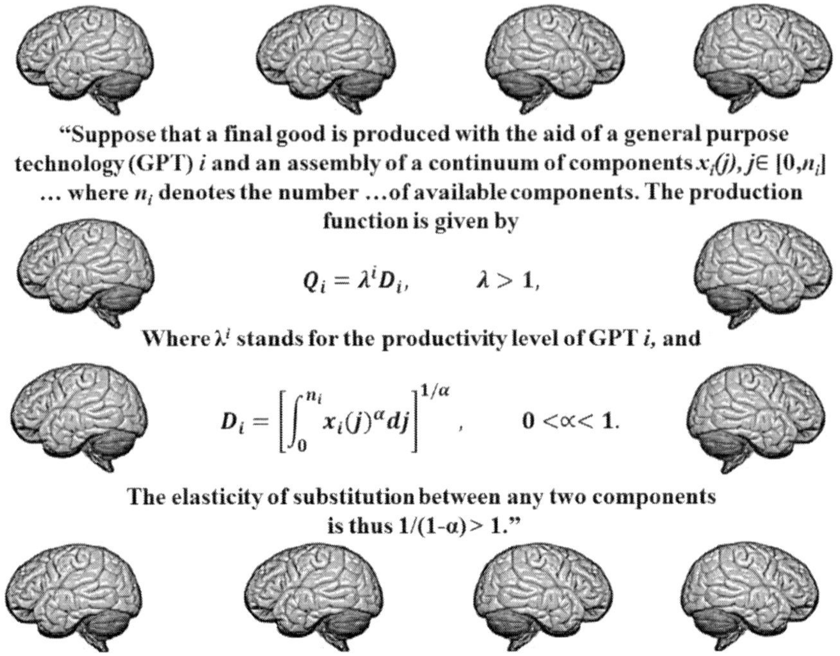

Figure 3.1 Merely the Beginning of Helpman and Trajtenberg's Brainy "GPT Model" Created by the author with reference to: Helpman, Elhanan and Manuel Trajtenberg. "A Time to Sow and a Time to Reap: Growth Based on General Purpose Technologies." In General Purpose Technologies and Economic Growth, edited by Elhanan Helpman, 55–84. Cambridge, MA: MIT University Press, 1998, 57. Brain Image by Wikimedia Commons, Shannan Muskopf (Own work), accessed May 6, 2017, http://tinyurl.com/lcx92ro.

In their chapter, the type of discussion shown in Figure 3.1 proceeds for the next, grueling, *twenty-six pages*, with only an occasional escape from the continuous mathematics. In these infrequent escapes from their seemingly endless onslaught of mathematical heavy lifting, the authors stop to offer some interpretations of the equations they have derived. As an example of these interpretations, Helpman and Trajtenberg state, "Thus the main inference from our analysis is that even if substantially more efficient, new technologies may barely make a dent at first in actual growth, since they have to await for the development of a sufficiently large pool of complementary assets to make a significant and lasting impact."[7]

I have argued that this main inference was based entirely on the strong assumptions that the authors used to design their model and on the impressive mathematical derivations that followed from them, independent of any single observation about how production processes actually work in the real world, or any reference to advanced knowledge in any field of science or engineering, even though the topic they purport to be analyzing is, indeed, technology. That is, they devoted twenty-six pages of mathematical formulae to analyze the mathematical consequences of the particular assumptions they started with—it was purely an exercise in the application of mathematics, not an analysis (in any true sense of the word) of "general purpose technologies" (assuming we can even agree on what the term really means in spite of fuzziness of how it was defined).

The Illusion of Accumulated Knowledge

Figure 3.1 above provides a small taste for the kind of strong assumptions that economic theory is generally based on, such as "constant elasticities of substitution among factor inputs." In actual production processes, such mathematical conveniences cannot possibly be realistic in most cases. As a simple example, some factor inputs are simply not substitutable with other inputs whatsoever, and there are in fact other economic models that are used to analyze what happens in such situations. Nevertheless, most of the assumptions that are made in model generation are simply adopted from assumptions used in previous literature, with no justification necessary except for the previous literature being assumed to be a reputable source by a reputable author (and of course, the more prominent the source, the less anyone might question its extended use). This perpetual recycling of the assumptions used in prior models, at a superficial level, promotes the perceived credibility of those prior assumptions. I am reminded of the saying "Fake it 'til you make it!"; in this context, advanced economic theory on technological change has definitely "made it," having been "faking it" for many decades.

As the theoretical literature essentially "builds on itself," it becomes regarded in the profession as a form of "accumulated knowledge." Theoretical economists thus simply use assumptions like constant elasticities of substitution whenever it will be convenient to do so for the new model that they are building. For these theoretical economists, it is as if it were a scientific fact that elasticities are constant, analogous to the constancy of the speed of light to physicists. The only catch is that, in reality, this is true for light, and not true at all for economic factors of production.

Each subfield of economics, like the economics of technology discussed in the previous section, thus has a core set of standard assumptions in its theoretical models. The top-ranked literature in that subfield tends to draw upon those assumptions first and then build more equations onto them. This creates a tendency of peer reviewers in the subfield to dismiss work that does not rely on the standard assumptions as an amateurish effort by authors who are ignorant of the topic. Moreover, even if the authors explain that they are aware of, but choose (for whatever reason) not to use the standard assumptions, they will then face an uphill battle in their challenge to the status quo of their subfield. Indeed, it may be an incorrect move on the chessboard in whatever game the authors are playing to advance their career, in view of the fact that they will be judged by the most prominent members of their subfield. The path of least resistance for them is often simply to build their models based on the most standard assumptions, regardless of how poorly those assumptions are connected to physical reality.

The "F-Twist"

The topic of this section has been analyzed extensively over the past six decades by experts on the history of economic thought. This section, however, will only have a brief look at the topic.[8] Our story begins in 1953 when Milton Friedman (who would be awarded the Nobel Prize twenty-three years later) wrote his famous book, *Essays in Positive Economics*. In it he argued that assumptions in economics do not have to be realistic, and in fact, as long as they have predictive value, *the less realistic they are, the better they are!* Here is the passage (with my emphasis in italics):

> In so far as a theory can be said to have "assumptions" at all, and in so far as their "realism" can be judged independently of the validity of predictions, the relation between the significance of a theory and the "realism" of its "assumptions" is almost the opposite of that suggested by the view under criticism. Truly important and significant hypotheses will be found to have "assumptions" that are wildly inaccurate descriptive representations of reality, and, *in general, the more significant the theory, the more unrealistic the assumptions* (in this sense). The reason is simple. A hypothesis is important if it "explains" much by little. . . . *To be important, therefore, a hypothesis must be descriptively false in its assumptions. . . .*
>
> To put this point less paradoxically, the relevant question to ask about the "assumptions" of a theory is not whether they are descriptively "realistic," for they never are, but whether they are sufficiently good approximations for the purpose at hand.[9]

Friedman had been widely criticized for this principle, especially by economists who understand science. Although I too find Friedman's statement to be incorrect, I also feel that his error was not that bad in comparison to the enormous damage that it caused for the next six decades after it was written, because of its even-worse misinterpretation by many economists thereafter.

With regard to this misinterpretation, I see the situation as analogous to the following scenario: A physician tells his patients, "Red wine is beneficial to your health because the antioxidants that it contains help to prevent heart disease. However, it should only be drunk in moderation—no more than two glasses a day." The patients then hear the first sentence of this two-sentence statement, but not the second, and become alcoholics who destroy their livers by drinking at least two bottles of red wine every day, all while thinking that they are improving their health, by the doctor's recommendation to drink red wine.

It appears that a similar situation has occurred in the economics profession as a consequence of Friedman's "unrealistic assumptions principle." For many economists, primarily theoretical economists, what registered was the first paragraph in the above long quotation from Friedman's book that "a hypothesis must be . . . false in its assumptions." What did not register is the second paragraph stating that it is still important for the assumptions to be "sufficiently good approximations for the purpose at hand." This second, largely ignored condition has an empirical element to it, since "approximation" implies the assumptions, though "unrealistic" as they may be, still have some predictive capability. In theoretical economic literature, there is often little or no effort to determine if the assumptions are, indeed, "sufficiently good approximations"—this requirement had been lost in the translation from Friedman's 1953 book.

Aside from this worst consequence of the Friedman's essay—its gross misinterpretation by the theoretical economics community—there has been substantial criticism, as well, of what Friedman actually did write in his essay. The best known of these criticisms was by Paul Samuelson in 1963 (who would be awarded the Nobel Prize seven years later). Samuelson wrote:

> [W]hat I and other readers believe is his [Friedman's] new twist-which from now on I shall call the "F-Twist," . . . is the following: A theory is vindicable if (some of) its consequences are empirically valid to a useful degree of approximation; the (empirical) unrealism of the theory "itself," or of its "assumptions," is quite irrelevant to its validity and worth. . . . The empirical harm done by the F-Twist is this. In practice it leads to Humpty-Dumptiness. Lewis Carroll had Humpty-Dumpty use words any way he wanted to. I have in mind something different: Humpty-Dumpty uses the F-Twist to say, "What I choose to call an admissible amount of unrealism and empirical invalidity is the tolerable amount of unrealism."
>
> The fact that nothing is perfectly accurate should not be an excuse to relax our standards of scrutiny of the empirical validity that the propositions of economics do or do not possess.[10]

In his article, "The Con in Economics" Noerpet explains a great deal more about why Friedman's falling-object example, as an excuse to ignore the validity of assumptions, is so very wrong:

> Newton's law of gravity, which Friedman calls the "law of falling" . . . turns out to accurately explain the orbit of the moon, which is moving in a vacuum.

> . . . And it also explains, despite Friedman's protestations, the movement of a feather dropped off the . . . roof and why it will eventually hit the ground even in a gale force wind. . . . Newtonian mechanics explains the motion of a feather provided we include all the forces acting on it as it falls. . . .The point is one cannot separate the theory of gravity from its assumptions. The assumptions are part of the theory and inform us when the theory applies directly and when we must consider other forces or better theories. . . .
>
> Friedman began with "assumptions that are wildly inaccurate descriptive representations of reality" and when caught instead of the expected mea culpa, he dug a deeper hole defending an untenable position with a weirder hypothesis. Why would such a smart person do this? In The Believing Brain . . . the psychologist Michael Shermer writes "smart people believe weird things because they are skilled at defending beliefs they arrived at for non-smart reasons." This is the Friedman Twist.[11]

However, even though economic students may no longer be required to read Friedman's *Essays in Positive Economics*, the F-Twist has remained to this day an *active curse* on economic thought, especially in its supportive influence over literature-only discourse. In spite of it simply being incorrect for all of the above-mentioned reasons, its resilience is attributable to two factors: (1) its telling many theoretical economists, who are not very familiar with scientific inquiry, exactly what they really want to hear, and (2) it was formulated by a brilliant economist who, to many of his admirers, could not possibly have gotten anything wrong. (This related to the "blind admiration" factor, mentioned below.)

The Convenience of Living in a Separate Reality

Suppose biologists are studying a particular phenomenon, but in their studies they find that the causality associated with that phenomenon may be better explained by accumulated knowledge in one of the other sciences (e.g., chemistry). When placed in such a situation, the biologists would defer to the expertise in that other field, consistent with the general perspective of there being only one objective reality, and the fields of science are simply divided in order to explore different domains within that same reality. In economics it is generally quite the opposite, as we saw in the above examples of the F-twist and GPTs: In economics, the accumulated knowledge of the natural sciences are, more often than not, simply ignored, as if science can be recreated by economists in their own separately defined reality, justified only by the official and recognized publication of their theoretical models. I discuss this topic further in chapter 10. Since many economic theories do not involve phenomena or principles that are studied in the natural sciences, this limitation may not appear to be a problem for most forms of theoretical economic literature. It does reflect, however, the broader problem that the economic theorists often have a tendency to view the universe complacently in a separate reality, which I discuss in chapter 8.

The incredible autonomy, or disconnect, of modern theoretical economics to other established (and often more reliable) disciplines has been observed at many levels. As another example, Deirdre McCloskey has spoken a great deal about "Max U" (for "maximizing utility")—the hypothetical entity that is assumed to be a human being as seen in the world of economic theory, which was historically also called "homo economicus" to distinguish the entity from homo sapiens or homo erectus as studied in biology and anthropology. She has argued that the dominance of the Max U perspective in current theoretical economics is horrific, where the hypothetical Max U, if he were a real person, would be regarded as a psychopath by experts in the field of psychology. This is because only a psychopath would have all of his behavior determined exclusively on the basis of maximizing his "utility" (as it is commonly defined in economics). As an example, McCloskey writes:

> Since the invention of Samuelsonian economics, *Vireconomicus* has been characterized as Max U. . . . Most young male economists nowadays simply can't understand a piece of economic reasoning that is not expressed as the adventures of Max U. . . . But it's an idiot savant's life. It's made worse by the techniques added on to the game-playing of modifying Max U assumptions endlessly, namely, existence theorems and t tests. . . . It's the particular techniques of existence theorems and t tests, widely practiced but never actually defended . . . that need to go into the rubbish bin. . . . Neither endless modifications of Max U nor existence theorems nor t tests tell us about the world as it actually is. If any of them did there wouldn't be so very many of them.[12]

Along the lines that McCloskey describes, it is simply incredible how pervasive theoretical economics have been in influencing the perspectives of economists. As an example, consider the very basic concept of fairness. Since economics has more to do with how income and wealth are distributed in society than any other field of study, one might expect the concept of fairness to receive some attention in economics, either directly or indirectly, though it is implicitly assumed that is not in Max U's vocabulary. In any case, I found it interesting how fairness is sometimes approached in economic theory.

Consider as one example a theoretical article published by Schneider and Zimmerman in *Review of Social Philosophy* in 2012 entitled "Fairness and Its Price." In it they write:

> [W]e have to distinguish between two situations of 'unfair trades', i.e., situations where the surpluses of consumers and producers are considerably different. . .

> . [W]e will not focus on trades between individuals in a narrow sense but—in accordance with welfare analysis—on trades between the group of consumers and the group of producers. This goes in line with Varian (1974), whose definition of fairness is related to the aggregate instead of the individual level.[13]

Simply how these concepts are presented I find fascinating. The authors do not say "we restrict our analysis to that of fairness between groups," but instead say that they accept a definition of fairness that excludes fairness to individuals, with the rationalization that one of the most prominent economists in economic theory—Hal Varian—had already assumed this in a model that he published in the *Journal of Economic Theory*. I would still give the authors the benefit of the doubt that, in their daily lives, they cannot have such an axiomatic perspective on fairness.

The Comfort of a Simpler World

While top-ranked literature often appears, by design and quite intentionally, to be highly complex and conceptually rigorous, it is actually quite the opposite: It creates a much simpler world for economists to think about, stress over, or attempt to understand. The mathematical derivations are of course complicated, even for the people who are good in mathematics, because there is a great deal of accumulated knowledge regarding those derivations, many of which are taught in advanced graduate courses. However, once these mathematical derivations become familiar territory, there is generally little for one to stress over. It is not unlike what happens when one studies a new language; it is difficult and stressful and first, but once fluency is achieved and is practiced daily, it becomes a cakewalk.

This situation is dramatically different from research involving the real world. Thus, in spite of the heavy lifting of the mathematics involved, life is so much easier studying literature-only discourse in economics than studying, and trying to actually make progress on real-world phenomena and circumstances. For this reason, literature-only discourse offers a simpler and easier life, which helps explain why many economists are attracted to it and continue to allow it to define their existence.

As an example, I once saw a conference paper written by an economist who was a well-published and recognized expert on productivity measurement, which is a subfield that is no stranger to literature-only discourse. The paper examined the productivity of hospital services, using as an indicator the average number of days that patients stay in the hospital. According to the paper, the fewer the hospital days are, the greater the productivity is of hospital services. The study found that the average number of hospital days per patient, over several years, did not decline, and thus, the paper concluded that the productivity of hospital services did not increase.

During the conference presentation, when it was time for questions, I asked the author if his analysis "normalized the hospital days by type of illness or by the age of the patients." At first he did not appear to fully understand my question, so I explained it further by way of an example: Suppose, for example, that through great strides in medical services, including hospital services, the average lifespan rises from eighty years to ninety years, and so the makeup of hospital patients changes to include many more people in their eighties and above, when before it did not. It is likely to be harder for people in their eighties and above to recover from their illnesses (or indeed be released eventually to hospice if they do not recover). Thus, the average length of hospital stays for this more recent pool of patients may not be lower than for the previous pool. Nevertheless, in the most basic sense, productivity in health services did indeed increase substantially by enabling people to live to much older ages. Therefore, if the data on hospital stays is not normalized by age of patients, it would not reveal this increase in true productivity.

The economist who performed the analysis, however, disagreed vehemently with my suggestion of such normalization of the data and the work it would involve. He had created a simple, convenient, and, in his mind, defensible indicator with which to measure productivity, and saw no reason to change it. He was perfectly comfortable in his greatly simplified world; and he could not understand why I was rocking the boat with epidemiological issues that was outside his purview and, in his view, outside economic discourse generally.

The Andersen Effect

I am introducing here the term "Andersen Effect," from Hans Christian Andersen's 1837 childhood tale, which in economic terms might be described as tale pertaining to quality measurement and marketing in the retail clothing industry. The tale is entitled "The Emperor's New Clothes."[14] Readers may initially be disappointed that such a cliché and "unscholarly" reference as this is being used here in this discussion. However, it is important to note that what is commonly remembered about the tale, or the cliché metaphor that has been taken from it, does not do justice to the brilliance behind Andersen's prose in the written work itself.

The well-known metaphor is that an emperor is wearing no clothes but has been told, and believes himself, that he is wearing magnificent clothes. In a parade before his subjects the emperor displays his supposed new attire, and his subjects cheer because that is what they feel they are supposed to do, until a young boy exclaims "The emperor has no clothes!" and the crowd realizes the fact. The cliché metaphor that has been used for close to two centuries thereafter has meant the following: something that is truly empty or vacuous is hailed as being wonderful because of a false reputation that it enjoys and the blind faith placed on it.

The written work, however, contained much more than this rather simple idea. In the tale, the charlatans who were selling the clothes to the emperor and his advisors explained that the clothes were, in fact, invisible to *those who were unsophisticated and feebleminded*, and the clothes were visible only to those who were *befitting of a high position in the emperor's society*. Thus, when the emperor and his advisors heard this description of the situation, they feared that, if they admitted to not seeing the clothes, they would be accused of being feebleminded and unfit for their professional positions. This was the underlying factor that had allowed the emperor and his advisors to fall for the charade.[15]

In economics it is quite common for graduate students who are exposed to top-ranked literature to question many of the assumptions made behind economic models, and to wonder whether so much advanced mathematics, built on those assumptions, is ultimately worthwhile. (Indeed, there must be a selection process where those who are most offended by it go off for a second degree in business, or public policy, etc. rather than "piling it higher and deeper" in economics.) The most naïve of those graduate students, however, and the ones who are most likely to become economics professors and add to top-ranked literature in their own careers, are inclined to hold back on any such skepticism, for fear that they, too (like the emperor's advisors), may be perceived as being feebleminded. Similarly, more advanced researchers who are impressed with the level of mathematics that underlie top-ranked literature may also dismiss their own skepticism, wondering how the authors of theoretical economic literature, who are so brilliant in math, could possibly be doing anything wrong. It is thus commonly believed that contributors to literature-only discourse in top-ranked journals are smart enough to see something that most other people are just not smart enough to see!

The Autonomy, Self-Regulation, and Self-Governance of Economic Subfields

Economic literature is divided into subfields, where each has a fairly well-defined group of individuals who are its senior advisers. These senior advisers are a very small group who generally know each other, forming, essentially, a club, with varying degrees of cronyism. The most prominent members of the club are often affiliated with a small set of institutions that have tended to provide individuals to serve as members of the club for decades. Those members who are not associated with these institutions often have an indirect connection to them in any case, such as by coauthoring papers with someone who is in one of these institutions. Occasionally, members of the club have internal feuds, but it is much more common for them to support each other's work, as, essentially, a mutual admiration society. Even when feuds do break out, the debate is usually beneficial to both sides by raising attention to the subfield, and by legitimizing and promoting a proliferation of the literature on the debate itself.

As an example, in the late 1990s and early 2000s, a debate raged within the "productivity measurement club" over whether computers have led to increased productivity—some saying they did, others saying they did not. This debate created no hard feelings on either side, but allowed both sides to benefit greatly from publications, speaking events, and research grants to further investigate the question.

New members of the club are generally brought in by invitation of existing members, especially the graduate students doing their doctorates under an adviser who is already in the club. This is done even to the point of identified "royal lineages," where an important credential for a person to have is to have been the student of a prominent figure in their subfield. Such a credential, and claim of "royalty," does have significance in the profession.

Research topics are generally established by the senior advisors of the club and are often informally assigned to junior members. The junior members are often given access to datasets that are needed for these research projects, which are not available to the public, thereby giving them exclusive rights to perform research on the topic. Under these circumstances, there becomes a clearly chosen elite group of junior members who are predestined to have their work published in the subfield.

Members of the club thus owe their careers and allegiance to the club, and this makes it taboo for them to ever criticize the club. It follows that criticism of what the club does can only come from outside the club. In turn, when such outside criticism is voiced, it is often dismissed by the club's leaders as being unqualified, since nonmembers of the club are seen as having less expertise in the club's subfield as the club's most prominent members.

Tolerance and Peace among Opposing Subfields

Although there are few, if any, real internal debates within the same subfield (or club), one might still wonder why members of one subfield might not criticize the work of another subfield if the two subfields tend to have conflicting perspectives or policy recommendations. If all subfields have a bent for mutual admiration and for theoretical models that tend to rediscover their own assumptions, however, then members of one subfield may be reluctant to criticize the members of other subfields, given how much they all have in common! The underlying principle here is simply that people who live in glass houses are usually disinclined to throw stones. Or, as the character Don Corleone (the Godfather) in the book and movie, *The Godfather*, expressed, when he wanted to keep the peace with the other Mafia families, "It don't make any difference to me what a man does for a living."[16]

I realize that peace and tolerance among groups of people with different views is often a good thing, but in this particular case I find there to be two sad aspects about it. The most obvious is the absence of scrutiny and of debate that it implies—without which there is less attention and interest within any of the subfields in finding truth or in solving important problems, and probably less progress made as a result. Less progress is made because less information or analytical arguments are shared that might bring people to improve the existing knowledge on any of the issues—in other words, each group exists in tranquility in the own version of the universe, with nothing to learn from the other group. Unless one group knows better than any other group on every possible issue, this implies a loss in potential knowledge that could be gained through debate between the groups.

The second sad aspect of such tranquility, and absence of debate, among differing subfields of economics, is that they reflect, and also foster, a complacency (if not an outright apathy) about finding the best way to look at things. Whether one is "right or wrong" becomes a mute question—everyone is both right and wrong, and so what difference does it make? Knowledge development then reduces to a matter of preferred style, and or simply luck-of-the-draw in terms of one's exposure to mentors from different schools of thought, and this ultimately discredits and dumbifies the pursuit of knowledge itself.

It is interesting to see historically how scientists who have been passionate in their quest for knowledge have engaged in fierce debates, not because they did not get along, but because they felt that debating over what they believed in was an important part the process of knowledge development. Economic theorists so often like to think of themselves as similar to theoretical physicists. Yet, it is quite rare to see the kind of debate that existed, for example, between Albert Einstein and Nicolas Bohr, where the first said, "God does not play dice with the universe," and the second replied, "Stop telling God what to do."[17] Similarly, I recall when a fierce debate in immunology was taking place in the mid-to-late 1980s over the question of whether the acquired immunodeficiency syndrome (AIDS) was caused by a virus or by some other mechanism. That debate was a crucial one, where the victory of those saying it was from a virus was a key component in our developing the knowledge to treat the disease. The relative absence of debates across subfields of economics is a discouraging reflection of an overall disinterest in finding truth and in finding the best possible solutions to existing problems.

Support for Graduate Students, and Their Rites of Passage

A great deal of the literature-only work in economics is expected as a "rite of passage" for PhD candidates. This is especially the case for the "job-market papers" that PhD candidates write as building blocks for their dissertations and also as essential credentials for their applications to teach after they receive their doctorates. As is commonly known in the profession, the job market paper is an especially important credential if it can be presented at the American Economic Association annual meetings or other prestigious meetings, or if it can be published in an impressive technical journal, or both. For either of these supporting mechanisms, it is extremely helpful for the graduate student to have a dissertation advisor who is a prominent professor at a top-ranked school.

Such work by graduate students to enter the teaching job market by contributing to top-ranked literature (or attempting to do so) is thus analogous to the hazing rituals of fraternities, or the grueling eighty-hour weeks that medical interns experience as their rite of passage to medical practice. The sacrifices that these and other groups make in their rites of passage generate feelings of entitlement to the advanced status and authority they will eventually acquire in their professions. There may then be confusion over whether the sacrifices that were made were actually useful in some way to their professions (e.g., perhaps the long hours of medical internships help train medical students in endurance and perseverance).

The opportunity costs of PhD candidates not performing research that is more valuable than literature-only research are incredibly great as costs to the student, to the profession, and to society overall. It is also remarkable how literature-only dissertation topics are often justified by dissertation advisors as a necessity for the altruistic cause of enabling students to receive grant money to support them in graduate school. Officials from granting institutions likewise speak proudly of their programs for supporting the income of graduate students, as if their grant programs were equivalent to social assistance programs for the homeless. Student grant applicants pursue literature-only research under the assumption that grant issuers are strong supporters of literature-only research, while grant issuers simply rely on the advice of leaders in academia who have built their careers on theoretical economic literature.

After writing an earlier version of this chapter, and sending it out it for review, I received a comment from one of the reviewers that my assumption about graduate students having a "rite of passage" was too strong. The reviewer wrote:

> A lot of grad students now have no "rite of passage". Most of them are now cannon fodder to keep Ph.D. programs either alive or well-funded. For the few star students there is a rite of passage into some form of club. An example is that 30 years ago no advisor would put their name on a dissertation for publication. That is now routine . . . a signal to employers that this one is okay.[18]

This use of graduate students as "cannon fodder" by graduate programs in economics is discussed in various ways in the chapters that follow.

The Ability of Intelligent People to Do Real Work after Playing the Game

Many economists contribute to literature-only work at some point in their career, and then change careers, essentially to perform more valuable work. At one extreme there are individuals contributing to literature-only work simply in association with their dissertation, before moving away from it. At the other extreme, there may be individuals who become highly prominent in literature-only work for almost their entire professional lifetime, but when approaching their retirement they might be offered a new position such as directing a government office as a political appointee, or directing a research project at an NGO, and they may then adjust to performing more useful functions.

When highly intelligent, resourceful, hard-working, and flexibly minded people become successful at doing useful work after they did a stint with literature-only work, the analysis of the ultimate effect of literature-only discourse can be easily confused. People might regard their experience with literature-only work as having given them a working background in the subject matter of their later practical work, even if that is not the case. And, it is generally in these individuals' best interest to claim (and perhaps even believe themselves) that their experience with literature-only work has enabled them to be qualified for their later position (for otherwise it would suggest that they were never qualified).

Naïve Pride in One's Success

As believers in markets, economists who perform literature-only research may naively believe they could be doing no wrong, since they are giving the technical journals and the organizations providing research grants precisely what they want. That is, they may see their actions as simply providing what the market system is requesting of them, and the market system knows best. Otherwise, according to their perspective, there would be no demand for theoretical economic literature, and the journals would not publish their product.

The flaw in this logic, however, ties back to the autonomy and self-admiration of the subfields, whereby the demand side that I just referred to is actually created by the supply side. The senior members of the subfields serve on the advisory committees of journals, the review committees of grant-issuing institutions, the selection committees for hiring economists, etc. There is virtually no "demand" that is not controlled by those who are already on the supply side of literature-only economics.

Blind Admiration of Prominent Figures

Coming full circle to the "Pretense of Scientific Merit" (the first factor that was mentioned) students who buy into this pretense the most are also most inclined to admire the prominent professors in their subfields. This admiration often comes with their confusion between (1) the impressive gray matter that their professors flex before them when presenting mathematical models and (2) professors demonstrating the actual qualities for which they *should* rightfully to be admired. Conversely, if students do sense, in their own minds, a whiff of skepticism that the esoteric theories that they are learning may be more show than substance, their admiration for their professors may create a type of blind-faith nullification of their skepticism. That is, in the language of psychology, some students may admire their prominent professors as a form of addressing their "cognitive dissonance" with regard to their internally repressed concerns they may have over the legitimacy of those professors' work.

The flip side of admiration on the part of those who do the admiring is arrogance on the part of those who are being admired. This yin and yang of admiration and arrogance within the profession creates a culture in which criticism of a prominent professor is often seen not only as ignorant (as described by the Andersen effect), or as disloyal (within the club that runs the subfield), but now as sacrilegious to those who greatly admire their famous (and in some cases charismatic) professors.

The Fact that Nobody Actually Reads the Literature

Along the same lines as the Andersen effect (with no one seeing the emperor's clothes), one of the greatest secrets that the economics profession as a whole has kept from the public about literature-only publications is that, in reality, *nobody reads them!* Actually, that cannot be true, because, presumably at least five people read them: (1) the one author (or two or more authors if there are coauthors, assuming the coauthors actually read more than only the sections of the article that they themselves write), (2) generally three peer reviewers who presumably read the article in order to approve it for publication, though how thoroughly they read has varied greatly, and often their graduate student assistants actually do the review for them, though that is not supposed to happen, and (3) the journal's one copy editor who plowed through the article to make sure the spelling, grammar, punctuation, etc. were all correct (depending on how one defines "read" since the copy editor most likely did not understand any of the economic theory in the paper). Furthermore, if the article had previously been a conference paper, it might have also been read by the "discussant" of the paper in the conference session in which it was presented.

Beyond these five or six individuals, the literature-only article will generally not be read by more than a handful of other people, in part by definition in the sense of our classifying it as a "literature-only" paper (as defined at the beginning of this chapter). For example, if an article becomes part of the assigned reading for a graduate class, then it fails to meet criterion #3 and thus it would not be a literature-only paper. But, the vast majority of top-ranked literature articles are not required reading for any class, and in general, they will hardly be read.

To many this will sound absurd so let me clarify that by "reading the paper" I do not mean perusing it, scanning, citing it in your own research paper, etc.—I mean actually reading it! These literature-only papers will certainly be scanned by many more people than the few people who will actually read it. It will be scanned by them for two general purposes: (1) the article could be scanned by prospective employers if it has been used by its author as a "writing sample" for a job application (including it serving as a job market paper for a teaching position), and (2) it could be scanned by prospective authors of other articles who are performing closely related work. Those other researchers may actually wish to glean some information from the article that they could use in their own research (the party-line basis for why the article exists), but more likely, they will scan it in order to learn just enough about the article to properly cite it in their own article. Thus, there may be a great many citations for an article, indicating how many other authors have scanned it in order to cite it. In this way, the authors who follow with related articles demonstrate that they have obeyed proper research protocol in recognizing the most current research on the same topic, and they have promoted comradely among the members of their subfield club (or avoided conflict that might otherwise exist if they "disrespected" previous authors by not recognizing their prior contribution). So, for example, perhaps there may be 200 people who might typically scan the article, 100 people who might cite it in their own research, 20 people who actually learned something from the article that influenced their current work (as opposed to citing it to reflect a thorough literature search), and 5 people (not including the journal referees) who actually read it from front to back.

This may beg the question, if nobody really reads the technical journal articles, why are those journals even published? Isn't the basic purpose of a journal to publish articles that will be read? To the extent that the journal articles are scanned, for the reasons described above, there certainly is some dissemination of information, even if the article itself is not truly understood by hardly anyone. However, that being said, *in actuality the technical journals that publish literature-only top-ranked articles do so, not as a product for the readers, but as a service for the authors. That service is to provide the authors with the publication credentials they need to advance in their careers.* This is very common knowledge in the profession, even though it might sound scandalous, as it rightfully should.

Occasionally, the journals do disseminate pathbreaking and highly valuable, top-ranked literature that truly advances knowledge in the profession, but this is a rare occurrence. (Some are, in fact, described and cited in this book.) This is one of the reasons that libraries and other institutions continue to purchase these journals, although the library may also be serving the needs of the larger number of "article scanners" described above, and the libraries are serving, as well, the authors of the articles.

Because the technical journals that publish literature-only articles already exist primarily for the benefit of the authors, and not the readers, they basically have little incentive to change their selection criteria and methods to make their articles more beneficial to their readers. In fact, the more they please their authors, the more proposed papers they will receive from authors, and the better able they will be to attract prominent authors who, in turn, will help promote their journal. That is, promotion of the journal will occur, not so much by the quality of its articles, but by the "big names" of its authors (and in most cases the "big-name institutions" to which those big-name authors are affiliated).

The journals also benefit by publishing articles that present research that has been supported by grant money. This adds to the journal's prestige by demonstrating to its subscribers that the journal is presenting the kind of research that is "earning big money," which to many researchers gives it higher status than research that does not earn money.

Thus, the journals depend on prominent authors, and those authors correspondingly depend on the journals, for the continuation of the status of both the journals and the authors. It is clearly a symbiotic relationship. But it is not a symbiotic relationship between *two separate groups*—these groups are hardly separate—they overlap enormously: As already mentioned, the professors who are prominent in the subfield associated with a journal generally serve on the journals' Board of Directors, or the Advisory Board that peer reviews the papers submitted to the journal for possible publication. In short, for most subfields, the professors in that subfield, and the officials who work for the journal and determine whether papers will be published, are all part of the same happy family.

The Misguided, "Theoretical-Physics Defense"

When I have shared my critiques of literature-only discourse in economics with other economists, I have been amazed at how often I have heard the response, "But don't the same problems exist in theoretical physics?" This idea had been expressed to me by Robert Solow in a letter several years ago, by economists serving with me in the same panel discussion on "Ethics in Economics" at the American Economic Association meetings, etc. Nevertheless, this "theoretical physics defense" is fundamentally flawed on a few different levels.

First of all, while this chapter is certainly critical of the economics profession, it makes no assessment of how economic literature itself fares in comparison to the literature of other professions. I am not qualified to make this comparison—economic literature is the only form of scientific literature that I feel qualified to assess to some extent. With regard to my own knowledge of physics, I only went as far as undergraduate classes in mechanics, and electricity and magnetism, quite a long time ago. Yet, I that feel my background in physics is usually no less than the backgrounds of those economists who frequently go around espousing the "theoretical physics defense." I cannot understand how this could be.

It appears that when economists say, "But theoretical physicists do the same thing," the following implicit argument is, in effect at least, in their minds: (1) We can assume that we all think that theoretical physicists are admirable in their efforts to pursue valuable knowledge, and that their work is uniformly accepted by all. (2) Ergo, if theoretical economists are accused of doing anything that theoretical physicists also do, then such criticisms of theoretical economists can be dismissed as either invalid or not relevant.

What makes this defense both adolescent and deplorable is that whether anything that a person does is right or wrong must, of course, be determined on the basis of the action's own merits and faults. Right or wrong should not be based on the childish excuse, "But other people do it too!"

There is an asymmetry here that many "but-what-about-physics espousers" probably do not see: Physicists should, and do, decide what to do with their own theoretical literature based on their own guiding principles and based on their own knowledge about physics itself and the physics profession. Physicists would not base their decisions about their own theoretical literature on any admiration they may have for *theoretical economists* or on any superficial impressions they may have about what theoretical economists do. So, if we economists, who so often suffer from "physics envy," truly want to be like physicists, then we, too, should proudly learn to stand on our own two feet in deciding what to do about our *own* literature (the way physicists care about *their own* literature).

Finally, the last time I checked, I have found that theoretical physicists are people too, as are the editors of their technical journals, the managers of their grant programs, the members of their committees that determine whether physics professors get tenure, etc. And, indeed, highly theoretical physics has not, by any means, been free of criticism. This is evidenced, for instance, by a book in 2006 by Lee Smolin entitled, *The Trouble with Physics: The Rise of String Theory, the Fall of Science, and What Comes Next.*[19] But, again, this is not relevant to the issue of whether literature-only discourse in economics is wrong, since that requires an independent assessment regardless of what theoretical physicists do. Needless to say, identical arguments are equally applicable to any substitutes for theoretical physicists, such as mathematicians.

Leadership for Public Relations Only

In 1994, Robert Solow had become a member of the National Science Board—the National Science Foundation's (NSF's) Board of Directors. Upon his arrival to the National Science Board, officials associated with running Board expressed their gratitude, before everyone in the room (where I was also in attendance), for Professor Solow's willingness to serve on the Board. He replied that he was happy to serve on the Board, saying that he and his colleagues have received considerable support over the years from NSF, and that he is now happy to return the favor to help NSF with its work. It was surely an innocuous statement, and one that might even be expected under the circumstances from any leader of a scientific profession.

I mention this as merely an example of the role that prominent economists have played with regard to (1) guiding the profession in terms of what work theoretical economists should do, and (2) representing the profession to organizations that financially support it, especially through research grants, but also through publications and teaching appointments.

Although Solow was there on NSF's Board of Directors, he had no input into NSF's economic grants program. His role was essentially (though not officially) that of a political advocate for public expenditure on basic research in science and engineering, where economic theory (some of which he was responsible for creating himself) would be used in such advocacy.

Reading between the lines, NSF had helped fund academic economic research, substantially, for over half a century, and so many of the academic leaders of the economics profession who have benefitted from that funding (and have seen their students, colleagues, and institutions benefit from it) have felt obliged to *return the favor*. Their returning the favor has involved helping NSF defend and promote its argument that the funds it has received in the federal budget, in order to promote scientific research, has been worthwhile for the nation. Indeed, this "economic return to R&D" was basically the main topic that my chapter addressed in the National Science Board's 1996 *Science and Engineering Indicators* report (which Solow reviewed for the Board).

The above discussion might suggest that I am hinting at a conspiracy of some sort, in the sense that economists might argue in favor of funding scientific research "in return" for some of that financial support going to their own economic research. Indeed, if scientific research were not extremely important for economic growth, then perhaps such a conspiracy might emerge. However, there is no conspiracy here because it should be obvious to all economists that scientific and engineering R&D are, most definitely, essential ingredients for economic growth. Barring exceptions in which technology may be used incorrectly (polluting the environment, etc.), it is certainly standard in basic economic thought that nations should promote scientific research (thereby advancing scientific knowledge) as a public good, and the economic success of nations could, in fact, depend on it. I would further argue that economists, because they may understand this better than many others, have a public responsibility to advocate government funding for scientific research, regardless of whether doing so might also be "returning a favor" to the foundations that have supported economic research as well.

I gave the above example about Robert Solow, however, to make a different point: As already suggested in the first chapter, the top leaders of academic economics, in terms of the positions they have held or the Nobel prizes they have received, have virtually no "global influence" on the direction of funding of economic research. They are essentially not involved in the grant-issuing process, and in the determination of what strategies or general principles should be followed, in determining the direction of funding (i.e., which areas should be funded more than others). In other words, the most prominent economic theoreticians may be called "leaders" in terms of the recognition they receive in the press, the large audiences they draw, their citation counts (which are important only in the academic world), and occasionally being asked to testify before Congress—all of the superficial things that one could list. *However, as suggested in chapter 1, with few exceptions (like Leontief and McCloskey), they have not been leaders in any real meaning of the term when it comes to taking responsibility for fixing the biggest problems that exist in the profession, such as the proliferation and dominance of literature-only discourse.* Their only role in influencing how economic research is directed is at two extremes: (1) expressing broad platitudes, directed at no one in particular, that appeal and plead for more valuable economic research, as the above-mentioned quotations in chapter 2 by Krugman and Stiglitz, and (2) participating as referees, at a miniscule level, in peer reviewing a handful of individual grant proposals and journal articles each year. They also have indirect influence in choosing their successors, in the hiring of their institution's professors, in determining which junior-level professors receive tenure, etc.

Some of these most prominent professors also write books that retrospectively analyze what should have been done (such as to have avoided the great recession), and some may say this does offer guidance into the future. However, it remains an open question as to what the motivation is behind these books, since the professors themselves are rarely actively promoting the changes they advocate by "putting their money where their mouth is" in terms of directly challenging the current system or using their power and influence to effect genuine change. They see themselves primarily as spokespersons for the profession (offering wisdom to those who want to hear them), or as advanced experts in very detailed aspects of their subfields, but again, not as leaders of the profession who are responsible for effecting any major change. In fact, most of them appear to support the view (at least publically) that no leadership of this kind is necessary—that the "market for economic literature" will ensure the value of economic literature (as discussed above and in chapter 1 as well).

Unintentional Support from Those Who Are Doing Real Work

Many economists, especially those who are not in academia (but many in academia as well), perform research and publish papers that are not literature-only papers. Many of these economists, of course, still use economic theory as a basis for the work they do. They may then browse through current journal articles to get more recent citations and the most recent and popular economic models that they can use to test their data against, in an honest effort to understand something valuable about the real phenomena they are studying. Along similar lines, they may browse a recent technical journal article and throw a sentence or two in their own paper to cite that article, thereby displaying in their paper that they did their homework in terms of performing an adequate literature review (especially for their work to be peer reviewed favorably). In doing so they are effectively endorsing the theoretical article they cited, even if they never understood more than the first 20 percent of the equations in that article.

The citation exercise for the researchers I am describing is simply a "cost of doing business" more than anything else. Yet on paper, it looks like the theoretical article that was cited was relevant to their paper. In practice, then, this "citation game" creates a great deal of confusion about the relevance of literature-only discourse, and can no doubt be used as empirical evidence for the alleged relevance of literature-only theoretical papers. Given the circumstances as I have described them, however, such evidence would be invalid.

NOTES

1. John Kenneth Galbraith, Economics and the Public Purpose (New York: New American Library, 1975).
2. Lester Thurow, Dangerous Currents: The State of Economics (New York: Random House, 1983).
3. Judea Pearl, Causality: Models, Reasoning, and Inference (New York: Cambridge University Press. 2000), 174–75.
4. Stephen Ziliak and Deirdre McCloskey, The Cult of Statistical Significance: How the Standard Error Costs Us Jobs, Justice, and Lives (Ann Arbor: University of Michigan Press, 2008), 2.
5. Steven Payson, Economics, Science and Technology (Northampton, MA: Edward Elgar, 2000).
6. Elhanan Helpman and Manuel Trajtenberg, "A Time to Sow and a Time to Reap: Growth Based on General Purpose Technologies," in General Purpose Technologies and Economic Growth, edited by Elhanan Helpman (Cambridge, MA: MIT University Press, 1998), 55.
7. Helpman and Trajtenberg "A Time to Sow and a Time to Reap," 73.
8. For additional background, see, for example: Mark Blaug, The Methodology of Economics or How Economists Explain (New York: Cambridge University Press, 1992); Alexander Rosenberg, Economics—Mathematical Politics or Science of Diminishing Returns? (Chicago: University of Chicago Press, 1992); Stanley Wong, "The 'F-Twist' and the Methodology of Paul Samuelson," American Economic Review 63(3) (1973): 312–25.
9. Milton Friedman, Essays in Positive Economics (Chicago: University of Chicago Press, 1953), 14–15.
10. Paul Samuelson, "Discussion," American Economic Review 53(2) (1963): 235.
11. Tony Noerpel, "The Con in Economics" Blue Ridge Leader, March 5, 2013. Accessed February 4, 2017, http://brleader.com/?p=10734.
12. Deirdre McCloskey, "Mr. Max and the Substantial Errors of Manly Economics," Econ Journal Watch 5(2) (2008), 201.
13. Andrea Schneider and Klaus W. Zimmerman, "Fairness and Its Price" Review of Social Philosophy 70(2) (2012):185.
14. Andersen, Hans Christian, "The Emperor's New Clothes," in Hans Christian Andersen, Fairy Tales Told for Children, (Copenhagen, Denmark: C.A. Reitzel, 1837).

15. Andersen, "The Emperor's New Clothes."

16. Mario Puzo and Francis Ford Coppola, Screenplay for the film, "The Godfather," 1972.

17. DaVinci Institute, "Niels Bohr and Albert Einstein," February 28, 2016, accessed February 2, 2017, http://tinyurl.com/jaofd8u.

18. William Charles Sawyer, email message to the author, November 8, 2013.

19. Lee Smolin, The Trouble with Physics: The Rise of String Theory, the Fall of Science, and What Comes Next (New York: Houghton Mifflin, 2006).

Chapter 4

How the Game Is Played

In the study of economics, no topic area could be said to be more important than the topic of incentives and what governs them. Indeed, an argument could be made that, in large part, economics itself is the study of incentives and how incentives affect production and consumption in our society. The importance of incentives in economic thought is evident everywhere, from the writings of Adam Smith to the latest reforms in health care policy and financial regulation. However, with very few exceptions, academic economists blatantly withhold their discussion of incentives as it may relate to the one profession, or service, that we would think should be closest to their heart—their own. This then begs the question of what incentives economics professors face and how those incentives affect the quality of their work. Most importantly, it begs the question of the extent to which those incentives actually promote the supposed, ideal goal that so many of them espouse, which is the advancement of useful knowledge. (As I have emphasized earlier, by "useful knowledge" in this context, I include knowledge that is valuable to have when it provides a better understanding to the world, regardless of whether it can be directly "applied.")

SALARY STATISTICS AND PROMOTION CRITERIA

From an elementary understanding of economics itself, it is fair to say that very few economics professors today would continue to maintain their university position if they were paid much less, and that many more people would try to be economics professors today if economics professors' salaries were much higher. Consider the salary statistics for economics professors, as shown in Table 4.1, in reference to the 2010–2011 academic year. Notice

Table 4.1 Average Salaries of Tenure-Track Economics Professors by Title and Type of Institution (Dollars in Academic Year 2010–2011)

Type of Institution by Degree Offered (and by Rank if offering Ph.D.)		*Title*		
		Full Professor	*Associate Professor*	*Assistant Professor*
Ph.D.	Ranked 1–15[a]	224,010	151,417	100,451
Ph.D.	Ranked 16–30[b]	181,518	133,932	
Ph.D.	Ranked 31–48	171,024	131,678	
Ph.D.	Ranked 49+	140,714	104,758	
Masters		106,953	84,803	79,492
Bachelors		103,262	80,382	74,677

Source: These statistics originated from Scott, C. S. and Siegfried, J. J. (2011): "American Economic Association Universal Academic Questionnaire Summary Statistics", American Economic Review: Papers & Proceedings 101 (664–667). They were presented in "Salaries in Economics in US Academia 2010-11," European University Institute, Last updated April 23, 2012, http://tinyurl.com/n6ux7d9.

Notes: [a]Includes California-Berkeley, California-Los Angeles, Chicago, Columbia, Harvard, Michigan, Minnesota, MIT, Northwestern, Pennsylvania, Princeton, Rochester, Stanford, Wisconsin-Madison and Yale. [b]Includes Boston University, Brown, California-San Diego, Cornell, Duke, Illinois-Urbana, Iowa, Maryland, Michigan State, New York University, North Carolina, Texas-Austin, Virginia, University of Washington, and Washington University-St. Louis.

that there is a threefold difference (2.9997 to be precise) between the average salary of an assistant professor at an institution whose highest degree is a bachelor's degree ($74,677) and the average salary of a full professor at a top-ranked, PhD-issuing institution ($224,010, in 2011 prices). Consider further the easily observable fact, which is widely recognized throughout the economics profession, that what separates these categories of economics professors the most is their accomplishments in theoretical economic literature, that is, their amount of publications in technical journals, weighted by the citations to those publications and by the relative prestige of the journals where the articles are published. In subsequent chapters I will provide a great deal of direct evidence for this causal relationship between the publication of theoretical economic literature and academic rank. The most obvious evidence, already known to all economics professors, is the official policies for promotion (especially for tenure) specified by academic, economic departments.

As an example, the following criteria are used by the Economics Department at James Madison University in its decisions to promote economics professors to tenure status or to a higher rank:

Promotion to Associate Professor or Receipt of Tenure Satisfactory:

1. A stock of research consisting of two (2) articles and eight (8) research points in total.
2. Exceptional: A stock of research consisting of three (3) publications, two (2) of which must be articles, and sixteen (16) research points in total.

Promotion to Full Professor Satisfactory:

1. . . . three (3) articles and sixteen (16) research points in total.
2. Exceptional: . . . thirty-two (32) research points in total.

B. NOTE: Research point totals must meet the following requirements:

1. Articles must account for at least 50% of the required total points.
2. Articles in ranked journals must account for at least 30% of the required total points.
3. For promotion to Full Professor, at least 40% of the required total points must have been earned in the base period and one article must be sole authored.[1]

In addition, JMU's guide to academic promotion goes on to state that the scoring system used generally is as follows: Articles in "top ranked journals"[2] earn eleven points, in "second ranked journals" [3] seven points, in "third ranked journals" four points, in "Other Journal indexed in the Journal of Economic Literature" two points, and in "Other refereed economics or cognate discipline journal" one point.

Does this sound at all like a game? Of course it does, and that is exactly what it is. While the evaluation of teaching ability has involved judgment on the part of the review committee that decides on faculty promotions, there is no apparent judgment related to the scoring game of publications. For example, by these rules, a fantastic article, from the standpoint of advancing useful knowledge that happened to be published in an unprestigious journal will always count as one-eleventh, or 9 percent, as much as an article in a top-ranked journal. This would be the case even if that that top-ranked journal article provided nothing more than an extremely esoteric, mathematical exercise that perhaps twenty people in the world found impressive, but otherwise offered nothing. The game is indeed well defined, and the stakes are extremely high in most cases—*essentially making or breaking the careers of economics professors.*

DO TOP-RANKED PUBLICATIONS CONTRIBUTE TO THE QUALITY OF LABOR?

Why Are Top-Ranked Journal Articles Given So Much Importance?

Basically, there are two party-line justifications for the existence of, and the focus on, top-ranked publications:

1. Top-ranked publications are beneficial to the rest of the world (outside academic scholarly discourse itself).

2. Top-ranked publications provide on-the-job training to improve the quality of economic professors' labor (by enhancing their knowledge and understanding of the world).

In addition, there are four other "under the table," or what I would dare call the *real reasons* for the focus on top-ranked journals in the promotion of economics professors:

1. This focus provides an incredibly convenient and extremely low-cost means of evaluation (no cost of acquiring information and no opportunity cost of the review committee spending any time to think about the basis of their decisions).
2. It may pass to most observers as an objective, noncontroversial method of assessment.
3. This game surely justifies and legitimizes (to naïve observers) the current ranks and hierarchical structure that already exists among academic economists.
4. The leaders of economics departments (and other departments that employ economics professors) simply do not know better and have never questioned whether these criteria are correct or should be changed. Rather, they are just maintaining a system they inherited when they first acquired any authority in the department, and they are happy to say to themselves, "Who am I to question it?"

In theory, however, these four real reasons could be defensible on the basis of the two party-line reasons. In other words, the publication game could be defended by the argument that top-ranked publications contribute significantly to the world and also reflect the labor quality of professors. It may further be argued that, the fact that top-ranked publications happen to be incredibly cheap to count, and that those counts are convenient to use, should not alone be held against them—all else being equal it is simply an added benefit for this system of evaluation.

The Irony of It All!

There are two incredibly ironic consequences of the publications game. Both derive from the fact that, for the vast majority of professors, the publication game, quite frankly, imposes an enormous amount of work—often grueling, often highly frustrating, and always very time consuming. It is common knowledge that the publication game takes away from professors the time that they could otherwise spend in better preparing their lectures (including performing research into the topics they should cover in class), and in speaking with and mentoring their students. In short, the publication game impairs their ability to be *better professors*, in terms of the main function that professors are *supposed to serve—the function of teaching*.

What I find most ironic about the publication game, however, is that it *ultimately reduces how much the publications are actually read!* By being forced to spend so much time writing and rewriting (in response to reviewer comments, etc.) the papers they submit to journals, on top of their classroom preparations, economics professors essentially have no time left to *read* the technical journal articles (other than their own) that they are supposedly producing for each other. It is analogous to farmers working so hard to produce an enormous amount of food that they find themselves malnourished because they do not have time to eat what they produce.

As a simple heuristic with made-up numbers (because the point is just conceptual and not worth the research for the actual data), say there are 50,000 economics professors, of which 30,000 are working their tails off in the publication game, and they publish 100,000 articles each year (or about two articles per professor, per year). Out of those 100,000 articles, perhaps only 20,000 professors find time to read seriously, on average, one article per year. (Again, I mean truly *read* an article, as opposed to scanning it, for instance, to ensure a thorough literature review in an article that a professor is writing themselves.) What if, instead, only 10,000 professors were producing only 10,000 articles per year, under no pressure to do so, and so their articles were much more self-motivated and designed to share useful ideas. In this alternate universe, perhaps all 50,000 economics professors would have the time and interest to read an article every month, and there would then be 600,000 read articles (counting a different one for each reader) instead of 20,000—a thirty-fold increase in dissemination of knowledge, and perhaps a 1,000-fold increase in the dissemination of *useful* knowledge. Of course these numbers are hypothetical—they are part of an illustrative model simply to explain the basic point.

Let us please reflect on this thought for a moment—the publication game actually has a net effect of making publications less read. It is paradoxical from a broader perspective: Publications have, essentially, *defeated themselves*, under the assumption that they exist in order to be read. Of course, if they exist for a reason other than to be read, then there is no paradox.

Outside of academia (e.g., in industry, government, and NGOs), the articles in top-rated technical journals in economics are simply hardly ever read and thus have essentially no effect on the world. There is one rare exception to this, however, in which one might see technical journal articles being used by a non-academic entity, but being used in support of academia. For example, if a research grant to an economics professor resulted in an article in a top-rated journal, the institution that provided the grant would be very inclined to refer to the article in its public relations efforts in support of its grants program. Furthermore, the same granting institution would be inclined to continue to issue grants to the same professors in the same research areas in expectation of generating even more articles that provide superficial evidence that its grants program has been effective at generating knowledge.

"On-the-Job Training" and "Quality Measurement"

For now at least, we are then left with the one remaining pillar that upholds the supposed legitimacy of the use of top-ranked journal articles as the basis for the promotion in academic economics—the idea that it effectively provides on-the-job training to improve the quality of economics professors' labor (by enhancing their knowledge and understanding of the world). Now, is this true? Indeed, we can approach the question in different ways.

One approach is to look at the academic's teaching as a service, whose quality is a function of their publications in top-ranked journals. In measuring the quality, or the value, of any good or service, there are four general approaches, which are not at all equal.[4] The first, most preferred approach is by acquiring information on the *revealed preference* of the consumer, which is basically observing what consumers are willing to pay for the product. Related to that is the revealed preference of the *characteristics* of the product, or the "hedonic price" approach, which basically asks how much consumers value the individual attributes of a product, and then adding those values together to derive the total value of the product. However, neither of these approaches can be used here, since there is little or no revealed preference in the selection of professors. Also, the consumer itself is ambiguous; the professors provide a service to the students, but also to the university to uphold the university's reputation and the value assessed by society of the degrees that it awards.

One might argue that the tuition students (or their families) are willing to pay for higher-quality professors might be used as a revealed preference of value, but that analysis would just not work for several technical reasons. Even controlling for the school, and for the specific economics class itself, students do not pay a higher tuition for classes taught by tenured professors with higher publication credentials than assistant professors with minimal publication credentials. Furthermore, tuition might be a little higher, on average, for top-ranked schools whose professors, on average, have higher publication scores, but the variance in tuition across schools would not be well explained by the average publication counts among schools, for a variety of reasons.

Without having revealed preference as the basis for assessing the value of the services provided by economics professors as a function of their publication scores, we are left with the two stepchildren of methods of quality measurement or valuation, which are: (1) *Contingent Valuation*, or stated preferences, where people are surveyed on how much they value alternate characteristics, and in this case on how much they value the services of professors with impressive publication records, and (2) *Input-Value*, valuing a product on the basis of the value of the inputs that were used to produce it.

Input-Value Approach to Quality Measurement

For reasons which should be obvious, the input-value approach is the only one that would make sense in this case for valuing the effect of publication scores on the services provided by economics professors. The logic behind the input-value approach is straightforward: The value of a product can be estimated as the sum of the value of the inputs that went into it. For some types of projects it works reasonably well, such as jewelry, where the value of the platinum or gold that was used to produce a necklace, and the value of the individual diamonds it displays, might reasonably reflect the value of the necklace, though the artistic appeal of the necklace is left out of the equation, unless the time of the jewelry designer's labor is assessed independently and imputed into the estimate. This input-value approach is indeed the methodology used in the US National Economic Accounts by the Bureau of Economic Analysis in valuing the entire government sector of the economy, which accounts for a very large portion of the GDP.

The input-value method of quality measurement, however, is not always reliable, in the sense that the producer may simply do a lousy job of creating a product of equal or greater value than what the producer spent on inputs. In fact, one might say that when companies go bankrupt, it is often because their product did not retain, in terms of revealed preferences in the market, the value of the inputs that they used to produce the product that they could not sell. In any case, one might fear that we are stuck in this case as well, since the only immediately identifiable and nontrivial "input" for professors' production of top-ranked publications is their labor. This creates a circular, indeterminate analytical paradox, since their labor is valued (in terms of salary level), to being with, on the basis of their publication scores. Nevertheless, there is a way around this circularity, which is to look at the "inputs behind the inputs"—namely, what it takes—what the professor needs to have and needs to do—to be successful at producing top-ranked journal articles.

If these, let us call them, "conceptual inputs," have inherent value in an intuitive sense, then we may see value in the top-ranked articles and, by extension, the value in the labor provided by those who have written them. If, on the other hand, these conceptual inputs appear to lack value, then the publications themselves have little value and so does the labor of the professors. These conceptual inputs present themselves indirectly in the next section of this chapter, which describes, by way of example, "what it takes" to produce a top-ranked journal article.

CHOOSING AN ACTUAL ARTICLE AS AN EXAMPLE

It is long overdue in this book that I provide an actual example of an economics article in a top-ranked journal, especially for those readers who may not be very familiar with them, and who might reasonably suspect that my criticisms of literature-only theoretical economics are simply too strong to be true. The article that I have chosen as an example for this analysis is by Jesse Rothstein, entitled "Teacher Quality Policy When Supply Matters," which appeared in the January 2015 issue of *American Economic Review* (AER).[5] I chose this article because of the interesting irony I saw in its title. The title subtly implies that the author is capturing some sort of *ethical high ground* by suggesting that educational policy should care about teacher quality. The irony, again, is that economics professors, like the author himself in this case, are often preoccupied with developing theoretical articles just like this one, at the expense of greater efforts to become higher quality teachers themselves.

Let us look at the article from the top down, and discuss the title a bit more. In examining "Teacher Quality Policy When Supply Matters," the term supply, in this case, means the supply of "quality." This article appears in a theoretical journal, and accordingly, its content is highly theoretical. That content is based entirely on assumptions and "simulations" that are run on those assumptions, without a shred of data, whatsoever, on observed teacher performance, or even anecdotal evidence of teacher performance. To the extent that this analysis is so highly hypothetical, one might ask what the term "policy" is even doing in the title—how can theory based on hypothetical, and arbitrary, mathematical exercises serve as a basis for policy? Is what is meant by "policy" simply a discussion of what policies should be adopted under alternative *hypothetical* scenarios? Would that then make the discussion simply a thought exercise without any identifiable connection to the real world, and without any "policy relevance" (since it could only be relevant if we know which of the hypothetical assumptions are closest to the truth)? Yet, by putting "policy" in the title, the author looks like a "policy expert" when one sees his curriculum vitae, or even reads the article's abstract or conclusions, which further expands the pretense of policy relevance, that is, the pretense that the article would be useful to policy makers in determining which alternative policies they should support.

What's in a Name? Only Everything

The author (or authors of such articles in general) is, in and of himself or herself, also an important part of the article. This is because the prominence of the author (i.e., the recognition of his or her name) makes a world of difference in determining whether the paper will be accepted for publication by the journal. The vast majority of academic economists will swear to this statement, and the vast majority of people who manage the journals (who are themselves prominent economics professors) will often deny it. The journal managers will argue, instead, that the reason that the top ten to twenty schools in economics heavily dominate the authorship in their journals, and also dominate among the referees who decide who gets published in these journals, is all merely because the top ten to twenty schools happen to have the brightest minds in the field. Considerable evidence exists against this explanation, however, which is presented throughout this book, as we have already seen.

A colleague of mine once told me that he had been extremely frustrated for several years because a paper he had written, and was proud of, was continually rejected by journals. He said that a friend of his then advised him to submit the same paper again, but to ask beforehand if a prominent professor who he knows could go in with him as a coauthor. The prominent professor agreed to do this *as a favor* (to help him get published) even though he did not contribute to the work. Sure enough, that addition of a prominent name as a coauthor enabled a journal to accept and publish the paper. This little story will admittedly be seen as quite boring among those readers who are familiar with the profession, since this aspect of the profession is very commonly known.

Rejection without Review—A Reflection of the Profession's True Colors

Highly disturbing evidence for this *big-name cronyism* is the following explicit statement made by the AER in its "Submission Guidelines": "*The AER reserves the right to reject papers without review.*"[6] This begs the question that if the paper is not reviewed, then on what basis would it be rejected, out of hand, by the AER? *What could a paper's rejection be based upon if it is not based on a review of its contents?* According to the American Economic Association, "The decision to return a manuscript without review is based upon a number of American Economic Review considerations, including expected probability of meeting the standards of the Review, breadth of topic, interest to the AER audience, and other factors."[7] One question, though, is how many people believe this, and another is how much sense does this make? For example, how can one determine the "probability of meeting the standards of the Review" without *reviewing it?* For that matter, how can one determine "breadth of the topic" (while the topics of published AER articles are often extremely narrow), or determine "interest to the AER audience" without reviewing it?

In terms of shear logic, the AER's policy of reserving the right to reject a paper *without* review would only leave rejection on the basis of the paper's title or on the basis of its authors' names (and their affiliations).[8] With regard to the titles of these papers, it is important to note that well-published, prominent authors are highly technical people who may know quite a bit about their area of study, but who may not be very adept at writing the best titles for their work. In any case, when it comes to books, as well as to journal articles, reviewers and editors will often suggest a title change for a work that is basically quite good, in spite of the work initially having a lousy title. On top of that, it is not unusual to see rather strange and obscure titles to published articles. The February 2015 AER, for example, had an article entitled "Thar She Blows? Gender, Competition, and Bubbles in Experimental Asset Markets." My point, which many readers would feel is too immediately obvious to have warranted this discussion, is that it is indeed extremely doubtful that when the AER states that it "reserves the right to reject papers without review," it is referring to rejecting a paper out of hand on the basis of that paper's title! What is then left is simply rejecting the paper on the basis of its authors (and their affiliations), without so much as reviewing the paper to give them any fighting chance to compete with the "in-crowd" of prominent individuals who are likely to be accepted by the journal with little or no review.

Begging the readers' indulgence here, allow me to reiterate the fact that what I am referring to here *is an explicitly stated policy of the journal*, not some deep dark secret or conspiracy of some kind that only I am claiming to expose. This is simply a widely known, publically announced, accepted practice, as if those who established and stated this practice could not, in their own minds, have possibly done anything wrong or anything questionable.

It is also important for us to note that, in order to submit a paper for consideration in the AER, at this writing, applicants pay a fee of $100 if they are members of the American Economic Association, and $200 if they are not members. It seems to me that paying $100 or $200 for a rejection that is made in an instant, without any review, on the basis of the author's popularity in the profession, is rather expensive—especially for the services of a nonprofit association that purports to represent "American economists" generally—not to mention unfair to the many individuals who made the payment out of their own pockets (as opposed to having received the funds from their own institutions).

The Author of This Sample Article

The author of the published paper discussed in this chapter, Jesse Rothstein, is a professor at the University of California, Berkeley, and his CV is quite impressive, which includes receiving a doctorate from Berkeley and serving as (1) associate director of Berkeley's Institute for Research on Labor and Employment, (2) research associate of the National Bureau of Economic Research, (3) senior economist for the President's Council of

Economic Advisors, etc. The most interesting credential, however, is that, since 2011, Professor Rothstein has been serving on the "Board of Editors of *American Economic Review*." Oh . . . did I mention that this article was published *in American Economic Review*? (I believe I did.) Thus, Professor Rothstein actually serves on the governing body that determines which papers will be published by the journal.[9] As I will discuss in chapter 8, the journal's policy has long been to exercise a peer review process that is not "double-blind" (a common term of art in peer review processes). This means, among other things, that whoever reviewed the paper knew who the author was. It follows that the decision to publish the paper was made by Professor Rothstein's close colleagues on the journal's Editorial Board. In other places such a thing would not be allowed to happen, that is, a potential author would simply not be allowed to publish in a journal that he helped manage, either as the policy of the journal or as a policy of the individual himself to demonstrate to the world that he can publish his research without the use of "obvious connections." Not so, apparently, for the AER, or for Professor Rothstein.

Conflicts of Interest in Publishing Research, and the AEA's "Disclosure Policy"

In the wake of the great recession, attention had been raised to an absence of integrity in the American economics profession and the need for the profession to improve in the area of professional ethics. This was brought out extensively in the documentary film *Inside Job*[10] and shortly thereafter by the inspirational book by Professor George DeMartino, *The Economist's Oath: On the Need for and Content of Professional Economic Ethics*, which received considerable media attention, worldwide (and will be discussed in chapter 9). An important aspect of this recognized need for greater integrity in the profession, though there are many other issues as well, is that many economists were performing research and reporting their findings as if they were acquiring purely objective scientific results, when they were, in fact, paid advocates for a particular position. That is, they were pretending to be working only for the goal of advancing scientifically objective knowledge, when in reality they were "hired guns" (the common term for it in the lobbying world of Washington, DC) who were paid to support the political agenda of whatever organization hired them.

As a result, the American Economic Association (AEA) in 2012 instituted a "Disclosure Policy" for articles in its journals, requiring the authors to disclose any potential conflicts of interest regarding their research findings. In other words, if they were paid to produce certain results, or were doing the work as part of their job in an organization that wanted the results to be a certain way, they were required by the AEA to tell this to the world, with the rightful purpose of adding reasonable suspicion regarding the objectivity and scientific validity of their findings. According to AEA's policy:

> Submissions to the AEA journals should conform to the AEA disclosure principles which state: (1) Every submitted article should state the sources of financial support for the particular research it describes. . . . (2) Each author . . . should identify each interested party from whom he or she has received significant financial support. . . . An "interested" party is any individual, group, or organization that has a financial, ideological, or political stake related to the article. (3) Each author should disclose any paid or unpaid positions as officer, director, or board member of relevant non-profit organizations or profit-making entities. . . . For published articles, information on relevant potential conflicts of interest will be made available to the public.[11]

The AEA's policy appears, however, to "have no teeth." That is, the disclosure policy states (with my emphasis):

> Failure to disclose relevant information at the submission stage *may* result in reversal of acceptance decisions. If the paper is already published, the journal *reserves the right to post a note on the journal's website and in its printed version notifying readers that the authors of the paper violated the AEA disclosure policy*. Violations of the disclosure policy will be brought to the attention of the Executive Committee of the American Economic Association who will decide on the appropriate course of action in each case.[12]

In other words, the AEA *may or may not* do anything with regard to violations of the disclosure policy, at the discretion of the members of the Executive Committee.

In any case, it is at least admirable of the AEA to mention that it will "make available to the public" "information on relevant conflicts of interest." Accordingly, as a "member of the public" who was studying this article by Rothstein, I looked to see if there were any disclosed conflict of interest by the author.

No disclosure statement appeared in the article itself, though I would think it might be much more convenient for the readers to be able to see one in a footnote or appendix within the article. Its inclusion in the article itself would, indeed, not take up much space: it would be smaller than some of the footnotes in the article and a tiny fraction of the three pages spent on the references at the back.

In any case, all that the article did have was a footnote that mentioned to the reader that they could go to a certain link—the "article page," "for additional materials and author disclosure statement(s)." I went to that link, and found, under a section called "Additional Materials," another link to

"Author Disclosure Statement(s)." Clicking on that next link, I found that it downloaded an obscure *.zip file, entitled "20121242_ds," containing two equally obscure subdirectories entitled "_MACOSX" and "DS," where, one might guess, the latter referred to "disclosure statement." Guessing correctly, I then opened the "DS" subdirectory, which contained a *.pdf file called "2012–1242_disclosures," and when I finally opened that, I luckily, and finally, came across the following text:

> Disclosure statement
> "Teacher Quality Policy When Supply Matters"
> Jesse Rothstein
> Funding
> I am grateful to the Institute for Research on Labor and Employment at UC Berkeley for research funding. . . .
> Potential conflicts of interest
> I have received compensation for consulting to teacher's unions and state Departments of Education regarding the design of teacher evaluations. In late 2013, I was retained as an expert witness on value-added models by the California Teachers Association and California Federation of Teachers to testify in the Vergara v. California case regarding California's teacher tenure and dismissal statutes. A portion of my testimony, delivered in early 2014, covered the analysis and results in this paper, as reported in a November 2013 draft that was completed before my retention.[13]

In short, after several minutes of "clicking away" and downloading an obscurely named zip file holding far less than a single page of text, one is able to learn that the author had been paid to perform the research for the purpose of advocacy and testimony in a legal case.

In the article's first paragraph, the author notes, "a California judge recently invalidated that state's teacher tenure law, finding that it 'impose[s]a real and appreciable impact on students' fundamental right to equality of education.'" With this powerful quotation the author only mentions this legal case—a case in which he, himself, served as a paid, expert witness who helped to cause this legal decision to happen. Yet, neither a footnote nor any other part of the article mentions this personal, and paid, involvement whatsoever.

Indeed, this advocacy aspect of the research was clearly hidden from the article itself, with the exception of clues to finding downloadable files from the AEA's website (outside of the article) that might indicate a conflict of interest for those with the time, patience, and interest to look for it. However, the language of the article itself was *highly suggestive of it reflecting independent work.* For example, in the article itself, the author writes, "I am grateful to three anonymous referees . . . and to the Institute for Research on Labor and Employment at UC Berkeley for research funding." This indicates that the research was funded by an independent research institute, and it probably was in part. This then raises the question of how the author was able to receive research funding from a supposedly independent source (thereby adding to the appearance of scientific objectivity) while receiving compensation from an advocacy group for obtaining his results.

Along these lines it may also be interesting to note that the institute that funded the research was an institute within the University of California-Berkeley, which in turn is a state school, essentially belonging to the State of California. Yet, the legal case in question was a case in which "California" was on the opposing side from the side that Rothstein supported with his paid testimony. So, was he able to receive support for his advocacy research from an institution that is part of the State of California, which then helped him testify *against California* in a legal case? I am not qualified to answer such as question, but I mention it because I thought readers would find this interesting.

Rothstein's research certainly appears to be a "good job if you can get it" and the author performed his job quite well. In the conclusion section at the end of the article, he writes the following, where perhaps only the last five words (with my emphasis in italics) will be comprehensible to judges, lawyers, and journalists:

> The simulations presented here suggest that the effects of policies aimed at improving teacher productivity will depend importantly on their interactions with the teacher labor market. If prospective teachers are uncertain about their own abilities or if their labor supply is less than perfectly elastic, performance-based compensation and retention policies *each require substantial increases in teacher salaries.*[14]

As often seen in the profession, some professors, like Rothstein, appear to possess a keen knowledge and strong sense of practicality when it comes to identifying "*which side their bread is buttered on.*" Here we see that he is being paid by the teacher's union, and by some strange coincidence his study concludes that substantial increases in teacher salaries are "required"!

There is Nothing as Good as Political Propaganda to Popularize a Journal Article

Note the initial premise underlying this conclusion—"the simulations presented here suggest . . ." Let us clarify what "simulations" are. They are, essentially, testing what happens, hypothetically, on *fake* data, using a particular model that was based on extremely strong assumptions. A different model, which might be equally defensible, and use alternative fake data (which might also be equally defensible), might generate completely opposite results. In fact, a great deal of economic literature exists which demonstrates this, as discussed earlier with regard to McCloskey's A-Prime C-Prime Theorem.

The conditional statement in the second sentence of the above quotation is somewhat laughable: Of course many teachers are "uncertain about their own abilities" (who isn't when they first start a job?). Furthermore, for those who understand the statement "labor supply is less than perfectly elastic," this will obviously be true for a variety of technical reasons, but the simplest reason that everyone might understand is that "nothing is perfect." Finally, who could argue against compensation to teachers being "performance based" and designed to support retention? Thus, the conditions here are dismissible to any casual observer, and to many lay observers, leaving us with the only conclusion possible from Rothstein's analysis that we must "require substantial increases in teacher salaries."

Here is your beautifully quotable line from the article—one that has certainly earned the author the compensation he received from the teachers unions in California, and one that will surely be quoted, and have his article cited, extensively. That quotable line will further help to make the article a "pivotal article" according to its citation counts, and in the same way help bolster the average citation counts of AER articles (a topic discussed in considerable detail in chapter 6). I would similarly expect policy analysts to only take this line from the article as well. Likewise, those who support higher teacher salaries will have the ammunition to claim: "According to a renowned professor at a top-ten economics department (UC-Berkeley), in an article written in the most prestigious economic journal in the nation, *American Economic Review*, the school teachers in California must have substantial increases in their salaries!" The fact that this conclusion relied on simulations (i.e., fake data tested by an arbitrary, unrealistic model) flies beautifully under the radar to anyone in this policy area who may be informed of the conclusion of this pivotal article.

The End Does Not Necessarily Justify the Means

As a quick aside, so as not to confuse any readers on this issue, I am personally not opposed at all to raising the salaries of school teachers. Having raised five children where I have taken their education very seriously, I have the utmost respect and admiration for school teachers, and I happen to believe that they are severely underpaid, given the importance of what they do. I believe that in many cases they are underpaid for two reasons: (1) They are among the people in our society who love children the most, and because of this they are willing to work as school teachers in spite of the relatively low salary they receive, given the demands of their jobs, and (2) the low salary of school teachers is still, to this day, an artifact of much older generations of teachers who were primarily women with strong skills and motivations, but who worked in an era when they could be paid less simply because they were women. While we have largely (but not entirely, of course) removed sex discrimination within each profession, the sex discrimination that might have existed across professions (with female-dominated professions earning less) may have still persisted to some extent. But, whatever I personally think about teacher salaries is irrelevant to any of this discussion, which is not about the policy itself, but lies squarely within the topic area of professional and scientific integrity.

What It All Really Means

Now let us take a much better look at what the article actually contains. Table 4.2 below translates the language in the article to common English so that we can see what it really says and does.

Articles in AER are brilliantly and meticulously designed works of art, in their own right. They typically begin by first explaining to the reader how important the topic is to any laymen who might glance at its beginning to acknowledge (without knowing any better) how the paper is important for providing a general understanding of vital phenomena (like quality of teaching). This the article does quite well in the first five pages. Then it creeps into advanced economic jargon to show that it belongs in the AER as a superior treatise on the topic, utilizing the most advanced and sophisticated "theory" (i.e., mathematical models, procedures, and techniques) that are currently in vogue at the most prestigious institutions. This it begins to do on the second page, but it goes into full force with this when it presents the second section ("II. The Model") on the fifth page. These are like the initial pawn and knight moves in a sound chess opening.

Paying Homage

Another key initial ingredient is to connect the work to famous predecessors, to demonstrate that the work belongs in the same club, and to respectfully bow to these predecessors so that they too, in appreciation and reciprocity, will welcome (or continue to welcome) the author and their article to their club. In theory, it is done so that the author gives credit where credit is due to ideas that the author used but learned from others. In reality, most of the citations are not to ideas that the author has actually used, but exist simply for the aforementioned superfluous reasons, and likewise (as mentioned elsewhere in this book) to play the game of "I'll cite you if you cite me" that is so heavily played

Table 4.2 Translation of the Language of the Article into What It Really Means

Quotation from the Article	*What it Really Means Between the Lines*
"This paper examines the selection effects of alternative teacher contracts."	This article will tell us how different kinds of contracts for teachers will get us better or worse teachers.
"I develop a stylized model of the teacher labor market . . . " (p. 101)	The article will use a highly theoretical, esoteric model that will be based on heroic assumptions which very few people will be able to understand (and few will even try, even if they are able to understand it). The journal's reviewers of the article, compadres of the author on AER Review Board, might bother to understand some of it.
"that incorporates heterogeneity in teaching ability, dynamic learning, and contracts that condition pay or retention on realized performance." (p. 101)	It is assumed that teachers have different initial abilities, and that they are rewarded more in salary and job security if they show they are better teachers.
"Given the extremely limited variation in extant teacher contracts, *I do not attempt to estimate the model.* Instead, I simulate the impact of alternative contracts using plausible parameters . . . ." (pp. 101–102) (my emphasis in italics)	The little actual data which the author has cannot tell us anything useful. Thus, in order to publish the article, and to make it appear as if the article actually discovered something about the real world, data will be made up, based on what the author thinks the data would look like if he had more of it.

Sources: First column are excerpts from Jesse Rothstein, "Teacher Quality Policy When Supply Matters," *American Economic Review* 105(1) (2015): 100–130. The second column was created by the author.

in the profession where citation counts translate to ranking and sometimes to salary levels (and at the highest levels, believe it or not, to nominations for the Nobel prize). Along these lines, the homage enters into full force on the third page, with sentences like, "My policy analysis is closely related to the personnel economics literature on incentive contracts (e.g., Prendergast 1999; Lazear 2000) and to studies of teacher firing policies (by, e.g., Staiger and Rockoff 2010; Boyd et al. 2011; and Winters and Cowen 2013a,b)."[15]

Assumptions to Feed the Mathematics, to Impress the Readership

As indicated, in the last cell of the above table, this extensive and prestigious research article deliberately reads as if it is actually discovering something about the real world by supposedly analyzing real data about the real world, when in truth it is merely a very sophisticated mathematical exercise conducted on data that were simply manufactured. The evidence for this and for the heroic assumptions used in this mathematical exercise are quite evident throughout the paper, even in simple enough language that nearly everyone could understand. As another example, the author writes, "In order to focus on the selection margin . . . Effort is irrelevant . . . and teachers cannot influence their actual or measured performance."[16] In other words, as I interpret it, though it is not clearly stated at all, the model assumes that teachers' abilities are strictly innate and only manifested at different stages of their professional development, so their personal effort to do better is not an aspect of the model. This alone should raise concerns about how useful the model is at developing an understanding of teacher behavior under different contracts. Along these lines, numerous other examples could be provided at the risk of beating this point to death. The model is simply an obscure, purely theoretical exercise whose only evidence of applicability is the author's assertion that it is applicable, and its publication in the AER, which, as had been argued extensively above, are far from independent.

Indeed, I would wonder how the leaders of the teachers union, which had paid Professor Rothstein for the findings he generated to use in a lawsuit that they filed against California, would have reacted to the idea that his findings were based on the assumption that "effort (by teachers) is irrelevant." On the other hand, I am fully aware of what Professor Rothstein and his colleagues managing the journal that approved the article would say in response to this point. They would most certainly say that I am interpreting the model's assumption of no effort way out of context—that I miss the point entirely that economic models need to make simplifying assumptions in order to "understand" and "focus on" one particular facet of the phenomenon being studied. They will tell me, as they tell their bright-eyed students and the public that is so impressed by their mathematical intellect, that this is simply what economic theory does, and what it must do, for the "promotion of knowledge and understanding." But, beyond their students and their sponsors, many people know better. Outrageous simplifying assumptions, for the express purpose of setting the stage for complex mathematical models, which in turn allow for "higher understanding," begs the question of "higher understanding *of what*"? Of how the mathematics in these models play out from their initial "structural form" at the beginning of the article to their "final reduced form" at the end of the article?

The pretense of the article was not to understand really cool, neat mathematical properties of models that can we create, but to acquire knowledge that will be useful for decision-making (such as legal decision-making in this case) that improves things in the real world. When the models go off into their own little world, it is debatable enough as to whether they do anything useful. However, even if we generously give them the benefit of the doubt of being in some way useful for higher understanding of mathematical properties, that still leaves us empty-handed when it comes to having useful tools for making important policy decisions.

The Proclamation of Policy Relevance

The first section of the article, entitled "What are the Policies of Interest," spends a little more than one page creating the pretense that the article is "policy relevant." Even in this short discussion, there is confusion over the motivation for the model itself, with an apparent focus on what the model can do, independent of its relevance to the real world. Table 4.3 below translates the paragraph in the article that appears at the top of page 103:

Table 4.3 Translation of the Language of the Article into What It Really Means

Quotation from the Article	*What it Really Means and Tells Us*
"A rich enough model can be used to simulate even the long-run effects of policies that have not yet been implemented."	The key word here is "simulate," which means, essentially, to pretend to know what will happen to the pretend data that we put into it. The fundamental question not being addressed here is how much commonality there is between the "simulation" and what will actually happen in the future. This is never tested, nor even addressed.
"I rely instead on parameter values informed by the best evidence from the literature" …	The author is just going to plug into my model information that appeared in other literature, based on whatever older data they may have used, and on whatever heroic assumptions they used. Moreover, the author can also adjust that information, and he will still be able to say that his assumptions were "informed" by the literature. This allows the author the freedom to pick and choose the results he likes best from any reasonably famous authors, and we know that those results vary enormously among themselves. In any case, no suspicious readers can make the accusation of there not being a "balanced literature review" with regard to the results selected from other studies. The selected, and possibly altered, parameters from other studies will not even show up in this article but will all be buried deep within the programming code of the simulation program.
"and present extensive sensitivity analyses that vary the parameters within plausible ranges."	No one can say that the model is not accurate, because this article will see and tell what happens when the author changes it in all sorts of ways. But the article will not address the fundamental question of whether the initial assumptions were the best to make, or how we can be confident of any conclusion when different assumptions produce different results.

Sources: First column are excerpts from Jesse Rothstein, "Teacher Quality Policy When Supply Matters," *American Economic Review* 105(1) (2015): 100–130. The second column was created by the author.

The paper commits about nine pages (pages 104–12) to develop and describe "the model" that is used to generate the fake data that will be produced in the simulation and to interpret those data, that is, to rediscover and reinterpret, essentially, the underlying assumptions that had been made by the author in the first place.

If anyone actually bothers to read carefully what the article actually says (though few will), and try to follow its logic, they will be confused on several points. For example, as mentioned above, this research assumes that teachers have an initial, innate ability and that they cannot actually improve in their ability. In fact, in the very first part of developing the model the author states, "Individual i has fixed ability i as a teacher. In the current pool of teachers, ability is normally distributed with mean 0 and standard deviation."[17] For those who have any knowledge of the development of economic models, it should be obvious why this assumption is being made—it is not because the author truly believes that teachers cannot improve. It is only because this simplifying assumption is necessary in order for the model developer to then pump into the model high-level, canned economic theory that has already been published, and this he certainly does. It is even highly questionable that he assumes teachers' abilities are "normally distributed" but he needs a convenient assumption about the statistical properties of their abilities in order to make up the data in the simulation (from random number generation) and, of course, a normal distribution is the easiest to use (in his programming) and to defend (since it is generally used by most scientists across all fields as the default distribution of random phenomena when the distribution is not known). Nevertheless, in the bigger scheme of things, the assumption of a normal distribution is merely a misdemeanor in contrast to the heinous crime (at different levels) of conveniently assuming that teachers cannot improve in ability. Yet, skipping to page 107 of the article, in which the author is describing his choice of "parameter values," he writes, "Many studies have found that teachers improve with experience but level off quickly; I draw r(t) from Staiger and Rockoff's (2010) estimates for New York City."[18] Here, "r(t)" is a "return to experience" that allows "output" to increase with experience. In this sense, there is some independent force in the model that allows teachers to be better at teaching over time, even though they cannot improve in "ability." What is "ability" then—only their *genetic disposition* to become good teachers?

These and many other concepts are muddled throughout the discussion of such simple terms like teacher ability. Most people, including, especially, experts in the field of education, would *not* regard "ability" to be something that is unchanging (like the teacher's DNA), while the teacher's "productivity," as manifested in the "quality of their output" (using economic terms), is expected to improve. In fact, teachers are specifically required to take training during their career to enhance their ability—implying that in the time span from before they had the training, to the time their training was completed, they did improve in quality (under the reasonable assumption that their training was not for nothing).

Nevertheless, in highly theoretical, economic literature, from the perspective of the authors of such work, why should any of that matter? They simply need to have the "ability parameter" fixed for their random-number generation in order to have the fake data that they need to acquire publishable results. To them, this is all very simple, and nothing for anyone to complain about it.

Picking the Assumptions You Want

In using estimates from Staiger and Rockoff's study on New York City, Rothstein is suggesting that even if New York City may not be representative of the rest of the nation with regard to its schools, their estimates might have still been the best available to him. As it happens, the Staiger and Rockoff study presented results for two cities, New York City and Los Angeles, and gave both cities equal attention and recognition in their study. Moreover, no statement is made in their study to even suggest that the findings for New York City were any more reliable than for Los Angeles.[19]

Now, let us think this through: Professor Rothstein lives and teaches in California; he is paid to do the research for evidence in a law suit against the state of California; and in the first paragraph of his article he even mentions the case referring to the decision of a "California judge." And yet, when having his choice over what findings to use in generating his fake data for his study, he chooses the results obtained by another study for New York City, and not the results of that same study for Los Angeles, nor even an average of the results of the two cities. Why? If there were any legitimate reason, why not just drop a short explanation in a footnote for anyone who was familiar with the literature and might be wondering the same thing? This is simply an example of how the fake data the author created to run his simulations were based on any assumptions we happened to like. It appears that none of these issues came out in any reviews of the paper before it was published, for if it did, one might expect the author to have used the data for Los Angeles, and not New York, or used a combination of the two.

At this Point, Enough is Enough

I could honestly spend a year and write another hundred pages, beating this poor article to death, but presumably, more than enough has already been said. Suffice it to say that the core reason the article exists is to show off all of the mathematical findings that it generated, based on the fantastic command the author has over the mathematics embodied in the assumptions he makes, to show off the additional mathematics he adds to those assumptions in building the model, and finally to show off the highly sophisticated interpretation of the fake data that he created to "test" the model.

Figure 4.1 illustrates this point, showing what the existence of this article was all about—*heavy lifting*. The figure shows three of the most impressive equations in the article in terms of size and complexity. There is no reason for the reader to try to understand any of these equations, which is why I do not provide the variable definitions here. I present them to show them as simply a metaphor for the dumbbells of the Olympic weight lifter, because that is

$$(3)\qquad \tau \mid \boldsymbol{\theta}_t \sim \mathcal{N}\left(\frac{t^{-1}\sigma_\epsilon^2\mu + (1-h)\,\sigma_\tau^2\overline{y}_t}{t^{-1}\sigma_\epsilon^2 + (1-h)\,\sigma_\tau^2}, \frac{1}{t\sigma_\epsilon^{-2} + (1-h)^{-1}\sigma_\tau^{-2}}\right)$$

$$(4)\ V_t(\boldsymbol{\theta}_{t-1}; C) = E\left[u(w_t) + \delta\left\{f_t V_{t+1}^f + (1-f_t)\max(\omega_{t+1}, V_{t+1}(\boldsymbol{\theta}_t; C))\right\}\middle|\boldsymbol{\theta}_{t-1}\right].$$

$$(5)\ E\left[E\left[e_{it'} \mid \hat{\tau}_{it}\right] \mid \tau_i = \tau\right] = E\left[E\left[E\left[E\left[e_{it'} \mid y_{it'}, y_{i,t'-1}\right] \mid \tau_i\right] \mid \hat{\tau}_{it}\right] \mid \tau_i = \tau\right].$$

Figure 4.1 The Highly Impressive, Heavy Lifting of Equations 3–5 in Rothstein's AER Article. Created by the author with reference to: Wikimedia Commons (Attribution: RIA Novosti archive, image #497570/Vitaliy Saveliev/CC-BY-SA 3.0), accessed May 6, 2017, http://tinyurl.com/zpfxwef.

what this is all about in terms of the ultimate psychological motivations of the academic professors who perform this kind of work.

The Irrelevance of Weight Lifting

We may want to watch Olympic weight lifters once every four years to marvel at their physical prowess, strength, and ability. Moreover, we may admire them, wish them well for what they do, and cheer for the ones who represent our nations in international competitions. However, when we are moving from one house to another and need to hire a moving company to transport our furniture, how interested would we be to hire a company that employs Olympic weight lifters to perform the work of moving our furniture? We would probably not be interested at all, or for that matter, we might prefer that the moving company *not* hire any professional weight lifters. As any reasonable person might see it, professional weight lifters have the core strength, of course, but not necessarily the knowledge or agility to safely move our furniture through tight doorways, to load it efficiently on the moving truck, etc. Thus, they will likely focus on showing off how much weight they can lift by themselves with their bare hands, at the expense of properly getting the stuff into the truck and moving it to where it needs to go, in the most efficient way possible. The same simple principle applies to the *mathematical* weight lifters who we may choose to hire as advisers on messy public policy issues, like figuring out if teacher salaries should be raised. They will be inclined to do simply the tasks that *they are good at*, regardless of how *irrelevant* those tasks might be, and avoid other tasks they are *not* good at, regardless of how *relevant* those other tasks might be.

PACIFICATION OF DESCENT AGAINST THE PUBLICATION GAME

As is commonly known, the population of economics professors in the elite castles of the top-ranked universities, who produce the vast majority of articles that appear in the top-ranked journals (which in turn is used to justify their positions in those institutions), account for a very small fraction of the profession. On the other side of the tracks lie the majority of academics who are clamoring for whatever publications they can get to support their careers.

The Exploited, Fourth Class in Academic Economics

The lowliest, and most downtrodden among the populous, lower class of academic economists, are foreign graduate students who are about to complete ("defend") their dissertations, or have recently done so, and who are desperately trying to acquire any teaching position they can find in order to remain in the United States (among the many who do wish to remain). The recent graduates, of which the largest group appear to be Chinese, cannot apply for any government positions in economics (with very rare exceptions) because they do not have citizenship, and likewise, it is difficult for them to acquire a private sector position at a firm that would sponsor their H-1B visas. In short, they may remain in the United States if they are hired to teach at a university, and if they are so lucky, will essentially be guaranteed to become a permanent resident and eventually a citizen of the United States. If they are not hired by a university to teach economics, their life path would be extremely different and, most likely, irreversible. Their entire future, in effect, rests on whether some university—*any university*—will hire them to teach economics after they complete their doctorate. *In turn, their future rests entirely on whether the papers they submitted to journals will be accepted for publication, since that will largely determine whether they will be hired or not.*

Imagine yourself to be one of these recent graduate students (if you are not one already) who, hypothetically, for the sake of argument, came from China to a graduate program in economics in an average-ranked university, and who recently defended their dissertation. You struggled for the last five years of your life to get through the program, surviving graduate school being taught in a language that is remarkably different from your own native language, to finally succeed in graduating. During all of those years of struggle you strove for a better life, envisioning that you could become an economics professor in the United States. Now your dissertation is completed, your grades are good, and recommendations from your professors are fine as well. However, there are two hurdles left: (1) Because your school is not in the top ten, or even the top twenty, Ph.D. programs in economics, you have a much harder chance of landing that teaching position, all else being equal, and (2) You need those precious publication scores in order to get in; otherwise there is essentially no point in applying. With regard to the second hurdle, universities require those publications as evidence that the new professor can, in general, produce published journal articles—the single most important indicator they use of a professor's worth.

Thus, there you sit, with the two (or if you are lucky three) papers that you have submitted to journals for consideration, waiting to hear if any are accepted. Many of these journals have very low acceptance rates. Suppose you have two submitted journals with a 20 percent acceptance rate. Then the odds of your getting at least one accepted is only 36 percent—the odds are against you! Hence, the odds are against your being able to enter upon the life that you had been working so hard to acquire. So much of it now rests on the whims of the few journal referees who have randomly been assigned to review your papers.

The desperation of many hundreds (more likely, thousands) of graduating students in economics each year in the United States to acquire teaching positions in situations like the one I just described is evident and well known within the profession. At every major economics conference, where recent graduates go to present their papers, you can sometimes see such desperation in their faces, and it comes out directly in their conversations. Paper applications to journals are, for them, essentially the same thing as a lottery ticket for immigration, and more broadly, a lottery ticket to a particular trajectory in life that they often have only "one shot" to get. In this sense, as the exaggerated metaphor goes, they would "give their right arm" for a publication acceptance, especially at a top-ranked journal.

I find the degree of insensitivity, of the "powers that be" within the profession to this predicament of thousands of foreign graduate students, to be unconscionable. Not only is the problem largely ignored, but it is sometimes a recognized source of exploitation. These graduate students and recent graduates (who might be working as "post-docs") will work very hard to have their name as a second or third author of a publication, and are thus at the mercy of any prominent professor who could use their work as a coauthor of a paper that they are likely to publish.

Chances at a Better Life versus Scientific Integrity

Along similar lines, one could only wonder where scientific integrity goes under such desperate situations. Realistically, suppose your paper had a much greater chance of publication if it had a regression result with a statistically significant coefficient. However, of the hundred data points you have, there are five outliers that make such a significant result impossible. You have no scientific or logical basis whatsoever to remove those five observations from your data, so you cannot remove them officially and explain it in your paper. Yet, what you can do is simply take those data out, pretend you never received them, and no one would be the wiser. Doing so would, of course, be unethical, and would clearly violate the most basic principles of scientific integrity. In turn, this calls into question why I am even mentioning such a possibility here in this book, but it is for the sake of expressing a more important point. The point is, if your entire future is riding on those lousy five data points, in a publication that hardly anyone would ever read and that would not make a difference in anyone's understanding of the world, and your actions would only be to score points in a game that is already corrupt in so many other ways, what would you do?

More generally, it is absurd to expect the paper authors to uphold scientific integrity when their entire lives often depend on deviations from it as in the above scenario, which might be quite typical. This, in turn, implies that we would be quite naïve to expect scientific integrity to be upheld in these publications overall, and the journals certainly do not enforce it (with very few exceptions, as will be discussed in chapter 9). It is a form of the economist's "prisoner's dilemma" problem, where, once certain people can be expected to violate scientific integrity, those who uphold it have much to lose (in terms of a lower probability of having their paper accepted), and nothing to gain (other than their own conscience, which of course should be important to them).

In this intensive, high-pressure environment within the lowest ranks of the profession to publish whatever they can to secure employment and, in many cases, to have a "nice place to live," there are naturally many concerns. The greatest concern is over how fairly their applications are being reviewed and evaluated by the journals. The journals may reject the application out of hand, as a function of the whims of the editor receiving the application, or, if it passes this first screening, it is sent to two or three referees to analyze and provide recommendations.

Referees and Their Reviews Are Highly Arbitrary

When a paper proposed to a journal is sent out by the journal to referees to review, what often happens is that one of the two (or three) referees likes the paper and the other does not, and the editor may then step in and reject the paper on the basis of it not being supported by both referees. This implies that the process is quite arbitrary, for example, if half the reviewers are expected to like the paper, and half are expected to dislike it, then if the reviewers are somewhat randomly chosen, the author has a 25 percent chance of having their paper liked by both reviewers.

Reviewers will eventually reveal their relative degree of kindness for authors: Some will be known as reviewers that reject almost everything; others as reviewers that accept most of the papers presented to them. Editors then, in choosing the reviewers, have great power in influencing the review outcome in their selection of who they feel should review the paper. Furthermore, the reviewers and the editors know who the authors are (they are usually not "double-blind" reviews), which means that there may be all kinds of nonobjective factors that enter into the review process.

So Much Riding on Chance, for No Good Reason

When people are evaluated on years of work (which is what often goes into the papers they submit), and those evaluations could make or break their careers or even their paths in life, they should naturally expect the process to be fair and objective. At the same time, it is common knowledge at all levels of the profession that the process is often arbitrary at best, and it exhibits favoritism, cronyism, and prejudice at worst. It can then be a source of outrage among those who feel they deserved much better than they received, and yet the vast majority of those who are personally outraged remain extremely quiet about it. They are quiet for two reasons: (1) If they have any hope of reversing their fate, they do not want to make waves with those elite leaders who might later give them a second chance. (2) They will most certainly be vulnerable to the dual accusation that their work is simply not that good and that they are too stubborn or obtuse to accept it (in some ways, the Andersen Effect in reverse!).

Another factor that enters into the review process is the fact that some journals ask those who are submitting their applications to provide the names of prospective reviewers whom they could contact to referee the article. (For example, the journal *Energy Policy* does this—I know from having recently submitted a paper to them.) This practice is clearly incredibly convenient for the journals, being saved from the trouble of having to find referees in these cases. It is also, of course, a situation that creates an absurd conflict of interest. In soliciting potential referees from the person who would be evaluated by those referees, the journal does state that the referees should not be from the same institution, as if this would seriously negate any conflict of interest. The instructions tend not to state that people should not offer potential referees who are close friends, or who owe them favors, etc., though even if they did instruct that the suggested referees should not know the author personally, how could the journal possibly enforce this? Of course, most applicants when offered this opportunity to suggest referees, especially those applicants who desperately need the publication for their career, will most certainly list the people they know, and perhaps can even rely upon, to review the paper in their favor. This creates an enormous advantage to those authors who already have prominent friends in the same subfield, and enormous advantage to those who belong to groups of friends who share the same philosophy of helping each other out whenever they can. In general, there is a "survival of the *cronyistic*," even when authors do not have the ability to suggest referees, but are friends with the referees the journal finds in any case.

A Presentation about "What Gets In"

At the 2016 Annual Meetings of the Western Economic Association International, the association's president, Professor David Card (from UC Berkeley), delivered his plenary Presidential Lecture on the topic of "What Gets In? Editorial Decisions at Top Economics Journals." At this writing there appears to be no published reference, not even on the web, on the presentation he gave at the conference. I wrote to Professor Card asking for a copy of his presentation and did not receive a reply. Thus, I can speak about his presentation only from memory (and my notes), having attended it when it was delivered.

I suggest we pause to consider the uniqueness of the academic economics profession to have a plenary presidential lecture delivered to all the attendees at a major conference, devoted to the topic of "what gets published" by economics journals. I have attended many conferences of other professions, such as those of the American Association for the Advancement of Science (the main association of scientists in the United States) and had never seen a presentation on a topic like "what gets you published in a science journal." The presumption, of course, is that important scientific discoveries are what get you published in science journals. Within academic economics, however, the culture has become oriented to winning at the publication game as the ultimate end in itself, so that this presentation seemed to fit in just fine for a room filled with thousands of economics professors, all curious about how they can be more successful at the game, as if the Western Economic Association were doing them all a favor to let them in on such "inside information."

Throughout his entire presentation, never once did Professor Card mention what qualities of papers editors were looking for, such as an important discovery or an advanced understanding of a topic. Rather, there was only one specific metric—the number of citations an article would receive, on average. At one point in his presentation, in fact, he specifically said that editors select papers on the basis of which papers they believe will receive the largest number of citations (and this feeds into the competition among journals for the number of citations they receive). Card then specifically recommended to the entire audience that if you want to get published in a top-ranked journal, the best strategy is to write a paper that you expect will receive a great deal of citations (as this is the one characteristic being sought by the editors).

His presentation involved a rather detailed econometric study, where he distinguished between papers that were accepted right away by the journal, and those that were required to "revise and resubmit." Among those papers that had to be revised and resubmitted, some were later accepted and published, and so you could see how citation counts differed among those that were accepted and those that were not accepted at first. Those that were accepted first received more citations than those that were not, leading Card to conclude that journal editors are good at choosing papers that will receive more citations. In other words, the takeaway from his presentation was that the editors of top-ranked journals *really DO know what they are doing* in finding the *best* papers to accept, on the basis of the assumption that citation counts measure a paper's ultimate value.

After his presentation someone (not me, by the way) asked whether it was valid to assume that the scientific merit of a paper should be based on the number of citations it is expected to receive, and that she, as a "scientist," had serious concerns about that criterion. Card's ten-second response was to say that yes, that is an assumption underlying his entire analysis, and this assumption should be questioned with further study.

In my view, Card's presentation at the WEAI conference, and other similar presentations and articles by high-ranking members of the profession, have provided propaganda to support the status quo of how papers are accepted for publication in top journals. On the surface it seems to respond to those who have expressed, and many more who have withheld, grave concerns that the process is unfair. That response was, essentially, equivalent to someone saying, "fear not—you have nothing to be concerned about—the process IS fair!" By having sophisticated econometric research behind its conclusions, his study appears to have thoroughly investigated the matter, for the sake of those who have concerns. For this he might also receive praise from other leading members of the profession—particularly those who manage the top-ranked journals—for having quelled the simmering outrage of the profession's second-class citizens.

His analysis, however, in spite of its sophistication and use of a great deal of data, was horribly flawed at many levels. As already mentioned, the presumption that citation counts measure scientific merit is basically wrong, as I argue in many ways throughout this book, and especially in chapter 6. Another aspect of his study is that he mentioned that he examined the top-five journals, except for the AER, which, as he put it, chose not to participate in the study. The absence of one of the five would suggest that what is found of the remaining four might reflect how the situation exists in general. On the other hand, an earlier study by Card himself (with Sefano DellaVigna) in 2012 mentioned that the AER "accounts for 40% of top-five publications."[20] This is quite a loss in the sample size, and it is, as many would expect, a rather biased loss. That is, if journals are approached and asked to participate in a study of their editors' decision-making, then I would expect the journals that opt out might have reasons for doing so related to what would be discovered about those journals. If a study is geared toward demonstrating to the public that a journal's decision-making is fair, then I would expect the leaders of a journal who believed their practices are fair to opt to participate, as good publicity for their journal. The decision not to participate by the leaders of one journal that accounts for 40 percent of top-five journal publications (at least at one time not long ago) does not reflect well on that journal. But, perhaps the AER is, indeed, quite fair in its selections, and its leaders simply did not want to be bothered with the study, in spite of it being good publicity for the journal. In all likelihood, we will never know.

What Makes Journal Editors So Successful at Picking "Citation Winners"

Let us consider what the journal editors might be doing to be so "successful" at picking for publication the papers that will receive many citations. Since they do see who the authors of submitted papers are, they may first decide if they know, or have heard of, those authors, and if those authors are famous they will surely know this. Those authors who are famous will most certainly tend to receive more citations for any new article they write than authors who are not known. Famous authors have greater followings in all kinds of ways, so more people are citing them to begin with. Thus, back to Card's analytical finding that editors are good at picking papers that will be cited more—yes, they are good at picking whoever is already famous, and on average those famous economics professors will receive more citations, on average, if for no other reason than *because* they are famous. How remarkable is this finding? How comforting is it to the people who are greatly hoping and praying each day to hear something positive from the journal to which they applied, to know if their paper was accepted or rejected, supposedly on the basis of its scientific merit? Recall the discussion earlier in this chapter about how the AER reserves the right to reject a paper, *without reviewing it*!

A GAME OF CHESS, PLAYED IN A TOURNAMENT

In this discussion, I will use the analogy of producing top-ranked journal articles as a game, and in particular, the game of chess as one might play it in a chess tournament. When it comes to producing articles for top-ranked journals, economics professors are, indeed, very much like contestants in a chess tournament. In both contests there is a well-defined fixed sum of wins that they could acquire in competition with each other, and a fixed sum of consequent "winners" in terms of high-ranking scores. Figure 4.2 below further makes use of this analogy by identifying six essential qualities that an economics professor needs to succeed at the game, metaphorically assigning each quality to each of the six different types of chess pieces.

Steps Just Large Enough for Only a Few People to Climb

With regard to the metaphor for the knight, the table mentions "the standardized compromise between explainability and mathematical impressiveness." This may be understood as follows: If the equations are "too understandable," where the reader is aided by more detailed explanations to help decipher them, then the paper appears to be too plebian and unprofessional to be worthy of publication in a top journal. On the other hand, if the equations

Piece		Features in Chess	Analogy for Publication	Key Elements
	Pawn	Numerous weak pieces, easily sacrificed	Use of student assistants and subordinate coauthors	(1) Ability to use (in some cases exploit) numerous student assistants and subordinate coauthors, who may or may not receive credit for their contribution. (2) Explains how some prominent authors can have impossible large numbers of publications per year: they receive credit for work primarily done by others.
	Rook or Castle	Movement in predicable straight lines	Building on work already highly recognized	(1) Recognition given to prior work to win favor with reviewers (who are often authors of previously articles, and who expect their work to be cited favorably). (2) Conveying an admiration for, and a sense of pride in understanding, what others had published, and reluctance to criticize prior publications.
	Knight	Jumping over pieces in a complex but precise way	Mastering stylized coverage of mathematical models	(1) The display of equations follows a calculus of its own, optimizing a compromise between explainability and mathematical impressiveness. (2) Often what might appear as a thorough and thoughtful analysis may simply be a repetition of earlier analytical work, with enough superficial differences in its appearance to pass for original work to the journal's satisfaction.
	Bishop	Movement in diagonal lines, not straight lines	Suggesting relevance to policy or current events	(1) Articles are often favored if appear to address policy relevant issues, even though they will rarely if ever be read by policy makers or have any effect on policy. (2) Having privileged access to a special dataset to analyze, perhaps from a recent survey. This helps infuse additional "newsworthiness" to the work.
	Queen	Powerfully combining straight and diagonal movement	Strategic Selection of Topics Most Likely to be Published	(1) Cleverly combining the use of well-established models (movement of the rook), while appearing to address current issues (movement of the bishop). (2) Choice of topic to avoid competition from other authors more likely to publish on it, or coauthoring with more prominent authors rather than competing with them. (3) Acquiring inside information on what topics are "hot" and likely to be published.
	King	Only piece that ultimately maters for winning	Preeminence of the author as recognized by the journals	(1) Reviewers will automatically accept the papers from prominent authors, assuming they only produce high-quality work (and their review would be suspect otherwise). (2) Authors who are not prominent may approach prominence by recruiting prominent coauthors, or be favored for their affiliation with a prominent institution, (e.g., MIT). (3) Authors may strategically acquire endorsements from prominent authors displayed in a footnote, or have their support indirectly conveyed to the journal reviewers.

Figure 4.2 The Chess Game of Publishing Economics Articles in Top-Ranked Journals: The Pieces and How They Move. Created by the author.

are too incomprehensible then the reviewers may be suspicious of a possible "sleight of hand" in the derivation of the equations. Thus, the optimal level of incomprehensibility is required for the work to appear as mathematically sophisticated as possible while still being trusted by the most adept reviewers who have studied the same models themselves.

Another analogy on the use of math in technical journal articles is that they are like pyramids, built of steps (as those in South America), that the reader is expected to climb to reach to top. In following the article's exposition of its equations, the reader is walking up those steps, with a new step for each subsequent equation. If these steps are relatively simple for anyone proficient in math to flow, for example anyone who is adept in multivariate calculus, then the steps up the pyramid are small, such as each being one foot high, enabling nearly all readers of the article to climb it. Once the step of the pyramid is, say, three or four feet high, some adults may be unable to climb them, though most might still be able to do it with enough time and effort. Once the pyramid step reached a height of say, six feet, then only the most athletic (and tall) adults, who could jump and pull themselves up to scale each six-foot step, would be able to make it up the pyramid. Those tall steps would require not only a familiarity with the math, but with the theoretical economic literature that has been produced on the topic at hand. Figures 2.3 and 3.1 in chapters 2 and 3 show us what these six-feet steps look like. They are deliberately designed to ensure that only a tiny fraction of all economists will be able to follow comfortably the explanation of the model.

This characteristic of how theoretical models are presented in technical journals begs the question of why the steps are not made smaller, so that readers who are not already familiar with such models might still be better able to understand the model presented in the article. It is surely not a matter of space in the article—it would hardly take any more space. Among other reasons, including some offered in the previous chapters, the profession simply has a perverse admiration for models that are incomprehensible to most people and even to other economists. This is an application of the "Andersen Effect"—causing more people to claim that they adore the emperors' new clothes, because if they admit that they cannot see his clothes, they will be accused of being feebleminded.

Also discussed with regard to the metaphor of the knight in chess is a willingness on the part of the authors of articles to recycle math that they have used before, dressed up as an original analysis. This thereby creates efficiencies in the production of new journal articles, and enables more to be produced. Conversely, those who have a distaste for such recycling are at a disadvantage in the game. Of course, there is no "expiration date" on the use of previous math, where work from researchers' dissertations, for instance, may be recycled for decades without scrutiny from reviewers, and it often is.

The Pretense of Addressing Current Issues

With regard to the pretense of addressing current issues, associated (somewhat arbitrarily, of course) with the chess piece of the bishop in Figure 4.2, the situation is analogous to that of Broadway musical. In the Broadway musical, the main attraction of course is its singing and dancing performances (like the article's mathematical models are the main attraction), while the plot (like its associated policy issues) exists primarily to provide the backdrop for those performances. In the case of the musical, however, there is no real deception here—simply a well-accepted and widely understood feature of that form of entertainment. In the case of the article, however, the backdrop of a policy issue pretends to add an additional justification for the article's existence which is often completely invalid.

NOTES

1. James Madison University, Department of Economics, "Criteria for Promotion and Tenure Decisions," Amended July 2010, accessed February 4, 2017, http://tinyurl.com/hkzp568.

2. JMU lists the top-ranked journals as follows: *American Economic Review, Economic Journal, Econometrica, Economica, International Economic Review, Journal of Economic Theory, Journal of Political Economy, Journal of the American Statistical Association, Oxford Economic Papers, Quarterly Journal of Economics, Review of Economics and Statistics*, and *Review of Economic Studies*.

3. JMU lists the second-ranked journals as follows: *Annals of Mathematical Statistics, Canadian Journal of Economics, Economic Development and Cultural Change, Journal of Money, Credit and Banking, Journal of Business, Journal of Economic History, Journal of Economic Literature, Journal of Finance, Journal of Law and Economics, Journal of International Economics, Kyklos*, and *Southern Economic Journal*.

4. My book on quality measurement provides some background on this topic: Steven Payson, Quality Measurement in Economics: New Perspectives on the Evolution of Goods and Services (Brookfield, VT: Edward Elgar Publishing Company, 1994).

5. Jesse Rothstein, "Teacher Quality Policy When Supply Matters," American Economic Review 105(1) (2015): 100–30.

6. American Economic Association, "The American Economic Review: Submission Guidelines," accessed April 7, 2015, https://www.aeaweb.org/aer/submissions.php .

7. American Economic Association, "American Economic Review," (Report of the Editor), *American Economic Review*, Papers and Proceedings, 104(5) (2014): 621.

8. The running joke that is commonly expressed in the profession is that the review is based on the submitter's *zip code*, that is, if the paper is coming out of Harvard, MIT, etc. Some might say, and the AEA would *probably* say, that what was meant by "without review" did not preclude the editor to looking beyond the author,

author's affiliation, and title, such as to read the abstract, or peruse the paper, etc. Nevertheless, if that were the case, then that would constitute a review itself, at least to some extent, and the language should have been "without detailed review" rather than "without review." I believe the AEA could be taken at its word here, that what they meant by "without review" was truly without *any* review, cursory or otherwise.

9. Jesse Rothstein, Curriculum Vitae, accessed February 4, 2017, http://tinyurl.com/zhopeba. For whatever it might be worth, I did not select this article as an example to discuss based on any of this. I simply first selected the article, as I mentioned, based on the subject matter being ironic, and only then discovered this extra tidbit when looking deeper into aspects of the article (and its author).

10. C. H. Ferguson, Audrey Marrs, Chad Beck, Adam Bolt, Matt Damon, Paul A. Volcker, George Soros, et al., Inside Job, 2011.

11. American Economic Association, "Disclosure Policy" accessed February 4, 2017, http://tinyurl.com/hm5tzgc.

12. American Economic Association, "Disclosure Policy," my own emphasis added.

13. From the downloaded file of the American Economic Association, as described in the text.

14. Rothstein, "Teacher Quality Policy When Supply Matters," 126.

15. Rothstein, "Teacher Quality Policy When Supply Matters," 102.

16. Rothstein, "Teacher Quality Policy When Supply Matters," 104.

17. Rothstein, "Teacher Quality Policy When Supply Matters," 107.

18. Rothstein, "Teacher Quality Policy When Supply Matters," 107.

19. Douglas Staiger and Jonah Rockoff, "Searching for Effective Teachers with Imperfect Information," Journal of Economic Perspectives 24(3) (2010): 97–118.

20. David Card and Stefano DellaVigna, "Nine Facts about Top Journals in Economics," National Bureau of Economic Research, Working Paper 18665, January 2013, 1.

Chapter 5

The Quest for Honest Truth in Economic Science

THE WELL-KNOWN, BUT STILL UNDERRATED, OBSESSION WITH MATHEMATICS AND CLEVERNESS

Personally, I have always loved mathematics, which is why I received a bachelor's degree in it, and also studied econometrics as one of my specialty fields as a graduate student. I would have enjoyed putting even more mathematics in my dissertation, and was even asked to do so, by one of the professors on my defense committee. I chose not to, because I did not see the reason for it. It would not have explained the ideas I was defending any better, and would have only distorted those ideas. The only benefit it might then have had would have been to increase the likelihood of my work being published in a top-ranking journal, which did not interest me enough at the time, nor at any other time thereafter.

To realize the extent of the problem, it is easiest to accept the simple statement that many academic economists believe in, and act in accordance with, the principle that economics is, essentially, a branch of mathematics. Fortunately, I do not believe that there is any mathematician or professor of mathematics who would agree with this. Though I am not an historian of economic thought, I know that historians of economic thought will agree that the epitomic creation of modern economics, and its relentless pursuit of more advanced mathematics, could be attributed in large part to an extremely famous book, not only for its time, but for generations thereafter. The book was *Foundations of Economic Analysis* by Nobel Laureate Paul Samuelson, who was a professor at MIT.

The criticism I am about to make should not, by any means, be misinterpreted as a condemnation or dismissal of Samuelson's contribution to economics. Indeed, Samuelson, in my view, was one of the greatest economists who ever lived, and this view is rightfully the consensus of the economics profession. Moreover, his contributions in making economics more mathematical caused, in my opinion, much more good than harm. Now, having said this, let us note the first words in that book by Samuelson, which are from a quotation by J. Willard Gibbs: "Mathematics is a Language." Here we see one of the most important and influential books ever written in economics, beginning with the recognition that economics is a manifestation of the glorious field of mathematics.

Along with the profession's growing admiration of the field of mathematics, to the point of an obsession, comes the confusion between mathematics and science. As most people, especially scientists, realize, mathematics is *not* a science, but is an essential *tool* of science. The key difference, of course, is that science addresses the causality behind known and observed physical phenomena, while mathematics focuses on ideas involving numbers without requiring observations of real-world phenomena. Nevertheless, without a clue as to what science is all about (or at least without a concern about it), many theoretical economists have come to believe and say that their reliance on advanced mathematics in their work makes their work "a science." This also reflects a cluelessness about all of the fields of engineering, which also heavily rely on mathematics but without engineers claiming that their work is science or that they themselves are scientists. Engineers rightfully have pride in their own fields of study, without having any compulsion to make the false claim that their work is a science because of its dependence on mathematics. Yet, the evidence is overwhelming that theoretical economists truly believe this in their case.

As an example, Bernt Stigum, a prominent economics professor at the University of Oslo, Norway, is noted for two books he had written, published by the MIT press: *Toward a Formal Science of Economics* (1990) and *Econometrics in a Formal Science of Economics* (2014). In its promotion of *Toward a Formal Science of Economics*, the MIT press writes:

> Toward a Formal Science of Economics provides a unifying way to look at the *concept of economic science.* It lays a foundation for the axiomatic method, focusing on applications in economics and econometrics, and including discussions in logic, epistemology, and probability theory. Each chapter deals with a topic *of fundamental importance to a rigorous science of economics* while illustrating an aspect of the axiomatic method.[1]

Like an advanced book on mathematics, this large book (with over 1,000 pages) on the "science of economics" is entirely theoretical, with no observations about the physical world. From my perspective I find it highly ironic that the main effect of *Toward a Formal Science of Economics* is to push economics directly away from being an *actual* science. In defending his formalist approach, Stigum has argued, "formalism in science is required for the purpose of confronting theories with data." That is certainly true, but the magnitude of formalism that he and many other academic economists promote (if not require of their students) has precisely the opposite purpose and precisely the opposite effect—it has enabled academic economists to make a career out of *avoiding* "the confrontation between theories and data." Formalism in economics is like salt in one's diet—a little is needed to survive, and too much will kill you. The amount we have now has not quite killed us, but has made us very sick.

Economics often overlaps with other fields, which is evident, in particular, by the placement of professors of economics in other graduate-school academic departments such as business studies, public policy, and international affairs. Thus, many people who acquire advanced degrees in economics have had courses in other fields where economics can be applied. Nevertheless, mathematics is the only other field besides economics that all graduate-level economics students must have a command over, as mentioned elsewhere in this book. As a result, there is a bias within economic research toward ideas that are more mathematically interesting (especially from the perspective of a scholar of mathematics) than they are interesting with regard to addressing relevant business-related, societal, or policy-related issues.

The kind of ideas that scholars of mathematics find most interesting are discoveries that fall under the category of "mathematical elegance." Mathematical elegance may be seen as occurring when we are considering certain concepts, where we would normally expect the relationship among them to be weak and complex, but we find, instead, that the relationship is surprisingly simple (though the explanation may remain complex). The most obvious example might be Euler's formula (sometimes called "the perfect equation") that offers an incredibly simple and profound relationship among the base of the natural logarithm (e), the "imaginary" square root of negative one (*i*), and the trigonometric functions of sin and cos. When such mathematical elegance is discovered, one finds what may first appear as a "coincidence," though there are no "coincidences" in mathematics, and so the apparent coincidence reveals a fundamental property of numbers that had not yet been realized. This is, indeed, the heart of what makes mathematics a field of advanced study.

In science, however, where actual physical phenomena are being studied, what counts the most is our understanding of the causal relations that exist among those phenomena. We may then create and use mathematical models to help us develop this understanding, but to remain valuable and consistent with our goals, those models must be tightly bound to our quest for understanding causality. When those models can then be broken away from their connection with the reality they were originally designed to understand, in fields of science, they would normally die (i.e., never be published or taught) for no other reason than their lack of relevance to reality. In economics, however, many such irrelevant ideas have found a way to survive, and even thrive, by substituting their relevance to reality by their mathematically elegant appeal among theoretical economists. In this regard, theoretical economists have effectively transformed themselves from scientists to mathematicians, but more precisely, to amateur mathematicians, for whom the threshold for producing mathematically elegant results is much lower than it is in real mathematics.

SHOWING OFF CLEVERNESS, WHICH MAY OR MAY NOT REQUIRE ADVANCED MATHEMATICS

In a broader sense, one might argue that my perspective on the overuse of mathematics in economics has been too limited. Some might say it has not captured the real problem in its entirety, because it is not mathematics *per se* that economics professors are obsessed about. Rather, many would argue that in academic economics there is an obsession to demonstrate overly complicated, intellectually impressive bodies of ideas, which just happen to be mathematical ideas in most cases, but the point is to show-off cleverness (in whatever form it takes) as a substitute for genuine, useful discovery (which is, of course, much harder to come by). As Harry Clarke, an economics professor at La Trobe University in Australia, has noted in a course he teaches on "Economics and Ethics":

> The criticisms of . . . {Ph.D.} curricula {in economics} stem from an excessive orientation to theory and technical skills rather than applications. These are promoted as being key to achieving career success. Surveys suggest that students . . . do not see either institutional knowledge or knowledge of economics literature as important. The pedagogical target was analytical cleverness not creative minds.[2]

CHASING AFTER STATISTICAL SIGNIFICANCE RATHER THAN SIGNIFICANCE

In chapter 3, I discussed the fallacy that association is causation, which could be quite subtle in cases involving multiple, confounding factors, such as in Simpson's paradox. As already mentioned, most economics professors will be quick to say that they are thoroughly familiar with the association-as-causation fallacy. However, we may still often find that fallacy crawling around inside their work when we turn over the stones of how they actually generated their findings.

Is Something That Is Statistically Significant, Significant?

As if this were not enough of a problem, there is another involving statistical inference that is arguably at least as egregious—the obsession (or "cult" as Ziliak and McCloskey have labeled it) that many members of the profession have with acquiring "statistically significant" findings that are actually quite unimportant. Moreover, this pursuit often occurs with little interest in what truly is important, though not statistically significant. This obsession comes from two ends: a "demand side" and a "supply side." On the demand side, statistically significant results are often required as a condition for the publication of those results in a journal article. On the supply side, many academic economists (and unfortunately many other economists as well) do not have a good understanding of the distinction between something being "statistically significant" and it being important. They seem to make the implicit assumption that the two are one and the same, or, among the most ignorant, they appear to make the implicit assumption that importance is itself defined by statistical significance.

Admittedly, my use of the term "important" here is somewhat vague and also subject to debate, since what I might call "important" someone else may not. Ziliak and McCloskey, who have written at length and profoundly on this topic, have used the term "oomph" as a synonym for importance in this context. They describe the concept as follows:

> The core problem is that statistical significance is neither necessary nor sufficient for testing an ethical, scientific, commercial, or material fact in a court of law or of scientific or business opinion. An insignificant coefficient can be substantively significant and important to real people or ecosystems if, for example, the possible loss from ignoring it . . . is large enough. And a statistically significant coefficient might be, economically irrelevant to the choice problem if, for example, the significance is caused by merely having a very large sample size or if the variable to which the coefficient is attached is not in any case a policy tool.
>
> What people want from the analyst is a demonstration of "oomph," of meaningful effect size, whether large or small. Probability comes in only as an inquiry into the odds of various levels of oomph.[3]

In my view, the most confusing aspect about all of this terminology, to many economists and to the public as well, is the ambiguity around the term "significance." In the above quotation, for example, Ziliak and McCloskey use the term "substantively significant" as distinct from "statistically significant."

Other economists who, unlike Ziliak and McCloskey, very wrongly believe that statistical significance is equivalent to "significance" in a broad sense greatly contribute to this confusion.

As a way to clarify all of this, I propose that we use a different word for what I meant by importance just now, or what Ziliak and McCloskey had referred to as "oomph." The word I propose is "significance"—defined by the *Oxford Dictionary*'s first definition as "the quality of being worthy of attention; importance."[4] Unfortunately (because it adds to the confusion) the *Oxford Dictionary*'s third definition of "significance" is, in fact, what is meant by statistical significance: "The extent to which a result deviates from that expected to arise simply from random variations or errors in sampling." Undoubtedly, this third definition came into being by people using the term "significance" to mean statistical significance for short.

For ease of understanding let us call the first definition "significance" and the third definition "statistical significance" and then recognize, as implied by the above quotation by Ziliak and McCloskey, that these are not at all the same. In fact, it is very possible for something to be significant without being statistically significant, and very possible for something to be statistically significant without being significant (as also mentioned in the above quotation).

As an example of the former (significant, but not statistically significant), suppose the women living in a certain area where the groundwater was contaminated with hazardous waste have experienced five times the normal rate of miscarriages. However, because the number of people in the area is small (thus, the "sample size" is small), and the data are only for a couple years (so the number of actual miscarriages is not very high), the data cannot demonstrate that the miscarriages are attributable to the hazardous waste beyond a 95 percent confidence level. That is, based on statistical principles and the available data collected, there might be, say, a 6 percent chance that the high rate of miscarriages happened by coincidence alone and a 94 percent chance (instead of a 95% chance) that hazardous waste really did cause those miscarriages to happen. This failure of the data and testing to demonstrate a 95 percent chance or above that hazardous waste was the cause of the miscarriages would mean that the results of such testing were *not* statistically significant. Would these results, however, be "*significant*" to the residents of the area—I would think so!

Here is an example of the latter (statistically significant, but not significant): People who are expecting babies, without, or before, receiving any information about the fetus, commonly assume that there is roughly a fifty-fifty chance of their baby being a boy or a girl. Actually, the odds are slightly higher for boys: 51 percent instead of 50 percent (and 49% instead of 50% for girls) in the United States.[5] This difference from the fifty-fifty assumption is highly statistically significant, given the enormous amount of data upon which it is based. Nevertheless, these differences from the fifty-fifty ratio, though statistically significant, are so small that they are *not significant* to anyone who is expecting a new child. That is, those expecting a new child may be free to believe they have a 50 percent chance of having a boy, etc., without any negative consequences whatsoever.

The economics profession, among some other professions, is indeed fixated with acquiring statistically significant coefficients in virtually all empirical studies that are performed in support of economic models, as a requirement for publication and, in many cases, under the misguided belief that such statistical significance is what makes their results important. This comes at the cost of the profession not focusing, instead, on what is truly significant, and the consequences are horrific in two respects: First, it has caused economists (and others in similar fields who share the fixation) to ignore whatever cannot pass the threshold of statistical significance (like the hypothetical hazardous waste example provided earlier). In their very important and highly acclaimed book, *The Cult of Statistical Significance*, Ziliak and McCloskey provide several examples of this, such as the past policy of the US Center for Disease Control (CDC) for many years to do nothing in support of regulating second-hand smoke, only because studies done on the effects of second-hand smoke could not pass the test of statistical significance even though it was strongly believed that second-hand smoke had very large effects. As Ziliak and McCloskey put it, "The official rhetoric of the CDC is: "Second-hand smoke is killing thousands annually. But is it statistically significant?"[6]

A Game within the Game

The other horrific consequence of the fixation is that it created *a game within a game*. That is, nestled within the bigger publication game described in the previous chapter is the game of playing around with as much data as you can, and as many mathematical options in your model that you could reasonably defend, in order to generate the statistically significant findings that you need for publication. This has encouraged much more "data mining" and use of spurious relationships in the statistical tests performed, including more fallacies of association as causation discussed earlier. As one might expect, this, in turn, often compromises the scientific integrity of the research, in ways that would be unimaginable to scientists in other fields.

Evidence from Conference Presentations

In my view there is quite a lot to be gained in understanding the mind-set of economics professors from witnessing them in sessions at economics conferences, where they present their research findings before their peers.

I have attended (and participated in) a countless number of these sessions at conferences since 1991. In the majority of the sessions I have attended, the following scenario happens very often: As part of the presentation, the paper presenter displays a table of statistical findings (what are often called the "regression results" of their model), with mixed feelings about the findings they acquired. Specifically, the presenter expresses happy and enthusiastic feelings about those coefficients that they found to be statistically significant, and disappointment and concern over the coefficients that were supposed to be significant according to the model, but just could not do their job.

As a hypothetical example, if the author hypothesized that a rise in the minimum wage would reduce employment, based on some kind of standard economic model, and found that it did in some cities but not in others, but enough to be statistically significant, then this would be satisfying to them (in the sense of supporting their model), and if it were not statistically significant it would be disappointing. For instance, if the results implied that a 20 percent rise in the minimum wage would be expected to reduce employment of low-income earners by as much as 20 percent, but those findings fell short of being statistically significant (for instance, by meeting the 90% confidence level instead of 95%), there would be disappointment. If the results implied that a 20 percent rise in the minimum wage would be expected to reduce such employment by as little as 0.1 percent, but this was found to be statistically significant (at the 95% level), then the author would be elated and claim that the "evidence supported their model."

In conference presentations I have attended, in which the authors could not acquire all the significant coefficients to support their model, they disappointingly expressed these results to the audience in the style and tone of a confession of failure, but also as an appeal for help. That appeal for help was hardly ever in the context of "How might I consider changing my understanding of the phenomena I am analyzing, since the data do not seem to support that understanding?" Rather, the appeal would be, "What can I do to my model specification or to my data to *get it to work?*" The author might then receive a variety of comments and suggestions from the audience, where it was not unusual for someone in the audience to have conducted a similar analysis in some way who could offer advice based on what worked for them. So in the session it would be common for the author to hear advice like: "Have you considered using this other independent variable in your regressions?" or "Have you tried this other kind of data?" etc.

On the surface, there is nothing particularly wrong with this—indeed, if it occurs in a scientific manner, then it might be said to justify precisely why economics research papers are presented at conferences. For example, in the case of studying the effect of minimum wage increases, the suggestion might be made that the researcher only include in the analysis those industries that tend to hire large numbers of minimum-wage employees, and leave out of the analysis those industries that do not. In his way, the "noise" associated with other factors in industries that are largely irrelevant for the analysis will not "dilute" the findings with regard to the specific effects being studied. It may well be the case that the increase in the minimum wage might lead to greater employment in some industries that will expand as a result of the minimum-wage increase. The expansion in those industries may occur because, once the minimum wage goes up, low-income workers might purchase more products in those other industries. All of this might be considered in such a study, for example. Thus, suggestions could be made that might essentially improve the science behind the research being conducted, and from that improvement the research findings themselves may become more useful and valuable.

Unfortunately, this is hardly ever the case in terms of the suggestions that are offered to researchers at economics conference sessions regarding how they might acquire statistically significant coefficients in their regression results. The discussion rarely captures the high ground of investigating the true causality and the underlying objective science of the phenomena under investigation. For instance, in the hypothetical example provided, if statistically significant statistics were not found to support the hypothesis that minimum wage increases reduce employment rates, then instead of making the suggestion of looking at the relevant industries, or even questioning whether the theory itself might be wrong, members of the audience will typically offer new ingredients to be thrown into the mix in the context of "repairing" the model so that it might crank out the needed statistically significant coefficients.

I would expect those readers who are not very familiar with these frequent conversations among academic economists (regarding how to harvest more statistically significant coefficients) to be somewhat skeptical of my description of them. In particular, why does it appear that I have assumed an absence of a scientific commitment—why should I not simply give these conversations the benefit of the doubt that they may mostly reflect a genuine interest in the causality of the phenomena under study even though such interest might not be blatantly obvious in the choice of words that come out in these conversations? I do believe it is important to give people the benefit of the doubt, but unfortunately, in this case, as the adage goes, "the devil is in the details."

As an example to shed light on the nature of the problem, I remember attending a presentation that discussed economic growth among the American Indian tribal nations in the United States, in which regression analyses were being presented in an effort to find a relationship between the type of governance those tribes had and economic statistics for the tribe. When the author expressed disappointment that their coefficients were not statistically significant, one of the commenters suggested that they use, as a variable in the analysis, the average "blood quantum" of tribes (the extent to which the residents of the tribe were not mixed races) which could be acquired from publically available data from the *1900* Census of the United States. This is not a typo—I wrote "1900"—and the study was not a historical one—it was investigating the world in the current time. The commenter's only justification for this suggestion was that they themselves had used this variable before and it worked pretty well for them. The author's automatic response to this was positive, writing the suggestion down in their notes, and then saying in so many words, "Thanks—I'll try that and see if it works."

CARING ABOUT THE ACCURACY OF NUMBERS AND WHAT THOSE NUMBERS ACTUALLY MEAN

In 1993, in his presidential address to the American Economic Association, highly acclaimed economist Zvi Griliches spoke on the fundamental problems that exist in measuring the economy—both conceptual problems and data problems.[7] During his speech, in reference to how we measure economic output, I remember him saying, as an aside that was not in the written, published speech, the following sentence in reference to the difficulty and ambiguity that exists in efforts to measure real output in the economy: "Take legal services, for example, we don't even know what *sign* to put on it!" (At that time, I was there in the room and heard him say it.) As soon as he uttered those words, there was laughter from the crowd, since most of the audience appeared to assume that he was expressing a "lawyer joke" of some kind. When this laugher occurred, Griliches reacted with a surprised expression on his face, because, in fact, he was quite serious about our not being sure what sign (a plus or minus sign, that is) to put on legal services when measuring gross domestic product (GDP). In other words, he was unsure whether to count the amounts of money that people spend on legal services as part of the overall output of economy, or whether to count it is as an expense that was only necessary to keep the output that we have, in which case it would only be subtracted from all our expenses.

What I strongly believe Griliches meant in that remark was that economists have uniformly treated most expenditures on legal services as output. In other words, if I spend an extra $1,000 on legal services, it would be the same as if I spent $1,000 on any other consumer good. Yet, how often is my expenditure on legal services not expenditure to get something new, but to maintain something I already have? For example, if I am falsely arrested, and hire an attorney to successfully defend my innocence in court, is that truly extra output that I am consuming, or is it only an extra cost to me for maintaining the level of freedom and justice that I already had? Is it not, in this sense, only an input to something already counted in the economy and not as an additional output? If so, it should be subtracted from total expenditures in deriving GDP, which should only measure those expenditures for final products (not intermediate ones). On the other hand, defensible counterexamples and counterarguments could be offered that legal services are a final output of the economy, so the measurement issue is ultimately ambiguous, at a philosophical level.

This is the kind of ambiguity in economic measurement that was sincerely identified by Griliches, the then-president of the American Economic Association. His basic point in that remark was, let us not kid ourselves—what we are measuring and calling economic output and productivity is fundamentally and inherently highly ambiguous. In other words, our findings and our conclusions are greatly dependent on measurement decisions that we have made, where many of those decisions were quite arbitrary. Needless to say, Griliches was not making these remarks as anyone with any "axe to grind" about how economists measure the economy. He was indeed someone who rose to prominence within the profession precisely from his substantial contribution to theoretical economic literature and applied economic literature. He was simply a recognized leader of the profession who was stating his views on economic measurement issues.

As another example, the United States experienced a shutdown of the federal government in early October 2013 for sixteen days because of an inability of Congress to pass a continuing resolution for the federal budget. Though hundreds of thousands of government employees were not allowed to work during that time, they were reimbursed by the federal government for their lost salaries. Would that reimbursement be considered part of GDP in the "government services" sector? Defensible arguments could be made that it should, and defensible arguments could be made that it should not. Indeed, the effect of the furlough on the national economy is rather complex, as reflected, in particular, by the 2013 White House report that estimated it.[8]

With regard to the topic of this book, what is most relevant about these measurement ambiguities is their implications for the validity of the analytical findings that economists acquire and publish, especially for those economists who are academics performing economic research whose findings are destined to be presented in technical journal articles. Such literature is usually supported by empirical regression analyses that back up the theoretical model featured in the article. In many and perhaps most of these empirical analyses that support an economic model, the variable GDP, or GDP per capita, is used as an input that has a crucial influence on the findings. Moreover, the empirical analyses of these economic models are typically highly sophisticated and highly sensitive to changes in the inputs that they use. It is quite conceivable, therefore, that an arbitrary decision about how GDP should be estimated, even if it results in a very small change, might be enough to throw the results of a model in an entirely different direction. For true scientists, or anyone for that matter who is committed to the honest pursuit of valuable knowledge, this dependency of results on arbitrary assumptions about measuring the real world implies that the results themselves are arbitrary and the their value needs to be scrutinized in light of this ambiguity.

Why Focus on GDP?

For better or worse, the one single measure that has been universally accepted by nations (and especially the United States) for "how well the economy is doing" is the GDP—the market value of all final goods and services produced by a nation over the course of a year. Quite simply, when GDP is up (or "real GDP" is up, after adjusting for inflation), then the economy has grown. When real, per capita GDP rises, we conclude that people are better off. When GDP falls, we announce that we are in a recession and, short of any major national disaster to attribute to the change (such as the incidence of a war), the public will blame the administration in power for having presumably allowed the recession to occur.

When we measure changes in the output of the economy we are measuring three types of changes: (1) changes in the physical quantities of goods or services, (2) changes in the quality of goods and services, per unit quantity, or what we might refer to as changes in the real value of output per unit quantity, and (3) changes in prices alone. The real GDP estimates that fall out of this analytical framework then serve as an input for many thousands of highly elaborate economic models that analyze the macroeconomy and study the factors that influence economic growth. In this respect, one might metaphorically regard the changes measured by (1), (2), and (3), although they are interdependent, as links in the chain from economic data collection (the first link) to the establishment of economic policy (the last link) based on the results of such model specification and estimation (the second-to-last link). This brings us again to Mayer's theory of the strongest link, where theoretical economists have tended *to act as though they believe a chain is only as strong as its STRONGEST link*, in contrast to the adage and truth that a chain is only as strong as its weakest link.

GDP measurement may not be, at all, the weakest link in the chain of economic analyses that have GDP as a variable, but in many cases it may well be, and, therefore, strengthening this link may directly strengthen the chain leading to policy development. Along these lines, many economists, including Nobel laureates like Joseph Stiglitz and Amartya Sen, have correctly and admirably been outspoken in their criticism of the overuse of GDP as a measure of the economic progress of nations.[9] Nevertheless, it remains the single most important economic variable in analyses of a nation's economy.

It also enters into many microeconomic analyses of particular industries or markets, in variables such as per capita income, where, for example, demand for a particular good may be seen as dependent on the per capita income of consumers.

Alternative Definitions of Value

For this discussion it would be useful to distinguish between three types of "value" associated with particular goods and services; however, the first type is something that philosophers might prefer to subdivide into any number of additional subcategories:

1. *Ultimate Value:* Value in terms of personal preferences and beliefs—how important the good or service is to the individual who consumes it, regardless of its market price and even regardless of what the consumer "is willing to pay for it."
2. *Economic Value:* How much someone is willing to pay for a good or service, in terms of exchanging money for it, or in terms of exchanging for it anything else that is a scarce resource to the consumer, such as the consumer's time or the consumer's health. (For example, if the item is offered for free but the consumer must wait in a line to receive it, the economic value would reflect how much time the consumer would be willing to wait to receive it, which might then be converted to a monetary value on the basis of the consumer's valuation of free time, as discussed further below.)
3. *Procedural Value:* The calculated value of a good or service based on standard procedures in economic methods, which economists use in calculating the GDP and many other economic variables used in economic analysis.

Economists who have been trained and indoctrinated to follow established procedures, and to define concepts operationally on the basis of those procedures, may instantly be confused between the distinctions expressed above between economic value and procedural value. Some of this confusion might derive from an absence of a scientific commitment to understanding true causal relations at the "lower level" (lacking prestige in the profession) of data collection.

The Choice between Being a Scientist and Being a Clerk

A committed scientist might conduct experiments on an entity in which they use a precise scale to measure the entity's weight at different points in time, hypothesizing that its weight is influenced by some particular phenomenon in the intervals between the times that its weight is measured. Suppose one of the procedures is to place the entity on a particular scale, and document the scale reading, and suppose the scientist hires a laboratory assistant, analogous to a "clerk," to perform this function. The scientist will understand that the weight of the entity is a measure of its mass for the purpose of the research; the clerk would not and would assume the scale reading is, in and of itself, the only information that is ultimately being sought. If anything would occur that might alter the scale reading of the weight from the true measurement of the entity's mass, such as the location of moon when the reading was taken (assuming very fine levels of measurement), the scientist, committed to measuring an object's mass accurately would be compelled to address such an issue and regard it as a problem for the research. The clerk, who is content with taking scale readings and collecting a paycheck in return, would be oblivious to such a problem, not necessarily being indifferent to the research being successful, but simply understanding the measurement by an operational definition: In the clerk's mind, the weight (or mass) is defined as whatever the scale says it is, without question.

This distinction carries further downstream to where the measurements are used to test theoretical models. Committed scientists would abhor the idea of using data to test a model when they have reason to believe the data are not accurate depictions of the reality that they purport to analyze and understand. On the other hand, *clerks in the form of theoreticians* may complacently plug into their models data that they ultimately realize are faulty but will provide "results," especially publishable results. Furthermore, they may feel their actions in doing so is granted immunity by a statement that they are happy to make toward the end of their published paper that their results are a function of the quality of the data they used, and that they cannot guarantee that the data they used are reliable, but they are the only data available (implying that the unreliability of the data is not their fault).

Understanding the difference between true economic value, and procedural value, then gets at the heart of whether economists act as clerks or as scientists. The core responsibility of economic science is to understand the causal relationships that truly exist, and that determine the actions taken by economic agents with regard to production and consumption. For example, suppose that consumers actually perceive an item as more valuable than another, and they are thus truly willing to exchange more for it. Yet, suppose further that existing procedures do not capture this perception, and willingness to pay, for greater value. It follows that these procedures have failed to serve their purpose, and by extension have failed to serve the purpose of economics or the role of responsible economists, regardless of the fact that such procedures may have been officially sanctioned by leading authorities and may have an historical precedence for their application.

Unfortunately, it is more often the case than not, that economic statistics used to test economic models are viewed by economic theorists in much the same way that hot dogs are viewed by fans attending a baseball game: They just want to have them, and use them for an immediate purpose, and do not care how they were produced. In addition, both economic theoreticians and baseball fans may argue that, from where they are situated, there is nothing that they can do to improve the ingredients of the economic data or of the hot dogs, respectively. This would not be true in either case, if either economists or baseball fans were committed to improving their respective situations. For economists, it gets down to a responsibility in leadership and in the culture in which their work is performed. There is a big difference between looking at the world as a scientist, and looking at the world as a clerk, regardless of one's superficial title and status.

Happiness and Societal Values

This framework for studying value, and the relevance of what economists measure as value, has something in common with a body of relatively recent literature on "happiness," which advocates alternative measures of societal success (or failure) on the basis of how "happy" people are, as opposed to measures of the economy like the GDP. However, I feel that the framework I am using here is preferable for two primary reasons:

First, the term "happiness" itself conveys a focus on hedonistic, personal satisfaction, for example, I am "happy" when I drink a piña colada while sitting on the beach at a tropical resort. It does not convey a sense of deep satisfaction that might be felt with regard to higher social or spiritual values. For example, people would not be included to say that their nation's management of a competent and effective military to protect them from foreign invasion or terrorism makes them "happy," though this sounds like something that perhaps a child could say. Rather the existence of the military capability is valued as a mandatory, social necessity as opposed to a "generator of happiness" like a tiki bar. In this sense "value" includes all that makes us happy, plus all that we hold as essential or highly important for any number of reasons. This broader definition is therefore more useful for understanding the big picture of the determinants of what people want in the economy and what motivates their actions as economic agents.

The second limitation of the "happiness" framework is that it assumes that "procedural value" and "economic value" are one in the same, that is, the economists, in their procedures, do a reasonably good job at estimating economic value. Thus, the happiness critique of economic measures of value focuses on the distinction between ultimate value and economic value, while the discussion here will focus on how economic value and procedural value are quite different.

Economic Value versus Ultimate Value

The only reason for our having procedures to measure economic value is to measure economic value as accurately as possible Thus, to whatever extent economic value and procedural value differ, this is a level of failure on the part of the economics profession. For many economists, and I would guess most economics professors, the distinction I have made among the three types of value would be perceived as confusing at best, and at worst, nonsensical. In particular, many may reject the idea that "ultimate value" would not still be reflected in the economic measure of the consumer's "willingness-to-pay" for a good or service. However, the "willingness-to-pay" concept that economists use are generally in the context of what individuals would be willing, as consumers, to pay for something out of their own pocket. This is very different from individuals promoting a social objective by supporting the establishment of government regulations or services which they know will create costs imposed on them through taxation, but where the consumers are focused, not on the precise costs that will be imposed, but whether it is the right thing for society to do. In his pivotal essay, "Cost Benefit Analysis: An Ethical Critique," Steven Kelman explains this difference:

> [T]he efforts of economists to impute willingness to pay invariably involve bundled goods exchanged in private transactions. Those who use figures garnered from such analysis . . . assume no difference between how people value certain things in private individual transactions and how they would wish those same things to be valued in public collective decisions. In making such assumptions, economists insidiously slip into their analysis an important and controversial value judgment . . . the view that there should be no difference between private behavior and the behavior we display in public social life. An alternative view—one that enjoys, I would suggest, wide resonance among citizens—would be that public, social decisions provide an opportunity to give certain things a higher valuation than we choose, for one reason or another, to give them in our private activities.[10]

Kelman further argues that individuals have societal preferences precisely because they see their revealed private preferences as unsatisfactory and incomplete:

> Precisely because we fail, for whatever reasons, to give life-saving the value in everyday personal decisions that we in some general terms believe we should give it, we may wish our social decisions to provide us the occasion to display the reverence for life that we espouse but do not always show. . . . In such cases, the use of private behavior to impute the values that should be entered for public decisions . . . commits grievous offense against a view of the behavior of the citizen that is deeply engrained in our democratic tradition.[11]

In terms of the economic measurement of the economy, public goods such as the enforcement of regulations are, in fact, valued in terms of the costs of the government's provision of that service (with regard to published measures of the GDP). However, their "ultimate" value cannot often be measured in this matter. The inherent fuzziness of ultimate value is also dependent on what is even meant by a good or service. As another important example, one might see government as having a role, and mandate, to reduce levels of poverty in the nation. To the extent that poverty reduction is a "government service," one might argue that the transfer of funds from the rich to the poor should increase GDP as part of this service, even though people have roughly the same amount of money both before and after the transfer. As it is now, only the amount of government expenditure to produce this transfer is counted as part of GDP, that is, the salaries and use of physical capital (e.g., computers) that such offices expend in administering these transfers. Some might argue, however, that the reduction in poverty, especially because it saves lives, reduces crime, etc., is ultimately worth more to society than what was spent in the administrative function to effect it.

Microeconomists should be quick to point out that the above paragraph is quite plebian—that I have simply left out of this discussion the all-important and widely recognized economic measure of "social welfare." They may also say that I have confused "output" (GDP) with "inequality" (which would include the proportion of the population in poverty), which would also be a correct criticism of the paragraph. As all economists know from the courses they took, social welfare is a function of both GDP per capita, and a function of how equally it is distributed, which has often been explained and illustrated in standard texts as concave curves in the two-dimensional space of the incomes of two individuals (simply for illustration). By this framework, one might argue that the concept of "social welfare" fits the bill for understanding the distinction between per capita income and what I have described above as "ultimate value."

As a simple example to explore further the distinction between ultimate value and procedural value, suppose that the air is quite polluted, but a new regulation is put into place that eliminates the pollution entirely. The regulation would have violators imprisoned for polluting the air, but none are imprisoned, because everyone chooses to abide by the new regulation. In addition, since people did not know enough about where they might move to breathe better air, there was no shadow market for living in places with better air which might allow an economist to estimate the value of the clean air from the cost differential in rents and home prices between the two places. In this case, the change from polluted air to clear air will have no effect on any measurement of the GDP—the economy will not have grown, or "improved," as far as economic analysis is concerned, and this example might just as easily be found in the "happiness literature."

ONE FAILURE SHOULD NOT BE AN EXCUSE FOR ANOTHER FAILURE

As Kelman suggested in the above quotation, societal promotion of the ultimate value of things—especially goods and services provided collectively by the government—is a topic that extends beyond the purview of economics, into all other fields of study for which ultimate value is considered, for example, philosophy, public policy, law, sociology, and religion. While the economics profession should rightfully *be excused* from the responsibility of measuring the *ultimate value* of economic circumstances, this does not excuse the economics profession from measuring correctly what they are *supposed* to be measuring, which is the *economic value* of goods and services. I have found there to be enormous fuzziness about the "blame game" that has been taking place with regard to this topic. "Happiness economists" (those who advocate the study of happiness that is) have properly accused public leaders, and the public in general, for paying too much attention to the GDP per capita as the criterion for assessing societal progress. Given the fact that the GDP cannot ever measure ultimate value, and the economists have neither the training nor the tools to measure ultimate value themselves (under the heroic assumption that it can ever be measured objectively), it follows that it is not the fault of economists if society pays too much attention to GDP. Of course, perhaps economists are guilty of publicizing their product more than they should, but the fault would lie equally with the consumers' (and particularly the media's) decision to "buy it."

On the other hand, what if GDP not only fails to measure ultimate value (for which it is supposed to fail) but also fails to measure economic value? Then, this would be a genuine failure, and GDP would be much less meaningful for economic analysis than it would be otherwise.

As a simple example of the kind of failure I mean, in the 1970s, in order to have pictures, people spent a nonnegligible amount of money on purchasing lower-end cameras, and the film (and film-processing services) to go with them. Modern cell phones today can now take as many pictures as one may want to have, at a resolution that is at least as high as the old lower-end cameras of the 1970s, at zero additional cost to the consumer who is already paying for the cell phone and its service. It still cost some money to acquire a print of a picture, while, on the other hand, one can electronically send the same picture to thousands of people or enable everyone to see it on a website. One can also manage, sort, and select among thousands of pictures at essentially no cost, while in the past one would sparingly take pictures so as not to waste expensive film. With all things considered, I believe it is reasonably clear that consumers derive substantial economic value from the photographic features, alone, of cell phones. Those features provide the same service as cameras.

Suppose, just for the sake of argument, that 80 percent of what consumers would have spent in the 1970s on cameras, film, and the processing of film is now replaced by these free features of cell phones, while the other 20 percent would still be spent on higher-quality cameras today. By the above-mentioned definition of economic value, and by basic principles of economics more generally, those photographic features of cell phones most certainly have substantial, positive economic value, which might even be estimated as the 80 percent of prior expenditures on cameras, film, and processing that would have been spent if these features did not exist.

Under these circumstances, it could be argued that there should be greater value assigned to cell phones on the basis of the fact that they are also valuable cameras, and this value could be added to the GDP. Put another way, GDP is underestimated because of our not including the full value of cell phones. This would certainly be a difficult adjustment to make, but not more difficult than many other adjustments that have been made over the years. In a broader sense, it is simply an example of the difference between economic value and procedural value (where economic value would include the photographic value of cell phones, and procedural value does not). Of course, the problem is made much more complex by all of the other applications offered by cell phones today, including their function as computers for many practical purposes, as well as small television sets.

While the economics profession has justifiably found room in their literature and deliberations to debate over the important differences between ultimate value and economic value (or the differences between ultimate societal goals and measured economic growth), there appears to be almost no attention paid to the failure of procedural value at measuring economic value. In fact, there appears to be a consensus that the distinction between economic value and procedural value (or simply the inability of estimation procedures to capture true economic change) is a minor problem, if a problem at all. The problem is dismissed generally for four reasons, which are provided in the next four sections:

Reason 1: Absence of Accepted Theory and Blockage of Alternative Theories

Much of economic theory on measuring economic value and related topics is produced by academics, though a significant amount is produced by government economists and private-sector economists. In the minority of cases, when it is pursued by nonacademic economists, these economists are still frequently working in collaboration (often as coauthors) with academics. Even when they are not coauthored with academics, the research is generally destined for technical journals or prestigious working paper series (such as the NBER working paper series), which are controlled and peer reviewed predominantly by academic, theoretical economists. Theoretical economic research is incentivized by research grant money, and by honoring the earlier work of prominent theoretical economists. Yet, here is the rub: The grant support in the area of economic measurement comes generally from government agencies, especially when the research is addressing what the government is doing in the area of economic measurement.

Research that receives such grant money in economic measurement usually occurs when it places already-existing methodologies in a favorable light. That research is only designed to fine-tune those already-practiced procedures with only minor tweaks. Such research venerates the existing methodologies by describing them in published technical literature, thereby suggesting that the agencies are already employing state-of-the-art techniques. In contrast, any research that calls for any major revision in the economic measurement processes performed by a government agency is very likely to receive a cold reception and discourage the government to provide further grants to those researchers.

Over the years there have been some exceptions, where research, in fact, questioned the existing methods, and was actually well received. For example, in the 1980s when personal computers began to capture a significant portion of the economy, "hedonic price methods" began to be used, and became officially sanctioned, to more accurately distinguish between quality change and pure inflation, by attributing quality measures to features like a computer's memory or speed. As another example, recent changes were made to the GDP estimates to include research and development (R&D) expenditures as an investment that builds a nation's capital, in the same vein as investments in physical structures and equipment. Beforehand, R&D was considered an intermediate expense (not a final product) and was not measured as a contributor to GDP.

Reason 2: Ambiguity between Technological Change and Changes in Tastes

When new products arrive on the scene, there is often a great deal of ambiguity in how they should be interpreted in relation to the products they substitute. In the example provided above about the cameras in cell phones, for instance, some people may be inclined to interpret the new situation as a new existence of "free photography," and that the value of cell phones should then go up by the value of the cameras they replaced (as already suggested). On the other extreme, some might argue that technological change has also occurred with regard to the creation of much higher-quality digital cameras, and that people who take photography seriously will purchase those cameras and not use their cell phone cameras, so for those camera-wielding individuals the cell phone feature has no value, and only forced them to pay more for a cell phone, since it is virtually impossible to buy a cell phone today without photographic features. Some might say that this ambiguity cannot be resolved without further research, which would cost money to support, and in the absence of that funding there is not enough analytical rigor to justify any methodological adjustment to the value of cell phones on the basis of their photographic capabilities.

The question then becomes whether this obstacle is a scientific one, or a bureaucratic one: If the magnitude of the change is substantial to any reasonable observer, resources should be found to address it, commensurate with the level of resources that are already spent to address changes that are comparable in size and effect. In contrast, if the ambiguity, or discomfort level associated with the novelty of the situation, serves as the reason for inaction regardless of the magnitude of the effect, then such inaction, and consequent lack of accuracy in the estimation of economic value, would not be justifiable from an analytical or scientific perspective.

Reason 3: Insufficient Data

An absence of data mirrors the problem of ambiguity that was just described, that is, we can conclude and announce, "Sorry . . . but we just don't have the data to effect any methodological change." For instance, we do not know the price of cameras, which are purchased separately, that are roughly equivalent to what is offered in cell phones, so that we might add that camera value to the value of cell phones. The relevant question, again, is whether the obstacle is justifiable on the grounds of prioritization of scarce funding for the most accurate estimates or not justifiable as a function of bureaucratic indolence or the topic being outside the comfort zone (or expertise) of those who, by virtue of their position, are most responsible for addressing it.

Reason 4: Presumption of a Small Effect

Often, the absence of sufficient data, the ambiguity of measurement, and an overall discomfort or lack of familiarity with the topic make happy bedfellows with the presumption that an effect of technological change on economic value must be relatively small and thus insignificant. This may be supported by the highly flawed logic that, if such an effect were actually significant, then there would already be literature on it, that is, some prominent people within the profession would have written on it. (In other words, if the emperor were actually wearing no clothes, someone would have already brought it to his attention.) This limited perspective relates to the scientist versus clerk heuristic described earlier, and to the misguided perspective among the practitioners of economic measurement that they need only look to academic scholars to know what they should do, without realizing that those academic scholars who perform research on economic measurement do so at the bequest of the practitioners who issue them their research grants, as discussed earlier.

SO WHAT *HAS* CHANGED IN ECONOMIC VALUE THAT HAS *NOT* BEEN MEASURED?

Many things have changed systematically over time, which have not been properly accounted for in the economic measurement of value. As mentioned at the outset of this chapter, it is important to note that these shortcomings in economic measurement are not a problem confined to the subfield of economic measurement alone. Quite the contrary, these sources of error have enormous impacts on all of economic analysis and policy because the unreliable statistics that result poison the waters downstream in the economic analysis of those statistics, the testing of economic models, and ultimately the establishment of policy. Some of these adverse consequences for policy are subtle, while others are quite obvious. In this discussion, the following three major sources of error will be identified: (1) free Internet services and time use, (2) effective equal recognition of past and present tastes, and (3) the true effects of health services and of biomedical R&D. There are surely many other sources of error in the estimation of economic value, and it is mere speculation that these three sources are the most important (assuming importance in this regard could be unambiguously defined). In any case, what matters is whether improvements could be made in these three areas through studies that academic economists could perform.

Free Internet Services

As all economists know, there is an enormous literature on "public goods," which are defined as having the following characteristics:

1. *Nonexcludability.* A person cannot be prevented from deriving the benefits of a good or service if they do not pay for it.

2. *Nonrivalrous Consumption.* One person's consumption of the good or service does not impair another person's ability to consume it (except at extreme levels in which there are crowding effects).[12]

An example might be a public beach. Another example for modern times might be the Internet, where a multitude of providers offer Internet access for free, in places like Starbucks and the Public Library, for those with their own laptops. Along with the prominence of the Internet, there has also been the influx of free information and entertainment-related services on the Internet. What is now greatly needed in economic thought, and especially in the area of economic measurement, is a category for the enormous number of services offered on the Internet that basically meets the public good criteria, once the Internet service has been paid and people own or can borrow the computer equipment for Internet access. Let us simply call these services "free Internet services." But, how can the value of free services be measured?

Time is the Answer

There is one unit of measure that is also a unit of value, and an unambiguous, basic physical unit by which the quantity of any free service (including Internet service) is consumed, and that is "time use." To make time use work for us, we need to distinguish greatly between (1) something that has our "undivided attention" (for the most part) and (2) something that is "on in the background" but generally does not have our attention. The former, of course, is "paid for" by the consumer's opportunity cost of time while the latter is not.

Admittedly, the value of time use as a cost paid by the consumer, for whatever the consumer does with their time, is not easy to measure. Such measurement must necessarily involve somewhat arbitrary assumptions in any theoretical model that is chosen, not to mention the problematic nature of data collection on time use and its interpretation. Nevertheless, the value of time use most certainly is measured, not only by academic researchers, but by federal government officials. As a case in point, the Department of Transportation (DOT) measures time use for the purpose of supporting policy decisions with regard to improvements in transportation systems. Along these lines the DOT calculates different "values of travel time savings" on the basis of whether it is business travel or personal travel, and whether the travel is for "surface modes (except high-speed rail)" and "air and high-speed rail." For intercity travel in 2009, these values ranged from \$16.70 per hour for personal travel and \$18.00 for business travel in surface modes, and from \$31.90 for personal travel and \$57.20 per hour for business travel by air or high-speed rail.

The basic idea of attributing the value of time savings to the value of time spent in being attentive to free services should be clear to any economist or economics student. If an individual is willing to give up, say, $20 to save an extra hour of travel where they generally are not able to enjoy other things (like free Internet services) while they are traveling, then this must mean that their free time is worth to them at least $20 per hour. If they spend, say, two hours per day on the Internet (with emails, Facebook, reading blogs, looking for jobs, doing online shopping, etc.) on their own time (outside of work), then that time spent must be worth at least $40 ($20 x 2 hours) to them per day (for the average person). Otherwise, they could sacrifice any of those two hours on a longer commute, on spending more time to prepare food instead of ordering takeout, etc.

Counting Only the Marginal Utility in National Accounting

The value of goods and services in the economy is measured on the basis of market prices, as opposed to the sum of the market prices and "consumer surplus." Consumer surplus reflects how valuable the product is to consumers beyond the price the consumer paid for it. For example, if a medication is sold at $10 per dose, but a consumer were willing to pay a maximum of $100 per dose if it were available in an auction, then the consumer surplus of that one consumer would be $90, and the total value of the dose to the consumer would be $100. In theory, the total value of any product in the economy could then be estimated as the sales of the product plus the sum of all the consumer surpluses of each consumer who purchased it. This would not be the GDP, of course, but a measure of how valuable the product is to society.

The trouble, of course, is that it is not possible, whatsoever, for us to collect and analyze data on consumer surplus at the level of all products in the economy. In contrast, market prices are much easier to acquire and analyze, though even market prices can be problematic to estimate under many circumstances. The unavailability of information on consumer surplus provides the economics profession a perfect excuse to measure the size of the economy on the basis of market prices alone, and an excuse to give up on measuring the immeasurable sum of all consumer surplus that might reveal how much progress humanity has made in terms of the true benefits of products to consumers. While I agree with this general excuse for GDP measurement, I cannot agree with how complacently the profession continues to use GDP growth as a measure of social progress, when by economic theory itself it is ignoring the well-established, economic principle of consumer surplus. In fact, ironically, in areas of policy decision-making, measures of consumer surplus (along with producer surplus, both comprising "social welfare") at specific micro-levels of analysis (for particular industries and products) plays a key role in determining the results of economic cost-benefit analysis. In other words, what the profession holds dear for evaluating the costs and benefits of public decisions, it ignores (for reasons of practicality) in its assessment of economic growth, while economic growth is used as a key measure of aggregate social progress.

To appreciate the full absurdity of this situation, consider the following extreme thought experiment that has a definite science fiction character to it: Suppose someone invents a special robot that can fuel, repair, and reproduce itself, which exists only to serve humanity, and its population produces all that humanity wants, so that human beings need no longer work nor spend any money on anything. That is, everything has become free. Under this extreme, hypothetical thought experiment, GDP would fall to zero, in spite of the fact that we will have all the things that we would want, only because everything would be free, and thus the market price of everything is zero.

Now, let us move away from that thought experiment, but keep it enough in our minds to imagine society simply moving closer to such a hypothetical situation. As we move closer to it we do see entire groups of products falling into the "free realm" that used to be paid for at significant costs: a great deal of information is free, much of communication is now free, and so is musical and video entertainment (which might be seen as a special form of information). For simplicity, let us do what economic theorists quite often do, which is to assume, for the moment, a hypothetical situation. In particular, let us assume that the things just mentioned (communication, library-type information, and audiovisual entertainment) have become free. All else being equal, measured GDP would fall by these products essentially falling out of the GDP measurement. Since these products are still being produced (at negligible cost per unit) and enjoyed by consumers, surely the loss in GDP would not reflect a decline in societal benefits. In fact, consumption of these products would likely expand by virtue of their now being free, so society will actually benefit from the change, at the same time that economic growth would be seen as negative.

As another science fiction thought experiment, suppose that a deranged dictator decreed that all communication, library-type information, and audiovisual entertainment were now illegal, and anyone found consuming these services would be imprisoned. GDP would fall in precisely the same way, as no one would be perceived as consuming any of these products (though not this time because of the movement toward a zero price), and society would suffer greatly this time, reflected by the loss in measured GDP.

Simply contrast two hypothetical worlds: the "happy world" where communication, library-type information, and audio-visual entertainment become essentially free (at near-zero cost per unit to produce) and the other "tortured world" being one that never experiences such technological advancement but where a totalitarian government outlawed these products, and so fiercely that no one dared break the law. The decline in GDP would then be identical in each case and no one would be able to tell the difference from looking at the GDP data alone which hypothetical world was in effect.

As discussed earlier, however, when something is free, in terms of not costing any money, it may still be far from free in its expenditure of the consumer's time. *A time-use survey of individuals in both of the above hypothetical worlds would explain their great differences.* The value of time in the happy world would be greater because, since people have a wider range of opportunity to enjoy their time, they will exchange more goods and services that they buy in markets to have that time. Adding to the GDP the value of the time spent on things that are free, based on the valuation of time, would clearly show the happy world to have a higher level of GDP than the tortured world.[13]

If Only There Were Data

The Bureau of Labor Statistics manages the American Time Use Survey (ATUS), which is implemented by the Census Bureau, to measure "the amount of time people spend doing various activities, such as paid work, childcare, volunteering, and socializing."[14] Though the data from the survey are invaluable to a great deal of other types of social and economic research, unfortunately, nothing in the ATUS data connects time use to the consumption of nearly free services like Internet usage for personal (as opposed to work-related) communication and entertainment. For example, anything done on the Internet through the use of a cell phone is categorized in the ATUS as "telephone calls."[15] However, there are other sources. For example, according to a survey conducted in May 2013 by the Bunton Group and Survey Sampling International, "US web users" spent an average of twenty-three hours per week on email, texting, and social media (e.g., Facebook).[16] Surveys like this might well be able to shed light on the true economic benefits of free, or nearly free, Internet services.

The problem, however, is there must be some interest and impetus in the profession to support the development of these data. Overall, there is none, because nonacademic economists have generally relied upon academic economists to initiate such new efforts, while academic economists have had no interest in doing so. Part of the problem is that any new kind of effort like this—to pose an argument for better data—does not easily support the goal of producing new journal articles, which is what academic economists focus on. Similarly, it would not be a mathematically impressive effort, and it does not build much on previous theory. Hence, this is the kind of research that hardly any academic economist would be interested in pursuing.

Changes in Tastes versus Knowledge Acquisition

There is an implicit assumption that is made in price measurement, which is that, if the physical characteristics of a particular good or service remain unchanged from one period to the next, then any price change is a "pure price change," that is, reflecting only inflation, and does not reflect any change in the value of the product. At first glance, the logic of this approach appears to be incontestable: If a product does not change physically, then how could its value change? Such is the simple perspective of economists who generally specialize in the study of price movements. Moreover, under this framework, if one were to pose the question "But what if people change their minds and value a product more in the second period than in the first?" the prevailing school of economic thought would be to provide the knee-jerk reaction, "Yes, then that would reflect a 'change in tastes,' but since the product did not change physically, we must still treat it as a pure price change and not a quality change." Yet, the effective disallowance of the quality of an item to change, when the item has not physically changed over time, goes against very basic economic principles that are applied to other economic concepts such as the valuation of assets. For example, if land that is purchased originally at a high price is then found to have hazardous waste in it, its assessed value is substantially reduced regardless of the fact that it did not change physically from when it was purchased. Its value changed because we learned more about it to enable us to change our minds about how much it is worth.

This kind of thinking could, and should, be applied by economists to assessing social progress. When new knowledge about products enables us to change our minds about how much certain products are worth, it is nonsensical for us to then say that we simply do not want to do the homework to reevaluate the economic implications of the new knowledge. Again, the problem lies in the disinterest of the profession to explore what really needs to be done to assess social progress from an economic perspective.

Our Final Frontier: The Prolongation of Human Life

Prior to the arrival of Europeans to the Americas, the ancient Mayan culture in what is now Mexico had many advances that were beyond those of the Europeans, such as a more accurate calendar and a superior medical system. They also had "pull toys" for children, which were toy animals with small wheels on their bottom to enable the toy animals to role when pushed or pulled. What many observers find amazing, however, is that while the Mayans had these toys with wheels, they had no wheeled vehicles of any kind—not even a wheelbarrow.[17] The technology for having wheeled vehicles was right under their noses, and yet they missed it.

In much the same way, economists apply the concept of the value of time to something that is relatively small in importance, such as the cost-benefit analysis of transportation projects (though of course the variable is important within this specific context). While the value of time is right under our noses, we miss the most important application of the value of our time there is—*how the value of our time expands with the prolongation of human life.*

Without a doubt, the value of time as it relates to an extended life span takes on a rather different nature from the value of time that economists are used to measuring as described earlier. However, the fundamental concept is still there that we may value the extra time that we are alive in a relatively healthful condition.

In recent years, life expectancy in the United States has been rising per year by about 0.1 years, and in 2012 (the year for which data are most recently available at this writing) average life expectancy at birth rose to a record high of 78.8 years.[18] A key consideration in the examination of life expectancy has been the adjustment of "life span" to "health span"—the number of years a person lives in a relatively healthy state, free of the debilitating effects of chronic disease.[19] Similar to the concept of the health span is that of the "disability-adjusted life year" (DALY).[20] In 2014, Dr. David Katz noted, "Life expectancy is greatly influenced by advances in medicine and the public health system, while the health span is most affected by lifestyle practices, in particular the quality of diet, physical activity and avoiding tobacco."[21] Nevertheless, medicine and the public health system surely play a very significant role in expanding the health span, by both keeping people alive longer and by reducing the causes of disability in older life, while advanced medicine and various other technological advances make life easier and more comfortable for those who experience the disabilities associated with old age.

NOTES

1. "Bernt P. Stigum," The MIT Press, accessed February 4, 2017, http://tinyurl.com/zolsv8l. (My own emphasis in italics.)
2. Harry Clarke, "Professional Ethics for Economists: Notes on DeMartino," August 12, 2013, accessed February 4, 2017, http://tinyurl.com/gv7ab93.
3. Stephen Ziliak and Deirdre McCloskey, "Lady Justice Versus Cult of Statistical Significance: Oomph-less Science and the New Rule of Law," in The Oxford Handbook of Professional Economic Ethics, ed. George DeMartino and Deirdre McCloskey, (New York: Oxford University Press, 2015), 353.
4. "Significance," Oxford Dictionary, accessed February 4, 2017, http://tinyurl.com/zlcmegg.
5. Gretchen Livingston, "The Odds that You Will Give Birth to a Boy or Girl Depend on Where in the World You Live," Fact Tank, September 24, 2013, Pew Research Center, accessed February 4, 2017, http://tinyurl.com/mjmwfgc.
6. Ziliak and McCloskey, The Cult of Statistical Significance, 10.
7. His presentation can be found at: Zvi Griliches, "Productivity, R&D, and the Data Constraint," (Presidential Address to the American Economic Association) American Economic Review 84(1): (1994): 1–23.

8. See: Sylvia Mathews Burwell, "Impacts of the Cost of the Government Shutdown," White House Report, November 7, 2013, accessed February 5, 2017, http://tinyurl.com/zgtaq9b.

9. .Joseph E. Stiglitz, Amartya Sen, and Jean-Paul Fitoussi, "Report by the Commission on the Measurement of Economic Performance and Social Progress," Report to the President of the France, September 14, 2009, accessed February 5, 2017, http://tinyurl.com/jafwpoq.

10. Steven Kelman, "Cost-Benefit Analysis: An Ethical Critique, " AEI Journal on Government and Society Regulation, January/February 1981, 38.

11. Kelman, "Cost-Benefit Analysis," 38.

12. Payson, Quality Measurement in Economics, 29–30.

13. This could be made more complicated by the inclination for the happy world to have less consumption of other things. For example, sales of books would be lower in the happy world, but given the limited purposes of this example, this level of complexity need not be addressed.

14. Bureau of Labor Statistics, "American Time Use Survey," accessed October 25, 2014, http://www.bls.gov/tus/home.htm.

15. Bureau of Labor Statistics, American Time Use Survey User's Guide: Understanding ATUS 2003 to 2013, June 2014, http://www.bls.gov/tus/atususersguide.pdf, 52.

16. .eMarketer, "Social Usage Involves More Platforms, More Often; Growing Interest in More In-Person Connectedness," July 2, 2013, http://tinyurl.com/p3hf46a.

17. Herman Smith, "Real Smart Folks, But No Wheel," accessed October 25, 2014, http://ambergriscaye.com/museum/digit4.html.

18. Larry Copeland,"Life Expectancy in the USA Hits a Record High," USA Today, October 9, 2014.

19. Steven Reinberg, "Americans Living Longer Than Ever: CDC," HealthDay, January 6, 2014.

20. World Health Organization, "Metrics: Disability-Adjusted Life Year (DALY)," accessed October 27, 2014, http://tinyurl.com/3rt842h.

21. David Katz, Director, Yale University Prevention Research Center, New Haven, Connecticut, who was quoted in Steven Reinberg, "Americans Living Longer Than Ever."

Chapter 6

The Effects of Electronic Files, Citation Counts, and Bibliometric Databases

The emergence of bibliographic databases like RePEc and Google Scholar, and their predecessor, the Social Science Citation Index, which still exists, have revolutionized the way that economists, and many other scientists and social scientists study their field, perform their research, and acquire the credentials they need to be promoted in their careers. As we know, these databases have created a public good in the information they provide, and also in terms of providing a supposedly objective, and unbiased, means through which the importance of literature can be assessed. The academic economics profession has wholeheartedly and very conveniently adopted the assumption that citation and publication counts measure degrees of scholarly achievement, to the point of making, or breaking, the careers of economics professors.

Though the "publish or perish" adage has been around for generations in all academic fields, over the last two decades the bibliographic databases in economics have put the publish-or-perish paradigm on steroids. With it comes a new question: To what extent are good ideas recognized in economics independently from the observable number of citations they have generated? Similarly, to what extent has the game of racking-up one's publication and citation scores, and the career advancement pressure to do so, all but replaced the long-lost scholarly pursuit of useful and important knowledge? The most fundamental question that follows from this is: To what extent does the genuine pursuit of useful knowledge coincide with the "citation game" and to what extent do the two conflict with each other? It should also be asked, how much pressure is there, within the academic economics profession, to score publication and citation points at the opportunity cost of what academic researchers truly believe is the best scholarly contribution they could make?

Ultimately, these questions boil down to nothing less, and nothing more complex, than the fundamental question of what academic economists are truly trying to achieve. Is it to advance useful knowledge in an admirable way, or to become celebrities or sports stars in their profession's most-watched sport of publication and citation scoring?

Perhaps academic economists have become too afraid even to ask these questions, for fear that performing research to answer them will not yield many citations to this research, or will never be published by a highly cited journal! By analogy, is the patient too sick at this point to survive ingesting any medication that would otherwise treat their disease? For many types of diseases, especially narcotics dependency, for example, the first step toward a cure is for the patient to recognize and accept that they are indeed ill, and that they must seek treatment. In this case, realizing that the citation-counting game is a problem for the profession will take us more than halfway toward the cure!

A PERVERSE ARGUMENT THAT *MORE* PUBLICATIONS REFLECT *LESS* ACCOMPLISHMENT!

I once heard Robert Solow tell a joke at a National Science Board meeting, when the question came up of whether researchers should use the number of publications as a measure of the output of scientific research. He was responding to the suggestion that, if there were more publications produced in one field of science than in another, then the one with more publications may be regarded as having produced more "output" from scientific research. His joke went as follows: "There are two very adept economists—one who has very many publications to his name, and the other who does not. Someone then asked the second one why he had so much fewer publications than the first, to which he replied, 'Well . . . mine are all different.'"

This was Solow's apparent way of saying that he was not a strong supporter of the idea that publication counts reflect output. In my own view, I could not agree more, in part from seeing for myself how frequently some economics professors and other economists "recycle" their same ideas in paper after paper, in order to maximize their publication counts to promote their careers, though I believe the majority do not do such extensive recycling. There is a more general principle, however, that the measure is, in fact, not only meaningless when one compares it across different fields, but one can even make the case that the number of publications in a field may be *inversely related* to the amount of new knowledge generated in that field.

That is, in a field that does experience rapid advancement of knowledge, many important genuine scientific discoveries are made continuously. When they are, professors are highly recognized for their important discoveries, such as Watson and Crick's discovery of DNA, or Einstein's General Theory of Relativity, to name the most extreme examples of valuable scientific discovery. When their important discoveries are recognized, these scientists have "job security" and recognition from their discoveries, without having to publish ten or more new journal articles each year to look good and get ahead in competing with their peers.

In contrast, in fields in which great discoveries (that are genuine and truly valuable) are rarely made at all, the only way for anyone to prove that they are superior in their field is to pile up an enormous number of publications to their name and citations to those publications. In this latter case, people have a greater incentive to recycle the same ideas with just enough cosmetic changes and mixing and matching ideas from different previous publications to make each new article appear unique enough to be published without the violation of copyright agreements with their previous publication outlets. The incentive to do this relies on the obvious fact that it is much easier to cut and paste, and paraphrase, from a few sources that already exist, than it is to produce brand new research findings. So, in this way, one can maximize one's publication counts while producing very little if any new ideas each year. In this sense, one may well expect fields of study that have more publications per researcher as discovering less than those with less publications per researcher. *In other words, publication counts may well be a SUBSTITUTE for genuine discovery, as opposed to a REFLECTION of genuine discovery as is implicitly assumed when we utilize publication counts as a measure of output.*

The plot thickens when we bring in coauthors, because counts of publications are usually not divided by the number of coauthors. Thus, if there are four authors and they each can write one paper, then each author winds up with only one paper. If they agree (or conspire) to all help each other with their papers, even if three authors on any one paper do almost nothing, then each of the four authors will have four coauthored papers to their name in the same time that it takes them to write one paper individually. So in publication counts and citation counts they all win, because the "advanced math" is not performed in most cases to normalize the publication counts by dividing by the number of authors.

Since citation counts do affect people's careers, in ways that will be explained in this chapter, it is common knowledge that friends often cite their friends as a favor, and journal referees are often not shy about requiring the author of a proposed paper to cite the referee's own work as a condition for its being published (though once in a while this may also be because the referee actually did write something that should rightfully be cited in the paper).

THE LOST, PSYCHOLOGICAL EFFECT OF THE HARDCOPY JOURNAL

For centuries, and up until the 1990s, economics professors tended to have something in their offices that had special meaning to them. It also had special meaning and to many of the students and colleagues who would visit them in their office: It was a bookshelf. What made the bookshelf so valuable was that it stood as a testament, or even a shrine in some respects, to their own published work and to the work of others whom they respected and admired. Along the same lines, the bookshelf paid tribute to economics journals, displaying the sheer bulk of the accumulated knowledge that they had documented. Many professors had entire walls of their office covered with published journals, as though to imitate the stacks of their university libraries, displaying their admiration for their profession's accomplishments.

Leontief's Presidential Address to the American Economic Association

The earliest volume that used to be on my own bookshelf (that I had acquired from an older economist who was getting rid of his collection of volumes) was the January 1971 issue of *American Economic Review* (AER) which began with the presidential address made to the American Economic Association (AEA; mentioned earlier in chapter 2). It was entitled, "Theoretical Assumptions and Nonobserved Facts." In the article Leontief supports his critique in part by quoting other leaders of the profession as well. For example, he remarks (with my emphasis in italics):

> To sum up with the words of a recent president of the Econometric Society, ". . . the achievements of economic theory in the last two decades are both impressive and in many ways beautiful. But it cannot be denied that *there is something scandalous in the spectacle of so many people refining the analysis of economic states which they give no reason to suppose will ever, or have ever, come about. . . . It is an unsatisfactory and slightly dishonest state of affairs.*"[1]

That prominent, physical presence of the hardcopy article in my daily work environment helped me realize, and retain my perspective on, how important that article was, and by extension, how important its ideas were.

Just to clarify, so there is no misunderstanding about what I have written here, there is no chance whatsoever that I would ever advocate the profession's return to using hardcopy literature—in my opinion that would defy all logic. The benefits of that digitalization are too obvious to be worth mentioning, and I would be surprised and disappointed if there are any readers who do not agree that there should be no "turning back" in this regard. Nevertheless, with all that is good, we must accept whatever bad comes with it, and try to mitigate that bad. Air pollution and automobile accidents do not justify the banning of automobiles, but they do require us to address the problem through policies and regulations. So too should we look as some of the negative consequences that the digitalization of economics journal articles has had on the economics profession, and not ignore them only because the good that came with digitalization outweighs the bad. To do so would be irresponsible, in the same way that it would be irresponsible of us to ignore the need for traffic and pollution policies on automobiles only because we believe that having automobiles is still worthwhile.

The Effect of Digitalized Journals

Now that journal articles are primarily digitalized, it has had a psychological effect on researchers—the effect being that we are less inclined to concern ourselves with what literature is better for us to have (as in devoting our shelf space to it)—the only constraint now is the time we devote to reading the articles. That is, the journal articles that we used to place on our shelves, in our file cabinets, and even much more recently in our saved electronic files are now (for the most part) instantly available to us online. There is nothing for us to save about them now other than whatever it might take to Google them so that they may instantly appear again on our computer screen.

As we already know, there is, then, often an overabundance of sources on any topic that might pop out instantly from any online search. When researching a topic in the past, perhaps there were only ten research articles that one could draw upon as references to that topic, to use in one's research, and that was based on what might be already available on one's shelf or what one might find in the library. Yet, if ten references seemed inadequate for the project that we were pursuing, we might devote a day of work to figure out, and perform the paperwork needed, to order ten more references through interlibrary loan, which might take a few weeks to arrive. Now, for the same topic, I might be able to find 100 references within the first ten minutes, and 1,000 references through one day of work, with electronic access to all of those references. In many respects this is a beautiful thing for humanity's pursuit of knowledge in general, especially if one might be investigating some crucial scientific issue like finding a cure to an epidemic.

Yet, if one is writing a paper on a topic in economics, and there are 1,000 potential references that one can use, then how does one now decide which ones to use, when one cannot read them all, or read even their abstracts for that matter. To many, the answer is to let the citation counts or the prestige of the journal weigh heavily on the choice of which references to use. Again, this is not necessarily a horrible thing—in some respects it offers an objective validity to such a selection criterion.

Psychologically, however, *it makes the researcher less confident in their own ability to decide what the best literature is.* In the past, when someone photocopied (or earlier than that, paid for a copy) of a journal article that they placed in a file cabinet for further reference, they were physically working on determining what was important enough to devote those resources to placing that article in their file cabinet. Now that the file cabinet is gone, the researcher is no longer forced to decide what articles are worth saving for current and future reference. As a result, whatever references are better or worse may freely "float" at the whim of the researcher, based on whatever the latest indicators of importance might be.

As a case in point, with regard to Leontief's pivotal presidential address of December 1970, I observed that, at this writing, the last time it was ever downloaded from the major source I was using (RePEc) was in 2007. (Honestly, I suspect it was me who downloaded it at that time!)[2] Furthermore, it has only been cited in the world twice, according to RePEc, since 2012. To this, the modern researcher in economics, like the DJ at a modern dance party, might say to our old friend Wassily Leontief, one of the most important "founding fathers" of modern economic thought as we know it, "Hey Wassily . . . about that Presidential Address you gave to the AEA a few years before you got that Nobel Prize . . . well . . . sorry, Baby, . . . you know we love you . . . but nowadays, you're just not on the charts."

WHAT CITATION COUNTS, PUBLICATION COUNTS, AND BIBLIOGRAPHIC DATABASES HAVE DONE TO US

What happens when a published rating system replaces whatever "debate" may be going on in our minds over what our preferences for references should be? The answer is that we stop debating and simply take the rating system's word for it. Some may argue, for example, that one baseball player is a better performer than another, but if the "stats" of both players are brought to the fore, the argument would cease—the stats provide the answer—the one objective measure. But here is the fundamental difference between the two sides of this analogy: a home run is a home run–any one home run is as good as another for the most part (without considering how many runners it brings home), and any strikeout is as bad as another, and so on. Thus, baseball stats do, indeed, provide a scientific, objective measure of the quality of a baseball player, within reasonably well-understood and agreed-upon definitions and statistical margins of error. Now, likewise, we have similar stats for the authors of economic ideas, and, horrifically (in my view), for their ideas themselves, as if those ideas can be rated as simply and as objectively as counts of outs, hits, and homeruns.

This effective parallel between baseball stats and "economic ideas stats" is ludicrous, because, as we all realize, the stats for the publication of economic ideas are not objectively generated, but are highly skewed toward the most mathematically impressive and obscure theoretical treatises. Moreover, they are based largely as well on an author's status within certain highly elitist and cronyistic circles, which may be associated with their institution long before their publications began to accumulate.

The emergence of this rating system has largely removed economists' interest and ability to judge the value of ideas, under the conformist and somewhat cowardly perspective of "Who am I to question the wisdom of the masses?" The rating system, in effect, promotes the enormity of elitism and cronyism that now exists within the profession, by pretending to be a reflection of some sort of objective endorsement of those who are already admired as being in the "in-crowd." Academic economists need to rid themselves of the convenience of using citation counts and the relative prestige of journals as a method of evaluating the value of ideas, as a substitute for the preferable, and much more honorable, method of applying their own advanced understanding of economics to assess the value of ideas.

Of course, some economists do not do this—some actually do apply their advanced knowledge to assess the value of published ideas. If those who do this—the "right thing" in this regard—then think that my critique here is aimed at them, when in fact it is not, then, naively thinking that they are representative of the profession, they will accuse me of falsely accusing them. Likewise, they may accuse me of painting an unfair picture of the profession as a whole. To them I would simply say, this is not about them, but they should *look around* and realize that it is indeed probably about most of their peers. Furthermore, if they are too blind to see how much others rely on citation counts and journal prestige to assess the value of ideas in economics, then this critique does, in fact, also apply to those who do the right thing, simply for turning a blind eye or deluding themselves about what others do in the profession.

Leontief was not blind when he wrote "Theoretical Assumptions and Non-observed Facts," which is about the same general topic of academic economists refusing to admit what was fundamentally wrong with the profession at that time, and which has since only become much worse. Those who believe they are honestly pursuing useful knowledge and who think I am exaggerating about this problem in the profession should indeed read Leontief's presidential address. In doing so, they can download the document from RePEc, and totally distort RePEc's download statistics, thereby proving (in the minds of those who put faith in those statistics) that his article really was valuable and important, notwithstanding the fact that it was written by a Nobel laureate in economics and that it was his presidential address before the AEA.

Scoring the Big Points with Top-Ranked Journal Articles

We have seen in previous chapters, and it is extremely well known within the profession, that academic economists are scored, as conditions for their career advancement, on their publication counts in top-ranked journals, based on a scoring weight attributed to different prestige levels of journals. For example, at James Madison University, an article in a top-ranked-journal gets you 11 points, in a second-rated journal 7 points, and in a third-ranked journal 4 points. Suppose one professor has one of each. Then their score would be equal to 22 (=11+7+4).

In a very similar way, studies done on the "Research Productivity of New PhDs in Economics" also count publications and weight them by the ranking of the journal, as in a study with this title by Conley and Onder that was published in 2014 in the *Journal of Economic Perspectives.* That study made the following argument (with my emphasis in italics):

> Raw counts of publications are imperfect measures of the research productivity of individual scholars because of the variation in the quality of those publications. We therefore use journal quality indexes from Kalaitzidakis, Mamuenas, and Stengos (2003), . . . to convert each raw publication into a number of American Economic Review–equivalent papers which we refer to as "AER papers." To give some sense of the weights we used, the following publication lists *(and it may be useful to think of these as entries on the curriculum vitae of tenure candidates)* are all roughly equivalent to one AER paper: (a) one paper in the American Economic Review or Econometrica; (b) one and one half papers in the Journal of Political Economy or Quarterly Journal of Economics; . . . (f) five papers in the Economic Journal, Journal of Public Economics, or Economics Letters; or (g) six to ten papers in high-quality field journals.[3]

As a case in point, the authoritative source for the weights provided in the above quotation—the 2003 study by Kalaitzidakis, Mamuneas, and Stengos —created the ranking based on the average number of citations per article in each journal. As an example, the authors of this study indexed the average citations per article so that the top-ranking AER has an index of 100, followed by the *Quarterly Journal of Economics* with an index of 59.6309, followed by *Econometrica*, etc. In their article, Conley and Onder do not provide the relative values they used for the lower-ranked journals, nor the Kalaitzidakis index numbers to which they are based. However, in 2010 Kalaitzidakis et al. provided an update of their 2003 numbers in which they expose their index numbers for each journal. While the numbers are an "update" of the previous ones, we can see from these new numbers the ballpark values that the previous index numbers were very likely to have. In the 2010 Kaliaitzidakas index, the AER continues to weigh-in as the gold standard, with an index value of 100. The *Journal of Post Keynesian Economics* (JPKE), where I once published an article myself, has an index of 0.0106.[4] Thus, by this index, and the Conley-Onder interpretation of it, one would need to write about 10,000 such articles (100/0.01) for those 10,000 JPKE articles combined to have a value equal to one article in the AER. Put another way, one article in the AER is more valuable than all of the articles that were ever published in the JPKE.

In November 2016, I presented the ideas of this chapter in a session at the Annual Conference of the Southern Economic Association. In my presentation I emphasized the absurdity of this overall approach by Conley and Onder, and by Kalaitzidakis et al, that leads to the conclusion that one AER article is estimated to be as valuable as 10,000 JPKE articles in the assessment of the productivity of authors, journals, and institutions. A colleague of mine who attended my presentation, and whose opinion I trust highly, agreed with many of the ideas in my presentation, but vehemently disagreed with my identification and emphasis of this 10,000-to-1 ratio in the alleged value of an AER article over a JPKE article. He said that most academic economists rely on RePEc's weighting scheme, based on the journal's "impact factor" (which will be explained shortly). By this measure, offered by RePEc, the JPKE is ranked #471 among economics journals, with a score of 0.021, in comparison to *American Economic Review*, ranked #17 with a score of 1.308. Thus, according to these alternative weights, the ratio is only 62 to 1, that is, it takes only sixty-two articles in the JPKE to make one AER article.[5] As my colleague recommended, it is quite likely that is a more realistic weighting scheme when it comes to how economics professors are hired or evaluated. (In addition, the high ratios implied here are clearly contradicted by the discussion of points scored for publications, in professors acquiring tenure, as discussed in the beginning of previous chapter.)

Is the AER Really the Gold Standard?

An important observation about these RePEc impact factor ratings, however, which the profession seems to have ignored completely, was already hinted at three sentences ago: The AER is ranked #17, even though nearly all (if not all) of the published economic studies on journal "productivity" uphold the AER as the highest, gold standard—the one journal for which all other journals can at most be equal, but nearly always are assigned a small fraction of its value, as we just saw in the Conley and Onder, and the Kalaitzidakis studies, which have been largely hailed by the profession as being the most authoritative on the subject. According to the same RePEc journal ratings just referred to in the AER/JPKE comparison, the highest scoring journal among the sixteen that are higher than the AER is *The Quarterly Journal of Economics*, whose score is 5.202—roughly *four times* the score of the AER! Why is it that there appears to be no literature whatsoever, or practices put into place, that would have us treat one QJE article as worth as much as four AER articles? I will now offer two interrelated explanations for this:

First, it should not be ruled out that the profession's entire approach to the analysis of citation scores, journal weights, etc. is conducted in the context of a pseudoscience, or, in more layman terms, as loosey-goosey arguments that defy more rigorous analysis. In short, the prescription for conducting such analyses is as follows: make up the weighting rules that you simply like the best, without needing any analytical justification for it, and then apply a complex numerical analysis thereafter to make it look like a thorough, scientific analysis that you can publish. As evidence of this, I will refer shortly to another study based on productivity weights, in this case for the institutions where the authors are located, which relies entirely on the *number of pages* in the "top 50"-ranked journals. Why the number 50, instead of another number, derived perhaps on the basis of data about the journals? The most obvious, highly likely reason is that fifty was the simplest round number that the researchers thought of in the few seconds they must have devoted to their decision. Yet, looking at the RePEc ratings of journals at this writing, the fiftieth-ranked journal is *Quantitative Economics*, with a score of 0.535, followed by the fifty-first-ranked *Journal of Economics and Management Strategy* (JEMS) with the *same exact score* of 0.535 (though presumably with a score that is lower with more significant figures). Recall that the AER had a score of 1.308, implying that one article in the JEMS is worth (by this measure) as much as 41 percent of an AER article, and by this account worth over twenty-five JPKE articles. Yet, in a study that has a cutoff of the top fifty journals, the JEMS is no longer on the charts, and its weight becomes zero. In short, there are no specific, objective, or established rules to this weighting game—researchers make whatever rules they want to make and report their results. The results from such arbitrary rules are highly dependent on what those rules are, for a wide variety of reasons. For example, those researchers who are most interested in management strategy, and who will therefore write for the JEMS (#51) will "fall off the bleeding edge," in a study that counts only the top-ranked fifty journals, and the JPKE and hundreds of other journals like it are given zero credit as well. Yet, such studies that analyze the relative value of different journals present their results as if they offered genuine, objective, scientific evidence of something important about how economic knowledge in economic literature should be valued.

A second possible (interrelated) explanation is that AER represents, in many respects, the prize possession and the flagship journal of the AEA, which in turn is the largest, and by far the most influential, organization of academic economists in the United States. At the AEA's annual business meeting, the AER's "impact score" is stated with pride as one of the organization's major accomplishments in the view of its leaders. Only one other of the AEA's journals is ranked higher than the AER in the RePEc rankings, which is the *Journal of Economic Literature* (#6). The AEA would, of course, like very much to have the AER continue to be seen as the profession's gold standard in the literature about valuing economic journals.

Let us now consider that the Conley and Onder study, which treated the AER as the gold standard, happens to have been published in the *Journal of Economic Perspectives*, which is ranked #20, and which contains *only articles that are provided "by invitation only."* That is, there is no application and selection process for articles in the JEP; the journal simply contacts authors and invites them to write certain articles. Now, who runs the *Journal of Economic Perspectives*? Why it is the *American Economic Association*, of course. By the way, what is the institution that sponsors and houses the *American Economic Association*? As all economics professors in the United States know, it is Vanderbilt University. OK, now guess where the lead author of the article (Conley) holds a teaching position, and where did the second author (Onder) do his graduate studies when their article was written? You guessed it—Vanderbilt University. Might this be a reason why the Conley and Onder study did not give the AER a weight of one-fourth the weight of *Quarterly Journal of Economics*, based on the RePEc scores? Would the situation be different if the QJE were a product of the AEA instead of Oxford University Press?

No, It Is Still OK for Economics Professors to Read

Let us start from scratch by asking the most basic of all questions with regard to assessing the value of economic literature, which is the question of what would make one article more valuable than another. The answer is not "citation counts." It is, of course, the extent to which an article *is actually read, and the extent to which its ideas are recognized as contributing to the advancement of valuable knowledge.* The knee-jerk reaction that I, and I suspect many others, would expect from most academic economists to this statement is "of course—we all know that!" However, as I have argued extensively in a variety of ways throughout this book, when we blindly assume that citation counts are a reliable indicator of readership and of the recognized contribution to valuable knowledge we are metaphorically attempting to jump from the cliff of one mountain to the cliff of another, with a huge crevice between them. We make that leap and delude ourselves into thinking we have reached the edge of the other mountain. In truth, we have fallen into the crevice between them, whose bottom deposits us directly into the underworld. This characterizes the current state of the academic economics profession when it comes to assessing the value of its own literature.

Back on topic, let us simply consider the concept of readership, which is rather easy to define, that is, it occurs when someone actually reads an article, generally from front to back. As discussed earlier, this is quite different from the article being cited, which, at an extreme, might take less than a minute of the citing author's time, and might be done from glancing at the article's abstract or from even glancing at a citation made to that article in some other article's reference section, without the article *ever being seen, let alone read!*

Average Citations per Article Says Nothing about Each Article

Another dimension to the absurdity, alluded to earlier, is that the journals can still be weighted or ranked on the basis of their average citations per article. However, our knowing the journal in which a particular article was published tells us essentially nothing about how many citations that particular article received. Thus, even if the number of citations is a measure of "quality," then we may only know the "average quality" of articles in a journal, and still know nothing from the journal about the quality of any one of its individual articles. As Engemann and Wall pointed out (with my own emphasis in italics):

> Before proceeding with our ranking of economics journals, we must point out that any ranking should be handled with a great deal of care when using it for decision making. *It would be a mistake, for example, to think that a journal ranking is anything like a definitive indicator of the relative quality of individual papers within the journals. First, any journal's citation distribution is heavily skewed by a small number of very successful papers, and even the highest-ranked journals have large numbers of papers that are cited rarely, if at all* (Oswald, 2007; Wall, 2009). Put another way, citation distributions exhibit substantial overlap, meaning that (i) large shares of papers in the highest-ranked journals are cited less frequently than the typical paper in lower-ranked journals; and, conversely, (ii) large shares of articles in low-ranked journals are cited more frequently than the typical paper in the highest-ranked journals.[6]

Let us now piece together and summarize what I have just described: (1) Top-ranked journals are defined as those receiving the most citations, because it is believed (by the powers that be in academic economics) that the importance or value of a journal is reflected in the *average* number of citations its articles receive (out of a highly skewed distribution where the vast majority of articles have very few citations, and only a small minority have a large number of citations). (2) Academic economists are evaluated by the numbers of *articles* weighted by the ranks of journals, and *not on* the number of citations, even though citation counts was our only measure of importance in comparing the journals, and the citation counts of the individual publications are readily available. So why we are not simply using citation counts as the direct measure of the professors' achievements, as opposed to the indirect, and highly imprecise publication counts?

This is somewhat analogous to people applying for loans at banks, where the banks have access to information on their individual incomes, but the banks decide not to base their lending decisions on that information. Rather, the banks prefer simply to rely on the average income of the different urban regions where the applicants live. For instance, hypothetically, if someone is living in Manhattan, the bank is willing to give them a mortgage loan of $500,000 or more, based on the average income of people in Manhattan, but if they live in Brooklyn, the bank will only give them a mortgage loan of $200,000 based on the average income of people in Brooklyn, regardless of the possibility that one person from Manhattan could have zero income (e.g., unemployed and homeless) and one other person from Brooklyn could be a multimillionaire.

It might also be amusing to note that there is significant literature that is well cited, which speaks against the use of publication counts and citation counts as a means of assessing the value of literature, some of which will be summarized shortly. This specific literature is ignored, for the most part, by the profession. In other words, it is the profession's position that publications and citations do reflect the value of ideas in literature, unless those publications and citations are written specifically *against* the idea that publications and citations reflect the value of ideas in the literature. It is the same logical flaw as the statement: everything that people say is valid, except when some people say that other people's statements are invalid.

So Why Not Just Use Citation Counts Instead of Publication Counts?

There are three reasons for the use of publication counts rather than citation counts to evaluate the performance of candidates for promotion in academic economics. In my view these reasons make the current practice somewhat defensible, but not entirely. The first of these three is reasonable, while the other two, though equally realistic, are a source of embarrassment for the profession and thus may be rarely admitted or expressed.

The first reason is that there is lag in time between the publication of an article and the citations it will receive for obvious reasons. This implies that citation counts would be severely underestimated the more recently an article had been published, relative to the citation counts it will receive eventually.

Another reason is that, in general, the publication counts for the majority of articles, regardless of the journal's rank, are miniscule. Those counts can very easily be less than five per year, or even zero in some years, even for articles in top journals. This, in itself, could be a source of embarrassment for the candidate and for the university, for paying so much attention to something that is so small in reality. Moreover, the citation itself (in the article in which it appears) could be rather obscure, such as a citation in an article that was written only in Japanese about a policy question addressed only in Japan, which no one in the United States might even understand. Thus, as an example, should one candidate be denied tenure for having a total of seven citations to their work each year, while another receives tenure for having as many as ten citations? The difference between seven and ten might simply be due to the existence of one friend of the candidate who tends to write three articles per year in which they always cite the candidate.

Finally, it is easy to see how citation counts could be gamed in all sorts of ways, which would make the process even more precarious. For example, if one is concerned about citation counts being delayed because the article is too recent, they might widely distribute on their own the "page proofs" of the publication before it is actually published, just to create a head start on the accumulation of citations. This would be done at the chagrin of the journal's publisher as it would violate the journal's copyright policies (which academic economists often ignore in any case). The greatest problem, however, in terms of the potential for gaming the system, especially since citations are generally very few in number, is for the candidate to solicit efforts by friends for the favor of citing their work in the articles that those friends are writing. In certain respects, such mutually beneficial arrangements already exist at different levels, from being explicit with a quid-pro-quo character, to being quite subtle and ambiguous. In any case, if citations counts were used instead of publication counts, we would expect such partnerships (implicit or explicit) to escalate greatly, with perhaps efforts on the part of academic economists to acquire such partnerships that would then crowd out (or partially replace) the efforts they might otherwise devote to writing a valuable article that could be useful to the profession.

As an example, when I was sending messages to several economists to promote a seminar I was organizing, one response I received was: "Thanks Steven, I'm already traveling on that day but please keep me informed of similar events – this looks interesting! PS I'm familiar with some of your work on the economics of product quality and have cited it!" I thanked the writer for his kind words with no mention of the additional thoughts I had regarding his response. Though the person's message was quite short, I find it interesting that nowhere did he say *what* he thought of my work on product quality, for example, whether he agreed with any of it or enjoyed read it. All that appeared to matter was that he "cited" my work thereby giving me points in the citation game. It is a game that I personally have no interest in playing, but he apparently assumed that I did, and that I would therefore appreciative of his citing it. Although I thanked him for his kind words, I wonder if he might have been disappointed that I did not reply "in kind" by my saying that I intend to cite his work as well.

With regard to the explicit or illicit agreements to "cite each other" (also discussed in chapter 4) some readers who are not familiar with the art of publishing articles in economics may wonder how this could happen, since one might except authors to mention and cite in their articles only prior literature that pertains directly to the topic being covered in the article. Such thoughts would be quite reasonable in a more perfect world, but are naïve in the current one. Any cleaver author can throw in a paragraph, or better yet, simply a footnote, somewhere in their article, that loosely connects whatever the paper is discussing to some other work published in economics, as long as some vague connection can, in fact, be found.

As already mentioned, of the three reasons mentioned above for using publication counts instead of citations, it is likely that only the first (involving the lag between publication and citations) would be offered as an official justification by leaders of the profession. However, that justification would be flawed, nevertheless. There is no reason, for example, for not having some general rule that counts average citations per year for articles that are at least five years old, and for those that are not, using the either their average citations per year from the author's previous publications, or the average number of citations per year among articles published in that journal—whichever is greater (giving the author a benefit of the doubt). Such solutions to analyzing statistical problems of this kind are what many economists essentially "live for," as reflected in their work. One could apply, for example, graduate-level, "Bayesian" econometric techniques to these citation counts. However, this one problem and the details of any solution to it are mute, because of the other reasons that exist for our not using citation counts.

What Most Citations Really Are

Along these lines we should recognize that the citations to other literature within an economics article are an all-or-nothing indicator that the cited work has some relevance, in some way, to the topic of the article, without any indication of the degree to which the cited article actually contributed to the ideas of the article. There is also confusion here because the cited work may not have actually contributed at all to the ideas in the article, but is simply being given credit for a well-known historical contribution. For example, an article might read, "This article explores, at a cursory level, how prices have changed for different goods over time. No effort is made here to develop price indices for them, though such indices could be made along the lines described in Fischer and Shell (1972)."[7] Thus, the relevance of a particular citation to the ideas presented in an article could range from (1) the cited work providing crucial background knowledge, without which the article could not exist, to (2) the cited work having virtually no relevance whatsoever.

Moreover, in admittedly rare cases, the cited work could be being criticized by the author, which would be worse than the cited work having no relevance. (That is, there are no "negative" citations that should be subtracted from the citation count, but conceptually they should exist, since citation counts are always assumed to reflect positively on the cited work.) This book, for example, contains a citation to Adolf Hitler's *Mein Kampf*—which is the absolute worst economics-related literature ever written in the history of humanity, which offers absolutely nothing of value other than the strong evidence it provides as to how horrific delusional minds can be, and how such literature could cause the absolute worst things that human beings can do. (Indeed, this is pretty much why it was cited.) Yet, in terms of citation counts, this book would be said, by the system used to promote economic professors, that I had "credited it." Similarly, many economists have written articles that have inspired a great deal of criticism from other economists, in many cases rightfully so. Ironically, the criticisms that those authors have received in articles effectively praised them in terms of the citations they received!

But Don't the Best Articles Receive the Most Citations?

In discussing these issues with academic economists, some have argued vehemently against the position I have espoused, insisting that, the very best articles do receive the most citations, and there is no such thing as a pivotal article in economics that has not receiving a great deal of citations. I will certainly concede this point, in the following sense: If we could somehow identify articles that fall in the top 1 percent of quality, and identify a subset of them that fall within in the top 0.1 percent of articles in quality, in other words the one-in-a-hundred articles and the one-in-a-thousand articles, then I would surely expect the typical one-in-a-thousand articles in quality to have more citations than the typical one-in-a-hundred articles in quality. The factor is visible at these extremes in the same way that people with a net worth of more than $100 million tend to have estates with more acres of land than people with a measly net worth of $10 million. However, once you get to more normal wealth levels the relationship between residential land area owned and net worth gets extremely fuzzy, or even reversed. People who may be impoverished in rural Montana may still have more residential land to their name (in terms of acreage) than very rich condo dwellers in downtown

Manhattan. The same statistical properties apply to citation counts. Yes, at the extremes they may actually mean something, but outside the extremes they do not. If one paper receives five citations and another ten, this says essentially nothing about which paper is of higher quality.

Are the Most Important Citations Even Counted?

I cannot help but wonder that perhaps my criticisms of publication counts and citation counts, as the metric through which academic economists essentially measure each other's value, may be interpreted by some as "sour grapes" on my part. That is, those who live for the purpose of increasing their own publication scores may think that my written opinions here reflect some sort of jealousy on my part for my not having many citations to my name. If this laughable hypothesis were, in fact, true, then it would have been quite childish of me for having written as I have on the topic. In any case, needless to say, I am not jealous at all for not having more prestigious publications or citation counts; and why should I be? As a nonacademic (except for the adjunct positions I have held) I have never felt a need to advance my career by accumulating publications or citations. With rare exceptions, the focus on (if not obsession with) publication counts that has dominated the lives of many or most economics professors is unique only to the academic sector. This alone should raise concern, if we believe that academic economics should contribute to private sector and government economics which in general have little or no interest in the publication game, or interest in knowing which economics professors are winning at it.

Having now said all this, I would like to provide a personal example to illustrate how questionable some of the citations counts are that are so often used by RePEc and other citation count providers to reflect on an author's supposed worth as a contributor to economic thought.

I have only perused some of the citations to my work, but there is one in particular that I must call my favorite, which I had known about all along (without needing to look it up in RePEc or anywhere else). It was in a news story article (as opposed to a technical article), in *Science Magazine* on August 25, 2000, entitled "Does Science Drive the Productivity Train?"[8] It was indeed an honor for me to find my work cited in one of the world's top science journals, in an article about what economists have said regarding the contribution of science to productivity in the economy. Also cited in the same article were Alan Greenspan (then chair of the Federal Reserve Board of Governors, long before his "fall from grace"), Adam Smith (for his contribution in 1776), Nobel Laureate Robert Solow, and quite a few other well-known, prominent figures in the profession. The work that was cited was my book *Economics, Science and Technology*, which was mentioned twice and discussed in eleven sentences in the article. As I was working at the National Science Foundation at the time, I was recognized in my work environment for having received that citation.

After the article had appeared in *Science Magazine*, I soon received an invitation to give a presentation of my book in an auditorium at Dartmouth College, with travel expenses and a stipend, as part of their engineering school's seminar series, which I was honored to do. My only point here is that the invitation was made possible because of that one citation to my work in *Science Magazine*. For whatever reasons, however, there is no existing record in any of the citation databases of my work being cited in that article—apparently the only evidence of it is in the article itself.[9] I am not interested enough in the reason why the citation is not listed to research it, nor do I think it would be of any interest to anyone else. My best guess would simply be that whatever mechanism exists to identify and count citations, it may not work for articles that are news stories, which do not contain reference sections at the end that could be easily fed into any database generating program that counts citations. In any case, my point is only that, as questionable as citation counts are, to begin with, they are also highly incomplete. If it is indeed true that they are not counted when they exist in news stories that might appear in *Science Magazine*, *The New York Times*, etc., then our system for counting them is often leaving out the most important citations that will actually have the greatest impact in terms of being read and in terms of influencing thought in any significant way.

There are still more arguments that can be made as to why citation counts, and publication counts are, for the most part, horrible indicators of the quality of economic literature, besides the many reasons already expressed above, and other reasons provided further along in this book. For example, I have not thus far mentioned the topic of "self-citation"—where authors can cite their own previous work—under the strong assumption that the measures taken by the system to eliminate these counts are effective. I wonder how effective they are, or how well they account for name changes, for example, for women whose name may change after marriage, which perhaps might create biases in favor of women able to cite themselves under a former maiden name, and receive credit for those citations toward their career advancement.

JOURNAL EDITORS AS BIG PLAYERS IN THE GAME

To complicate matters even further, the journals themselves are not passive in this—they, too, (or their editors to be precise, avoiding "anthropomorphisms" here) are big players in the game. They compete with each other to become higher-rated journals by gaming the system to have more citations to their journals. Along these lines, I received the following comments from a colleague who has served, himself, as an economics journal editor. I am allowing his comments to be anonymous here, and am making the journal to which he referred anonymous as well, for obvious reasons:

> The problem lies with the editors of journals. *It is now unfortunately common for an editor to accept a paper conditional on the author adding X number of citations to the journal.* I think this originally came from the misbehavior of the Journal. . . . They have always been notorious for citations to their journal in order to manipulate the rankings. This behavior has now spread to many journals outside of the top 50 or so. The only plausible way I can think of to shine a light on the problem would be to do a massive survey of the profession and find the offenders and publish the results. This would be interesting but extremely time consuming. (Anonymous, my highlighting)

The practice of the editors of economics journals, who are nearly all academics, to force the authors of the journal's articles to include citations to other articles in the same journal is, indeed, reprehensible. It reflects the incredible game-playing environment that characterizes the world of publications in economics journals, where the contribution to useful knowledge is so easily compromised by petty interests and pursuits. Moreover, even though some journal editors may not explicitly impose this requirement on authors, the requirement may still be imposed implicitly. In particular, all else being equal, the article that has many more citations to the same journal's earlier articles than another article may be expected to be looked at as being more favorable by the journal in its impact on the ratings. So, it is conceivable, or perhaps even expected, that some authors will go out of their way to add citations to articles by the same journal in the hope that this will win favor with the journal to help improve their chances of acceptance. In such a petty environment, one might also wonder if journals may be hostile to the papers that cite other journals more than their own (especially when those other journals compete in the same subfield).

The High and Mighty "IF" ("Impact Factor")

Journals likewise compete with each other according to a similar, well-known indicator (or game in effect) called the "impact factor" (IF). The IF (mentioned earlier in reference to the RePEc journal rankings) measures the average number of citations that the journal's articles received (in journals other than itself), for its articles over a particular time span, for example, two years prior or five years prior to the year in question.[10] Though this measure is considered in journals across all fields, the economics profession seems to be particularly obsessed with it. There is a growing body of literature, in fact, about the IF, because of all the wonderful numbers in databases that it offers, enabling all kinds of statistical tests as if to offer wisdom on how IFs could be used better to guide the academic economics profession in how it may apply publication counts in its hiring and promotion decisions.

In a recent analysis, which happened to appear in one of the most prestigious, top-ranked journals—the *Journal of Economic Literature*—David Stern, at the Australian National University, raised concerns that the IF is just too statistically unreliable to determine which journals are better than others:

> My analysis does show . . . that IFs themselves are quite uncertain and a broad range of journals can have statistically indistinguishable IFs. It does not seem to be justified to give a researcher more credit for publishing in the Journal of Applied Econometrics than in the Oxford Bulletin of Economics and Statistics . . . , for example, *if what we care about is potential citation impact.* As long as research assessments and search committees wish to evaluate very recent publications, it seems inevitable that they will use some form of journal ranking as a proxy quality indicator. This paper shows that though this may be justified to some degree, for the majority of journals fine distinctions in rank are not possible using IFs.[11]

This uncertainty exists even after we made the heroic leap that "what we care about is potential citation impact." The above quotation also relates back to the earlier discussion that citation counts themselves from the candidates' articles would not work for "very recent publications" (because citations take time to happen), thereby requiring some scoring simply on the basis of the journal's rank. In this case, Stern is saying that those ranks are very fuzzy if based on impact factors. Yet, when journals are ranked on the basis of their average citations alone, matters may be even worse, since the impact scores at least weed out the citations that journals have to themselves, thereby, if little else, reducing the game-playing behavior of journals when they pump up their own citations to themselves, as discussed earlier.

NARCISSISM GALORE IN THE FORM OF A PSEUDOSCIENCE

In short, academic economists have shown a key interest in devising scoring schemes of various kinds to determine who can get more points toward hiring and promotion, on the basis of data on publication and citation counts. All of this is occurring as if these data actually reflect, in a systematic way, the value of accumulated knowledge—an assumption that is incredibly wrong, as reflected by at least half of all the things this book discusses. Yet, the profession's obsession with these statistics proceeds undaunted, ignoring the warnings that appear in its own well-cited literature about it. It is as if our in-depth mathematical analysis of these statistics will somehow legitimize their use in the hiring and promotion of economics professors, regardless of the underlying garbage-in, garbage-out problem that it so obviously has.

I do not use the term "obsession" lightly in describing the effect citation counts and publication counts have had on the way academic economists look at themselves, and at each other. The RePEc website has done much to capture the hearts and minds of academic economists, especially by providing a mechanism for them to be ranked completely among each other. At this writing I am examining the webpage entitled "Top 10% Authors, as of May 2016." The page states:

> This page shows one of the many rankings computed with RePEc data. They are based on data about authors who have registered with the RePEc Author Service, institutions listed on EDIRC, bibliographic data collected by RePEc, citation analysis performed by CitEc and popularity data compiled by LogEc. . . . The average rank score is determined by taking a harmonic mean of the ranks in each method.[12]

To me these rankings have the same psychological appeal that Billboard's top recordings have for teenage music fans, and that the ranking of sports teams have for sports fans. On the RePEc page one can toggle down to find the rankings of the "top 5 percent" of academic economists, from (at this writing in June 2016) #1—Andrei Shleifer (at Harvard), all the way down to #2,369 Simon Grant (at the University of Queensland in Australia). After those 5 percent, listed sequentially by their rank, we then see the next 5 percent, listed in groups of the top 6 percent (after the 5%), top 7 percent, etc. Given that 2,369 people were 5 percent and the next 5 percent are shown, there are roughly 4,738 people's names listed on that one webpage. For the first 5 percent, RePEc shows a table where each one of the 2,369 individuals is listed in a row. The table has one column for the rank (the left-most column), followed by another column for the name, and then, after that, a total of thirty-seven other columns of statistics. Table 6.1 displays only the first row of the 2,368 rows (of the top 5%), where I used several rows to display that one row on the webpage, since the webpage had too many columns to fit on one page.

One is reminded of similar mechanisms that have existed historically for people to do something that enables their name to be displayed in a public list, where they may look upon the listing of their name with pride or sense of accomplishment. We see this everywhere, as in, for example, the listing of honor roll students in a high school, or the "Dean's List" in college, and the "Who's Who" books (if they even still exist) that used to charge a handsome fee for including your name and seem to be most important only to those who shelled out the money to be listed. So, too, has the top 10 percent

Table 6.1 The *First Row* of 2,369 Rows in RePEc's Table of the "Top 5 Percent" of Authors; Name: Andrei Shleifer, Ranked #1

Column #	*1*	*2*	*3*	*4*	*5*	*6*	*7*	*8*	*9*	*10*
Column Heading	Score	Nb Works	DNb Works	Sc Works	WSc Works	ANb Works	ASc Works	AWSc Works	Nb Cites	D Cites
Indicator Value	3.05	21	115	1	1	147	6	14	1	1
Column #	11	12	13	14	15	16	17	18	19	20
Column Heading	Sc Cites	DSc Cites	WSc Cites	WDSc Cites	ANb Cites	AD Cites	ASc Cites	ADSc Cites	AWSc Cites	AWDSc Cites
Indicator Value	1	1	1	1	4	4	4	4	4	4
Column #	21	22	23	24	25	26	27	28	29	30
Column Heading	H Index	NCAu thors	RCAu thors	Nb Pages	Sc Pages	WSc Pages	ANb Pages	ASc Pages	AWSc Pages	Abs Views
Indicator Value	1	1	3	11	2	2	48	7	7	5
Column #	31	32	33	34	35	36	37			
Column Heading	Down loads	AAbs Views	ADown loads	Stu- dents	Close	Bet weenn	NEP Cites			
Indicator Value	14	40	61	5	197	128	1			

Definition of Columns:
1. Score (This is a summary Score)
2. Number of works
3. Number of distinct works (115) (I do not know why it is larger than the number of works)
4. Number of distinct works, weighted by simple impact factor

5. Number of distinct works, weighted by recursive impact factor
6. Number of distinct works, weighted by number of authors
7. Number of distinct works, weighted by number of authors and simple impact factors
8. Number of distinct works, weighted by number of authors and recursive impact factors
9. Number of citations
10. Number of citations, discounted by citation age
11. Number of citations, weighted by simple impact factor
12. Number of citations, weighted by simple impact factor, discounted by citation age
13. Number of citations, weighted by recursive impact factor
14. Number of citations, weighted by recursive impact factor, discounted by citation age
15. Number of citations, weighted by number of authors
16. Number of citations, weighted by number of authors, discounted by citation age
17. Number of citations, weighted by number of authors and simple impact factors
18. Number of citations, weighted by number of authors and simple impact factors, discounted by citation age
19. Number of citations, weighted by number of authors and recursive impact factors
20. Number of citations, weighted by number of authors and recursive impact factors, discounted by citation age
21. Number of "h" works that have at least "h" citations (reflecting number of publications and number of papers per citation)
22. Number of registered (with RePEc) citing authors
23. Number of registered citing authors, weighted by rank
24. Number of journal pages
25. Number of journal pages, weighted by simple impact factor
26. Number of journal pages, weighted by recursive impact factor
27. Number of journal pages, weighted by number of authors
28. Number of journal pages, weighted by number of authors and simple impact factor
29. Number of journal pages, weighted by number of authors and recursive impact factor
30. Number of abstract views in RePEc services over the past twelve months
31. Number of downloads through RePEc services over the past twelve months
32. Number of abstract views through RePEc services over the past twelve months, weighted by number of authors
33. Number of downloads through RePEc services over the past twelve months, weighted by number of authors
34. Record of graduates (definition not clear from webpage)
35. Closeness measure in coauthorship network (average number of degrees of separation through coauthorship)
36. "Betweenness" measure in co-authorship network (a complex measure)
37. Breadth of citations across fields

Source: IDEAS/RePEc, "Top 10% Authors, as of December 2016, with Details," Accessed June 20, 2016, http://tinyurl.com/hgnxbc8

in RePEc become a *high-school honor roll* for economics professors, greatly distorting what economics professors should see as important to them and to society. Besides its harmful psychological effects and distortion of incentives, the citation/publication ranking system of course serves to legitimize the profession's obsession with publication and citation counts as the primary basis upon which it values and evaluates its own members. It is a clear case of "supply creating its own demand" where the plethora of publication and citation measures, and the way they are presented with ranks and effective honors to those who have them, has created a greater attention to them and desire among academic economists to want them and study them. RePEc, especially, has done a fantastic job at marketing its product, and it has sold wonderfully within the profession.

Citation Rankings as Player Rankings in a Sport

Let us pause for the moment and consider the concept of the ordinal ranking of people, especially when the rank bestows on everyone an assessment of their worth, as also described by RePEc and others when they name lists of "top economists," etc. In theory, an ordinal ranking of people in the same field has the advantage of clearly distinguishing who is better than whom, and by how much. It is most useful to have under two situations: (1) where it facilitates hierarchical authority (as in a military rank) and (2) where the measure coincides with an important linear measure that truly indicates a person's worth (as in the fastest runner among Olympic contestants for the hundred-yard dash).

In the sciences, one rarely finds such an ordinal ranking of persons. Even though chemists, physicists, biologists, etc. could be ranked by their publications and citation counts, and might well be ranked in this way in some of the "scientometric literature" (explained below), culturally we just do not find that they, themselves, think of each other in the context of one scientist being *better* than the other in the form of a ridiculously simple ordinal rank, where it can be determined, among any two randomly selected scientists, which one is better that the other.

The more carefully one actually thinks about such a situation, the greater its absurdity reveals itself. In fact, I would suspect that most scientists, in just about any field of study (other than economics!), would be appalled at the idea of such a linear ranking of each other, as would many other professionals in many other fields, from engineers, to attorneys, to elementary school teachers. Among scientists, including economists who are scientists, it is their ideas—not them—that are valued in the field. This is extremely important in the sciences so that ideas can be considered objectively, and that disagreements may be addressed head-on and in the right way at many levels (both analytically and culturally). That is, if biologist A believes in theory X, and biologist

B believes in theory Y, which contradicts theory X, then the debate is over theories X and Y, and that is all, without any consideration of whether biologist A or B is higher on some sort of publications scale. Even if the scientists personally harbored such thoughts secretly to themselves (that one of them is more famous for publications than the other), that kind of thinking would be regarded as highly irrelevant, and highly unprofessional and distasteful to enter into any open discussion or debate among them. This is how scientific debates generally work, and of course, this is how they are supposed to work.

In some respects it may even be said to be an important difference that separates adults from children. When we hear children arguing with each other over a point, we may not be surprised if one says to the other, "I'm right and you're wrong because I am smarter than you." We would not expect that kind of behavior among adults (with few exceptions, unfortunately). But, we have created an implicit mind-set that is analogous to that argument in the perspective of many economists (whether or not they can admit it to others or even realize it themselves).

Most importantly, perhaps, the general absence of such superficial and linear rankings from professional, scientific discourse allows the scientists to value their own ideas and not value themselves in the process. In contrast, if they believe that they are already inferior as scientists, because they have been ranked lower for whatever reason (most likely a bad one), they may easily value themselves and their own ideas less, and will be strongly discouraged to pursue their ideas further or to share them with others. *They will not believe in themselves if the culture around them does not believe in them!* Conversely, those who are in the top ranks may easily fall into a level of arrogance that would not exist otherwise, and such arrogance may easily compromise good leadership or good scholarship.

Graduate Students with Head Starts

Graduate students in economics who are pursuing a doctorate already have a huge head start in the publication game if they are in the top-ranked graduate schools, where their professors (and dissertation advisors especially) are ranked highly in publications. Of these students who decide to pursue an academic career, many of them will find themselves "scoring big" in the publications game soon after graduating, as they start to rack-in the points they need for tenure (as described in chapter 4). They will thereafter join the royal family of high-ranking professors on the RePEc website, while their cohorts from the less-prestigious institutions will have a much tougher road to follow (as discussed in chapter 2). The person-by-person ranking by RePEc in this way indirectly promotes the elitist mentality that pervades the academic economics profession, which seems to be indirectly supported by the profession's elite. As I have argued elsewhere in this book, however, the wisest and most honorable among the economics professors are also inclined to have the most humility, and they are the ones who are most likely to find the profession's elitism, and associated ranking system, to be distasteful, or worse.

Bring on the Fan Clubs!

Many economics professors have shown no shyness or shame in their reliance on such ranking systems to express who, among their peers, they believe are better than others. To top it off, they have sometimes reverted to personal, idiosyncratic, and unprofessional perspectives in these comparisons. For example, in displaying their love for baseball, McPherson, Kim, Dorman, and Perera, out of the Economics Department of the University of North Texas, wrote the following in an article in 2013 on "Research Output at US Economics Departments":

> Because tenure and promotion standards vary according to programme quality, we rely on the ranking of American institutions according to pages published in the top-50 journals in economics between 1994 and 2009, created by McPherson (2012). Following earlier work, this ranking divides 240 programmes into four quality tiers. *Adopting the terminology from professional baseball, there are 19 schools in the 'major leagues', 30 in 'AAA', 50 in 'AA' and the remaining 141 in 'A'.*[13]

For any baseball fans who might be reading this, it might appear to have been petty on my part to begrudge the four authors from expressing their love for the sport simply on the grounds that it reflects, in my view, a rather unhealthy way that economics professors should look upon one another. However, there are two other points that I feel are useful for me to make about their one, four-page article in *Applied Economics Letters*. The first, somewhat-trivial point is that the authors of the above finding published it in a journal ranked #390 (by RePEc). Therefore, by their own way of looking at the world their institution—the University of North Texas— belongs in a *first-grader t-ball team.* Would they demean themselves in this way, based on their own methodology, or have they not thought it through that far? I would never demean the author's own institution in this way—the University of North Texas is a perfectly good school, and the four authors are perfectly good economics professors for all I know. But they should ask themselves what we should all ask ourselves, which is: *Who are WE* to have the right to place our peers in major leagues, or minor leagues, etc.? This is, again, the kind of childishness that has horribly inflicted the academic economics profession.

CITATIONS ARE NOT MEASURES OF OUTPUT!

In their article, McPherson, Kim, Dorman, and Perera have one sentence at the end of its first paragraph that I found particularly disturbing, because it gets at the heart of the problem. They stated, "*Measuring research output is not without difficulties, but in many respects it is simpler than measuring contributions to teaching and service.*"[14] This is the kind of statement that can be easily made when there is little thought behind it. In this simplistic perspective, "output" is, for the most part, tautologically defined as "the quantity" according to whatever metric you decided to use.

Consider food for example. If we measure it in pounds, then the output of food is easy to measure. However, if we prefer to measure food output in terms of a vector of calories, grams of protein, grams of carbohydrates, etc., then measuring food output is rather complex, but for the right reasons! We must purchase food all the time, and we must address the complexity that comes with measuring food because it is important to us. We do not go to the grocery store with the preconceived notion of going there to buy thirty pounds of food. Deciding to measure food in pounds makes it *easy* to measure food output, yes, and it is also defeats our very purpose for measuring food! Our calling pounds of food "output" is meaningless to us, and in the end we have achieved nothing useful in the exercise. The same holds for measuring the output of economic literature. When we find an easy way to measure it, which has nothing to do with *why we even want to measure it*, then we have accomplished nothing, or perhaps worse than nothing by deluding ourselves into thinking that we have accomplished something!

The only reason why "research output" is "easy" to measure, according to so many academic economists who have not thought this through at all, is that all you have to do is count publications and weight them by the prestige of the journal (by its citations). One might also go the extra mile of weighting them again by number of pages (as some have done), make adjustments for coauthorships (giving each of two coauthors half credit), etc. Then, abracadabra, you have your measure of the "research output" of academic economists. It is easy for only one reason—because *you made it easy* by design—but your measure of "output" is a worthless façade, which does nothing but harm to the profession and to pursuit of useful knowledge.

The Quality of Economic Literature

In my book *Quality Measurement in Economics*, I analyzed in considerable detail the concept of what is meant by "quality," how it is truly distinguishable from "quantity," and how quality change over time reflects patterns of technological change, which I will discuss in chapter 10. (By the way, according to RePEc this book does not exist either.) As I was finishing that book I added a final chapter entitled, "The Quality of Economic Literature." My motivation was rather simple: I had already looked extensively into the question of what is meant by quality measurement as it relates to all goods and services. Since the most important product in the economics profession is, arguably, economic literature, which in turn affects all things that economics can affect, it dawned on me to write this chapter to help the profession assess the quality of its own output, using general principles of quality measurement. To my surprise at the time, the review of the book in Britain's *Economic Journal* suggested that the problems that I was criticizing with regard to measuring the quality of economic literature in the United States paled in comparison to those that exist in the United Kingdom. This is because of additional state support for those simplistic measures of literature quality, independent from the games that are played to acquire publications. The review article wrote the following about the chapter:

> In a fascinating chapter 8, he turns his attention to the quality of economic literature and analyzes the process by which economic ideas gain currency. One instantly recognizes the censorship, intolerance, cronyism, and excessive appeal to sterile formalism which he describes. As an American, Payson has been spared the UFC {the Universities Funding Council in the U.K.} 'Research Selectivity Exercises': he would be horrified to learn that his British colleagues face a very similar system, but one which is reinforced and imposed by a State agency.[15]

An Unlikely Winner, to Say the Least!

The Wikipedia entry for Professor Andrei Shleifer at Harvard has, as its third sentence, the statement "IDEAS/RePEc has ranked him as the top economist in the world, and he is also listed as #1 on the list of 'Most-Cited Scientists in Economics & Business.'"[16] Likewise, at the end of his short bibliography on his Harvard University website, we see the sentence, "According to RePEc, Shleifer is the most cited economist in the world."

Notice the language here, which is seen in many other places—Shleifer is not described as "the *most-cited* economist in the world"—no. He is the "top economist in the world." Furthermore, he is not the "top economist in the world" for any particular reason that any reasonable person might suspect, like developing a strategy to eliminate poverty that was proven to work, or proposing theory that will greatly reduce the risk of future financial crises. No, he is the "top economist" for scoring highest in citation counts—which is all we need to know about him to call him the "top economist." Of course, if we wanted more information about *those citation counts*, we have thirty-seven parameters to see on Shleifer (see Table 6.1), but still without our knowing a single thing about his supposed contribution to valuable knowledge.

This simplified and presumptuous nomenclature of "top economists" or "top authors in economics" rather than "top ranking economists in citation counts" does well to promote the RePEc website. After all, how appealing is it have a website that only lists ranks by "accumulated citations" (even though that is actually all it does!), when there is a site that will tell us who the "top ranking *economists*" are! It may not be a coincidence then that the language in the RePEc site itself shares this kind of favored wording.

From my own unique perspective in writing this book, it is as if, *by the grace of God*, that I should discover something that serves as perfect evidence in support of the points I have been making in this chapter, and many of the points that I make in this book more generally. This discovery is that the "top economist in the world" is someone who, perhaps, should be very thankful, or consider himself very lucky, *for never having to serve jail time*. Specifically, he "was found by a judge to have conspired to defraud the federal government by making personal investments in Russia while advising the country on the United States' behalf."[17] As reported in the *Harvard Crimson* (Harvard's own daily newspaper):

> Shleifer, the Jones professor of economics, was found liable by a federal court in 2004 *for conspiracy to defraud the U.S. government* while leading a Harvard economic reform program in Russia as it transitioned to capitalism in the 1990s. *Shleifer settled the case for $2 million*. . . . Federal prosecutors have charged that Shleifer and his wife, hedge fund manager Nancy Zimmerman, violated State Department conflict-of-interest restrictions by investing in Russia beginning in 1994.[18]
>
> Last August, Harvard paid $26.5 million to settle the lawsuit, in addition to $2 million that Shleifer paid himself. . . . The controversy reignited on campus in February, as professors cast the details described in the Institutional Investor article as instances of favoritism and misconduct by Lawrence H. Summers. The outgoing University president is a close friend of Shleifer, and the article suggests that Summers shielded his fellow economist from disciplinary action by the University. . . . Indeed, there has been no known action taken against Shleifer yet. . . . While some professors outside the economics department have lambasted the University for not taking any action against Shleifer, many economists here have publicly defended their John Bates Medal-winning colleague as a vital intellectual asset.[19]

What does this tell us about citation counts as a means of evaluating the quality of professors, and about economics professors' commitment to professional ethics?

In 2016, I attended the annual conference of the Southern Economics Association which had only one distinguished, plenary guest lecturer—numero uno himself—Andrei Shleifer. The audience of 2,000 people welcomed to see and hear him as a major celebrity in their profession. In introducing the guest speaker, the association's president (Professor Peter Boettke) described the kind of work that Professor Shleifer had done, but made no mention of any particular discoveries that he had made (as opposed to a scientist who might be credited for having discovered something important). However, Boettke did make mention, as the highlight of his introduction, Sheifer's status in Google Scholar and RePEc as the most cited economist, in the same way that one might introduce an economist as having won the Nobel Prize (or an Olympic champion having won a gold medal). The room's reaction to the introduction was comparable to that as well. In short, those who are at the top of the publication charts in academic economics are at the top of the charts in general in the minds of most academic economists as honored celebrities who draw large audiences and quite a bit of admiration, including admiration by those who have never read a single word they wrote, but who have put their faith in the publication counts. And, in Shleifer's case, his *citation-count stardom* has long washed away the negative publicity of his having been sued for conspiracy to defraud the government.

More Sensible Approaches

There is a field of study known as "Scientometrics," defined by the *Journal of Scientometrics* as "concerned with the quantitative features and characteristics of science and scientific research. Emphasis is placed on investigations in which the development and mechanism of science are studied by statistical mathematical methods."[20] In many respects, all of this new discourse in economics that counts and analyzes publications and citations in the literature may be classified as studies within the field of scientometrics, especially since scientometric studies often analyze the same kinds of statistics. However, the connection between economic studies of publications and citations and the field of scientometrics is extremely weak. This new, little, "cottage industry" within the economics profession, which might be named "economic scientometrics," might also be considered "*amateur* scientometrics by economists," since that is essentially what it is.

Fortunately, some scholars have made attempts to find more relevant and useful measures of citations and publications counts than the ones currently in existence, with the intention of constructing measures that are more closely tied to a publication's actual usefulness. For example, in 2005 Yolanda Kodrzycki and Pingkang Yu published a study on "New Approaches to Ranking Economics Journals" in which they noted, "Our final method ranks economics journals according to their influence on . . . policy journals. This ranking may suit the interest of scholars interested in reading or writing for economics journals that have substantial influence on policy analysis and research, and, ultimately, on policymaking."[21] As I have repeated throughout this book, useful knowledge does not necessarily have to be "policy relevant" if it, instead, improves our genuine understanding how the world works. In any case, Kodrzycki and Yu's measure at least attempts to do something to help us separate out economic literature that is primarily self-serving to the authors and whomever they cite, and economic literature that is likely to serve a useful purpose and should thus have a broad appeal throughout the profession. I am confident that another, similar effort could be made to identify useful economic theory, though this would be challenging and would require, in my view, a fair amount of ingenuity.

While Kodrzycki and Yu's study might offer a glimmer of hope in certain respects—that we might put into place measures of relevance and usefulness regarding economic literature—there is one major problem: Neither of the authors are academics; they are both affiliated with the Federal Reserve Bank of Boston, where Kodrzycki is a senior economist and policy advisor and Yu a former policy analyst and advisor. Their study was not published in an economic journal, but as a working paper of the Federal Reserve Bank of Boston. I believe this is not at all coincidental. These authors did not have to play the game described in chapter 4 to get their study published, and I am sure that it was peer reviewed by nonacademics at the Federal Reserve Bank of Boston in a rather different way than it would have been peer reviewed by academic economists for a journal article.

In June 2016, I used the principle of citations and RePEc to see the fairly long list of citations to their working paper. I was glad to see that it had been cited by about thirty articles and working papers since it was published, and some of these appear to have actually studied and gained knowledge from their article, as opposed to providing lip service to it. In other words, by these citations, and by seeing how they appeared in the publications, we can, in fact, observe that their article did "make a difference." It made a difference in being recognized by a small number of researchers all over the world. Unfortunately, we all know that in the bigger scheme of things, it will most likely not make any difference in the way citations and publications are counted for the hiring and promotion of academic economists. It was simply "preaching to the choir"—and a rather small choir at that—of those with like-minded beliefs in the principle that publications should advance useful knowledge. Their study fell on deaf ears with regard to all those who do not share this perspective, and it is those without that perspective who will continue to determine the rules of the game in how publications get counted in the hiring and promotion of economics professors.

The Root of the Problem, and Its Consequences in Hiring and Promotion

Let us now finally ask the most fundamental and obvious question: *Why are publication and citation counts most often used as the main measure of an economic professor's worth (especially in the most prestigious and highest paid positions); why are we not using, instead, a direct assessment of their true contribution to knowledge in economics?* First of all, many readers who see this may be fortunate enough to be professors in departments where this is not true. My first inclination would be to compliment them for finding a good place to teach! However, their good fortune should not distort their perception of what is happening in most other parts of the profession, which is easy to see if one only looks around a bit.

As also argued elsewhere in this book, the only seemingly defensible answer—the party-line answer—that the profession could offer to this question is that economics professors' work is both too prolific and too complex for the members of any selection committees to make such an assessment of their contribution to the field of economics. With regard to the complexity issue, it is argued (or effectively assumed at least) that members of the review committee which determines hiring and promotions do not themselves possess the expertise within the candidate's particular subfield to make such a direct assessment.

I believe this two-part excuse—lack of time and lack of knowledge—is, for the most part, simply a convenient excuse and, for reasons I am about to provide, a completely unacceptable one. The real reason for why review committees do not directly assess the value of a candidate's contribution is that those committees consist of people who simply do not want to perform that direct assessment. However, in many cases, to their credit, in a way, their disinterest in performing that direct assessment reflects an honesty on their part that they are ultimately unqualified or incapable of performing that direct assessment.

As an economist, my first inclination is to consider the resource constraints that would be faced by the members of a review committee (consisting primarily of the highest ranking professors in the department) with regard to the time they need and their capabilities for making determinations on hiring and promotions. The vast majority of the members teach at least two courses per semester, and thus they must prepare and present lectures, and prepare and grade exams. These teaching constraints on their time, however, probably occupy much less than 50 percent of their working time. In the most prestigious institutions especially, these professors are spending large portions of their time performing their own research, and advising their doctoral students on their dissertations. They also apply for grants (for the research they perform) and they may often serve as reviewers of grant proposals.

Most ironically, however, many (and my guess is most) of the members of these review committees are also on the advisory boards of technical journals, where they review the papers submitted to the journal and determine, essentially, whether those papers will be accepted for publication. In this sense they are already involved in reading and evaluating research papers in their specialized subfields. They do this as well when they serve on dissertation committees, and as discussants (reviewers) of conference papers, etc. Moreover, in the preparation of their classes they must continually familiarize themselves with the latest literature in their subfields (or they are at least expected to do so). Indeed, as they most certainly should, economics professors do spend significant amounts of their time examining economic literature, even if they only do this in a very selective way (i.e., perusing it and extracting from it whatever interests them the most).

Imagine the argument from this perspective: Suppose, in the course of a year, that a full (senior-ranked) professor at a university reads ten papers per year as a reviewer for a journal, for which they recommend which papers should be accepted for a publication and why. Suppose the same full professor is on the review committee to determine if a candidate qualifies for tenure. It would be absurd for the professor to argue that they would not have time to read and evaluate the quality of the candidate's research, and because of this they must rely on publication counts, when the same professor is reading the work of other economists and determining the quality of their work as input in determining whether those economists will be able to have more publications that can be counted in their applications for tenure. *So, in truth, it is not about the time and resource constraints that review committee members have—it is about their mindset.*

The most important pillar that has held up the reliance on publication and citation counts as a basis for hiring and promotion in academic economics is pure and simple *tradition*. Let us remember that it has been a ritual for generations of economics professors—similar to the dissertation defense. Those senior faculty who sit on the review committees had been through the same process themselves, at the other end, earlier in their careers, and had been successful at pumping out the publications that they themselves needed when they had been candidates, and this has been going on for generations of economics professors. They have largely been indoctrinated into the system and have become devout followers in it, perhaps without ever thinking to question it.

The system is not completely frozen—it does appear to have evolved over time, but, lately, it has been evolving precisely in the wrong direction! Publication and citation counts have grown even greater in importance, in part because of technological changes created by RePEc, Google Scholar, and other facilities in providing new, easily accessible measures of publications and citations. The situation has gone from a bad and misguided ritual to an even-worse obsession, which has poisoned the mind-set of the profession into a tolerance for cronyism and elitism, a perception of economics as a game for publications and citations, and an effective disinterest in the advancement of valuable knowledge.

NOTES

1. Wassily Leontief, "Theoretical Assumptions and Nonobserved Facts," 2.
2. It was in support of a presentation I was giving on ethics in economics in 2007, many years after I sadly and grudgingly disposed of that collection of AER volumes that I had.
3. John P. Conley and Ali Sina Önder, "The Research Productivity of New PhDs in Economics: The Surprisingly High Non-Success of the Successful," Journal of Economic Perspectives, 28(3) (2014) 207. My own emphasis in italics.
4. Pantelis Kalaitzidakis, Theofanis Mamuneas, and Thanasis Stengos, "An Updated Ranking of Academic Journals in Economics," The Rimini Centre for Economic Analysis, WP 15_10, April 2010, accessed February 4, 2017, http://tinyurl.com/jcxq2k8. The index number of citations/article for the AER, of 100, can be found on in row 1 on page 9, and the one for the JPKE of 0.0106 can be found in row 191 on page 13.
5. "IDEAS/RePEc Recursive Impact Factors for Journals," accessed 11/27/2016, http://tinyurl.com/jnf2ybg.
6. Kristie Engemann and Howard Wall, "A Journal Ranking for the Ambitious Economist," Federal Reserve Bank of St. Louis Review 90(3) (2009): 128.
7. Franklin M. Fisher and Karl Shell, The Economic Theory of Price Indices: Two Essays on the Effects of Taste, Quality, and Technological Change (New York: Academic Press, 1972).
8. David Malakoff, "Does Science Drive the Productivity Train?" Science Magazine, August 25, 2000, 1274–5.
9. See, for example, IDEAS/RePEc, "Economics, Science and Technology," accessed June 16, 2016, http://tinyurl.com/znca9kr.
10. See, for example, IDEAS/RePEc, "Simple Impact Factors for Journals," accessed February 4, 2017, http://tinyurl.com/z3pvmf5; and Social Capital Gateway, "Ranking of Economics journals based on the Impact Factor," accessed February 4, 2017, http://tinyurl.com/jkpodms.
11. David Stern, "Uncertainty Measures for Economics Journal Impact Factors," Journal of Economic Literature, 51(1) (2013): 188. (My own emphasis in italics.)
12. IDEAS/RePEc, "Top 10% Authors, as of December 2016 (with details)," accessed June 20, 2016, http://tinyurl.com/hgnxbc8.
13. Michael A. McPherson, Myungsup Kim, Megan Dorman, and Nishelli Perera, "Research Output at U.S. Economics Departments," Applied Economics Letters, 20(9) (2013): 890.

14. McPherson et al., "Research Output at U.S. Economics Departments, 889. My own emphasis in italics.

15. Donald A.R. George (Book Review), "Quality Measurement in Economics: New Perspectives on the Evolution of Goods and Services. By Payson (Steven)." Economic Journal, 105(428) (1995): 233–35.

16. "Andrei Shleifer," Wikipedia, accessed June 24, 2016, http://tinyurl.com/z757fu5.

17. Steve Sailer, "Economist Andrei Shleifer Demoted by Harvard," The Unz Review: An Alternative Media Selection, October 15, 2006, accessed February 4, 2017, http://tinyurl.com/gobf4qn.

18. Nicholas M. Ciarelli and Anton S. Troianovski, "'Tawdry Shleifer Affair' Stokes Faculty Anger Toward Summers," The Harvard Crimson, February 10, 2006. My own emphasis in italics.

19. Anton S. Troianovski, "Shleifer to Resume Teaching," The Harvard Crimson, April 24, 2006.

20. Springer, "Scientometrics," accessed February 4, 2017, http://tinyurl.com/hjxapuz.

21. Yolanda Kodrzycki and Pingkang Yu, "New Approaches to Ranking Economics Journals," Federal Reserve Bank of Boston Working Paper 05–12, 2005, accessed February 4, 2017, http://tinyurl.com/zaoht8d.

Chapter 7

Scholarship, Though Beautiful, Cannot Save the Academic Economics Profession

THE CURSE OF TOO MUCH SCHOLARSHIP, AND THE NEED FOR SOME

I have previously written on how economists often violate principles of scientific inquiry, but for me and many others with the same or similar views, it would be an enormous amount of work to publish such ideas in any of the standard technical journals.[1] And, if such work were, in fact, published, the audience for which it was designed would have no interest in reading it. A technical publication on the topic of scientific integrity in economics would require a detailed discussion referring to a comprehensive, scholarly review of the history and philosophy of scientific inquiry as it relates to economic thought. It would need to provide a review of the literature by Lakatos and Popper, etc., and discuss positivism, instrumentalism, descriptivism, etc. The vast majority of economists who really need to learn something about scientific integrity have no interest in any of this, and they would run for the hills at the sight of such historical names and philosophical terms that they have never seen before. That is, they might be able to hear a simple criticism that their efforts violate scientific principles, but they would not be able to hear it when it is couched in a scholarly paper about the philosophy of science, which they would ignore and avoid as something completely outside their knowledge base and most certainly outside their comfort zone.

Scholarly discourse thereby places yet another curse on economic thought that effectively precludes the consideration of the most important issue of all in economics—the issue of how to determine if the work performed by economists, and for top-ranked literature in particular, is relevant, valuable, useful, and worthwhile. Making that determination would involve philosophy;

but most economists do not do study philosophy, and the ones who do only write to each other and have no effect on the rest of the profession.

Put another way, while the unscientific theoretical economists are having their own brand of self-gratification by sharing their beautiful models with each other, with no real intention of advancing progress in human understanding of the real world, are the advanced scholars of the history of economic thought so different? They, too, are having their own brand of self-gratification in their own way, by conversing in their own esoteric, philosophical language, and by sharing their own type of love for historical writings and for philosophical positions espoused by renowned writers of the past, like Adam Smith, Nassau William Senior, Tjalling Koopmans, etc. Are they not simply amusing each other and doing little more than that by studying bodies of work that are otherwise never considered or used by applied economists, or even by scientific theoretical economists, and most certainly not by policy analysts? To whatever extent such a scholarly group is perceived as being self-serving, the group will be taken less seriously by those outside of it, and will attract less scholars who actually do want to work toward improving the profession.

While advanced study in the history of economic thought will not, in fact, do much for the profession, the fundamental basics of what is important for economics cannot be ignored either. Currently, education in economics horribly fails to engender students with a sense of responsibility to uphold the intellectual history of their discipline, and to think beyond the set of mathematical models that they are required to digest and regurgitate in examinations. In his book *Debunking Economics-Revised, Expanded and Integrated Edition: The Naked Emperor Dethroned?* (2011), Steve Keen writes:

> Economics students . . . graduate from master's and PhD programs with an uncritical and unjustified belief that the foundations of economic analysis are sound, no appreciation of the intellectual history of their discipline, and an approach to mathematics which hobbles both their critical understanding of economics, and their ability to appreciate the latest advances in mathematics and other sciences.
>
> A minority of these ill-informed students themselves go on to be academic economists, and then repeat the process. Ignorance is perpetuated.
>
> The attempt to conduct a critical dialogue within the profession of academic economics has therefore failed, not because neoclassical economics has no flaws, but because—figuratively speaking—neoclassical economists have no ears. . . . So then, 'No More Mr Nice Guy.' If economists can't be trusted to follow the Queensberry Rules of intellectual debate, then we critics have to step out of the boxing ring and into the streets.[2]

As Keen implies, intellectual arguments on how economics should be improved remains largely outside the interest of most academic economists, who have been trained at model memorizing, not critical thinking. They have received that training simply because it was all that many of their professors had learned themselves, and thus it was all that those professors could offer to their students. Furthermore, as I have argued in the first chapter, Keen takes the same position that, when members of the profession are too arrogant to engage in any meaningful discussion on improving the profession, a more forceful voice (as reflected in the tone of this book) may be necessary to evoke a response.

SCIENCE ACCORDING TO SCIENTISTS, RATHER THAN PHILOSOPHERS

Those who often contribute to the scholarly literature on how economics should be more scientific appear to put all of their eggs in the wrong basket by assuming that the scholarly writings of the philosophers of science hold all the answers. Their perspective is understandable to some degree because this is what these writers find most interesting and what they themselves care about the most. Thus, the philosophical papers that some academic economists have written on how economics should be more scientific seem to rely on the naïve belief that unscientific, theoretical academic economists are willing to be trained to act like scientists, if only provided the opportunity to read these papers. However, as I argued in *Economics, Science, and Technology*:

> For a true scientist, proper thinking is something that one expects to do for a lifetime. Therefore; in natural science itself, science educators take a much different approach from that of philosophers. They have generally realized that what their students, or new scientists, need most is a simple understanding of basic guidelines. These are guidelines that they will maintain in their long- term memories and always put into practice throughout their careers. What they do not need are detailed philosophical and axiomatic rules. If such rules were required for their courses, they would likely soon forgot them once they regurgitate them on the final examination.[3]

As an example, in explaining the scientific method to their students, David Keeports and Dean Morier distinguish between "science" and what they termed "pseudo science." They proposed to their students: "Let's hypothesize that the Earth is flat. From this hypothesis we might then correctly predict that some portion of the Earth's surface, such as a particular field in Kansas, should be flat, and that all people on Earth should feel like they, stand upright." From this they argued, "A failure to acknowledge the possibility of a false hypothesis leading to true predictions through sound reasoning lies at the heart of pseudoscientific belief."[4]

In this argument they basically take the position, as scientists, that is diametrically opposed to the most common perspective in academic economics—Milton Friedman's F-twist perspective—which was discussed extensively in chapter 3. Although my discussion here will most assuredly be considered plebian and shallow by philosophers of science, I hope it might still be beneficial to readers who are not so interested in the intricacies and nuances of the topic, but simply in the up-front, bottom line. The scientific perspective—the one that science teachers teach, and the one that scientists live by—is that it is essential to know that the Earth is not flat, regardless of the fact that it can be usefully approximated as such in many cases. Science students are taught in their classes to dislike any theories that blatantly ignore the most accurate view of reality (which make them obsolete), only for the sake of convenient approximation, while economics students are taught to embrace such theories and to ignore or dismiss the fact that they deviate substantially from reality.

It is rather rare for economics students to learn about the "scientific method" in their economics classes, and I believe many economics graduates would be at a loss if asked to explain what the scientific method is. In academic economics, an understanding of the scientific method might only be expected from a "history of economic thought class," or similar type of class, though such classes rarely exist anymore and are no longer required.

Students of the natural sciences also rarely, if ever, take a history-of-thought class involving the philosophy of science. However, they are expected to understand the scientific method throughout every science class that they might take. The situation in completely different in the training of economists, where the study of methodological principles is a highly specialized subfield, as already argued.

In sharp contrast to the study of methodological issues in economics, there is the study of the *culture* of natural science. In natural science *culture*, methodological issues pervade over just about everything that is ever done, and everyone who performs research in the natural sciences is fully expected to have a solid grasp of the importance of having the appropriate methodological framework. For practicing scientists, methodological awareness and competence is rooted in basic common sense combined with a simple but strong commitment to understanding causality through an objective lens. This culture is supported not only in how natural science is taught but also from the hands-on experience that scientists and science students gain in performing scientific research. Along these lines, Derek Hodson has argued:

> Though necessary, conceptual knowledge and knowledge about procedures that scientists can adopt, and have adopted in particular circumstances in the past, are insufficient in themselves to enable a student to engage successfully

in scientific inquiry. That ability is developed only through experience. In other words, one can only learn to do science, and one can only experience science as a mode of inquiry, by doing science.[5]

There is, however, a rich body of scholarly literature in economic thought on how economics simply cannot be like natural science, supported by various ideas, such as the idea that economic entities (firms, workers, etc.) are always changing due to institutional factors and the like, so that we cannot have "laws" that remain constant, like $E=mc^2$. There is also a completely opposite literature which borders on propaganda, in favor of experimental economics, which argues, primarily, that economics can be just as much a "science" as any other "science" by virtue of the fact that economists can, and have, run economic experiments. This argument will be discussed extensively in the next chapter. Nevertheless, the extent to which economics can, or should, be similar to natural sciences is a rather large philosophic question, which I will not be addressing here. Rather, I am simply focusing on aspects of the way economics is taught in comparison to the way the natural sciences are taught, in the context of the subject matter of this book, which is "how economics professors can stop failing us." Regardless of how different economics is, or should be, from the natural sciences, I strongly believe that the way that economics is taught should have much more in common with the way the natural sciences are taught, with an emphasis on the importance of understanding true causality. In particular, the fact that economics differs from natural science in various ways should not be used as a free license, on the part of economics professors, to focus on the beauty of esoteric mathematical models at the expense of the relevance of economics to understanding the real world.

In one of the chemistry classes I had when I was in college, I will never forget an enlightening trick question that the professor asked of our class. Before he asked that question, he covered in the class one of the laws of chemistry that showed the relationship between the temperature of a gas and its pressure and other chemical properties (known as the "Ideal Gas Law"). He then asked the question, "If you were performing an experiment in the laboratory, and for your results you needed to know the pressure of a gas, how would you find it out?" Having just been given this wonderful formula, students started answering the question by saying how they would use that formula to find out the pressure of the gas. The professor said no, that was not the right answer, and the class was stumped. The best way, he then explained, to determine the pressure of the gas would be to measure the pressure directly using a pressure meter. The obvious point that he was making, for which the class was embarrassed (as scientific thinkers), was simply that, if we are trying to observe something about reality, then we should indeed rely on direct observation, rather than rely on a model that can only tell us what the observation is supposed to be according to a certain theory. This prioritization of direct observation over theoretical findings is something that should be taught to economics students, for obvious reasons, but it is not. I do not recall a trick question like this ever being asked in any of the economics classes I have ever attended as a student, though I would sometimes ask it myself in some of the economics classes that I have taught. When I did, the students were stumped as well, and then they generally reacted quite favorably to the exercise, leading to a discussion about how "theory is theory" but measureable economic variables like income, prices, employment and gross output are all real, and measuring them directly helps us to realize and appreciate our stronger connection with reality.

ORMEROD'S *DEATH OF ECONOMICS* AND LANCASTER'S THEORY OF THE SECOND BEST

I recently came across a book whose title was not shy by any means—*The Death of Economics*, by Paul Ormerod (1994).[6] The book says quite a bit about the shortcomings of what I have been referring to as "unscientific economic theory," which it refers to (in politer terms, despite the book's impolite title) as "orthodox economic theory." Like many books that have sharply criticized the academic economic profession, *The Death of Economics* was written by a highly acclaimed and highly accomplished economist. The book's cover accredits the author as follows: "Paul Ormerod studied economics at Cambridge and Oxford Universities and worked as head of the Economics Assessment unit at *The Economist.* He was Director of Economics at the Henley Centre for Forecasting and has been a visiting Professor of Economics at the Universities of London and Manchester."[7]

In my view, Ormerod's critiques of the economics profession's misuse of, and obsession with, economic theory mirrors many of arguments that I have written in this book, and often in a somewhat similar tone. For example, Ormerod writes:

> In a famous passage in Alice in Wonderland, the Red Queen declares that she often believes six impossible things before breakfast. The model of competitive equilibrium appears to be requiring us to move into this kind of world. And especially so in the case of companies, where the evidence from over a hundred years of economic history provides powerful evidence against the validity of the theory as a description of reality.[8]
>
> The profession in fact resembles the revelers in Edgar Allen Poe's chilling story "The Masque of the Red Death." Everyone is having a splendid time,

> indulging "joyfully in virulently esoteric chat." But some, at least are aware of the existence of a presence among them that will ultimately cause the party to end in tears.[9]

Aside from certain similarities in tone, Ormerod's approach to the topic was much narrower than mine, and more rigorous at explaining some of the problems with "orthodox economic theory" from an understanding of fundamental principles of economics.

I will share one of the points that Ormerod made in his book, because I believe it has long been recognized as extremely important by many economists, and I strongly suspect that readers (even those who are not economists) will agree with this as well. I am also proud to say that it involves the work that had been developed by my own dissertation advisor (Kelvin Lancaster) in collaboration with another prominent economist (Richard Lipsey).[10] Although Ormerod does not mention the name of the specific economic theory to which to which he refers in his argument, it, indeed, has a name that all theoretical economists should recognize—the "Theory of the Second Best" which was published in the journal *Review of Economic Studies* in 1956.

The Theory of the Second Best reflects, in my view, economic theory, and economics itself, at its very best. The theory is not self-serving, nor a reflection of any effort at self-gratification or effort to display the authors' prowess in mathematics. Rather, it provides an important basis for understanding a fundamental principle of economic thought.

In his book, as reflected in the above quotation, Ormerod wrote largely about the economic theory of "competitive equilibrium"—what happens in the economy when there are no monopolies of firms, or monopolies of workers (in the form of labor unions), and when, as a result (of basic economic theory) the production and consumption of goods occurs in an "optimal way." Competitive equilibrium is often the baseline, or ground floor, upon which economics is first learned. We then explore what happens when things get complicated, and there is no longer a competitive equilibrium, such as when a monopoly arises. Once the economic system deviates from competitive equilibrium then "suboptimal" things can happen. For example, a regular monopoly will tend to produce fewer products and charge more for them. Consumers will be forced to pay more for products that cost less to produce than their price, and the monopolist earns "monopolistic rents" at the consumer's expense. In addition, the firm, overall, produces less than it would under competitive equilibrium.

The overall finding of the Theory of the Second Best is that, if there is more than one obstacle to optimal, competitive equilibrium, then removing any one of the obstacles may actually do more harm than good. For example, if we start with two obstacles, and we remove one, then this could (though not necessarily) result in a worse, more "suboptimal" situation. In this sense, certain obstacles to begin with may counterbalance each other to some extent to make things better. We might envision this with various metaphors. For example, if a husband and wife continually scream at each other, then that would easily be seen as suboptimal to a situation in which neither screamed at the other, but if we prevented only one of the spouses from screaming at the other, the situation might be worse in certain respects than when we started.

In *The Death of Economics*, Ormerod provides a simple example in which he proposes that there are two obstacles to competitive equilibrium: (1) All firms cannot control the price of their products (as it is instead determined by supply and demand in the market), except for the auto manufacturer General Motors, which can, and (2) no labor union could determine the salary of its members, except for the Union of Automobile Workers. If both General Motors and the Union lost their power over prices and wages, respectively, then we might conclude, on the basis of economic theory, that the economy would be more optimal. However, if only one of them lost their power, then according to the Theory of the Second Best, it would not be possible to determine whether the economy would be any more or less optimal.

As mentioned in Columbia University's biographical webpage on Kelvin Lancaster:

> His best-known paper of that period is his remarkable work (with Richard Lipsey) on The Theory of Second Best, an important theoretical breakthrough which had, in the best tradition of economic theory, enormous policy impact. Stated briefly, this paper established that the necessary conditions for the optimal allocation of economic resources have to hold in their entirety; if one of them is violated then adhering to the remaining conditions is no longer optimal. The implications of this principle reach into all fields of economics.[11]

As Ormerod recognized in his book, the implications of The Theory of the Second Best is that any policy to increase competition in the economy need not be the correct policy in terms of improving the economy—rather "each proposal to increase the degree of competition in an economy must be treated on its own merits."[12] Nevertheless, a great deal of theoretical economic literature, as Ormerod documents, simply ignores all of this, and assumes the opposite—that all movements toward more competition are preferable. *It is an example of how academic economists often do not take economic theory itself seriously.* For many of them there is no assumed responsibility to identify which theories are truly more reliable and why. Instead, many appear to take on the much lighter responsibility of identifying whatever theories they enjoy the most, and whatever theories they should study and cite in their work to maximize their chances of publishing in the highest ranking journals.

False Assumptions as a Crime, or Just Part of a Sport?

Allow me to diverge from the topic at hand, just for a moment, with the promise that I will soon demonstrate the relevance of this diversion. This diversion will focus on the question of whether a "punch to the face" is a crime or just part of a sport. Consider what happens when a person is walking down the street, and a man comes to him insisting that he give that man all his money. When the person refuses, the man punches him in the face and continues to insist on receiving the money with the implicit threat that he will punch the person again if he does not receive it. Of course, if an undercover police officer were nearby witnessing all of this, the officer will instantly arrest the mugger, and throw him in jail for assault and attempted robbery.

Now contrast this situation with that of the same undercover police officer sitting in the audience of a boxing match, watching two men continually trying, and occasionally succeeding, at punching each other in the face. Needless to say, the officer will do absolutely nothing, since the face-punching in this case is simply an expected part of a sport that has been mutually endorsed by the audience and participants, and accepted as legal by society.

Now consider those people who are seriously involved in analyzing the world for an important purpose, such as those performing medical research, or those performing public policy research that is based on economic analysis. For these people, suppose their analysis is found to rely on a false assumption, which is not merely a simplifying assumption for purpose of approximation, but a very wrong assumption that will quite probably lead to false analytical findings, thereby defeating the very purpose of the intended work. This kind of assumption, to those who must rely on reasonably accurate assumptions, is a crime—it is an assault to their work and their goals—it is, in this sense, a punch (or at least a slap) in the face.

Let us contrast this to a research paper published in a journal that had relied on rather arbitrary assumptions that were arguably wrong, and those assumptions determined the findings of the paper. Someone else then comes along and writes a follow-up article, in which they argue that the assumptions underlying the first paper were wrong, and led to wrong findings. The second person further argues that their own paper used much more reliable assumptions, thereby enabling them to acquire more reliable results. Here, in this situation, we are in the sports mode. In the vast majority of cases the first author would not consider the second author's critique as a punch in the face, in the sense of it coming from that second author, or in the sense of it coming from the wrong assumption that the first author used (if he believes the second author's argument).

Likewise, one might wonder whether the journal editor who published the first article, having supposedly instituted a thorough peer review to validate the claims of the first paper before publishing it, might be disturbed by this situation one way or the other. That is, one might wonder whether the journal editor would be disappointed with the first author for possibly fooling the journal with an analysis that was not quite legitimate, or disappointed with the second author for possibly unfairly criticizing the first author's work. Yet, of course, the editor, like either of the authors, would be not disappointed. *Rather, everyone is at peace in this sports-like La, La Land of journal publications on economic theory.* Indeed, the first author would likely thank the second author for the interest they have shown in the first paper and, of course, for the citation to it. The punches taking place here are punches in a sporting event designed to entertain the audience, and to promote the careers and incomes of both contestants, in an environment where no one is seen as having done anything wrong.

In the vast majority of cases, scholarly critics of existing economic literature are themselves absorbed into the scholarly debates that are seen by the profession as simply self-serving and isolated discourse, removed from their own areas of expertise. Imagine, again, the scene I described earlier involving a police officer arresting a mugger on the street for assault. Suppose that, in the process of the officer arresting the mugger, the mugger fights back and a boxing match ensues on the street, with either one of two results: If the officer wins the fight, the mugger will be arrested; if he loses, the mugger will run off scot free. Further suppose that, as this fight is occurring, the officer appeals to some citizens on the street saying, "help me capture this man—I am arresting him for assault." Finally, suppose the passersby respond, "No thanks, boxing has never interested me—I much prefer golf" as if the passersby were being invited to participate in a sporting event rather than to take a responsible position to correct a wrong. *This has essentially been one of the major problems with scholarly critiques of economic discourse—the confusion between responsibility and entertainment, and how it has led to complete inaction, with those criticisms simply falling on deaf ears.*

The Death of: The Death of Economics

Paul Ormerod, a highly distinguished economist as both a scholar and as a practitioner, went through the trouble of writing an entire book which he called *The Death of Economics* in order to warn people of the how the self-serving nature of economic thought (primarily from academia) has led to disaster—indeed, to a "death" of the profession. Admittedly, and perhaps quite obviously, I am attempting to do something similar here with my own book. I feel that my book is necessary, because, in part, Ormerod's book, published 23 years earlier, *changed nothing*, even though it sold very well at first. In Amazon, his book is ranked #833,443 among books, and #4,072 among economics books,[13] which is not terrible, but still within the realm of generally being ignored. Ironically, one of the reviews shown at the back of his book, from *The Washington Post*, mentioned that the book "should be required reading for Economics 101 classes"—something that unfortunately never happened.

Ormerod made a gallant effort to expose how the majority of economic models that are generated by economists can actually be proven false by better economic theory, and by economic reasoning itself, such as by consideration of the Lancaster-Lipsey Theory of the Second Best. The failure of his arguments to be heard is that he used economic thought and theory to fight economic thought and theory—and that had the effect for many readers believing they were seeing a spectator sport, presented before them for their amusement, instead of a scandalous exposé which they could have acknowledged and acted upon in their own way. This is what happens in general to scholarly arguments that have been made to improve the profession. As I have argued throughout this book, the authors of these works wind up either feeling dissatisfied for having hardly been read, but are comforted by having developed these works as publications. They are also comforted by their like-minded colleagues, as reflected by the metaphor of "preaching to the choir." Along these lines, poor Paul Ormerod who declared "The Death of Economics" did not see the death of economics as he had predicted after his book, but the death of just another book that predicted the profession's demise—his own. My previous book in 2000, *Economics, Science and Technology*, which discussed how economists should be more like scientists (as I have argued in this chapter as well) suffered the same demise (actually much worse), as have countless other books that have identified the same or similar problems with appeals for the profession to change. Here are just a few other examples, though if I did enough research I am sure that I could find at least ten times as many (as well as a countless number of corresponding journal articles):

- *Why Aren't Economists as Important as Garbagemen? Essays on the State of Economics* (David Colander 1991)
- *Debunking Economics* (Steve Keen 2001)
- *Truth Versus Precision in Economics* (Thomas Mayer 1993)
- *The Vices of Economists, the Virtues of the Bourgeoisie* (Deirdre McCloskey 1996)
- *Naked Economics: Undressing the Dismal Science* (Charles Wheelan and Burton Malkiel 2010)
- *Dangerous Currents: The State of Economics* (Lester Thurow, 1983)
- The Economist's Oath: On the Need for and Content of Professional Economic Ethics (George DeMartino 2011).

In fact, I believe another reason why such books fall on deaf ears is that the majority of their intended audience has already decided to ignore them, so that the marginal value of yet another book is near zero. *This is why this book had to be different, by attacking the core of the problem—the culture of the profession itself—instead of focusing on how some of the theories are wrong on the basis of economic reasoning.*

WISDOM FROM *THE PICTURE OF DORIAN GRAY*

From my encountering the vast body of scholarly literature that has criticized the economics profession, I am reminded of the story written in 1891 by the famous American novelist, Oscar Wilde, entitled *The Picture of Dorian Gray*. It was about a rich, spoiled and handsome young man who had just acquired a portrait of himself, while simultaneously fearing that eventually old age would destroy his beautiful world. He thus made a pact with the devil when he looked at the picture and said, "I shall grow old, and horrible, and dreadful. But this picture will remain always young. . . . If it were only the other way! If it were I who was to be always young, and the picture that was to grow old! . . . I would sell my soul for that!"

Back in 1996 I wrote about *The Picture of Dorian Gray* in the article I mentioned before in the *Journal of Post Keynesian Economics*, entitled "Regardless of Philosophy, Economics Will Not Be a Science Until it is Based on Science." At that time, I wrote that the first concerns about the scientific validity of economics were in Nassau William Senior's (1827), "Introductory Lecture on Political Economy." I then mentioned that, in 1983, Alfred Eichner wrote *Why Economics Is Not an Evolutionary Science*, in which he referred to Veblen's (1898) essay, "Why Is Economics Not an Evolutionary Science?" Eichner noted then, in 1983, that over eighty years had passed with the issue of unscientific economics still unresolved. There is a clear pattern here which I described in my analogy to Dorian Gray. Back in 1996, I wrote that Eichner had passed on, and that his book on economics as science is quickly being forgotten. Right now, at this current writing, I am sure that Eichner's work has indeed been completely forgotten. Yet, scholarly treatises on the topic have never ceased, nor even slowed down. As I described in that 1996 article:

> The philosophical and sociological factors that account for the absence of science in economics have already been discussed and analyzed *ad nauseam*, and any attempt to review this vast body of literature would be befitting of nothing less than an encyclopedia, authored by dozens of scholars who have devoted their lives to the topic. . . . Like Dorian Gray, economists who espouse the

> concept of 'economic science' have continued to appear young and attractive to economics students and to the public, while, like Dorian Gray's portrait, the historical literature continues to age, growing ever older and more decrepit, while hidden from most observers.[14]

Nevertheless, I do not believe, whatsoever, that it is futile for us to try to cure the enormous problem of unscientific theoretical economics. I strongly believe that it *can, indeed, be cured*, but by rather different means than the perpetuation of the flow of scholarly appeals that will fall on deaf ears. Those other means require a less scholarly approach, and more economic approach, which is to address directly the incentive system and resources that perpetually support unscientific theoretical economics: the approach that I have in fact taken in this relatively "unscholarly" book.

If anyone still thinks, after all this discussion, that scholarly discourse is still the only way they are willing to address the problem, then I will ask them, in one last desperate plea, to take a moment and look more broadly at the results that scholarly arguments have had, *in general, in our society*. Let us ask ourselves how often scholarly arguments play a major role in encouraging people "to do the right thing," and to "stop doing the wrong thing"? Begging the reader's indulgence, I feel obliged to make the following, somewhat facetious, remark: If scholarly arguments alone could cure society's ailments, then what a wonderful world, indeed, we would be inhabiting—a world without any need for things like law enforcement, military defense, or even financial audits—a world in which just the advancement and dissemination of scholarly knowledge would solve our problems.

No, unfortunately, our universe does not work this way, and scholarly arguments cannot be relied upon to fix the horrific problems that exist in academic economics, no more so than scholarly arguments have fixed injustices in the world. If they could, they would have done so nearly fifty years ago, for example, with Leontief's presidential address to the AEA. Indeed, the fact that the scholarly arguments have failed, over many generations, to change the academic economics profession's problems was one of the main reasons that I felt compelled to write this book, in which I could offer an alternative approach that just might work.

NOTES

1. Fortunately, the *Journal of Post-Keynesian Economics* did allow me to do this, in part because it is more open to discourse of this kind than the "standard" journals.
2. Steve Keen, Debunking Economics-Revised, Expanded and Integrated Edition: The Naked Emperor Dethroned (London, Zed Books, 2011), 41.

3. Steven Payson, Economics, Science and Technology, 16.

4. David Keeports and Dean Morier, "Teaching the Scientific Method," Journal of College Science and Teaching, September/October 1994, 45–50.

5. Derek Hodson, "Re-thinking Old Ways: Towards a More Critical Approach to Practical Work in School Science," Studies in Science Education, 22 (1993), 125.

6. Paul Ormerod, The Death of Economics (New York: John Wiley & Sons, 1997).

7. Ormerod, The Death of Economics, back cover of book.

8. Ormerod, The Death of Economics, 71.

9. Ormerod, The Death of Economics, 77.

10. R.G. Lipsey and Kelvin J. Lancaster, "The General Theory of the Second Best," The Review of Economic Studies 24(1) (1956): 11–32.

11. "Kelvin John Lancaster," Columbia|Economics, accessed February 5, 2017, http://tinyurl.com/hlgroux.

12. Ormerod, The Death of Economics, 84.

13. "The Death of Economics," Amazon, accessed December 8, 2016, http://tinyurl.com/jnb2qw6.

14. Steven Payson, "Regardless of Philosophy, Economics Will Not Be a Science Until it is Based on Science." *Journal of Post Keynesian Economics*, 19(2) (1996): 257–58.

Chapter 8

Academic Economics at Its Dumbest and Ugliest

MANY ECONOMICS PROFESSORS HAVE NO CLUE HOW IMPORTANT THEY ARE

The degree of influence and authority that economic professors have as a group in our society is enormous—it does not require much thought to recognize this fact. The subject of economics provides the intellectual pillar that upholds the very nature of how resources on our planet are extracted and used, and how goods and services are produced and distributed. In turn, it is the economics teaching profession that upholds the subject, teaching our society about it, and filling some of the most powerful and influential roles among our society's leaders: the chairman of the Federal Reserve Board of Governors, members of the President's Council of Economic Advisors, the assistant secretary for Economic Policy in the Treasury Department (if not the secretary of the department, itself), the leaders of the World Bank and the International Monetary Fund, etc. Such positions are led by hand-picked members of the academic economics community who are usually simply borrowed temporarily from their universities. For better or worse, their perceived qualifications for their incredibly important roles in our society have been based on their prominence as economics professors, which in turn was at least partially based on the incredible success that each of them had to have at playing the publication game described in previous chapters.

At a very superficial level, some people might think that physicians play a more important role than economics professors in our society in the sense that they directly save lives. Some might argue the same for high-ranking officials in the military. Yet, I have encountered, over the years, prominent physicians who, in their retirement years, decided to become volunteers in organizations that provide medical services, or conduct medical research, in less-developed countries. It is interesting to see them coming back from their experiences abroad and presenting lectures to audiences of physicians as if they were economics professors teaching a course on economic development. In their lectures they explain how they learned that life expectancy in the countries they visited could be vastly improved by a much greater distribution of safe drinking water and soap, greater supplies of food and safer preparation of it, etc. In other words, those physicians come back looking very much like economic development professors, realizing that economic development is the field of study that might, in many cases, be even more relevant to saving lives on our planet than the provision of specific medical services to those who fall ill.

Likewise, high-ranking military officials seem to be highly adept at understanding economic issues and making economic decisions that are integral to military operations. They often follow the recommendations of their economic advisors, whose knowledge, in turn, is based on the economics courses they have taken from the professors at their military academies.

People who understand how the world generally works know, of course, that good economic policies save lives, from raising living standards (and the consequential effects that has on health) to reducing the incidence of terrorist acts or war, and vice versa for bad economic policies. It then follows that it is economics professors, more than any other group (including other types of economists), that society entrusts the most to guide us, either directly or indirectly, in establishing the best economic perspectives, advice, and policies.

Juxtaposed to this enormous responsibility, as commonly seen by the public, is an extremely opposite view held by many economics professors themselves. For many of them, their job is to deliver their lectures, prepare and grade their exams, all based on standardized material that they feel they have little influence over, and otherwise have fun, essentially, in whatever intellectual pursuits might tickle their fancy (as long as they can get the publications they need out of it). *There is no profession on earth where there is so great a discrepancy and disconnect between the incredible responsibility that society rightfully expects of the profession, and the minimal level of responsibility that most members of the profession appear to have.* In this chapter I provide examples of this incredible, unbelievable discrepancy.

LIVING IN LA-LA LAND

Let's face it: Many academics, in many different fields besides economics, live in "La-La Land." In the arts, literature, philosophy, and other subject areas it would be expected, if not required. Of course, my use of the term "La-La Land" in this context is surely demeaning and belittling. In my mind, however, it conveys a level of direct honesty about this topic that could not be conveyed as effectively, or as efficiently, through the use of politer, or more technical terms, like "preoccupation with obscure and often idiosyncratic interests that do not connect well to practical applications or to a useful understanding of the world." In any case, I am abstaining from making any judgments about the "La-La Land characteristics" of fields in the arts, other than to defend those characteristics as being within the rights of experts in those fields, because those experts are not being hypocritical or irresponsible to society by choosing to live their lives in the way they have chosen. They are doing what they are supposed to do, and as far as I could tell, they are doing it well. In fact, if universities adjusted their budgets to hire less economics professors, in order to hire more arts, philosophy, and humanities professors, I would have no objection to that.

The way economics is taught, in itself, may often reflect economics professors' desire to live in La-La Land. As a simple example, consider the following excerpt from a very widely used introductory, graduate-level textbook in economics, which I was required to study back when I was in graduate school: "[C]onsider demand and supply behavior. Here one group of economic agents determines how much they wish to demand of some good as a function of its price. This determination of demand is presumably the result of some underlying maximization, *or at least can be modeled as such*."[1]

I would guess that 95 percent or more of the economics graduate students who read the above passage, or one very much like it, would comfortably fly right through it without a glitch, including the last phrase that I placed in italics. However, let us pause for a minute to consider what this phrase truly implies. It implies, essentially, that we are free and even encouraged to explore economic demand as a "maximization problem" regardless of whether *it truly is or is not a maximization problem in reality*. Whatever it is, in reality, is apparently not a relevant concern for the author of this text, because *as long as we can MODEL it as a maximization problem*, we are in the clear from his perspective to move forward with it to further analysis. In other words, if our work on studying economic demand as a maximization problem is expelled from the land of reality on the basis of relying on an assumption that is simply not true, we are still granted refuge and sanctuary in the "modeling region" of La-La Land to live as we please. To me this begs the question of what our study will ultimate produce, if we have ignored its remoteness from reality. The standard answer economics professors will often provide in response to such a question is that "our study will enable us to better understand how demand works." The more truthful and comprehensive answer, of course, would be, "Our study will better enable us to understand of how demand works *in the La-La Land that we have created*."

In discussing economic models in classes that I have taught, I have always tried to emphasize that it is not enough for the model to be intellectually interesting, regardless of how interesting that might be. The bottom line is how relevant it is to enabling us to understand reality. At many times in my classes, and in my career in working with economists and policy analysts, I would occasionally refer to an old riddle that I had heard several decades ago. Before asking the riddle I would preface the question with the remark that nearly all of the practicing scientists, statisticians, and empirical applied economists, to whom I have asked the riddle, would get the right answer, and the very few who did not were embarrassed when told the right answer. The riddle is, "How many legs would a sheep have, if we decided to count its tail as a leg?" Sometimes I asked students to write their answer on an anonymous piece of paper, and then tallied up their responses in front of them. The vast majority of the answers from students was "5," and some were "1" (apparently believing that the riddle assumed that *only* a tail would be counted as a leg).

The correct answer to the riddle, of course, is "4." This is because our deciding to count the tail as a leg *does not make it a leg*. This is the kind of thinking that is horribly absent within the theoretical economics community—I fear the logic of the answer may even bewilder some theoretical economists who have spent so much time living in La-La Land, that they cannot even understand the point. For the most hardcore theoretical economists, there is no independent reality of any relevance to them (at least not one they would ever like to talk about)—only the separate "interesting" reality that they have created for themselves in their models. We can see this about them when we engage in conversations with them, and I am sure that most non-theoretical economists who are reading this already know exactly what I mean (as many theoretical economists know as well).

Many Economics Professors Just Want to Have Fun

It is not uncommon to see academic economists making no secret of their joint interests in advancing knowledge while also "having a good time." This is evident, for example, in the blog on "Economics and Ethics" maintained by the Association for Social Economics. The association, in fact, lists the precise words, "have a good time," as one of its five objectives, which I suppose is quite harmless for a blog. However, I am more disturbed by the caption under the blog's title, "Economics and Ethics," which reads "An occasional examination of economic theory, practice, and policy, informed by philosophical ethics (*and a dash of whimsy*)" (my own emphasis).[2] As many of us know, the term "whimsy" means "Playfully quaint or fanciful behavior or humour."[3] I would have liked to think that the concepts that preceded the qualifying term "(and a dash of whimsy)" were fairly serious, and that this qualifier undermines their seriousness. Obviously, I personally believe that the study of "economics and ethics" should not be approached with "a dash of whimsy."

For a comparison, I searched for a few blogs on medical ethics and how they described themselves, along with a few blogs on legal ethics and business ethics, and none of them offered any suggestion that one of their objectives was "having a good time," nor any suggestion in any way (or in any similar words) that their contents included "a dash of whimsy." It appears that the vast majority of intellectual groups that study ethics simply do not have the joint objective of (1) advancing useful knowledge that might improve the world, and (2) having a good time in the process. Many academic economists appear to be different in this regard; their unique desire to have fun when studying ethics is something they must have picked up from their frequent travels to La-La Land.

The Greater Reality of Interdisciplinary Approaches

Addressing more substantive issues, however, we might observe that contentment with life in La-La Land often precludes economics professors from adopting an interdisciplinary approach to whatever phenomenon they are studying, even when such an interdisciplinary approach would provide a much greater understanding of that phenomenon. This is because that better understanding would only be a better understanding in the real world, and not in La-La Land. Other social science disciplines generally approach the topic of interdisciplinary research in a very different way—consider the field of psychology for example. In comparing economics and psychology, the excuse that academic economists often give for their frequent reliance on unrealistic assumptions—the limitations they face in studying human behavior—could just as easily be made by academic psychologists, since psychology, by definition no less, is devoted to the study of human behavior. Within psychology, one of the most interesting subfields is abnormal psychology. In this subfield, many of the theories (or "models"), such as those by Jung and Freud, have been largely impossible to verify. Nevertheless, even in abnormal psychology there is a strong commitment by psychologists to develop theories that are grounded in, and have positive results in, *reality*.

For instance, I remember an introductory text on abnormal psychology, which I had read quite some time ago, in which the authors embraced the importance of truth and interdisciplinary knowledge in the study of Abnormal Psychology:

> Increasing one's knowledge means not just storing new facts; there must be a growth of sensitivity, and increase in perceptiveness, that makes it possible to

> reach intimate terms with the subject under study. . . . Because the field includes disorders that are somatogenic, in whole or in part, he [the practitioner of abnormal psychology] must perceive these problems with the eye of a biologist. Because it includes a wide range of psychogenic phenomena, . . . he must [view] . . . things with the eye of an experimental psychologist. . . . Because disordered personal behavior occurs in a social setting . . . he must be able to assume the outlook of a sociologist.[4]

I have seem similar appeals in some areas of economics, particularly in the subfield of economic development, where it is often conveyed that, in studying why countries are less developed, one must consider a wide range of subjects, including the nation's culture, physical natural resources, means of governance, etc. Unfortunately, it is far more often the case, especially in other subfields of economics, where whatever analysis is performed, it is performed squarely within the borders of the La-La Land of economic theory.

Near Worship of Past Heroes

I know one economics professor who is a devout and zealous follower of the great economist Adam Smith, who is best known for his work in 1776 on *The Wealth of Nations*, and who in many respects is the "founding father" or at least one of the "founding fathers," of the field of economics itself.[5] By a zealous follower I mean that the professor's perspective on Adam Smith's writing is characteristic of the perspective that a religious person might have of the writings of an important religious figure. So, for instance, if you were having dinner with him in a group, and the topic of "sharing" came up (as in someone suggesting "shall we order a bottle of wine and just share it?"), the professor might say something like, "Ah yes . . . sharing is a very important thing that people should do . . . as Adam Smith wrote in his book entitled . . ." (and then a book title would follow). It is characteristic of how some people speak who clearly spend great blocks of their time studying scriptures, and who might then randomly affirm a simple point being made in a conversation with a reference and citation to those scriptures.

As a case in point, Adam Smith has often been quoted for his recognition that people generally act in their own self-interest as we have seen quoted in this book as well. Many scholars of the history of economics, however, while they have not denied this about Smith, have devoutly criticized this simplification of Smith's perspective, and have committed themselves to setting the record straight by saying that, in his writing, Smith has also recognized the importance of people caring for others and of people assisting others who need their help and cannot fend for themselves. Unfortunately, in many of these cases, I believe the logic shared by the participants in this debate is as follows: (1) Smith is recognized as a great leader and thinker, so we should follow what he says. (2) Some of his writing appears to be supportive of capitalist greed, and that is what he is most often quoted as supporting. (3) People are therefore inclined to believe that capitalist greed is good, because they know that Smith said it is good. (4) I know that Smith also cared about others and also wrote that greed is not always good. (5) Thus, I can be effective at reducing society's support for greed, and be effective at helping people care more about each other, by revealing to people that Adam Smith was misrepresented, in part, and that Adam Smith also advocated that people should care about one another.

There are two aspects of this bus stop in La-La Land that are absurd; the first should be obvious to everyone, and the second obvious, I would hope, to most people. First, any self-respecting, reasonably intelligent and responsible person should be able to form their own opinions on issues like "the importance of greed" and "importance about caring for one another" independent of what one particular smart guy wrote about it some 240 years ago. Nevertheless, if they do want some input into their decision, then perhaps they should look to leaders of fields like religion and philosophy before feeling they need to take the advice of famous economists on issues pertaining to religion and moral philosophy.[6] The second obvious element of absurdity is that, if you take any prolific writer like Adam Smith, whose body of work is huge and available to the public, you can find him saying *just about anything you want him to say!* This, in itself, makes the quotations and references irrelevant—they are a function of whatever homework had been done to find whatever it is that the quoter wanted to find.

To bring this point home, in case any readers do not believe it, I will offer two quotations from Adam Smith. The first one supports the very theme of this book, that economic professors have failed us. (If the professor I mentioned earlier had been tasked with writing this book, he would have surely used it in the book's introduction.) The second will support a "blasphemous" argument that Adam Smith was a racist, who was not very smart about a lot of topics, and who "had a thing" for Irish women! Both quotations are from The Wealth of Nations, in fact. Here is the first:

> *[T]he teacher . . . His interest is, in this case, set as directly in opposition to his duty as it is possible to set it.* It is the interest of every man to live as much at his ease as he can; and if his emoluments are to be precisely the same, whether he does, or does not perform some very laborious duty, it is certainly his interest, . . . *either to neglect it altogether, or . . . to perform it in as careless and slovenly a manner as that authority will permit. . . . In the university of Oxford, the greater part of the public professors have, for these many years, given up altogether even the pretense of teaching.*[7]

I inserted my own italics in this case; the reference here is to all professors, not economics professors, as economics did not exist yet. In the first italicized sentence Smith says, effectively, that what professors actually do could not be more different from what they are supposed to do. The remaining italicized words simply demonstrate how nasty Smith could be in criticizing professors. I will be happy to claim then, that the title of this book follows directly from the teaching of Adam Smith in its consistency with Smith to harshly criticize professors, if I were delusional in believing that such a claim would have some significance.

Here is the second quotation that would surely never be used by Smith's admirers to demonstrate his assumed brilliant powers of observation and deduction:

> In some parts of Lancashire it is pretended, . . . that . . . oatmeal is . . . heartier . . . than wheaten bread. . . . I am, however, somewhat doubtful. . . . The common people in Scotland, who are fed with oatmeal, are in general neither so strong nor so handsome as the same rank of people in England, who are fed with wheaten bread. They neither work, so well nor look so well; . . . But it seems to be otherwise with potatoes. The chairmen, porters, and coal-heavers in London, and those unfortunate women who live by prostitution, the strongest men and the most beautiful women perhaps in the British dominions, are said to be, the greater part of them, from the lowest rank of people in Ireland, who are generally fed with this root. *No food can afford a more decisive proof of its nourishing quality, or of its being peculiarly suitable to the health of the human constitution.*[8]

The interpretation of this is straightforward: According to Smith, the most buff men, and the most beautiful women, are the Irish who eat potatoes. They are then followed by the "people in England" who are not bad looking and are decent workers, who eat wheat. Then, at the lowest rung, according to Smith, are the "people of Scotland" who are "neither so strong nor so handsome," who eat oatmeal. According to Smith, this represents "decisive proof" that potatoes are more nourishing than wheat, which, in turn, is more nourishing than oatmeal.

My point is simply that, if Adam Smith can, quite definitely, write incredibly stupid things on occasion, then how valuable (for evidence) is his written testimony on any issue? The value placed on anything that he writes, in reality, is the value that the reader places on that writing to begin with, and perhaps the value of the time they spend to find the particular quotation they needed to support their argument. Yet, such arguments have not been heard in La-La Land.

Along similar lines, in a recent economics conference that I attended, a paper was presented that examined the topic of how one historical figure in economic thought had been influenced by an earlier historical figure. The more recent one, whose work was written primarily in the 1930s and 1940s, wrote on topics that were quite obsolete, and such work has never been referred to in modern times. New graduates with PhDs in economics would have likely never heard of either of the two figures discussed in the paper. Yet, for the professor, this topic of how one of the figures had influenced the thoughts and writing of the other was a major research project which served as input to several of his publications and which helped define his unique contribution to the academic economics community. He was also a popular professor—many others admired his work, and encouraged him to continue with it, as it was, to them, so interesting and admirable.

At the early part of his presentation, the professor mentioned that he had been extremely lucky, and he explained why: He had learned that the more recent historical figure, whose work he was studying, had owned copies of books that had been written by the prior historical figure. Those books, the professor discovered, were being auctioned, and he was able to acquire them at, in his mind, a very reasonable price (around the order of $1,000). As he boasted about this in his presentation, some members of the audience expressed both praise and jealousy. He showed that what made these used books so valuable (in his mind) was that the more recent historical figure had written his own notes, scribbled in the margin of many of the pages, displaying what he thought of the ideas being expressed in the book (written by the prior historical figure). In one of the professor's presentation slides, he showed a picture of these handwritten notes in one of the book's pages, which he also presented in an appendix to his paper.

In my view, this research effort offered no useful knowledge with regard to the practice of economics. The research was designed for the tiny audience of scholars of the history of economic thought who are big fans of both of the historical figures studied, and who would then find the work interesting to read as a form of entertaining their fanaticism. At the same time, the research demonstrated the most advanced study available in this minute, idiosyncratic niche of economic scholarship, making the work easily qualifiable for a journal publication.

For me the type of research that I have just described is analogous to my being happy to know something about the song written by Don McLean, in 1971, called "American Pie." Don McLean explained in an interview, shortly after the song was a success, that its lyrics were in reference to the 1959 plane crash that took the lives of famous rock stars Buddy Holly, Ritchie Valens, and "The Big Bopper" Richardson. It is interesting to me because I am a fan of these musical artists, and so I find such trivia to be quite fun to know, as I would suspect many other people might if they are my age or older and if they too remember these artists.

Nevertheless, such idiosyncratic, *intellectual candy* is not intellectually nutritious, nor does it have any relevance, or convey any useful knowledge to the vast majority of other people who are not interested in such trivia. In my view, preoccupation with such intellectual diversions on what one great scholar of economics nearly a century ago might have personally thought about the work of an even-older scholar of economics, is extremely wasteful, and should be embarrassing for the profession.

The seeking of such fun by academic economists is not restricted at all to research in the history thought, as some might have inferred from the above discussion; it is more common, in fact, at the level of obscure, highly advanced mathematics, where many economics professors take great pride in displaying their prowess in certain very specific areas of mathematics. In their fun with math they are often confused regarding the distinction between such expertise in math and expertise that would be valuable for economic science. The next section is also about economics professors just wanting to have fun, with another, entire subfield, devoted almost entirely to having fun, and little else.

Sports Economics

I have long found it both fascinating and bewildering as to why there is an incredibly large subfield of economics called "Sports Economics." It is committed to the economic study of sports, such as how the salaries of star players is determined, how much money sports teams get, what it cost to build a sports stadium, etc.

Now, I just used the term "large subfield," but what does that mean? Here is what it means: First of all, there are a great many economics professors who perform research, teach, and publish in this particular subfield. Also, consider the *Journal of Economic Literature*'s classification of fields in economics, which is the classification system for fields of economics that is most widely used, by far, in the United States. That classification system devotes an entire *major category* of economics to "Z2 Sports Economics." Examples of other *major categories* are: "A2 Economic Education and the Teaching of Economics," "E5 Monetary Policy, Central Banking, and the Supply of Money and Credit," and "N6 Manufacturing and Construction." In addition, there already exists one other major category called "L8 Industry Studies: Services." This particular major category includes, as one of its ten subcategories, the subcategory "L83 Sports, Gambling, Restaurants, Recreation, and Tourism." So, I remain perplexed as to how "Sports Economics" grew to be so large as to climb its way out of this S83 subcategory, and then out of the main industrial category of *all services*, and finally into its very own major category, in parallel with all of "services"!

Likewise, the subfield enjoys its own technical journal (*Journal of Sports Economics*), and there is the North American Association, and International Association, of Sports Economists. There are, as well, numerous classes offered at universities specifically on "Sports Economics," while there are none, for example, on the entire, major, industrial category of services, of which sports it is a tiny part (in terms of expenditure levels). Similarly, in economics conferences there are often many papers presented on sports economics, in entire sessions devoted to sports economics.

According to the recent (2015) statistics by the Bureau of Economic Analysis, all of the industries under the much broader category of "performing arts, spectator sports, museums, and related activities" account for a miniscule 0.56 percent (about half of 1%) of the entire US economy (by value-added the most standard metric for measuring shares of the economy). Of course, one might argue that, if we include the construction of sports stadiums, for instance, it would be higher, while the statistics I was looking at was including it under the category of construction. Nevertheless, given the fact that the larger category I just mentioned also includes the "performing arts"—such as theater and movie production and theaters, along with museums, etc., it is fair to conclude that the sports industry is truly a miniscule sector of the entire economy. (Also think, for example, about how much people pay for their houses, their food, their fuel, their taxes that in turn pays for the national defense, public schools, etc., and compare all those expenses to how much people pay to watch sporting events, for which half of 1% sounds about right!)

As an example of the attention that Sports Economics receives among economics professors, consider one conference that I recently attended (in 2016), which is the second largest economics conference in the United States each year—the annual meetings of the Western Economic Association International. Each session of the conference typically lasted for one hour and 45 minutes, and typically involved the presentation of between three and five papers. Of the 328 sessions at the conference, as many as 14 sessions (4.3% of the conference) were devoted to Sports Economics with the following session numbers and titles:

35. Grad Paper Session {on only sports-related papers by graduate students}
53. Economics of Baseball
70. Economics of Soccer I
91. Economics of Soccer II
111. Economics of Basketball
131. Economics of the Individual {with papers on sports stars only}
148. Economics of Football
173. Economics of the NCAA
190. Sports Economics: The Individual

211. Competitive Balance {in professional sports}
230. Sports Economics I
247. Sports Economics II
267. Sports Economics: Revenue and League Structure
284. Sports Economics: Economic Impact

In comparison, there were less than half as many sessions on food and agriculture (which would include topics such as food and its distribution, agricultural production, fisheries, forestry, cotton and wool for clothing, coffee and tea, tobacco, etc.).

What could possibly warrant the huge, highly disproportionate, attention that sports economics receives within academic economics? Besides sports being a tiny part of the economy, is there any particularly *strong policy reason* for the attention it receives, as would be the case, for instance, with health economics or international trade studies, which, by the way, involve much larger shares of the economy in any case? Would the focused study of this tiny sector of the economy save more lives (as the study of health economics), or create more employment (as the study of labor economics), or help prevent the next financial crisis (as the study of financial regulation), or raise and address fundamental questions about how economics should be studied and taught (as the study of economic education), etc.? Surely not.

There is *only one reason* for why sports economics is such a huge field, which should be extremely obvious, but I will announce it here anyway: Many academic economists are particularly interested in the subject of sports, because—you guessed it—*they like sports!* They like to think about sports, to read about which teams have made more money, to find out how much their favorite players are being paid, etc. To my surprise, I learned that this field also includes discussions about *game strategies* that have essentially nothing to do with economic principles. Sports Economics is big only because it is fun for the people who study it—what a surprise!

To verify this "theory" to my own satisfaction, I attended the first session of the conference on Sports Economics—#35. The Grad Paper Session, at that 2016 Western Economics Association conference. The first paper presented was apparently on a graduate student's favorite topic in baseball—the strategies that pitchers use in throwing "borderline pitches," in or out of the strike zone, and the "effect of a borderline pitch being called a strike." Figure 8.1 shows pictures that I took of the presentation. The room was populated by sports fans who had a keen interest, and incredibly advanced knowledge, in pitching strategies in major league baseball, and an impressive knowledge of the baseball statistics associated with particular teams and players. (Unfortunately for me, with my background being only in economics, and some public policy and natural science, I was horribly unqualified to enter into any of their discussions!)

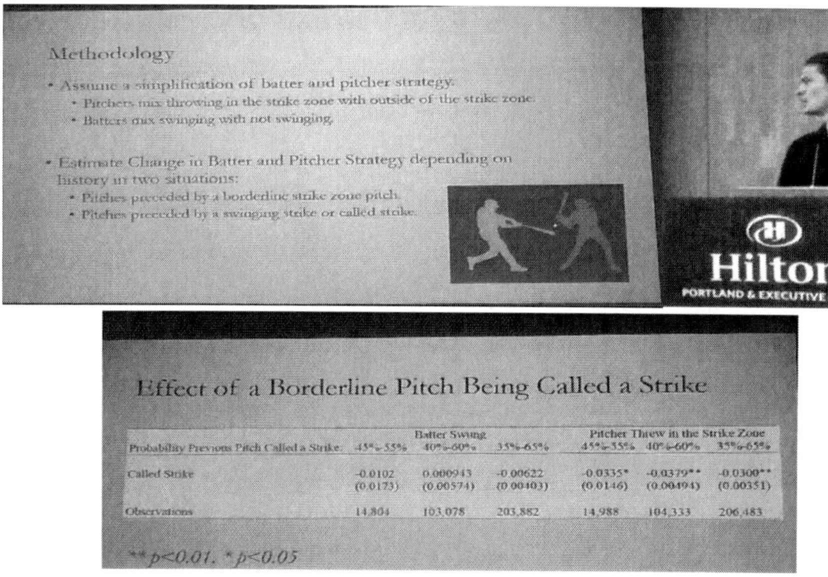

Figure 8.1 Conference Presentation of an Economics Paper on Pitching Strategy in Baseball. Created by the author.

If one were to video-record these presentations, and edit out the occasion mention of an economics term like "Nash equilibrium" or "regression coefficient," which entered into no more than 5 percent of the conversation, the result would be quite revealing. One would see essentially no difference between the presentations in these sessions and televised SportsChannel commentaries on sports topics (like pitching) that a group of friends might see and discuss at a party in someone's family room. The only things missing from the room where the economics session was held would be the sofas, chips, and beer.

Along these lines, if the purpose of economic discourse is to have fun, then this begs the question of why there is not a larger subfield of economics called "Rock and Roll Economics," or for that matter, "Swim-Suit Modeling Economics." Or, going the extra mile, why not "Sex, Drugs, and Rock and Roll Economics"? Actually, there is, in fact, an "American Association of Wine Economics," with their own conferences and journal, and likewise the "Beeronomics Society" that does not appear to have a journal or conferences—just a website. However, the "wine and beer economists" appear, for the most part, to be legitimately studying their own respective products and industries, without claiming to be so important as to have their own economics classes or their own major category of economic literature.

Economics Professors Setting the Example—Often a Bad One

Professors in any field, in certain respects, teach two different things (though these things are interrelated): (1) the technical knowledge of the field, and (2) the culture of the field, which includes an understanding of what is important to the people who choose the field as a profession. With regard to the cultural aspects of the field, one of these aspects—of the many there are—is the extent to which enjoying one's work, while performing the work, influences *how* one performs their work. Consider two extremes in this regard: (1) a musical composer and (2) an emergency room physician. Since the musical composer is creating something that is being designed for people's enjoyment, it is natural and quite reasonable to expect musical composures to seek enjoyment themselves as they are performing their work, the same way that a cook may taste-test the sauce that they are preparing for a dish. Indeed, it would be quite strange even to think of a musical composure who was not enjoying what they were composing as they were composing it, since that enjoyment itself is assisting in the feedback needed to produce the desired product.

Now consider the other extreme—the emergency room physician. Of course, the emergency room physician could be happy in the job they perform, primarily in the sense of accomplishment whenever they are able to save lives, and perhaps even when they are not so successful but still feel that they were able to offer the patient the best care they could possibly give them. At the same time, no one would expect an emergency room physician to enjoy the work itself as they were performing it except as it might relate to any specific accomplishment as the work was progressing (such as stopping a patient's bleeding). Surely, whatever options that an emergency physician might face in performing their work, their choice of which option to take must be completely dependent on whatever maximizes the odds of success from a purely scientific perspective, and not dependent on what option the physician would enjoy doing more. Indeed, the very idea of the doctor choosing options for the sake of enjoyment itself, independent of what is medically best for the patient, in the case of a medical emergency, is horrific and would easy warrant the termination of the doctor from their position.

Quite simply, part of a profession's culture involves the expectation regarding how much fun one is expected to have in the choices they make as they are performing their work. In the field of economics, in particular, one might ask, how much fun should I have in deciding what research topics I should pursue, what models I should develop and how I should develop them, what famous economists from the past should I study and quote in my research, etc.? Overall, as I have indicated in the section above, and will indicate in another section below (on scapegoatism and dehumanization), many economics professors find a great deal of fun in the choices they make in the work that they perform. They convey, either directly or indirectly, the importance of "fun in economics" to their students, helping to preserve, from generation to generation, a culture of having fun in academic economics.

I remember when I was about to receive my doctorate in economics, one of my advisers asked me what I intended to do after graduating, and at that time I answered that I would like to teach. He smiled and joking replied, "It sure beats working!" I laughed—recognizing it was only a joke—but it does reflect that, within academic economics, there is a strong sense that economics professors have chosen an easy and enjoyable way of life.

In my view, the greatest constraint in all of this is not in convincing others that economics professors place too much weight on personally having fun, given the incredible responsibility that they have in society regarding issues that greatly affect people's lives. I believe most people who know anything about economics and how it is taught in the universities would already agree with this. One significant problem, however, is addressing how anything could be done about it. To me, the larger problem, however, is in getting anyone *even to think about it*. It is just too simple a problem, and too obvious to most people, to attract their interest, and so it is dismissed from any discussion on this basis of it being uninteresting. Getting people to attend to the problem, especially within the academic economics community, is an uphill battle, made worse by the fact that it is "not fun to hear" when "having fun" often governs people's choices of what to study and what to discuss.

DOUBLE BLINDNESS ABOUT DOUBLE BLINDNESS

In July 2011, the Executive Committee of the American Economic Association (AEA) changed its policy for selecting papers for publication in the AEA's journals, from a "double blind" review process to a "single blind" process. That is, before this change, paper authors would not know who their reviewers are, and the reviewers would not know who the paper authors were (hence a "double-blind" process). After the change, paper authors would continue to be unaware of who the reviewers are, but the reviewers would be explicitly told who the paper authors were. The executive committee expressed and published a rationale for this change as follows: "The Executive Committee maintained that easy access to search engines increasingly limited the effectiveness of the double-blind process in maintaining anonymity."[9] Now what does this mean? It can only mean one thing, which is incredibly obvious, even though it is stated in vaguer terms in the above quotation: The executive committee has reasoned that, even though it might be against their policy for reviewers to know who the paper authors are, those reviewers are still physically capable of defying and undermining that policy by spending their own extra time to utilize search engines in order to find out who the authors are. Therefore, according to the executive committee's reasoning, since there is no physical barrier to prevent reviewers from undermining and violating the policy if they chose to do so, the only recourse is for the executive committee to remove that policy, regardless of its originally intended benefits.

I find there to be an astounding logical flaw in this policy change. Since the executive committee appears to be oblivious to this logical flaw, and so, apparently are all groups of paper authors, in the sense that no concerns have been raised about it from their perspective (as far as know), I have titled this section "Double Blindness about Double Blindness."

As discussed in previous chapters, having one's paper selected in one of the "top journals" of the AEA, like *American Economic Review*, can be an extremely important contribution to the advancement of an academic economist's career. Indeed, in many cases, depending on the circumstances, it might generally "make or break" someone's career, especially at critical times when assistant professors are "up for tenure." It is also commonly known, and actually measured quite extensively and published by the executive committee itself, that the selection of papers to these journals is extremely competitive. In 2011–2013, for example 1,645; 1,648; and 1,714; papers were submitted (respectively by year), and 122, 130, and 121, papers were accepted,[10] amounting to acceptance rates of 7.4, 7.9, and 7.1 percent, respectively. In other words, if you submit a paper, your chance of the paper being rejected is about 92–93 percent. These odds, of course, make the publication a highly valued "prize" for many economists' career, analogous to winning the lottery.

It follows from this, though it appears to be less obvious within the profession, that reviewers who determine "which papers shall live, and which papers shall die," have enormous power and control over people's careers—perhaps not quite as influential as determining "which people's *careers* shall live, and which shall die," but close to it, in many cases. More generally, they wield great power, as well, over entire research directions in the field of economics itself. If, for example, a paper on a relatively unique topic, or on a unique approach to a topic, is published, it might lead to significant revisions in the way economics is studied in that particular subject area.

What is less known to many economists is the level of pride and pomp that ensues among the executive committee members (including the journal editors) when the topic of publications in their journals is raised. I noticed this while attending one of the annual business meetings of the AEA's executive committee, which took place in the early evening on January 4, 2014, at the AEA meetings (and I have attended others as well). These meetings typically convene after a short break following the AEA presidential address at the conference, in the same room—a room with the capacity to seat thousands, and it indeed seated thousands during the presidential address. However, at the business meeting the enormous room was almost completely empty, with only about twenty people in attendance; I was surely one of the only individuals in attendance who was not affiliated with the executive committee as a member, former member, or volunteer. Given the number of free and luxurious receptions at the conference taking place at the same time, it was understandable that the opportunity costs were too high for nearly all of the conference attendees to attend the AEA's business meeting, even though it was explicitly billed as being open to everyone in the conference. (Actually, because the doors to the room were locked from the main hallway, and open only in a more remote side hallway, the policy of the meeting being "open to the public" may have not been fully realized.)

During the meeting in 2014, AEA president Goldin asked the audience to give a round of applause, and a "standing ovation" (in her precise words) for the editors of the AEA journals. Actually, she asked this twice—once for each of two editors—and so it was done twice. With much laughter and cheer, and the loudest clapping that one could imagine from an audience of only twenty people, with the two standing ovations resounded in the huge room. Not a single observation was offered at the meeting about anything the editors had done in particular to warrant the request by the president for these standing ovations—all that was said to explain them was the simple assertion by the president that the editors had done an "excellent job."

Getting back to the topic of the AEA removing the double-blind review process, allow me to propose a simple thought experiment: Suppose we were to go back to an earlier time, back before the days of search engines that could easily identify anonymous authors, and back when AEA journal referees were adhering to the rules of a double-blind review process. The behavior of the referees at that time was rooted in a supposed commitment to the objective measurement of scientific merit and to a system of review that was designed to be as fair as possible. Suppose further that, in these days of yore, a referee were given a paper to review and were personally curious about who the author is, but had no way of finding that out. Now suppose that another individual who was not the author or the referee happened to know who the author of that paper was and who that referee was. This might be possible through any number of scenarios one could imagine, such as that individual simply being a friend of both the referee and the author, and knows this information through personal conversations with each. Finally, for this thought experiment, suppose the individual who had this inside information—let us call this person the "informant"— approached the referee and told them, "I know for certain who the author is of the paper you are reviewing. Would you like me to tell you who it is?"

By all widely recognized and all widely accepted standards of professional ethics, any reasonable person would expect the referee under these circumstances to reject the informant's offer. We would expect that referee to say, "I do not want to be given this information—please keep it to yourself—because I have agreed to referee the paper on the basis of a double-blind process." In short, it would be "unethical"—plain and simple— for the referee to receive that information from the informant, if the referee had the ability to avoid receiving it, such as simply telling the informant "no thank you".

There are, of course, many principles that referees for technical journals are required to follow, even if they can easily "get away with" violating them. They are required, for example, to recuse themselves if there is a significant conflict of interest in their review of a paper. Likewise, they are not supposed to exercise any personal or political prejudice toward specific topic areas of a paper, which would be peripheral to their assessment of the paper's scientific merit, etc. In short, they are already asked, and are already ethically bound, to adhere to a wide range of principles in their peer review of a paper, regardless of the fact that they can get away with violating those principles if they chose to do so. It is assumed that they will not violate those principles, because it is assumed that they already possess professional integrity—end of story.

Of course, if the executive committee or any other individuals or groups wanted to dispute this argument by claiming that this assumption about other principles is false—that in fact, referees are free to discriminate or play favorites, etc.—then that might indeed counter this entire essay, and have the great benefit of allowing us all to know more valuable information than this discussion here could possibly provide. Nevertheless, for the sake of argument, at least, let us make the assumption (however heroic some might think it to be) that referees do indeed recognize an obligation to exercise sound, objective judgment in their selection decisions. That is, let us assume that they do not make selections on the basis of cronyism or other unethical factors, regardless of the fact that they may be "able to get away with it."

Now let us revisit the logic (or absence thereof) of the executive committee's decision to eliminate double-blind review, and even announce to referees who the authors of papers are. The expressed rationale was essentially this: Gee-whiz, why keep the author's name a secret when referees can just Google the paper's title, or something like that, especially if it were a previously presented conference paper, and find out anyway? By *this same logic*, according to the executive committee, there would be nothing wrong with the referee in the thought experiment that I just proposed earlier to say to the informant, "Sure, I'm curious about who the author is—please tell me." In this case the information was even easier for the referee to acquire, without needing to spend any time using a search engine.

If there were an ethical, fairness principle associated with the double-blind review, and surely there was since otherwise it would have never existed to begin with, then there is no reason that referees cannot be asked, and required, to abide by it, regardless of the fact that they can easily *get away with* not abiding by it. As mentioned, there are already other principles that they must still abide by, even though they can get away with violating them as well, so why should this one be different? Why not simply maintain the double-blind process, since there is an ethical reason to maintain it, and simply tell reviewers, "No, you cannot use search engines or make any effort whatsoever (using any other resources) to learn who the anonymous authors are." How is this any different from, "No, you cannot approve papers for publications on the basis of the authors being your friends, while rejecting papers by people who you personally do not like."? How simple is it to understand that the guidelines for the ethical behavior of referees are *not* based on *what people can get away with and what they cannot, but simply on doing the right thing?*

The members of AEA's executive committee are quite proud of their own individual achievements in areas of economic theory, and I am not saying that they should not be. But, while they are in the business of establishing rules that essentially make or break the careers of many thousands of economists, and which steer economic discourse itself into various directions, perhaps their pride has distracted them from making the most responsible and mature decisions that they should have make in managing the peer review of proposed journal articles.

As already discussed in chapter 4, papers submitted to the AER can be rejected "without review." This absolute absurdity, giving a free license to pure favoritism, cronyism, elitism, and discrimination, reflects how far the AEA's peer review system has fallen from basic standards of fairness and scientific integrity, revealing its true colors. The leaders of the AEA must wake up to fix this, reinstitute double-blind review, and implement the requirement that their referees abide by basic ethical standards. If they cannot do this, because either they simply do not want to do it or are even amused at the prospect of it, then at least those institutions that fund the AEA and its members should step up to the plate. Those other institutions that can influence the AEA should do something about this, for the sake of better economics and a better economics profession, governed by fairness as opposed to cronyism.

THE PROMOTION OF SCAPEGOATISM AND DEHUMANIZATION BY MANY ACADEMIC ECONOMISTS

Defining Scapegoatism/Dehumanization

There is only one thing that any of us should like about "scapegoatism," which is the fact that it is a real word that can then be used legitimately in our discussions. Dictionary.com defines it as "the act or practice of assigning blame or failure to another, as to deflect attention or responsibility away from oneself."[11] In addition, the *Collins English Dictionary* defines it as "the practice of scapegoating or blaming a scapegoat."[12] Of course, this begs the question of what a "scapegoat" is, which the *Collins English Dictionary* defines as "a person made to bear the blame for others."[13] There is also a biblical reference which is clearly where the word originates: From the Old Testament, it is a goat used in the Jewish ritual of Yom Kippur (Leviticus 16:22), which "was symbolically laden with the sins of the Israelites and sent into the wilderness to be destroyed."[14] At a personal level I find it ironic that the word "scapegoat," and much of the concept itself, is traceable to the most important holiday in the Jewish religion—the irony being that, in the history of the world, Jews, more than any other group of people, have been scapegoats, especially for the economic problems encountered by empires and nations.

Note that the definition of scapegoatism refers only to the concept of blame, but in the vast majority of cases of scapegoatism there is something else involved which is much stronger, and much worse, than "blame"—namely *dehumanization*. Dehumanization is the psychological process of demonizing the enemy, making them seem less than human and hence not worthy of humane treatment.[15] Although scapegoatism and dehumanization appear to occur simultaneously, more often than not, I have not been able to identify a single word that captures the simultaneity of both concepts, so I will just refer to combined concept as "scapegoatism/dehumanization."

Scapegoatism/Dehumanization by Economics Professors

In 2008, I attended the annual meetings of the Southern Economic Association which in that year was held in Washington, DC. In the very first session I attended, a professor began his talk with a joke, which went like this: Upon traveling to Washington for the conference, he read some of the local news which said that, in the face of the cold weather the city was having, the heating systems in government buildings were inadequate. The professor said that the article he read therefore recommended the replacement of the old heating systems in government buildings by new heating systems. Then, in a serious tone for the shock jock effect that it would have for the audience, the professor said that he "agreed with half of the article." That is, he said that he agreed with the idea of removing the existing heaters in government buildings, and he then said, in an emphatic tone, that he disagreed, however, that any new heating systems should be installed in their place. (His joke was implying, in other words, that he would like to see the federal employees freeze in the cold.) He then paused as if to wait for laughter from the audience from his joke, though none arrived. Perhaps he had not considered that, by the Southern Economic Association's conference taking place in Washington, DC, that year, many of the people in the audience would be economists who are federal employees, who work in heated government buildings, and who might not have found his joke to be as amusing as he did.

It was rather evident that the professor had been accustomed to a very different audience, where any random forms of government-worker-bashing would be welcomed and appreciated. This also begs the question of whether the audience to which he was more accustomed to speaking are the students of his classes, and further begs the question of what he has been teaching his students from his leadership position as their professor.

Although it does not appear in the formal literature very often, I believe that scapegoatism/dehumanization is very relevant as a motivating factor that lies underneath how many economists approach public policy issues, and how they reach their analytical conclusions. This is because scapegoatism/dehumanization resides within the personal, and very private, belief system that many economists hold, which in my view substantially influences much of economic discourse, especially in the public policy arena.

An Illustration of How Critical Discourse Factors in to Economic Discourse Overall

Figure 8.2 presents an illustration of economic discourse in a broad, and admittedly abstract, perspective, though a perspective that I hope will help illustrate points that I intend to make shortly. The first space in the figure is what might be considered standard discourse in the sense of existing primarily in textbooks, standardized lectures, and well-circulated technical journals. This discourse, and the ideas covered in them are separated into well-known subfields, such as economic development, tax policy, industrial organization, international trade, etc. I illustrate these subfields as overlapping gray clouds in the diagram.

The next space is shown by dark clouds, representing the discourse that, essentially, *criticizes* the standard discourse. I have shown them as dark clouds only in the sense of their being critical in nature, though in many respects they may be seen as the brightest clouds, addressing some very important limitations and often legitimate concerns about the standard literature. Let us use the simple term "critical literature" to mean the body of literature that tends to criticize the standard literature.

As I have shown in the diagram, the critical literature tends to take on two general forms: (1) questioning the motivations and assumptions underlying the standard literature, and (2) questioning the scientific validity of the findings reported in the standard literature. An example of the former would be questioning a "multiplier model" in which any increase in government spending would lead to economic growth, under questionable assumptions that

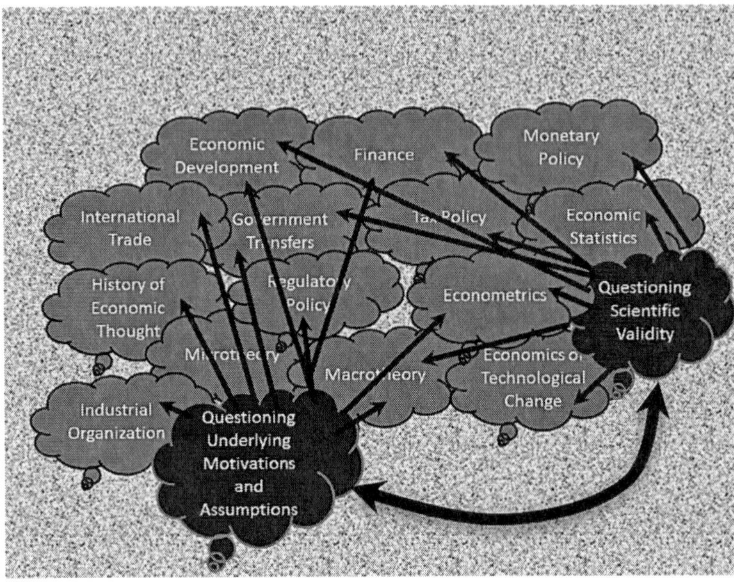

Figure 8.2 A Perspective on the "Space" of Economic Discourse: The Important Role Played by the "Dark Clouds." Created by the author.

ruled out the possibility that government expenditures may simply replace (or "crowd out" in economic jargon) private expenditures, thereby having no net effect on economic growth. An example of the latter might be a critique that the data which the study used were unreliable, or that the econometric methods employed to obtain the results were flawed. Yet, there can easily be overlap between these two types of criticisms under a variety of scenarios.

Figure 8.3 displays another perspective on the spaces occupied by (1) Literature on Economic Models and Related Discourse, at one end of the spectrum, and (2) Literature on the State of the Economy and How to Improve It, on the other. In between the two ends there is generally a mixture of both. Also playing an essential role in this discourse is the unique area occupied by critiques of the existing literature and related critiques on the state of the economy.

The figure populates these spaces with three kinds of economists:

1. Those who focus on methodology, especially from an academic and theoretical perspective,
2. Those who focus on the history of economic thought, and
3. Those who tend to apply generally accepted methods, in studying economic models, or in assessing the state of the economy (or in elements of both).

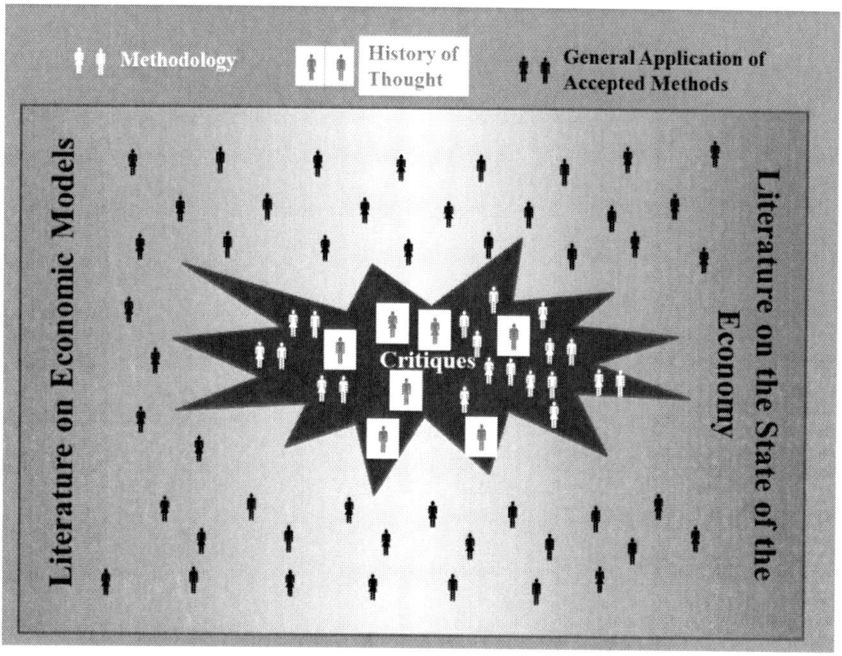

Figure 8.3 Illustration of the Dichotomy between Literature on Economic Models and Literature on the State of the Economy. Created by the author.

As shown, the critical area is populated primarily by the first two types of economists (methodologists and historians of economic thought), while all other areas are populated by the third type (practitioners of standard economic models). As I will argue shortly, it is within the important area of criticism that, unfortunately, scapegoatism/dehumanization can reside to a substantial degree.

Economic Scapegoatism/Dehumanization in a Historical Perspective

Let me now discuss scapegoatism/dehumanization in economic thought from a bit of a historical perspective, especially as it relates to the topic of the state of a nation's economy. Figure 8.4 illustrates four major examples from the writings of Karl Marx, Adolf Hitler, the Ku Klux Klan, and Joseph McCarthy. Of the four examples, Karl Marx may be said to be the only true scholar, and for this and other reasons he should not be placed in the same figure as the other three protagonists (or groups of protagonists) of scapegoatism/dehumanization. Nevertheless, I included an excerpt from the Communist Manifesto here, coauthored by Marx, to illustrate that the communist revolutions

Karl Marx, Communist Manifesto: "The **bourgeoisie** ...has drowned the most heavenly ecstasies of ... chivalrous enthusiasm, ... it has substituted **naked, shameless, direct, brutal exploitation."**

Adolf Hitler, Mein Kampf: "Look at the **ravages** from which our people are suffering daily as a result of being contaminated with **Jewish blood**."

Ku Klux Klan, Pamphlet in 1920: "The **supremacy of the White Race** must be maintained, or be overwhelmed by the rising tide of **color**." (Source: "Ideals of the Ku Klux Klan," Jackson Sun, October 1960, Accessed May 7, 2017, http://tinyurl.com/l9zyqaa)

Joseph McCarthy, (speech in 1950, West Virginia): "The reason why we find ourselves in a position of **impotency** is ... because of the **traitorous actions** of ... **Communists.**" (Source: "History Matters" Accessed May 6. 2017, http://tinyurl.com/goemde4.)

Figure 8.4 Examples of Historical Scapegoatism/Dehumanization in Criticisms of the State of a Nation's Economy. Created by the author. Marx: Wikimedia Commons, Accessed May 6, 2017, http://tinyurl.com/kbf7lab; Hitler: Wikimedia Commons, Accessed May 6, 2017, http://tinyurl.com/muhhbcz (Attribution: Bundesarchiv, Bild 146-1990-048-29A / CC-BY-SA 3.0); Ku Klux Klan: Wikimedia Commons, Accessed May 6, 2017, http://tinyurl.com/kutun8j; McCarthy: Wikimedia Commons, Accessed May 6, 2017, http://tinyurl.com/mbpcasj.

were not waged on the basis of scholarly discourse. Rather, there was a definite "let's get the those bad guys" mentality that underlay the support for those revolutions—the scapegoatism/dehumanization of the bourgeoisie was certainly a significant part of that revolutionary mentality, and Marx played a hand in promoting that mentality with statements like the one shown. Just to clarify, none of the protagonists shown in the figure are economics professors, so the figure in itself does not present a criticism of academic economics. It simply demonstrates the nature of what scapegoatism/dehumanization is so that we can understand it more clearly.

Modern Day Scapegoatism/Dehumanization in Academic Economics

As a first example of modern-day scapegoatism/dehumanization, Economics Professor Thomas DiLorenzo has a recent book entitled, *Organized Crime:*

The Unvarnished Truth about Government.[16] By its title, alone, the book accuses government workers of being criminals. Let us just consider a few excerpts from the book (with my own emphasis shown in italics):

1. "Government enterprises are *notorious for being lazy, slothful, inefficient, and corrupt*. The very notion that they should be in charge of business decision making . . . is *a farce that is destroying capitalism* in America."[17]
2. "[G]overnment bureaucrats, not individuals and their doctors, inevitably determine who will get medical treatment and who will not. . . . They assume totalitarian control over the industry, in other words."[18]
3. "*[L]owly government bureaucrats* became powerful economic dictators."[19]
4. "Politicians will only take the advice of . . . advisors if the advice promises to increase the state's power, wealth, and influence even if the politicians know that the advice is bad for the rest of society."[20]

In his book DiLorenzo glorifies the famous economist, Ludwig von Mises. Not surprisingly, then, the institute that is named after the famous professor (the Ludwig Von Mises Institute) glorifies DiLorenzo's book, to the point of posting his book on their website, in its entirety, for the public to freely download.

On the Ludwig von Mises Institute's website, I found an interesting historical account of Professor von Mises' life, but that account seemed to be missing something about von Mises that I found in Wikipedia. What was missing in both the institute's account and in everything said about von Mises in DiLorenzo's book was that, like Albert Einstein, early in his career, von Mises had also been a "lowly government bureaucrat" (using DiLorenzo's terminology—not mine, as I do not consider myself, or my coworkers, to be lowly). In addition, for many years thereafter von Mises served as a high ranking adviser to supposedly, as DiLorenzo would put it, "lazy, slothful, inefficient, and corrupt" "government enterprises."

I wonder how von Mises' serving as a government adviser matches up against the last quotation shown above by DiLorenzo, which says that the only advice government officials take is to increase government. It must mean that von Mises' advice was not taken, or that his advice was to increase the state's power—neither of which seems very likely, given von Mises' expressed principles. Although I am not a historian, and do not know much at all about von Mises, it just seems to me that someone who served himself as a government employee, and then as a chief government adviser may not share DiLorenzo's dehumanizing distain toward government employees that DiLorenzo so transparently displays in his book. Similarly, while I realize that von Mises was a libertarian and was most definitely critical of government bureaucracies, as are many government employees themselves, I would not expect a distinguished scholar of von Mises' caliber to condone the level of hateful dehumanization toward government workers that is so blatantly promoted by an institution that named itself after him. It would indeed be hypocritical of von Mises to harbor such hateful views of people whom he advised in the height of his career, when the same kind of hateful dehumanization was what forced his own exodus, as a Jew, from Europe to the United States, in order to escape the Nazism that was overrunning Europe at that time.

I noticed that DiLorenzo teaches economics at Loyola University of Maryland, which in my view has a very admirable "vision statement." The first sentence of that vision statement contains the words: "The education of men and women of compassion . . . represents the enduring aspiration of Loyola University." I would have thought, though, that the university's expressed commitment to compassion might apply to all groups of individuals in our society, even those who one of their professors publicly describes as "*notorious . . . and corrupt.*"

Along similar lines, Economics Professor Daniel Klein, at George Mason University, wrote an article entitled, "The People's Romance: Why People Love Government (as Much as They Do)," in *The Independent Review*, in 2005. The article questions why people "love" the government while the article simultaneously presents a dual attack on the both the government, and on a hypothetical group of people outside the government whom Klein sees as allegedly "loving" the government. The article presents a conspiracy theory in which government officials are said to capture people's hearts and minds through what he calls TPR—"the people's romance." As an example of what the article contains, we see the following (with my own emphasis in italics):

> Why are *government officials* and enthusiasts often *hostile* to leading corporations such as Microsoft, McDonald's, Wal-Mart, and *Martha Stewart*? Why are they often *hostile* to other bases for independent private cultural power such as *private builders, private schools,* and *talk radio*? Part of the answer may be that they are *jealous* in *guarding their role as medium and focal point in TPR*. Why are they *hostile* to . . . *private communities,* private shopping malls, *the private automobile*. . . . Because these practices are means of withdrawing from TPR.[21]

The above quotation is a perfect example of scapegoatism/dehumanization that is on par with the kinds of ideas expressed in Figure 8.4 above. Having been a federal employee myself for twenty-six years at seven different agencies, and having known and worked with federal employees since the Carter administration, I am quite amazed at how Professor Klein may have reached his conclusions. I have gone to lunch over the years with federal colleagues who insisted on eating at McDonalds, as that was their preference. Similarly, I remember many high-ranking officials over the years who demanded their office use Microsoft software when alternatives existed, and, needless to say, I have never heard federal employees ever say negative things about Martha Stewart! Klein probably confused the remark about Microsoft with an effort at one time by the Federal Trade Commission to address Microsoft's monopoly power, the rationale for which is based on standard principles of economics, and federal law, that Klein is supposed to be teaching in his economics classes. Likewise, perhaps he noticed some federal agency, like the Food Safety and Inspection Service, keeping an eye on McDonalds to ensure food safety standards, or a law suit against them for some reason—who knows? I also wonder if Klein realized that the vast majority of government buildings are built by private contractors that the government hires, rather than by government employees, and this is only because the government prefers to use private contractors for this purpose. Of course, I could go on and on in describing the absurdity of his remarks about how government workers hate all that is good in life, but that would surely be absurd as well. The best punchline, however, is the completely delusional conspiracy theory that he is espousing, which is that government workers possess such distain for all good things in life because those good things will cause the public to *love* them less. I have found no better proof that academic economists are capable of writing absolutely anything, regardless of how absurd it may be, and getting it published.

Of all the thousands of economics professors in the United States, surely it should not be surprising to find some at the extreme end of the bell curve when it comes to expressing juvenile discrimination of others, as I have found here, and by no means am I implying that most economics professors could harbor or espouse similar beliefs. Let us bear in mind, nevertheless, that Professor Klein is not a standup comedian, nor a patient in a psychiatric facility (in spite of the potential he may have for either), but is a full professor at George Mason University, where he also serves (at this writing) as the "JIN Chair" of the Mercatus Center at George Mason University. He is also the chief editor of the online journal *Econ Journal Watch*, and the list of his leadership credentials in the academic economics community goes on and on. Furthermore, the above quotation of his text was not found in an unprepared speech he made to a group of friends at lunch gathering, but part of a published journal article, supposedly peer reviewed and deemed to have been publishable, given its *scientific merit*, by the journal's editors and advisory board. Looking at the journal's website, one finds that *The Independent Review* is an arm of the libertarian organization *The Independent Institute*. The journal itself provides no mission statement, just many testimonials from some famous economists.

In a similar article of his, Klein asks the question, "If Government is So Villainous, How Come Officials Don't Seem Like Villains?"[22] The basic answer is twofold: first, according to Klein, government officials are simply sneaky enough to have their villainous behavior go undetected, and second, the victimized public is gullible enough to fall for it. The character of his argument is quite disturbingly similar to the scapegoatism/dehumanization that characterized the changes experienced in German society during the 1930s. Indeed, since George Mason University is in the Washington, DC, area, I wonder how many of Klein's students are the sons and daughters of federal employees who work in the area. I find it rather strange that some of his students may be receiving his lectures that are espousing how their parents are "villains."

Fortunately, I am happy to reiterate that the kind of explicit scapegoatism/dehumanization espoused by professors DiLorenzo and Klein, as described above, is certainly not common among economics professors. The vast majority of economics professors have the sensibility and decency to produce work that is devoid of scapegoatism/dehumanization. And, one can easily find scapegoatism/dehumanization in certain circles of economists outside of academia, especially at institutions that are on the extreme left or right. Needless to say, however, the presence of scapegoatism/dehumanization in circles outside of academia does not in any way excuse its existence in academia, which is often believed to uphold the higher ground on such topics.

The Mentality of Scapegoatism and Its Influence Over the Profession

Unfortunately, while the vast majority of economics professors do not explicitly espouse scapegoatism/dehumanization I am concerned that a large fraction of them—especially those who critique standard methods—are motivated by a mentality that embodies some degree of scapegoatism/dehumanization. Let us step back from scapegoatism/humanization for the moment to ask a broader question, which is: *What Motivates Economists to Write Criticisms of the State of a Nation's Economy, or of Work by Others to Analyze the Economy?* I believe there are four general, separate answers to this question:

1. A strong interest in, and commitment to, *understanding methodologies* and proposing how they may be improved (and publishing in this area).
2. Interest and background in the history of economic thought and how it may apply in various contexts (and publishing).
3. A deep-rooted belief that our economic problems are caused by a certain group of people, and so removing or disempowering that group would solve the problem—what we might call the "Scapegoatism/Dehumanization Solution."
4. Tapping in to a populist sentiment, that is, producing work that will be read and popularized by the general public.

Now let me revisit the perspective that I displayed before on the continuum of economic literature on economic models and on the state of the economy, shown again in Figure 8.5. Within this space of discourse lies the critical literature, which I have described as being populated by work on methodology and work on the history of thought. We may now ask the question: How are criticisms of the literature generated with regard to the motivations underlying them? How many of the contributors are motivated most by a desire to share an understanding of methodology or an understanding of the history of thought? And, how many of the contributors are motivated primarily, not by either of these, but by the third motivation I describe as a deep-rooted belief that our economic problems are caused by a group of bad people, whose recognition and power should be diminished, as the one simple solution to these problems.

It may well be the case that the contributors to critical economic thought are motivated more by scapegoatism/dehumanization than by anything else. The reason you do not see more scapegoatism/dehumanization written directly into the literature is a reason that I expect most, if not all, of us already understand: Scapegoatism/dehumanization simply does not look good for

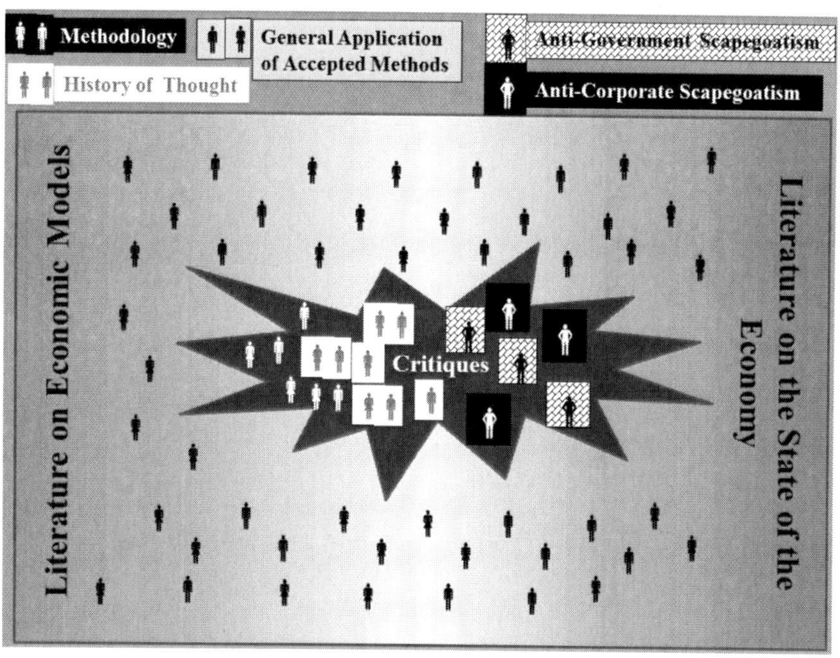

Figure 8.5 Where Do Economists Go to Work, Based on Motivation? Scapegoatism/Dehumanization plays a major role in populating the group of economists who criticize economic literature and especially the state of the economy. Created by the author.

most scholarly audiences, so it is usually not directly displayed. Nevertheless, we can observe how widespread the motivation for it is, based on the personal conversations that often exist within the profession. When one attends a conference event, for example, organized by academic economists affiliated with organizations like the Ayn Rand Institute and the Ludwig Von Mises Institute, the conversations one hears implying scapegoatism/dehumanization often fills the room. I am certain that most of the people who have ventured into these rooms, either deliberately or by accident, would confirm this.

One may then ask why there is an attraction to scapegoatism/dehumanization in critical economic discourse. The most basic answer is that it exists in academic economics for the same reasons that scapegoatism/dehumanization has always existed in human society:

a. It conveniently provides simple explanations and simple solutions to otherwise highly complex problems, without the need to trouble ourselves with data or analysis (or struggling to find *real* solutions).
b. It provides an excuse for blame and hatred among those who unfortunately feel a disturbed, psychological need to harbor and share such feelings.
c. By definition, it absolves the accuser (and any group to which the accuser belongs) of any guilt or responsibility for any existing problems—the "scapegoat" has absorbed all of humanity's sins.
d. It provides a social function, where proponents of scapegoatism/dehumanization may belong to clubs in which they are easily able to make friends and express comradery among their like-minded compadres.

Secondly, within certain communities of critical economists scapegoatism/dehumanization can foster a degree of "shock-jock amusement"—a comic relief from "political correctness," among those who personally object to political correctness. Finally, in the most common case of scapegoatism/dehumanization, which is against government workers, many economics professors can easily acquire *financial support* for such research, and publications. Such support is widely available from several well-endowed institutions, which encourage, support, publish, and endorse *government-bashing*. These institutions are financed, in large part, from contributions they receive from highly successful entrepreneurs, many of whom have harbored a disdain for government, perhaps, in part, because of all the taxes they incurred over the years.

A Final Remark about Scapegoatism/Dehumanization in Academic Economics

My final conclusion of this section may well insult the intelligence of many readers—though, of course, that would not be its intent. I simply feel that we must have some degree of adequate closure on such an important topic. For this closure I will answer the most basic question we could ask: *Why is scapegoatism/dehumanization, as an underlying motivation in critical economic discourse, wrong and should be eliminated?* Here are the obvious reasons:

1. In its most extreme cases, it is factually wrong, unethical, shameful, low class, unprofessional, and despicable (and, as clearly demonstrated in my use of these words, deserving of the same level of shock jock criticism that it dishes out).
2. It promotes irresponsibility, and in its most extreme form—hatred—which in academia defeats the purpose of economics education at many levels.
3. It makes it much more difficult for the profession to improve its genuine understanding of economic science, because:
   a. It crowds out (in literature and professional positions) those economists who are committed to developing useful and productive analyses.
   b. It discourages solid scientists from entering the profession, by their seeing, and certainly being offended by, this worst side of the profession.
4. It rightfully casts public doubt on the reliability of the profession, when the public observes this level of adolescent and irresponsible behavior.
5. It discourages conscientious and hard-working people from entering into public service, or into corporate enterprise, if they naively believe the arguments that they would be traitors, acting against the people in their communities, if they did.

Here are other questions we may wish to consider: Do the economics professors who are sympathetic to such scapegoatism/dehumanization rhetoric honestly believe that most government workers (or whatever other group is the scapegoat, such as greedy corporate executives) have such *evil in their hearts* as to wish harm to others in our society? Do these economics professors honestly not recognize how interchangeable the roles are among economists? (For example, how many economics graduates enter into academia, or into government, or into the private sector *quite arbitrarily*, often simply depending on wherever they can land a professional position once they have acquired their final degree?) Do the government-bashing economics professors not recognize that government so often contracts with the private sector, in economic studies as much as anything else, and that the highest-ranking leaders in government economics are so often former distinguished economics professors? Personally, I think the answer to all these questions is "no." In other words, it is highly doubtful that the economics professors who espouse scapegoatism/dehumanization actually believe what they are writing, or advocating, or joking about in their conversations. Ultimately, it is all a shallow exercise of irresponsible show business and self-amusement and nothing more. Self-amusement is not necessarily a bad thing in itself, but it is quite a shame when it substitutes for important responsibilities, and *when it reflects the ugliest and most embarrassing aspect of the profession.*

THE DELUSION THAT CONDUCTING EXPERIMENTS MAKES ECONOMICS PROFESSORS "SCIENTISTS"

I had strong reservations about writing this section on "Experimental Economics" for the reason that it will cast a shadow over a huge subfield within the profession—one that has enjoyed remarkable success by many standards, including, for instance, Vernon Smith's winning the Nobel Prize in economics in 2002 for his work in the area. Because of this, many readers might instantly question this book's validity: How could the author dare to include one of the most widely acclaimed subfields in economics—Experimental Economics—in a chapter on "Academic Economics at Its Dumbest and Ugliest"? Another reason for my reluctance to write this section is that the topic itself is simply not quite as dumb as the topics of the other sessions, and the way that it is dumb is fairly subtle and requires some thought.

Nevertheless, with regard to my first reservation, I believe the problem can be solved by emphatically stating that this section is not meant to discredit the entire subfield of experimental economics. What it does criticize is not so much the research and writing that is done in the subfield—much of which is quite good and quite beneficial—but the way in which the subfield is generally perceived and understood within the economics profession. That general perception and understanding of experimental economics, in my view, is quite wrong, and also quite harmful, in ways that I will explain shortly.

Experimental economics is arguably one of the easiest subfields of economics to define, because it does not look into any particular aspect of the economic system itself, like employment or international trade, nor does it fall under any particular purpose for economics, such as health care policy or environmental protection. Rather, it is defined in terms of its use of a specific method of acquiring information, which is "laboratory" experiments using human subjects. I expressed the term "laboratory" here in quotes because it is not a laboratory as one might imagine one for biology, chemistry, or physics, but it is a controlled environment that is typically performed a classroom where each subject sits before a computer screen. The subjects are usually students, who receive minimal compensation for participating in an organized exercise, such as a hypothetical auction. The experiment measures the subjects' actions, such as their bids in an auction, which generates data that will then be analyzed using econometric tests, and which may validate particular models of "economic behavior."

A True Story about My First Encounter with Experimental Economics

Back around 1993 I was working on the economics of food safety, at a time when food safety was a hot topic, shortly after a horrific *Escherichia coli* outbreak had occurred in a Jack in the Box fast-food chain.[23] Experimental economics was also emerging at the time, especially in the area of auctions, implying that any research which might combine experimental economics on auctions with food safety would have double odds of receiving a research grant and being published in a top journal. At that time, researchers who were indeed tapping into both fields had performed a study and were going around presenting their findings. I thus found myself, one day, in a large audience (of about hundred people) to attend such a presentation.

At this presentation we learned that the researchers had performed experiments which involved many students who were paid to participate in an auction game. How it worked was that students were asked to imagine that they were given a sandwich, which had a certain probability of being poisoned with salmonella (a deadly bacteria that often caused food poisoning). Of course, in reality, none of them ever received a poisonous sandwich—they were only asked to imagine it. They also had an allotment of money, and were asked to bid to acquire a 100 percent safe sandwich, that is, one that was known with certainty not to contain any poison. Their bidding in this experiment, in different phases under different scenarios, generated a wealth of data that the researchers then used to derive an estimate of their supposed "willingness to pay" for food safety, and "willingness to accept" certain safety risk in the food they purchase.

The presentation, and the research itself, focused on the data and on sophisticated econometric methods involved in analyzing the data. Thus, the study was much more about econometric methods than it was about purchasing behavior as it relates to food safety preferences, even though behavior regarding food safety was supposedly the topic at hand and the motivation behind the study. Accordingly, during the question-and-answer session at the end of the event, my colleagues in the room, especially those who were quite adept at econometrics, asked the presenters question after question about their econometric techniques, and were generally impressed with the presenters' responses.

During this question-and-answer period, I asked a question of my own in trying to understand the study's findings. My question related to the actual measures they acquired of the willingness to pay for food safety. In one of their experiments they had the imaginary risk of salmonella in the sandwich set at one in a hundred, and in another experiment they had it set at one in a thousand. I asked my question simply in the context of my trying to understand the results: to me, from the numbers they were displaying, it looked like the subjects with the 1/1000 chance of having a salmonella-poisoned sandwich were willing to pay *a higher price* for a guaranteed safe sandwich than the subjects with a 1/100 chance of having a poisoned sandwich. I politely and respectfully asked if I were interpreting this correctly, and if so, how could this result be possible—one would think that the higher the risk of the sandwich being poisoned, the more people would be willing to pay for a completely safe sandwich.

The lead presenter's reaction to my question began with a smile and a pause, but his answer was refreshingly honest. He explained that these experiments were run with students in the room who were sometimes just getting carried away in different random ways to the instructions they were receiving. It just so happened that the particular group that was given the hypothetical 1/1000 chance of a poisoned sandwich had certain students in the room who were more enthusiastic about bidding for a safer sandwich than the group with the 1/100 chance of a poisoned sandwich. (Again, it was all hypothetical—everyone was fully aware that none of the sandwiches were actually poisoned.) Such, counterintuitive inconsistencies were not uncommon at all in these types of experiments, he explained. I simply responded to his answer with a short, neutral acknowledgment, saying something like, "Oh, OK . . . I understand—thanks."

My colleagues in the room, however, knew that I would be extremely disappointed with that answer to my question, and it became a topic of discussion among us later on. I naturally thought it to be ludicrous that an incredible multitude of data was being collected and analyzed extensively, on what was, essentially, a fun game being played by students that they were not even taking seriously. Thus, I viewed the exercise as suffering from a basic, garbage in, garbage out problem, which no sophisticated econometric testing of the data thereafter could cure, and my coworkers who were also studying food safety in serious manner, basically agreed with me.

Several months after the presentation, one of my colleagues peaked into my office and asked me if I remembered that presentation on experimental economics. I replied that I sure did, and I then repeated to him what I thought of it. He then laughed and said, "Hey, guess what? It was just published in *American Economic Review*!" and he handed me a copy of the journal (since he rightfully suspected that I would be in disbelief without seeing the evidence).[24]

The Unique (Untold) History Underlying the Creation of Experimental Economics

One of the most important things to understand about experimental economics is that its rise to prominence in economics, in the 1980s and 1990s, essentially from nowhere, was not because it was suddenly found to be a new source of discovery and advancement of economic knowledge. It did lead to certain discoveries—that is true—but the main impetus for its growth was that there was a particular interest in promoting the field itself by those who, from the beginning, wanted to promote it. This is primarily because the field supports an image of economics as being "scientific," especially, unfortunately, among those economists and others who may not have a strong understanding of what it truly means for a field to be scientific (as I have discussed in previous chapters).

Why, one might ask, is it so important, then, for economics to look like a science, to the point that people with influence and authority strive to promote the subfield primarily because it supports this image? The answer lies in another true story, and it is a story primarily about only one institution—the National Science Foundation (NSF)—and one individual within that institution who ran the economics program for about three decades.

Just for clarity, and to prevent any misunderstanding here, the economics program at NSF overall has done much more to benefit the academic economics profession than it has to harm it. In particular, the NSF, probably more than any other institution in US history, has done more to promote the integrity and objectivity of research in academic economics. Frankly, as critical as this book is of the academic economics profession, I shudder to think of how much worse things would be without the NSF's influence.

After receiving a doctorate in economics at the University of Virginia, and teaching at the State University of New York, Binghamton, Dr. Daniel Newlon first entered NSF as a deputy director of the economics program in 1974. He then directed the program (or directed the division that included the economics program) for twenty-nine years, from 1980 to 2009.[25] Throughout his career he faced very difficult challenges to secure the survival of NSF's grant program in economics, in spite of continual efforts by members of Congress to shut it down.

Along these lines, Mata and Scheiding provide a detailed and interesting account of the situation that NSF faced, in which they note, "Throughout early 1981 there was widespread rumour that the social sciences were going to experience drastic cuts in their research funding. The anxiety was well justified."[26] They also describe a major effort made by many of the nation's leading economists at the time, and by the AEA, to save the NSF's budget. In particular, eight Nobel laureates wrote a letter in 1981 to the Reagan Administration stating:

> [NSF funding] is all the more important because the National Science Foundation is the only disinterested source of funds for research. Research supported by private industry and by government agencies with specific missions are very

> important for practical purposes, but usually are too directly targeted to permit the genuine innovation that comes with freedom to inquire and are not without some pressure to conform to preconceived outcomes.[27]

Mata and Scheiding note that the letter also stated that "the foundation of all useful knowledge in economic understanding and policy, has been supported by NSF funding." [28] Through this and other similar threats to the NSF's economics program, Daniel Newlon, nearly single-handedly defended the fort from attack, and was rightfully praised for his success. Mata and Scheiding remark:

> The 1970s and 1980s crisis of government patronage of social science enabled the development of a network of professionals that engage in the soliciting of public funds and in their distributions to the disciplines. Dan Newlon is an example of this advocate career. The 1996 COV {Committee of Visitors to NSF}, at another hard time for the funding of the social sciences, acknowledged in writing the role of Newlon's leadership that 'the Economics Program exemplifies a number of best practice activities. . . . He has impeccable taste in research and intellectual quality. [29]

At this point, readers may well be asking what all of this has to do with the growth of experimental economics. The short answer is "everything," as I will explain shortly.

I had known Daniel Newlon since 1994 when I first started working at NSF, not in its economics program, but in its Science Resources Studies Division, where I worked on the economics of R&D statistics and related topics. After I had left NSF in 2001, I remained in touch with him occasionally for the next ten years or so, primarily to help him promote occasional events for economists. Although he and I did not work on the same projects at NSF, the community of economists there was not large, and so we all tended to know each other. However, my relationship with Newlon first began on very rocky terms. This is because, shortly after joining NSF I had authored the article I mentioned earlier in the *Journal of Post-Keynesian Economics* on "Regardless of Philosophy, Economics Will Not be a Science Until It is Based on Science." Although this work had nothing to do with my work at NSF, and I affiliated myself with the university where I was an adjunct professor at the time, it made Newlon rather upset, as did some of my other writing that would follow along similar lines. What bothered Newlon so much were my arguments criticizing economics for not being more of a science. However, as far as I could tell, it bothered him only politically—not intellectually.

Unbeknownst to me at first, Newlon had fought the good fight of defending NSF's economics program from budget cuts, and he fought those battles through various arguments, one of which being that economics is a legitimate science, and as such it belonged as one of NSF's grant programs. This science-based defense of the program served to fend off not only attacks from the "outside" (by the Congress and Office of Management and Budget in particular), but from attacks within NSF itself (from officials in other fields of science). Thus, Newlon, in league with other directors of social science programs, and with the support of the most prominent economists in the nation, was standing his ground, insisting that economics *is* a legitimate science, and arguing further that this is why economic research needs to be funded by NSF. My, then, showing up on the scene in 1994, not only as an economist but as another NSF official, calling into question whether economics truly is a legitimate science, was naturally seen by Newlon as a betrayal of his efforts to defend his program. I understand his position of course, and learned to appreciate it more over the years.

During one of our lunch conversations, I believe when I was still at NSF, Newlon had shared with me how pervasive and threatening some of the earlier rhetoric in Washington had been against NSF's economics program. He mentioned, for instance, that sometime in the 1980s he had gone to a dentist's appointment, and while he was sitting there in the waiting room the radio was on and broadcasting the news. The news that day included the latest items in Senator Proxmire's "Golden Fleece" awards, which allegedly identified the worst cases of government waste and abuse of funds, most of which were actually completely misunderstood by Proxmire's team and were not forms of waste at all. Nevertheless, at the time, the public was paying attention to them and taking them seriously. So, while sitting there at the dentist's office, Newlon heard on the radio that one of the "Golden Fleece Awards" had just been given to a project that his own program was funding. He said that it was then that he realized that he needed to take aggressive measures to ensure the survival of his program. Although Newlon did not mention this to me, it was also obvious that it was not only his own program that was in jeopardy, but his position at NSF.

In finding every possible means that he could to save the program from the critiques it was receiving, Newlon supported new initiatives in *experimental economics*, which, until then, had hardly existed as a subfield. This would certainly make NSF's Economics Program appear to be more scientific and more scientifically valid to many observers, especially at a superficial level, and especially to observers who are only looking at the issue from that superficial level. Whether it truly made the program more scientific (discussed below) remains an open question, but that was not the issue at hand. The issue was saving the program all together, which was already supporting a great deal of excellent and important research that would have otherwise all been lost if the program were terminated.

Thus, it might be argued that even if the new surge in support for experimental economics did not in itself contribute substantially to useful knowledge, its ability to help keep the program alive might have alone made it worthwhile. I strongly suspect this idea had entered into Newlon's decision to offer strong financial support for experimental economics in the 1980s, 1990s, and beyond. As Eckel, a former director herself of the economics program at NSF after Newlon, has noted:

> In the early years, National Science Foundation (NSF) support was very important for experimental research and contributed greatly to its growth. . . . The first experimental grant was to Tom Schelling at Harvard in 1960, and Vernon Smith in 1962. . . . [I]n 1974, Dan Newlon became {associate} program director for the economics program at NSF {and director in 1980}. Newlon appreciated experimental research, and under his guidance the review panel has included at least one experimentalist since then. I do not think Newlon realizes how important his support has been for the development of the field {of experimental economics}.[30]

Thus, as the Egyptian Empire is said to be the "gift of the Nile," the subfield of experimental economics may best be understood as "a gift of the NSF," for better or worse. Whether Newlon absolutely had "to play this card" in order to save the program is something we will never know. While this chapter is entitled, "Academic Economics at Its Dumbest and Ugliest" readers should not think for one second that I am implying here that Newlon's decision to support experimental economics was dumb or ugly—it most certainly was not.

Experiments versus Science

Now, what *is* the problem, however, is how so many proponents of experimental economics (though Newlon is not one of them) have *propagandized* experimental economics as, essentially, the *only* subfield that makes economics "scientific." This is far more than a semantic issue—it gets at the very root of academic economists' understanding of their role and responsibilities. If economics professors think that they are more scientific, or are better scientists, if they run experiments in their research than if they do not, then they are very wrong, and they understand very little about science. What is most important in science is being committed to, and understanding, what truly causes things to happen in the real world. It is not about whether you run experiments, or, as discussed elsewhere in this book, it is not about the use of advanced mathematics.

It may be noted that good science has proceeded in the absence of experiments, as in the case of astronomy, where experiments are pretty much impossible to conduct, for obvious reasons. Yet, scientists may find opportunities to make use of new data from unique situations, like a solar eclipse, in which, in a certain way, nature has offered the astronomer with an experiment that they can study. Thus, if the question arises as to how much society wants to pay for certain levels of food safety, one possible source of information might be the added increase in expenditures after a food safety incident in terms of the media attention it received, the number of additional inspectors the government assigned to prevent future incidences, the fines or imprisonment imposed on individuals who caused the problem, etc. None of this would involve experiments, but simply the gathering of important facts that would enable us to understand the relative value that society places on food safety. Such a study could be very scientific in the sense of its commitment to analyzing and understanding what is actually happening in the real world. On the other hand, one could pay a bunch of students to sit in a room and play a computerized auction game with each other using hypothetical poisoned and safe sandwiches that no one will ever eat, and apply sophisticated econometric tests on the thousands of data points collected, and claim that they are being more scientific by virtue of the fact that they have conducted experiments. In my view, such a wrong-headed understanding of science would be an embarrassment to the profession of economics, and more importantly, could be potentially harmful to society if academic economists espouse the rhetoric that their experiments will generate more "scientific" results than other analytical methods.

Not surprisingly, the concern that I expressed—that the experiments run by economists take place in a different world which may have no relevance to the world in which we live—has been addressed substantially in the economic literature for several decades. For example, Daniel Friedman and Shyam Sunder expressed this concern in two parts: (1) "Do the data permit correct causal inferences?' and (2) "Can we generalize our inferences from laboratory to field?"[31] Those who do research in experimental economics will be quick to say that none of this is new, that these concerns have existed in the field since day one, and that they have been thoroughly addressed. I certainly agree with this, and commented on some of this literature myself in my book in 2000 on *Economics, Science, and Technology*.[32]

Nevertheless, experimental economists have not gone far enough in admitting that these concerns are quite applicable to nearly all of the work that is done in experimental economics, and that these concerns also explain why, in fact, experimental economics has not expanded more than it has to address other economic questions. This is what truly limits the usefulness of the field, which will never change regardless of how many additional grants may be issued for new economic experiments. These hard truths about the limitations of experimental economics need to be stated and understood clearly in order to prevent projects that will ultimately suffer from the garbage in, garbage out problem. Academic economists should not be performing such studies if their only reasons for doing so are to receive funding for them and acquire publications.

The "Economic Science Association"

What I personally find to be one of the most disturbing aspects of the experimental economics subfield overall is that its members belong to an association that they have chosen to call the "Economic Science Association" (ESA). The ESA was established in 1986 by a small group of "experimentalists" as Eckel defined them.[33] Its academic founders were never interested in promoting economics as a science in a general sense, and were only interested in the use of experiments. This is made evident on the association's website, which states, "The Economic Science Association (ESA) is a professional organization devoted to using controlled experiments to learn about economic behavior."[34] In *Economics, Science and Technology*, I raised the following concern regarding this association's identity:

> It is ironic that experimental economists often defend economics as a science to funding institutions, to the press, and to their students, using their own work as examples, but, indirectly, through their own self-proclaimed status, they effectively criticize the rest of economics as being unscientific. If experimental economists truly believed that other subfields were also scientific, then how could they have established an "economic science association" that would have only experimental economists as its members? Conversely, if other subfields were as scientific as the experimental economists, why would members of those other fields not protest experimental economists' pronounced, exclusive entitlement to "scientific economics"? The only explanation for the current status of the Economic Science Association is that most economists simply do not care whether they are viewed as scientists or not. That is why the experimental economists can lay claim to the concept of "economic science" without our resistance.[35]

Along these lines, the leaders of the ESA would surely laugh at my suggestion that they change their name to the Experimental Economics Association, or something of that nature. A legal name change would impose an enormous burden in terms of paperwork and expenses, so much so that it might be easier for them to start fresh by establishing a new association, populate it with the same leaders, and then abandon the ESA altogether while letting it draw people to the new one.

In any case, it simply remains irrational that many economists, myself included, feel that we have been practicing "economic science" for our entire professional life, while probably never, or rarely ever, performing a "laboratory experiment" in economics. Likewise, NSF has been funding research in "economic science," though most of this research has not been in experimental economics. The association's name is thus offensive to economic scientists who do not perform experiments, and to institutions that support economic science projects that do not necessarily involve experiments. Moreover, as I already remarked, the performance of experiments is not the same thing as the practice of science; the implicit belief that all there is to science is the performance of experiments reflects an ignorant view of what science is, and what good science should be. Perhaps NSF should request the ESA to change its name (informally of course, as it would never make such a request officially), because NSF supports a great deal of economic science that is not experimental but is still scientific. To many people these ideas may sound delusional—no one will be willing to do any of this—and so, in all likelihood, nothing will change. For those economists, like myself, who do take science seriously, however, it remains a bitter pill to swallow.

NOTES

1. Hal R. Varian, Microeconomic Analysis: Second Edition (New York, NY: W.W. Norton & Company, 1984), 3–4. My own emphasis in italics.
2. "Economics and Ethics," accessed February 5, 2017, http://tinyurl.com/h4h5kny.
3. Oxford Online Dictionary, accessed February 5, 2017, http://tinyurl.com/zfmsg8c.
4. Robert W. White and Norman F. Watt, The Abnormal Personality (New York: The Ronald Press Company, 1973), 43.
5. I mean no gender bias in my using these common terms.
6. Yes, some will say that Adam Smith was also a philosopher, but there are so many others besides him.
7. Adam Smith, "An Inquiry into the Nature and Causes of the Wealth of Nations (Cannan ed.) Vol. 2 [1776]," accessed February 5, 2017, http://tinyurl.com/gszbea2.
8. Adam Smith, An Inquiry into the Nature and Causes of the Wealth of Nations (London: William Strahan, 1776) Book I, Chapter 11. My own emphasis.
9. American Economic Association, "American Economic Review," 621.
10. American Economic Association, "American Economic Review," 622.
11. Dictionary.com, "Scapegoatism," accessed March 4, 2007, http://tinyurl.com/hyjjpqc.
12. Collins English Dictionary, "Scapegoatism," accessed March 4, 2007, http://tinyurl.com/j99t9gs.
13. Collins English Dictionary, "Scapegoat," accessed March 4, 2007, http://tinyurl.com/j72yuyr.
14. Dictionary.com, "Scapegoat," accessed March 4, 2007, http://tinyurl.com/zqro5g3.

15. Michelle Maiese, "Dehumanization," Beyond Intractability, July 2003, accessed February 5, 2017, http://tinyurl.com/2nhpaz.

16. Thomas DiLorenzo, Organized Crime: The Unvarnished Truth about Government (Auburn, Alabama: Mises Institute, 2012).

17. DiLorenzo, Organized Crime, 16–17.

18. DiLorenzo, Organized Crime, 28.

19. DiLorenzo, Organized Crime, 47.

20. DiLorenzo, Organized Crime, 10.

21. Daniel Klein, "The People's Romance: Why People Love Government (as Much as They Do)," The Independent Review, 10(1) (2005):20.

22. Daniel Klein, "If Government is so Villainous, How Come Government Officials Don't Seem Like Villains? With a New Postscript, in The Dynamics of Intervention: Regulation and Redistribution in the Mixed Economy (Advances in Austrian Economics, Volume 8), ed. Peter Kurrild-Klitgaard, 223–44 (Bingly, UK: Emerald Group Publishing Limited, 2004).

23. See "1993 Jack in the Box E. Coli Outbreak," Wikipedia, accessed February 5, 2017, http://tinyurl.com/pgaoxvs.

24. The article was: Jason F. Shogren, Seung Y. Shin, Dermot J. Hayes and James B. Kliebenstein, "Resolving Differences in Willingness to Pay and Willingness to Accept," *American Economic Review*, 84 (1) (1994), 255–270.

25. "AEACGR: Contact the Committee: Government Relations Office," American Economic Association, accessed February 5, 2017, http://tinyurl.com/zmuefh3.

26. Tiago Mata and Tom Scheiding, "National Science Foundation Patronage of Social Science, 1970s and 1980s: Congressional Scrutiny, Advocacy Network, and the Prestige of Economics," Minerva 50(4) (2012), 423–49.

27. Letter from Nobel Laureates to the White House (Reagan Administration), 1981. Cited in Tiago Mata and Tom Scheiding, "National Science Foundation Patronage of Social Science," 439. The eight Nobel Laureates were Kenneth Arrow, Lawrence Klein, Tjalling Koopmans, Simon Kuznets, Wassily Leontief, Paul Samuelson, Theodore Shultz, and Herbert Simon.

28. Cited in Tiago Mata and Tom Scheiding, "National Science Foundation Patronage of Social Science," 439.

29. Tiago Mata and Tom Scheiding, "National Science Foundation Patronage of Social Science," 445.

30. Catherine Eckel, "Economic Games for Social Scientists," in Laboratory Experiments in the Social Sciences, ed. Murray Webster, Jr. and Jane Shell (Burlington, MA: Elsevier, 2007), 499.

31. Daniel Friedman and Shyam Sunder, Experimental Methods: A Primer for Economists (New York: Cambridge University Press, 1994).

32. Steven Payson, Economics, Science and Technology.

33. Eckel, "Economic Games for Social Scientists," 498.

34. "Economic Science Association," accessed February 5, 2017, http://tinyurl.com/zwapz88.

35. Payson, Economics, Science and Technology, 51–52.

Chapter 9

Violations of Professional Ethics, Whether by Ignorance or Intent

ORGANIZING OUR THOUGHTS ON ETHICS IN ECONOMICS

No consensus exists on what is meant by "ethics in economics." For this statement, one need look no further than the recent *Oxford Handbook on Professional Economic Ethics*, by George DeMartino and Deirdre McCloskey in 2015. Its many chapters cover a wide range of topics, written by individual economists, most of whom are prominent economics professors.

Categories of Professional Ethics Issues in Academic Economics

There are basically seven different general frameworks for considering ethics in economics, though these frameworks certainly overlap. Most academic economists are not aware, and appear to be generally disinterested, in this diversity regarding what is meant by "ethics in economics." As far as I know, few efforts have been made to understand this diversity, and without this understanding it is that much easier for economists to dismiss work in the area, seeing that work as being outside what they themselves consider to be the most important in the study of economics. Thus, it is not so much that economists disagree on ethical issues (though this is certainly the case to some extent), but the larger problem is that economists cannot even agree on what they want to discuss among each other when it comes to ethics in economics. On such topics they often talk past each other, if not ignore each other altogether, for reasons that will be provided shortly.

The seven frameworks are first briefly defined below, and they will then be discussed in greater detail:

1. Prevention of Simple Wrongdoing. This category is the simplest and most obvious of them all—it is the avoidance of corruption, deception, falsification of data, plagiarism, bribery, fraud, etc. Violations of ethics in this regard involve circumstances that the public would generally understand and condemn, and that all economists would publically oppose if questioned before an audience about how they personally feel about such unethical behaviors. Nevertheless, some of these behaviors, such as plagiarism, have been shown to exist extensively throughout the profession, as will be demonstrated shortly.

2. Scientific Integrity and Responsibility. This involves the ethical principle that economists should present their theories and analyze them in a manner that is consistent with an honest commitment to understanding how the world actually works. An example of this ethical principle being applied is when an economist develops a theoretical model, which reflects a simplification and approximation of the behavior of a complex system, but nonetheless contributes, in some useful and meaningful way, to an improved understanding of the world. The counterexample, however, is when is an economist performs disingenuous research for the purpose of constructing a highly complex model that serves only the purposes of mental self-gratification, impressing peers with mathematical weight lifting, and publication in prestigious technical journals, while in actuality offering no contribution to how we may better understand the world. In most cases, the public would not be able to distinguish between these two situations, and may then naively assume that whatever might be published in a technical journal must have scientific merit and scientific integrity, when this is may not be true at all.

3. Doing No Harm and Consideration of a Code of Ethics. This category focuses not on whether the work done by economists is scientifically valid, but whether it is ethically or morally correct. This is probably the most difficult category to address because it crosses into alternative moral philosophies that economists might possess. If theoretical ideals are advocated without regard to the specific consequences they may have on individuals' lives, then the economist is essentially playing god. That is, they may be guided in this case only by the arrogant belief that economic theory alone prescribes what is right and wrong for society, and has precedence over all other cognitive and empirical approaches to public policy, including precedence over preventing unnecessary human hardship. (As discussed earlier, the simplistic perspective ot advocating a theoretical ideal, like removing any barrier to competition, could also run counter to more advanced economic theory itself, as we saw with regard to the Lancaster-Lipsey Theory of the Second Best, explained in chapter 7.)

4. Due Diligence and Regulation in Financial Operations. The previous three categories involved principles that may apply to any sector of the economy. Of all the sectors, however, one sector, in particular, has drawn more attention to issues of ethics and integrity in economics than any other—the financial sector, and this, of course, has especially been the case with regard to the financial crisis of 2007–2008. Ethics and integrity in financial markets and the regulation of those markets has thus earned a category of its own, not only in economic discourse and literature, but in new government offices like the Consumer Financial Protection Bureau, new legislation, recent best-selling nonfiction books, and even Hollywood films like *Inside Job* and *The Big Short*.

5. *Scholarly Review and Critiques of Historical Literature*. Many, if not most, academic economists look upon ethics in economics as an independent, scholarly field of study, focused primarily on an understanding of what the "the great historical scholars" have said on the topic. Such scholarly, historical analysis would fall under this category, where the work being done is not investigating any wrongdoing that might exist, but in studying the principles that various authors have historically espoused.

6. *Upholding Scientific Integrity in the Face of Potential Policy Bias*. Many economists actively support what might be called "social causes," which range from the extreme left to the extreme right, and everything in between. On the left such causes are often associated with concepts such as "social justice"; on the right they are associated with concepts such as "liberty" (in support of libertarianism). The proponents of these causes often regard it as ethical to promote their particular cause, and unethical not to do so, or unethical to do the bad things that their cause is fighting against. For example, economists who are outspokenly concerned about global warming may feel it is an ethical responsibility for other economists to express agreement with their concerns. Libertarians may likewise consider it an ethical imperative to speak out against government involvement in the economy (as discussed in chapter 8).

In a broad sense, it is, by definition alone, ethical for economists to identify and support ethical causes, and even to use economic thought and economic theory to promote these causes. The question of which causes are correct or most important is far beyond the scope of this book. Nevertheless, a separate issue involving scientific integrity arises out of this discourse, which is whether there is a policy-related bias in economic analyses that purport to be objective and policy neutral. In other words, was the analysis (in its selection of data, underlining assumptions, etc.) slanted toward certain results that would support a particular policy? To a large degree this issue might be seen as contained within the broad issue of scientific integrity and responsibility (#2 above). However, when the analysis involves potential policy bias, I would argue that this is an important enough, and unique enough, area to warrant its own category and discussion.

7. *Addressing Sociological Aspects of the Profession*. This category is probably the smallest in terms of the amount of discussions and literature that

might fall into it. It might be regarded as professional ethics in economics at the macro level, in contrast to the first category of the prevention of simple wrongdoing, which might be regarded as professional ethics at the most micro level. For example, within this category one might study the question of whether the economics profession as a whole should pay more attention to the topics of professional ethics and scientific integrity, and if it should, what could be done to effect that change. Also connected to this topic is how other major entities, like government or the media, could help to foster more ethical considerations in the economics profession. Other sociological factors that might be considered are the forms of cronyism that exist in the profession, and how cronyistic orientations and behavior by economists might lead to unfairness in the acceptance of publications and in hiring and promotion decisions.

Additional Topics that Transcend the Categories

In addition to the above seven categories, there are also five specific topics that cut across these categories, and which also deserve, and have often received, particular attention in their own right. These topics, defined below, will also be discussed in detail later in the chapter:

1. *Plagiarism in Academic Economics.* This problem has been surprisingly quite prevalent for generations, in spite of some occasional, high-profile efforts within the profession to address it. This topic may fit in the category of "prevention of simple wrongdoing" but it also fits into "scientific integrity and responsibility." Moreover, when we might try to understand how the problem has prevailed for so long, it brings us to the category of "addressing sociological aspects of the profession."

2. *Reproducibility in Economic Research.* In any science, if one acquires data, analyzes those data to acquire particular findings, and then publishes the findings, then it should be assumed that the findings were completely determined by the data used and by the specific methodology of the study. That is, it is assumed that, if any other reasonably competent scientist were handed the exact same data, and the exact same equations that had been previously used to analyze those data, then that scientist would be expected to reproduce the exact same findings that the previous scientist had acquired. Reproducibility in this regard is essential to the proper conduct of any field of research. When reproducibility cannot be achieved, it calls into question whether the initial experiments were run properly, or whether the initial researchers were honest in the reporting of their findings. What is meant by "reproducibility" here, however, is not about acquiring the same results with a different experiment (which would essentially mean with different data from a different

source), but about acquiring the same results from the same, exact dataset, and from the same exact equations that were used in the first study.

It is sometimes possible for the same data and equations to yield a different result in a test of reproducibility without there being any deliberate attempt by the first researcher (or by the second) to deceive the audience. For example, one of the researchers might have simply made an unintentional error of some sort, such as having a typo in the code that ran the statistical test that rendered erroneous results. In some cases, there may also be bugs or subtle nuances in the researchers' software that might create differences in results from the same data and the same formulas. However, as should be obvious, such discrepancies do not happen so easily, especially if researchers are diligent in ensuring the validity of their work. Moreover, when the discrepancies occur as a result of subtle differences in how, for example, alternative software packages process statistical regressions, we would expect the observed discrepancies to be quite small in most cases. It follows that when non-reproducibility occurs to a substantial degree, it is likely to reflect a high level of sloppiness, a lack of candor, or some combination thereof, on the part of the researcher.

3. Objectivity and Transparency of Findings. This topic relates primarily to issues of scientific integrity, addressing the question of how reliable and generalizable a study's findings are, when there may be obvious circumstances that would allow any reasonable person to question those findings. Such circumstances may include utilizing biased data, or questionable assumptions that might then make the study's findings highly deceptive. Examples of this type of problem have been provided throughout this book.

4. Fairness in the Hiring of Academic Economists. The "job market," as it is commonly called in academic economics, pertaining to the process by which academic institutions hire new economics professors, is ridiculously competitive and fraught with concerns over fairness. It is extremely difficult to underestimate the importance of how the job market works to the future of the profession, though I have yet to find any research (other than my own) that has approached this topic. Quite simply, the future of the academic economics profession will depend on precisely who enters into it in the upcoming generations, where only a minority of those who earn PhDs in economics will make it in (or even want to make it in). Who makes it in, and whether they even want to, is determined greatly by the characteristics of the how the job market works. Unfortunately, in many cases the job market enrolls future professors who will be most adept at perpetuating the professions worst problems, and least adept at correcting them.

5. Whistle-Blower Protection in Academic Economics. There is often the impression in our society that academics have the most freedom of speech among professionals in any sector. This is quite far from the truth, however, when it comes to their speaking out broadly against negative aspects of their own profession. Those on the left may comfortably and freely bash "corporate greed," and those on the right "government intervention and incompetence," but when it comes to statements about their own profession we find that economics professors in general are quick to stand up straight and salute their profession's flag. There is, indeed, a tendency for academic economists to "know what side their bread is buttered on" and to act accordingly, by "not making waves." As a case in point, I believe that very few full-time academics (as opposed to adjunct professors as I have been) would be able to write a book like this (or even an article like any one of this book's chapters) and still remain in good standing with their employer or grant provider. This general problem is a major obstacle to the profession's overall capacity for improvement, since the first step in correcting any problem is to recognize that it even exists.

Sources of Information on Ethics in Economics

In 2006, when I first established the Association for Integrity and Responsible Leadership in Economics and Associated Professions (AIRLEAP), one of our first initiatives was to develop a web-based survey on ethics and integrity in economics (for all economists). The effort was a failure because many people were simply uncomfortable with the questions, or too uncertain in terms of how they should respond to them, and so the participation rate was abysmal. This in itself was revealing however, implying how much disinterest there was in the profession with regard to ethics and integrity, and/or how much reluctance there is to participate in any function that might be perceived as "making waves."

This overall disinterest and shyness (if not fear) might be attributable, in part, to the selection process that determines who decides to become economists—a topic which David Colander, in particular, has written about at various times over the years, in work that had been based on surveys.[1] However, there are two other rather obvious problems with any survey that might ask economics professors about their views on professional ethics: (1) biased selection—those who agree to participate in the survey are much more likely to be altruistic (as they are those who are willing to donate their time for the implicitly perceived cause of the survey in promoting professional ethics), and (2) many participants would be naturally inclined to answer the survey questions with a posture that is more ethical and reflects more integrity than what might actually be revealed by their own actions.

In lieu of a survey of economics professors, however, I have acquired a great deal of information in a less formal sense, primarily from my role in managing AIRLEAP for more than ten years and by managing ethics and integrity discussions in a range of forums from which I have seen the viewpoints and heard the opinions of hundreds of academic economists. In conference sessions and seminars that I have organized, and in many more that others have organized and that I simply attended as another speaker or member of the audience, I have heard what economics professors have to say about professional ethics.

Perhaps my most objective source of information, however, was when I was staffing an exhibitor's booth at the annual meetings of the American Economic Association (AEA),[2] where I encountered thousands of economics professors (as well as nonacademic economists) who spoke to me as they passed by the booth. Unlike the attendees of a seminar on ethics, which would include only people who were interested enough in the topic to attend, the passersby of the exhibitor's booth offered a much more "random sample" of economics professors. They were in the exhibitors booths for a wide variety of reasons, such as to peruse the books and journals there and to acquire free review copies of textbooks from publishers. Since I aggressively introduced myself and my organization to everyone walking by (and not just those who made the effort to come speak with me), I acquired what I believe to be a strong sense of how economics professors overall tend to approach ethics and integrity in their field. By the way, although the conference is always held in the United States, the attendees are quite international.

Those Who are Interested, and Those Who are Oblivious

The most obvious pattern that I noticed from initiating these conversations at the exhibitor's booth is that economics professors tend to fall into two distinct camps: (1) those who automatically react with interest to the topic of professional ethics in economics, and (2) those who are oblivious to the topic, who react in a way that suggests they have given very little thought to it. Unfortunately, the vast majority of passersby fell under the second category.

Some interesting observations might be made about this second group of individuals who are oblivious to the topic. One is that they varied greatly in terms of the tone of their reaction. At one extreme, some react in a manner that is polite and diplomatic, displaying respectful attentiveness to the topic, while apparently entertaining the idea in their minds that such a topic area might, in fact, be important, as there is, indeed, an exhibitor's booth devoted to it in front of their eyes. At the other extreme, the reaction was condescending laughter, or an instantaneous confrontational assertion, often with a sarcastic tone, such as the remark "Oh really! And how do you even define professional ethics!" With this negative end is either the automatic dismissal of the topic as something that is simply uninteresting to them or a somewhat hostile, paranoid reaction as if I were implying that I was accusing them, personally (though I had never met them), of being unethical (as if they assumed that I was making an accusation against all economics professors or against all economists). Fortunately, for whatever it may be worth, of these two extremes (the first being genuine ignorance combined with curiosity, and second being condescending amusement and hostility), the first was much more common.

Another fortunate finding was that whenever a prominent academic economist happened to pass by the booth (at least those who were prominent in the sense that I was already familiar with their name and accomplishments as well-known authors or leaders of organizations), the reaction was either automatic interest in the topic or, at worst, respectful attentiveness to the topic. There might be a few obvious reasons for this, such as, in their role as a prominent professors they may have held positions such as department chairs, in which they were expected to address professional ethics in the positions they held. They may also simply have more experience in, and be more accustomed to, conversing with people diplomatically and respectfully, and more cognizant of their being "public figures" who always need to watch continually what they say and to be friendly in public regardless of the topic of discussion. Some actually knew or were familiar with work by a couple of AIRLEAP's own prominent directors, especially Deirdre McCloskey. Of course, I would also like to think, wishfully at least, that most prominent economics professors would be attentive to discussions on professional ethics simply because they tend to be intelligent enough to recognize its importance!

Another tendency that might be worth noting is that, among those who were oblivious to the topic and who were not prominent professors, the distribution among the continuum of reactions, from genuine interest to condescending laughter, seemed to be completely independent of the age or status of the passerby. That is, the chance of observing a smug response to the topic was about the same regardless of whether the passerby were a graduate student, an assistant professor, or a tenured professor. One exception to this, however, was that virtually all foreign graduate students seemed to be interested in the topic, or at least not dismissive of it. Two possible explanations for this might be that, being less familiar with American culture, they might simply be more open to topics that they have not yet encountered, allowing for the possibility that they are learning something new about the culture. Another, completely different, factor is that many of those graduate students are from developing countries (or former developing countries like China) and might already be familiar with the topic as it relates to economic development issues, or corruption issues, in their own countries.

CATEGORIES AND CHARACTERISTICS OF PROFESSIONAL ETHICS AMONG ACADEMIC ECONOMISTS

Table 9.1 summarizes the seven categories of issues, and additional five particular topics, identified earlier, with regard to six characteristics that may

Table 9.1 Categories of Issues on Ethics and Scientific Integrity, and Their Characteristics

	Category of Issues Regarding Ethics and Scientific Integrity in Economics, and Specific Topics	*Most Professors Unaware of It*	*Often Not Taken Seriously*	*Assumed to be Handled Adequately*	*Seen by Vast Majority as Outside Their Expertise*	*Perversely Diminishes Interest in Ethics*	*Substantial Literature on It*	*Often Overlaps With Categories*
1	Prevention of Simple Wrongdoing	X	X	X	X	X		2, 3, 4, 7
2	Scientific Integrity and Responsibility	X	X	X	X			1, 3, 7
3	Doing No Harm and Consideration of a Code of Ethics				X		X	1, 2, 4, 5, 6
4	Due Diligence and Regulation in Financial Operations			X			X	1, 2, 3
5	Scholarly Review and Critiques of Historical Literature		X	X	X	X	X	3
6	Upholding Scientific Integrity in the Face of Potential Policy Bias		X	X	X			2, 3
7	Addressing Sociological Aspects of the Profession	X	X	X	X			1, 2
A	Preventing Plagiarism in Academic Economics	X	X	X		X		1, 2, 7
B	Reproducibility in Economic Research		X	X		X	X	1, 2, 7
C	Objectivity and Transparency of Findings	X	X	X	X			1, 2, 3, 6, 7
D	Fairness in the Hiring of Academic Economists	X	X	X		X		1, 7
E	Whistle-Blower Protection in Academic Economics	X	X	X	X	X		1, 2, 6, 7

Source: Compiled and created by the author.

be of interest: (1) whether most economics professors are aware of the category, (2) whether it is often not taken seriously, (3) whether it is assumed to be handled adequately; (4) whether the majority of economics professors see it as outside their expertise, (5) whether it perversely diminishes interest in ethics, and (6) whether there is substantial literature on the topic. Each one of these characteristics is considered separately in the sections that follow.

Most Economics Professors Are Unaware of It

This characteristic in Table 9.1 identifies whether most economics professors are aware of the category or topic as something that is particularly problematic in their profession. As shown in the table, only five of the eleven categories/topics appear to be recognized by most academic economists, that is, economics professors *are* reasonably aware of them: Doing No Harm, Due Diligence and Regulation in Financial Operations, Scholarly Review and Critiques of Historical Literature, Upholding Scientific Integrity in the Face of Potential Policy Bias, and, to a lesser extent, Reproducibility in Economic Research. The category Doing No Harm is recognized because of its connection to the many billions of dollars that are provided each year by the World Bank and many other institutions to support economic growth in developing countries, where these institutions have been continually scrutinized for possibly causing "more harm than good" in certain situations. Similar situations have occurred with regard to austerity programs that have been promoted by the International Monetary Fund and by other powerful financial institutions.

Due Diligence and Regulation in Financial Operations surely receives a great deal of attention for obvious reasons. Scholarly Review and Critiques of Historical Literature is recognized as well, because many economics professors simply make their living from researching, publishing, and teaching in this area (though much less than in previous generations). Similarly, many academic economists are fully aware of the issue of Upholding Scientific Integrity in the Face of Potential Policy Bias, simply because policy biases receive a great deal of attention in the media and in public debates.

Ten years prior to this writing, reproducibility in economic research was a little-known topic. More recently, however, it has received attention from the Berkeley Initiative for Transparency in the Social Sciences (BITSS), which is a well-funded and high-profile effort to address the issue. This organization will be discussed in some detail later on in this chapter.

Often Not Taken Seriously

Most economics professors tend to show little serious interest in issues associated with professional ethics, perhaps, in part because some may have the perspective that they are powerless to change anything, so why should they worry about it? The two categories that do receive serious attention, however, for reasons that were already suggested, are Doing No Harm, and Due Diligence and Regulation in Financial Operations. In contrast, the other two categories that economics professors are generally aware of—Scholarly Review and Critiques of Historical Literature and Upholding Scientific Integrity in the Face of Potential Policy Bias—appear to be taken seriously only by those who are actively working in them.

Assumed to be Handled Adequately

Most economics professors tend to assume that most of the categories are being handled adequately by the profession's leadership, with one exception: Doing No Harm. It is easy to see how most feel reasonably secure with regard to Due Diligence and Regulation in Financial Operations, as there has been so much that has been done in this category since the financial crisis of 2007–2008, in the form of new financial regulations, new governmental bodies (like the Consumer Financial Protection Bureau), and new policies and practices by financial institutions (and by the Federal Reserve in particular). Reproducibility in Economic Research seems to be something that the BITSS has suggested they are handling with strong efforts, and some economics journals have expressed support for these efforts as well, which I believe have largely pacified the concerns of most economics professors in this area.

Seen as Outside Their Expertise

Academic economists tend to view the majority of the categories of, and particular topics involving, ethics and scientific integrity as being associated with background knowledge, theories, and literary arguments that are outside their own areas of expertise. Thus, they are reluctant to think much about them, as they are not confident in forming their own opinions in these areas. The categories/topics which most economics professors do generally have confidence to think about are: Due Diligence and Regulation in Financial Operations, Plagiarism, Reproducibility of Findings, and Fairness in Hiring. The first of these is a very newsworthy area, on which many professors have had to deliver lectures. The other categories/topics involve areas that economics professors must also be familiar with as researchers, and as individuals involved in the "job market" as candidates or as hiring officials.

Perversely Diminishes Interest in Ethics

For many economics professors, what they think about most when they hear "professional ethics in economics" is the prevention of simple wrongdoing, such as making up data or engaging in an inappropriate relationship with a student—essentially "smoking guns" in the nature of a tabloid news story, that would get a professor in big trouble with their institution's "ethics office." This perspective on ethics in academic economics greatly diminishes the relevance of the entire topic to most economics professors, who may then look upon the topic as the business of the university's Ethics Office, or the Dean's Office, or journalists, or prosecuting attorneys, but otherwise has nothing to do with them or their work.

Similarly, as I have argued thoroughly in chapter 7, the perception of professional ethics in economics as a scholarly issue (confined to the category of the Scholarly Review and Critiques of Historical Literature) has provided an extremely convenient excuse for many economics professors to think or say that they are simply unqualified to address it. Likewise, the topic of Upholding Scientific Integrity in the Face of Potential Policy Bias may cause economics professors to think that "ethics in economics" is simply "politics in economics" where some of the policy advocates are evoking the concept of ethics in support of their policy position. They may then be uninterested in professional ethics in economics, seeing the entire topic area as too involved in politics for their tastes. Not unlike the category of Simple Wrongdoing, the specific topics of Plagiarism, Reproducibility, Fairness in Hiring, and Whistle-Blower Protection may also be seen as a sort of "law-enforcement" issue that economics professors might consider too plebian and unscholarly to be worthy of their attention.

Substantial Literature on It

There is substantial literature on only three of the seven categories, and only one of the five topics: Doing No Harm, Due Diligence and Regulation in Financial Operations, Scholarly Review and Critiques of Historical Literature, and, as discussed earlier, Reproducibility in Economic Research. All of the other categories and topics are simply not investigated very much by the academic economics profession, in spite of their incredible importance.

We can now examine each of the categories and topics in more detail, having defined them earlier.

EXTENDED DISCUSSION OF THE CATEGORIES AND SOME OF THE CROSS-CUTTING TOPICS

Prevention of Simple Wrongdoing

Simple wrongdoing, or, in more precise terms, lying, cheating, and stealing, etc., does of course happen everywhere, in all fields and all walks of life. There is, indeed, a literature on the economics of crime, and many economists and economics professors have specialized on the topic. Of all people, then, economics professors should know that, all else being equal, wrongdoing occurs most when there are great incentives to support it (an effective "demand pull" for it), and when those who might commit such wrongdoing are more inclined, for whatever reason, to do just that (a "supply push" factor, in effect).

In my view, and from my experience, there are four areas of simple wrongdoing that have been pervasive in the academic economics profession, which cannot be dismissed as simply occurring everywhere. The first of these has actually been substantially exposed (especially in the documentary *Inside Job*) and has "officially" been addressed to some extent by the profession, though far from adequately. The other three are very well known among the profession's members, and yet the profession has kept an extremely low profile on them—they are, in certain respects, the profession's "dirty little secrets." These are: (1) conflicts of interest in the research performed by economics professors (discussed in chapter 4), (2) cronyism and favoritism in the publication and citation games (discussed in chapters 4 and 6), (3) exploitation of many graduate students, especially foreign students, to support the work of their advisors in their desperate attempts to win in the publication game (discussed in chapter 4), and (4) deliberate efforts by some members of the academic economic community to generate propaganda against online learning in economics.

As I have argued in various ways throughout this book, and especially in chapter 7, the emphasis on scholarship and intellectual muscle-flexing, or the simplistic view that we, as intellectuals, should be above talking about the kinds of topics that might appear in tabloid journals, has created a huge obstacle to the correction of the profession's simple wrongdoing. This posture of "raising above the fray" has indeed helped to prevent economics professors from admitting these problems exist.

I have attended many conference sessions, for example, on "Ethics in Economics," where the presenters had papers arguing for a commitment by the profession for "honest truth" in the models we develop, where these arguments were supported primarily by explanations of how great thinkers of the past supported this goal. In many of these ethics-in-economics sessions, the speakers would preface their presentation by saying that they are by no means accusing the profession of any wrongdoing, but simply "contributing to a discussion on what the goals of the profession should be." This would sometimes even be said with pride, as if to imply that the speaker is capturing the high ground, as opposed to the less admirable, accusatory, low ground. In my view, by our doing this, we have essentially *thrown away the baby with the bathwater by suggesting that these issues are nothing we should really get ourselves upset about—or issues we need to do something about—they are only issues we can have fun exploring and discussing.*

Another contributing factor to the profession's cases of simple wrongdoing is, of course, its cases of *more complex violations* of ethical principles and violations of scientific integrity. If people find themselves in an environment dominated by dishonesty at a *complex* level, like the complex dishonesty in the assumption that their worth is measureable by their publication counts alone, then they will of course be more inclined toward dishonesty at the simple level. (Recall the hypothetical example provided in chapter 4 where I suggested that the high stakes of getting a paper published, vis-à-vis unfair cronyism in that competition, will make some authors more willing to "massage their data" if they believe it will help to get the paper published.) Thus, any efforts to fix complex wrongdoing will have positive spillovers in fixing simple wrongdoing, and vice versa.

Scientific Integrity and Responsibility

As might also be obvious, there are enormous "gray areas" over the issue of when actions reflect scientific integrity or not, or to what degree they may reflect scientific integrity. For example, as discussed in chapter 7 and elsewhere, an economics professor might publish a journal article which presents a model and findings, where the findings merely rediscover, mathematically, the assumptions underlying the model. More broadly, the findings of such a paper may ultimately be arbitrary and unreliable, because they were based on arbitrary and unreliable assumptions, and if a different set of equally defensible assumptions had been made, then entirely different findings would result (the McCloskey A-Prime C-Prime Hypothesis). It appears that the vast majority of economics professors who publish research like this personally believe that they are firmly grounded in "scientific integrity" because somewhere in their article they mentioned that their assumptions and model could have been different in some way, which would have led to different findings. In essence, their study is like an algorithm with a big "IF" pasted in the heading of each page (analogous to something like "Draft" or "Confidential"). That is, IF these assumptions are true, THEN such and such would happen. As a child (or childish adult) might sometimes argue, "Listen! I never said they WILL happen—I said IF!"

Where it gets shaky, however, is how the study is presented and how it is truly perceived by those who read it and who draw conclusions, in their own mind, from it. The situation might be analogous to when evidence is presented in a trial, and then declared "inadmissible" after making a permanent impression on the jury. The assumptions underlying an economic model are often presented with the same confidence level and conviction as if the model's findings were observed facts or verified laws of nature, and the mere fact that such assumptions were published (especially in a top-ranked journal) conveys to many readers, and the community overall, a false sense of knowledge and understanding that is simply unjustified.

Many economics professors seem to believe that their mathematical storytelling, and the delusion (by others and sometimes themselves) that such storytelling always offers a higher understanding of the world (when often it does not), is something that is confined only to the academic community. That is, they view this lack of scientific integrity (if they do recognize it as such) as a problem that academic economists had simply created for themselves, and that it is thus not anyone else's concern who is outside their community. What must be realized is that this lack of scientific integrity has created and continues to create much more harm *outside* the realm of academic economics than *inside* it. The financial crises of the prior decade are a case in point.

What is somewhat perverse is that the harm that is caused by a lack of scientific integrity occurs in two very different ways: One is when the lack of integrity is not known, and the other is when it is known. When it is not known, the underlying, heroic assumptions of fanciful models work essentially as propaganda, or as misinformation, that can easily sway public opinion and influence policies in ways that may simply be erroneous and detrimental. This effect may be accidental, or it may be by design if the researcher has a particular agenda to promote a policy—either a personal agenda or an agenda supported by a research grant or other compensation from an institution that is promoting that agenda (as discussed, for example, in chapter 4 with regard to Jesse Rothstein's American Economic Review (AER) article on "Teacher Quality Policy When Supply Matters").

When lack of integrity in economics *is* known, then the public adopts a cynical outlook on the field of economics overall, and many public leaders adopt the expectation that economic theories are meant primarily to be used as propaganda in support of political agendas. (I have seen this first hand, sometimes on a daily basis, for over thirty-five years as a professional economist in Washington, DC.) Under this situation, two rather bad things naturally happen: One is that economists (whether in academia or elsewhere) are then often expected by their superiors to perform studies and to generate findings that support a particular agenda (often specified to them directly) under the assumption that principles of scientific integrity will not enter into the scene as an obstacle. If scientific integrity does still sneak in as an obstacle, then those superiors might conclude that the economist they hired was not a typical one (as they would have expected), and that they should go find another one who will be better in doing what they are told. Indeed, there is a reason why economists in this situation have, for many decades, been referred to as "hired guns." This situation, in turn, in some ways creates a Darwinist advantage to the economists who are most deficient or disinterested in upholding scientific integrity, as they will be more in demand by those who expect economic thought and economic theory to exist for purposes of advocacy alone. This Darwinist tendency then helps to perpetuate and exacerbate this problem from one generation to the next. It is the survival of the invertebrates, and the extinction of the vertebrates (i.e., an extinction of those who have a backbone).

The other bad thing that happens (as if this were not enough!) when the public assumes that economists lack scientific integrity is, what might be described as, a boy-who-cried-wolf effect, or its equivalent, the principle behind the adage, "Fool me once—shame on you; fool me twice—shame on me." That is, in the world of disbelief in economists as legitimate scientists, when someone does "tell the truth," or does present reliable findings from an objective study that was motivated only by an honest effort to gain knowledge and understanding, many people will simply dismiss it, assuming it is unreliable propaganda, especially if it does not support their own agenda. In short, when enough economists lack scientific integrity, or are at least believed to lack scientific integrity, then the assumption is made, by the public and by societal leaders in particular, that all economists lack scientific integrity and thus cannot be trusted. This gives free license for any political figure to propose just about anything that might please their constituents and win votes, and recruit an economist to produce an economic study to support it, and I am sure most readers agree that the evidence for the existence of this effect is overwhelming.

Doing No Harm and Consideration of a Code of Ethics

One might wonder how I might start a new section on "doing no harm" when the previous sections, as well as the sections that follow this one, involve the identification of harm being done in one way or another. In this particular section I am focusing on the overall lack of interest in "doing no harm," and on the idea that economic policies are too often adopted on the basis of how popular or intellectually appealing the theory is, irrespective of their true effect on society. This problem is at its worst when austerity policies are imposed on developing countries, sometimes resulting in rather inhumane consequences, including fatalities.

One need not look far to see that societal policies are not, in general, founded solely on principles of economic efficiency. For example, we do not commit people who are elderly to death once their productivity and accumulated wealth fall below their level of consumption, as a policy that would in theory promote economic efficiency and thereby achieve higher per capita income in the nation overall (among those who would still be alive). Economic efficiency is surely one of several societal goals that enters into the complex trade-offs that govern societal and governmental policies. Causing no harm, and especially causing no *unnecessary* harm (where the same goals could be achieved without such harm), is an essential principle that economists, as social scientists, and more generally as responsible human beings and societal leaders, must understand and apply in their policy prescriptions. But, if economists arrogantly assume that it is only their responsibility to advocate economic efficiency on the basis of economic theory, and leave it to policymakers and the people who vote for them to weight that recommendation against the principle of doing no harm, then economists are essentially promoting a situation that increases the probability that harm will, indeed, occur. In short, many economists often have, effectively, caused harm, as a result of their apathy, whether they are willing to accept this conclusion or not.

Economists most certainly do have the ethical responsibility to identify how harm might occur as a result of the policies that they have advocated on the basis of economic principles. For economists *to play god* with these principles, and at the same time, *to play dumb* in saying it is up to others to weigh in the other factors associated with reality, is simply unethical and morally reprehensible, regardless of how economists are compensated or how they may have been trained (or how they have based their views on what their own economics professors taught them when they were students).

Many writers on ethics in economics have argued in favor of establishing a code of ethics for economists, though others have argued against one, saying it is not needed. Of course, any code of ethics for any profession will still always beg the question of how well that code of ethics is taken seriously by its members. Nevertheless, it conveys an important message to the members, and especially to new entrants into the profession who are presumably susceptible to such influence.

At present there is no professional code of ethics for economists (in all fields or industries) in the United States, and, as suggested by many of the points made in this book, there is certainly *no code of ethics for academic economists in the United States.* There are three exceptions (or near exceptions) to this for specific fields or industries: (1) the National Association of Forensic Economists, which has a "Statement of Ethical Principles and Principals of Professional Practice" that in my view is rather impressive,[3] (2) the American Finance Association (assuming for the moment that finance may be considered a field within "economics" in its broadest definition), which has a newly established (in 2016) "Code of Ethics and Guidelines,"[4] and (3) the Society of Government Economics, or government economists in general, who do *not* have a stated code of ethics, but all those who are employed in government service are required to take an oath upon entering federal service, and are thus subject to a long list of officially established, ethical standards that would apply to any of their work, including economic analysis. (I have left out AIRLEAP which of course has a code of ethics but is admittedly a small organization, at least at this writing.)

In his personal website, Professor George DeMartino lists ethical codes for economists that have been established in Belgium, France, Germany, and Sweden.[5] This leaves out quite a lot of nations, such as the United States, Great Britain, China, and Japan, which do not have codes of ethics for economists. If there is any organization within the United States that would be responsible for establishing such a code of ethics or code of conduct, for all economists, or for academic economists in particular, everyone knows that it would be the only organization large enough and influential enough to make it work, and that is the AEA. As mentioned early in chapter 1, many years ago the governing board of the AEA, as a group, had broken into laughter as a letter was read to them recommending that they adopt a code of ethics. Hopefully, today the idea is not as great a source of amusement and humor to the AEA leaders as it was then, but their fundamental posture on this issue has thus far remained unchanged. (Perhaps this book will help them think about it further.)

It is actually amazing how economists in the United States do not have a professional code of ethics, while just about every other profession does. As mentioned in previous chapters, economists, especially academic ones, rely quite heavily on mathematics and greatly admire the field of mathematics. Economics professors might then be interested in knowing that the American Mathematical Society (the main American association for mathematicians) has long had a "Statement Policy on Ethical Guidelines."[6] As also discussed in this book, academic economists who focus on theoretical models may often be said to suffer from "physics envy." Well, as it turns out, the American Physical Society (the American professional society of physicists) has its own "Guidelines for Professional Conduct."[7] Economics professors also perform a great deal of research involving statistical (econometric) analysis, and so they might like to know that the American Statistical Association has "Ethical Guidelines for Statistical Practice" (discussed in detail below).[8] Unfortunately, like the AEA, the Association for Public Policy Analysis and Management (APPAM), the leading public policy association of the United States, also seems to lack a code of ethics, so economists are not exactly the "only ones" who do not have it, but "one of the few" who do not have it. Given the severe problems that the academic economists have in the area of professional ethics, however, the adoption of a code of ethics by the AEA certainly would not hurt, and might actually help, especially if instills a commitment to "do no harm" as a professional economist.

In his essay on "Creating Humble Economists: A Code of Ethics for Economists,"[9] Colander proposes a rather elaborate, five-page-long "Code of Ethics for Economists" which he says he adapted from the "Code of Ethics for Engineers." As he admits, Colander basically took the code of ethics of engineers and replaced each incidence of the word "engineer" with "economist" and then he writes that he was amazed to see how little was inappropriate for economists. In my view this claim is debatable, but what we can certainly accept in Colander's proposed code of ethics for economists is its "fundamental canons," which are as follows:

Economists, in their fulfillment of their professional duties, shall:

1. Hold paramount the safety, health and welfare of the public.
2. Perform services only in areas of their competence.
3. Issue public statements only in an objective and truthful manner.
4. Act for each employer or client as faithful agents or trustees.
5. Avoid deceptive acts.
6. Conduct themselves honorably, responsibly, ethically, and lawfully so as to enhance the honor, reputation, and usefulness of the profession.[10]

Such ethical standards need to be recognized in the economics profession, and for all the reasons provided in this book, they are especially needed in the academic sector of the profession.

George DeMartino mentions the following in a presentation that he gave in 2015 regarding his highly acclaimed work, *The Economist's Oath*:

> Essentially in that book I argued that economics, as a profession, is ethically deficient, in that it isn't engaging in a serious, systematic way the ethical challenges that arise in the context of economic practice. Unlike law, and medicine and several other professions that have spent a lot of time worrying about the ethical burdens that their practitioners face, economists haven't done that. It is not that they just overlooked the issue. Having gone through the AEA {American Economic Association} archives as far back as they go—the late 19th century—I found that this issue was raised repeatedly . . . and the AEA Executive Committee . . . always resolutely rejected the idea that this was an area that required attention. . . . [W]e need this for a very simple reason: Economists have an enormous impact on the lives of others, by design, . . . but we . . . haven't paid attention to the ethical entailments of having influence over the lives of others.[11]

Certainly, many individuals and various institutions do assume responsibility for the ethical issues associated with their actions. For example, a governmental regulatory agency will assess (and is required to do so by law) the societal costs and benefits of any major regulation, and will be held accountable to public scrutiny if its analysts ignore such effects. Similarly, even though a private corporation exists primarily to make profits, the corporation must also be very mindful of its public image and careful to avoid actions that might be seen by the public as unethical (even if its only reason for doing so is to maximize its profits by minimizing negative publicity).

These ethical concerns are essentially "retrofitted" onto the profession in the absence of any systematic educational foundation for ethical considerations that economics students might otherwise receive in their education. This is quite the opposite for medical students who will receive ethics training from their medical school professors, and law students from their law professors, etc. (Of course, this does not make them invulnerable to unethical tendencies in spite of their training, but at least gives them an initial vaccination, of sorts, to fight off those tendencies, for whatever it may be worth.) Training in ethics is, for the most part, absent in the academic sector of economics, not only in terms of there being essentially no formal course material on it, but simply in terms of a basic disinterest in the topic among most academic economists, as has been demonstrated by numerous examples throughout this book.

Due Diligence and Regulation in Financial Operations

As mentioned above, this category is unique in that it pertains to a particular sector of the economy—the financial sector—though this one sector is arguably the most important one with regard to the field of economics. It is also a unique category for another reason: It is the only one that is not largely driven by academic economists, though academic economists still have considerable influence over it, especially if we were to include among academic economists the economics professors who are borrowed by major financial regulators (like the Treasury Department, the Federal Reserve System, or the International Monetary Fund) to hold major leadership positions in these organizations. For the most part, however, it is these regulatory agencies that are "doing the driving" to ensure prudency in financial operations, and, of course, to prevent, as much as possible, any future financial crises. It is also important for us to realize that there is a rather fuzzy distinction between the field of economics and the field of finance, though there is definitely a distinction between them nonetheless. That distinction may even be seen as a fundamental difference in terms of the nature of the subfield, whether it is a science or a professional practice. That is, we very often see the economics departments of universities located within the university's "graduate school of arts and sciences" (and the like), while the finance department (if there is one) or simply the advanced courses on finance themselves are offered in the university's business school. There are exceptions, and the smaller the university the more likely it is to have its economics department, or economics classes, contained within its business school. Nevertheless, it is important for us to recognize the field of finance as existing primarily within the category of business studies and not so much in the field of economics.

The one area where the overlap between finance and economics is greatest is in the study of monetary policy, and especially the topic of predicting the future of financial markets—a topic that has combined macroeconomics, finance, and econometrics. It is in this topic area in which *academic economists contributed greatly to the financial crisis of 2008–2009* by, in large part, being totally oblivious to the fundamental flaws in the financial system, especially related to housing bubble. This failure on the part of academic economists is widely recognized, as had been discussed in chapter 1.

The financial crisis of 2008–9 led to a cottage industry of articles, blogs, books, and even popular movies that have sharply criticized the economics profession, the finance profession, and the financial regulators as having been responsible for the crisis, as indeed they were. At this writing that crisis is no longer fresh in people's minds, and it has become a topic of history. We can now see what effect the crisis has had—what changes have taken place to ensure that it will not happen again. Fortunately, many good changes have taken place in the aftermath of the crisis in the areas of financial regulation, and to some extent in the education of economists, with regard to a greater appreciation for how easily such a crisis could happen, and how we cannot always rely on rosy assumptions about the financial industry. *What has NOT been learned from the crisis, however, is the ultimate problem of academic economics existing as an autonomous field, where ideas are developed and promoted primarily in isolation of fundamental changes in the world.*

The regulations and offices put into place as a result of the financial crisis created an effective "autopilot system" to protect the economy from another similar crisis. In this sense, on the bright side, we are now safer while academic economists remain sleeping at the wheel. However, if, in the future, the pendulum swings against financial regulation, as people (and especially voters) forget what happened in the past, the academic economics community simply may not be able to come to the rescue to remind us of what happened in the past.

Scholarly Review and Critiques of Historical Literature

Proponents of "pluralism" in economics (simultaneously considering multiple perspectives and frameworks) tend to address ethics much more, on average, than those in the more traditional core of economic discourse. This connection between ethics and pluralism is so strong, and so obvious in many cases, that some economists might go as far as believing that "ethics in economics" is simply a "pluralist" topic as opposed to a topic for "mainstream" economists to explore. These economists may then dismiss the topic as inappropriate for *them* since they do not consider themselves to be "pluralists." (I realize that this sounds weird—it *should* sound weird, but it is often true, nevertheless.)

Of all the categories of ethics in economics, this one is the most remote from the real world and from usefulness to the profession, or to humanity more broadly. As discussed in the previous chapter, one will find scholarly debates concerning whether one particular famous scholar, who lived, say, 100 years ago, was significantly influenced by an earlier famous scholar who lived 200 years ago. Indeed, it is amazing to see how much written discussion there is among the academic scholars over the topic of which famous scholars influenced which other famous scholars, and what evidence they have proudly found for it.

Such literature appears to be quite similar in nature to literature in the humanities, such as literature on how the ancient Greek philosophers had influenced the ancient Roman philosophers. To their credit, however, humanities professors offer only the claim of knowing about their highly restricted field of study, while economics professors often use their knowledge of a similar nature to prescribe solutions to society's greatest problems—a role for which they are horribly unqualified. Yet, their arrogance, arising from their advanced and thorough knowledge of the history of economic thought, and from the teaching podium provided to them to proclaim their views, does not allow them to realize this.

Upholding Scientific Integrity in the Face of Potential Policy Bias

When I was a graduate student at Columbia back in 1985, the university campus was experiencing student protests against South African apartheid, which called for divestiture of all financial assets that the university had that could be tied to South African enterprises. This was, in fact, a wide-spread protest movement taking place throughout most major universities in the United States, and in many other nations as well. It had been occurring for a few years, in fact, by the time it peaked at Columbia in 1985 when one of the buildings was occupied by students who were also on a hunger strike.

Soon after these protests had begun, one of the prominent economics professors who specialized in international trade and development devised a new economic model that offered proof (under the necessary assumptions) that apartheid was economically inefficient for a society. He then motivated many of the students by devoting a lecture to the model. In theory, an argument could be made that there is no breach of scientific integrity here, in the sense that apartheid was a real issue confronting society at the time, and it is, indeed, the responsibility of economists to apply economic thought to important social issues, if such thought could actually contribute to a useful understanding of the issue. In this sense one cannot pass judgment against the development of such a model and lecture to students.

On the other hand, there is one aspect of this I find particularly troubling, which is the suggestion that the apartheid issue is something that would need an economic efficiency analysis behind it in order for economists to advocate its removal. This reflects a somewhat "intellectual totalitarianism" among economic theorists, where there appears to be an implicit assumption that ethical issues must be based on economic efficiency arguments to warrant the interest of economists. Also troubling was the suggestion that, if you are an economist and you have a cause you are fighting for, then you can always concoct some theoretical model, which, with the right assumptions and data, will support your cause. Of course, *if* this was the main perspective behind the model on apartheid that was presented, then it "crossed the line," by going outside the boundaries of scientific integrity, and into the realm of misleading propaganda (in the form of a mathematical model), regardless of how worthwhile its cause might have been.

Many of the concerns that I have expressed regarding scientific integrity in the work economists perform may be generalized to be concerns that apply to all practitioners and scientists, in all fields of study, who rely on statistics to generate their findings. In the area of statistics, the leading organization among professional statisticians in the United States is the American Statistical Association (ASA), which, as recently mentioned, has long-established standards of professional conduct for statisticians. In its "Ethical Guidelines for Statistical Practice" the ASA lists the following responsibilities of employers of statistical practitioners:

> Recognize that the results of valid statistical studies cannot be guaranteed to conform to the expectations or desires of those commissioning the study or the statistical practitioner(s). Any measures taken to ensure a particular outcome will lessen the validity of the analysis.
>
> 1. Valid findings result from competent work in a moral environment. . . .
> 2. Make new statistical knowledge widely available in order to benefit society at large. . . .
> 3. Support sound statistical analysis and expose incompetent or corrupt statistical practice. . . .
> 4. Recognize that within organizations and within professions using statistical methods generally, statistics practitioners with greater prestige, power, or status have a responsibility to protect the professional freedom and responsibility of more subordinate statistical practitioners who comply with these guidelines.
> 5. Do not include statistical practitioners in authorship or acknowledge their contributions to projects or publications without their explicit permission.[12]

In my view, these are wonderful guidelines, and they should be adopted wholeheartedly by the economics profession as well, especially given how much economics is based on the application of statistics. Many members of the ASA are, in fact, economists, including economics professors. Furthermore, as many of us already know, there is indeed a major subfield of economics devoted to the study and application of statistics in economics—econometrics—which is a required course for all economics students, along with micro- and macro-economics. Yet, econometric societies (especially "The Econometric Society"—the international 500-pound gorilla in the room) appear to have no explicitly stated ethical guidelines at all (other than a few publishing guidelines against plagiarism, etc.). Again, how is it that such an incredibly influential profession as economics (arguably the most influential profession of all), whose most important work is based on statistical analysis, has no stated ethical guidelines comparable to those that have long existed among statisticians? The unacceptable answer to the question is that the economics profession has always looked upon academic economists for leadership on such philosophically based topics, and frankly, the economics professors have *failed us* in this respect.

Addressing Sociological Aspects of the Profession

This book focuses primarily on the behavior of economics professors, as individuals, as opposed to the overall behavior of the institutions where they work, and the other organizations (like the AEA) that influence them. In a broad sense, however, the universities where they work do influence their behavior and beliefs. I think it is useful then to separate the organizations that influence economics professors into two groups: (1) Those that provide *money* to economics professors, directly in the form of income, or indirectly in the form grants and contracts issued to their academic institutions to become part of the professor's research budget. (2) Those that provide publication outlets (i.e., the technical journals and the associations that publish them) and other credentials through which economics professors may improve their employment status (such as conference presentations, serving on advisory boards of government agencies, etc.) In many cases, of course, the two overlap. For example, the World Bank might provide a professor a contract to perform a study, and might also publish that study as a World Bank report. This perspective on the influence that organizations have over the behavior and beliefs of economics professors is facilitated by the schematic provided in Figure 2.4 of chapter 2, entitled "The Circular Flow that Determines Theoretical Thought and Literature."

To an extent it could be argued: Let us not *blame* the individual professors themselves, but blame the organizations that influence them. There is, of course, a bit of a chicken-versus-egg problem here: Are the beliefs and behaviors of the organizations, themselves, the independent phenomenon that then affects the individual beliefs and behaviors of economics professors? Or, did the beliefs and behaviors of individual economics professors, and what they had in common in this regard, come first, which then caused organizations to develop their own beliefs and behaviors? In reality, of course, we would expect a mixture of both, especially in cases where the organization is populated primarily by economics professors, such as most of the associations that publish technical journals. Those organizations that are inhabited primarily by individuals who are not economics professors, such as government organizations and industry-based associations, have tended to influence economics professors more than they have been influenced *by them*. However, it is important to note that such organizations are influenced by economics professors, nonetheless, in various ways. The key question is, to what extent do the influencing organizations stand to benefit from enhancing professional ethics in academic economics? This is surely a question that leaders of the organizations should ask, though many organizations ask it either too infrequently or not at all. What is needed is an independent watch group to assess professional ethics in the work of economics professors, when the organizations those professors work for, the organizations that fund their research, and organizations that publish it have too little interest or investment into ensuring professional ethics.

Plagiarism in Academic Economics

In 1996, when I was working at NSF, I had written a chapter on the "Economic and Social Significance of Scientific and Engineering Research," for an NSF publication entitled, *Science and Engineering Indicators*. Technically, the volume was said to be written by the National Science Board (NSF's board of directors, appointed by the president).[13] However, the acknowledgments section of the report mentioned the "primary authors" of each chapter.

A couple years after the report was published a professor sent me a paper of his for comments. I did not know him and thus do not know why he sent it to me, but probably I was on some kind of list of economists working on the economics of technology and he was writing to everyone on that list. As I looked at his paper, a large part of it looked awfully familiar! Indeed it *was* familiar, because the paper had copied, *verbatim*, several pages from my *Science and Engineering Indicators* chapter. My guess was that the author of the paper thought the chapter had somehow been written by the National Science Board, and he had not bothered to see the acknowledgments section of that report to know that I actually wrote the chapter!

As it happens, anything that is published and provided to the public by the federal government is in the "public domain" and enjoys no copyright protection. Thus, it was not *illegal* for him to do what he did; it was only *ethically reprehensible*! Also, it was a paper that he was simply distributing for comment, as opposed the work actually being published by a journal. In any case, it was good for a laugh among my colleagues, where, along these lines, I would say that I am comforted in knowing that at least one person liked my chapter!

Economists who have studied plagiarism in economics, like Professor Gary Hoover in particular, who was one of AIRLEAP's first directors in 2007, often became interested in the subject of plagiarism after they themselves had become a victim of it. They also learn, as Gary Hoover has shown, that institutions, like universities and journals, do very little to stop it, or to make amends for it after it occurs.[14] As Hoover found, when journal editors discover plagiarism, they are often reluctant to do anything other than to send an essentially phony response to the proposing author saying the journal does not accept their paper—the same kind of form letter they would send to any author whose paper was rejected for any innocuous reason. In other words, many journals basically *chicken out* in confronting the plagiarist author or in informing the institutions (usually a university) where they work about it.[15] Surveys and statistics have been collected on the topic which reflects a disappointing lack of interest among journal editors to capture the high ground of professional ethics and responsibility on the issue, thereby helping to perpetuate the problem for many decades.

The four published studies that Hoover has coauthored (listed on his website)[16] present a great deal of survey results and even an economic model showing the "inefficiency" caused by tolerated plagiarism. On the one hand, I think this area of research is quite important and I believe the authors of this research should be commended, as should the journal editors to have decided to publish such work in their journals, in spite of the fact that this research does not always show the editors of economics journals in a favorable light.

Having said this, I also have a strong reservation, however, about the research that has been conducted in this area thus far. Unfortunately, in the typical fashion of most published research findings by academic economists, the studies have focused and expanded the "strongest links" and largely ignored the most important weakest links, leaving our fundamental understanding of the situation of plagiarism in economics extremely weak. Hoover and Enders conducted a survey, which they tabulated in 2004, in which they asked economics journal editors "what types of behavior constitute plagiarism," "how often they have experienced a clear case of plagiarism," and "how they would respond to a clear case of plagiarism."[17] They conducted a very similar survey of journal editors after that, along with a survey of "rank and file economists" (obtaining results from as many as 1,208 of them) which they tabulated in 2006.[18] They provided a variety of statistical summaries of the opinions of editors and authors from the rich data they collected—clearly one of the strongest links in the chain, which might be described as filling the bill for empirical analysis.

Another even stronger link in the chain, which nearly always seems to be the case in academic economics publications, is the "development of models" to explore the topic. As an example, in describing their own work and the work of others on the topic, professors Arce, Enders, and Hoover write the following, which readers may simply glance over to get a feel for the nature of this discourse:

> Yet the effect of ethical standards on the marketplace for ideas, and editors' role in establishing them, remains largely unexplored. . . . Consequently, a secondary contribution is re-establishing the dependence of misbehaviour on the frequency of monitoring and the punishment for violations in strategic (game-theoretic) models of enforcement/monitoring. Andreozzi (2004), among others, has shown that the (mixed strategy) Nash equilibrium of enforcement games under imperfect information often results in a counterintuitive independence between the incidence of violations and their corresponding penalties. We provide an alternative mechanism for establishing the dependence between violations and penalties under the conditions of incomplete information.[19]

We can see here that, as is so typically the case in economics literature, the analysis ventures into the La-la Land of "game-theoretic models" where we are essentially exploring the mathematical properties of the particular models we just created, as an intellectual exercise, independent of observations about what is actually happening in physical reality. Along these lines, Figure 9.1 shows what some of the theory *looks like* with regard to the model proposed by Arce, Enders, and Hoover in their 2008 article. [20]

In contrast to this approach I would interject two questions, which I would call the weakest links in the chain: (1) What deliberate measures have editors been using to detect incidences of plagiarism? (2) How much plagiarism *is there*, in economic journal articles? Related to this second question, *has*

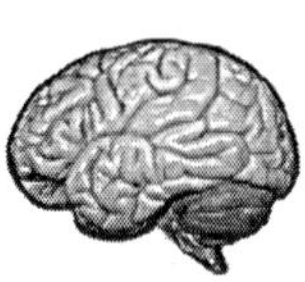

Result 1. In the (perfect) Bayesian equilibrium of Figure 1 the author does not publicize his/her work prior to submission if

$$\rho \le \text{Min}\{(\nu - \omega)/(\nu + \pi), (\nu^* + \nu)/2\nu^*\} \quad (1)$$

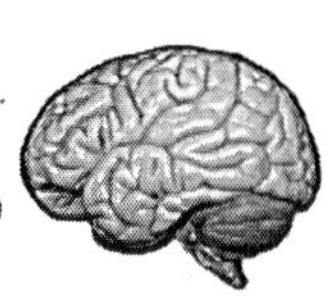

Figure 9.1 What Some "Economic Theory" Looks Like, Applied to the Topic of Plagiarism. Created by the author with reference to: Daniel Arce, Walter Enders, and Gary Hoover, "Plagiarism and Its Impact on the Economics Profession," Bulletin of Economic Research 60(3) (2008): 239. Brain Image by Wikimedia Commons, Shannan Muskopf (Own work), accessed May 6, 2017, http://tinyurl.com/lcx92ro.

anyone tried to find out? Arce, Enders, and Hoover might first appear to address this as follows in their 2008 article:

> Second, the editors were asked how often they have experienced a clear case of plagiarism. The 97 editors responding to this question reported that, on average, they experienced 0.38 instances of plagiarism per year (for a total of 37 cases/year across all reporting editors). Although this number is not especially large relative to the total number of submissions, it is probably biased downward since some instances of plagiarism go undetected and editors do not always acknowledge some forms of plagiarism.[21]

However, these incidences involve only the "clear cases" of plagiarism—where, in essence, the editors have not been looking for such cases, but where these cases basically jumped out of the pages of the proposed paper, and slapped the editor in the face, saying, "Look at me! I'm right here!" As an example, from their 2004 article on plagiarism, it appears that either Enders or Hoover became initially interested in the topic because one of them was serving as a referee for a journal, and when the journal had asked them to review a proposed paper, they discovered that the paper they were reviewing had copied their own work![22]

Frankly, this is what I cannot understand about the entire situation of how the academic economics profession is attempting to address the issue of plagiarism in economic journal articles: *Why are the editors of the journals not making any deliberate attempts to discover incidences of plagiarism using existing methods—methods that they must surely know!* There are indeed specific tests, using modern software, or equivalently, there are services to which an organization can subscribe, that will very often determine incidences of plagiarism as long as the original material was in print or was *ever* on the Internet (that may have since been deleted but can still be found).

Over a decade ago, when I was teaching a class on the economics of technology at Georgetown University, I received a term paper from one of my students that looked suspicious. That is, the paper had many references to articles posted on websites, but none of those articles were recent—the most recent one was a couple years old, and there seemed to be quite a few that were a couple years old. The paper was a Word file, and so as a curiosity, I went to information on the Word document that shows the author's name. Rather than seeing the student's name there, I found the name of another person who had already graduated. In theory, this alone could mean nothing; for example, the student and other person could be living together, and the student could have simply started to write the paper on the computer that the other person owned. However, the combination of this and the other circumstantial evidence about the age of the references was quite suspicious, so I mentioned this to the dean of the program under which I was teaching.

The dean asked me to provide him with what I had about the case, and that he and others would gladly "take it from there" to investigate it and make a determination. The dean told me that the university subscribes to a standard service that is used to identify cases of plagiarism.

Interested in what services of this kind might be available today, in about ten seconds (much less time than it is taking me to write this sentence) I found on the Internet an article entitled, "Top 10 Free Plagiarism Detection Tools For Teachers."[23] Similarly, as the editor of the 2014, three-volume set *Public Economics in the United States*, which contained forty-four chapters by about sixty authors and coauthors, I had worked extensively with the publisher to investigate all cases of potential plagiarism, after the publisher had run a thorough test of the entire manuscript. The publisher also used a special service, which I believe was not free, but more comprehensive than the free services.

If we were to ask journal editors why they have not used similar services to detect potential incidences of plagiarism, perhaps some (though I am only guessing here) may be quick to say that these services will likely find many incidences where the same authors have simply posted in the Internet, for comments, earlier versions of the same paper. Nevertheless, such cases could be easily identified and dismissed in seconds. What is important is that the same service would also detect genuine plagiarism, which should be the journal's responsibility to find!

Topics Similar to Plagiarism in Economics

A similar topic is the situation in which researchers, especially graduate students, write articles for others, like the professors for whom they are working as research assistants, where only the professor's name is listed as the author. This is not unique to the academic sector—it is pervasive throughout all of the sectors that hire economists, and of course, it happens in many other fields as well. This happened to me and to other graduate students I knew, for example, when we were working as research associates at the Inter-American Development Bank, although the fact that we were receiving a reasonable salary for our work took the edge off of the "exploitive" nature of the situation. In any case, leaders of the academic economics profession should take a stand against it, instead of remaining silent about it. They should do this for the incredibly simple and obvious reason that such behavior reflects unethical exploitation of those who do not receive credit for their work, as well as illegitimate credit for those who do not deserve it.[24]

Reproducibility, Objectivity, and Transparency

There is so much overlap in the discussion of these two factors that I thought it more efficient to discuss both into one section. The topic of reproducibility in economic research can be approached from two completely opposite ends: (1) from the advanced studies and scholarly literature that have been written on it, much of which have been quite recent, and (2) from the institutions that have supported or at least accepted research into this area. With regard to the first approach, a recent study (in December 2016) was performed by economics professors Garret Christensen and Edward Miguel at the University of California-Berkeley. Entitled "Transparency, Reproducibility, and Credibility of Economics Research," it was published as a National Bureau of Economic Research Working Paper.[25] This paper addresses a variety of issues associated with ethics and integrity in economics, not just reproducibility.

One of the issues discussed in the paper is "publication bias," which is quite basic. Explaining it in much simpler terms here, suppose there were 200 independent researchers all trying to prove that some factor A causes some factor B, all with different datasets, and there were no independent researchers trying to prove the opposite, that factor A does not cause factor B. As a hypothetical example, suppose there were a group of researchers who wanted to demonstrate that schools with lower student-teacher ratios, all else being equal, have students who perform better on standardized tests, implying that there is a strong justification for increasing a school's budget to have lower student-teacher ratios in classrooms. In this case, factor A is a lower-student teacher ratio for a school, and factor B is the school's average standardized test score. It is easy to envision 200 researchers all trying to prove that A causes B, but none wanting to prove the opposite. In any case, suppose that there is no actual relationship between A and B, at least for the range of values of A that there are. Nevertheless, if they all have different data, and significance at the 5 percent level is needed to ensure the study will be published, then on average about 5 of those 200 researchers will simply be lucky enough to find a statistically significant, positive relationship between lower student-teacher ratios and higher test scores. (There would also be five researchers on average who will find a statistically significant *negative* relationship between the two, though those researchers would most likely then assume that they were simply unlucky and that their research findings are inconclusive and would not try to publish them.) The world will then wind up with five published studies "demonstrating," by tests of statistical significance, that there is a positive relationship between low student-teacher ratios and student achievement, with the policy implication that some school districts should hire more teachers. This would be in spite of the fact, of course, that there actually was no positive relationship between the variables (in this hypothetical thought experiment).

Another issue that is commonly discussed with regard to reproducibility is as simple as the problem of data availability—whether the researchers who want to replicate and thereby verify what other researchers have published can even get their hands on the data from the original researchers. In some cases the verifiers cannot receive the data because of confidentiality issues. However, as the study suggests, these legitimate excuses for the lack of data sharing is much more the exception than the rule. What is more common is that the original researchers simply choose not to provide the data to others who want to verify the findings by replication.

The topic of "Specification Searches" is also often discussed which could, depending on the circumstances, account for another way in which results that appear to be statistically significant are essentially *phony*. However, we should first realize that there is nothing wrong with "specification searches" themselves—specification in this case meaning "finding the right equations that work"—finding the "specifications" of those equations. For example, if Isaac Newton were trying to find the equation that calculates the distance of a falling object, he may have concluded that it is the equation where an object falls at a constant rate of acceleration of about 10 meters per second, per second. Specification searches are then, in many respects, the workhorse of the empirical sciences, or at least one of the workhorses.

When "specification searching" is listed in the literature as a category of factors that could lead to phony results, however, it means something a bit different. In this case the words "specification searching" is meant to mean excessive specification searching that tries so many possibilities of equations, that when it finally gets one that works, it is probably only by chance alone, rather than reflecting a true causal relationship. This topic is therefore, another version of the fallacy of association as causation, discussed previously in chapters 3 and 5.

For example, let us go back to hypothetical example of a study that is trying to find a positive relationship between lower student-teacher ratios and test scores, or equivalently, a negative relationship between class size and test scores. Suppose the researcher had data for a total of 1,000 classes, all of the same grade, that is, 1,000 observations with the class size and average test score per class. Now suppose the researcher first tried to test directly whether class size made a difference in the average test score and found that it did not. However, not giving up, the researcher thought of adding other factors into the model, to see what could happen—perhaps the age of the teacher matters, for example, since more experienced teachers might be better at teaching and thus their students might have higher test scores. So they try it! If it works, they grab those statistical coefficients while the grabbing is good, and write their paper with its statistically significant findings. If it does not work—no problem, just try something else . . . how's about the per capital income in the county where the school is—would that work? It doesn't . . . darn! . . . I know . . . let's try the proportion of the population of the county whose first language spoken in the home is not English . . . etc. Indeed, this is the same significant-coefficient-hunting game that was described in chapter 5.

I would hope at this point that some readers might think, "Now wait a minute—wasn't it just said that specification searching is part of the process of scientific discovery?" And, if another variable is added to a model that renders more statistically significant findings, then isn't this a form of genuine scientific discovery? For example, maybe it is indeed *true* that household income, and whether English is spoken in the home, makes a difference in test scores in addition to class size, and so the model that incorporates all of these elements, and finds all of them to be statistically significant, is simply a legitimate finding, reflecting good, scientific use of statistics to learn how the world actually works.

Such a statement would reflect sound logic. The test of the truthfulness of the model, however, would then depend on how well the same model worked on simply a different set of comparable data. Suppose it worked for a particular dataset with 1,000 classes (observations). What if we could then test it again on each of ten other datasets, where each one of those other datasets had 1,000 other observations of its own? Suppose further that, when these other ten tests were tried, the same model worked the same exact way, with significant coefficients for, say seven of the ten, and the other three of the ten did not have quite the same results but they were somewhat similar. Then, in this case we would have strong evidence that the model is offering a truthful understanding of reality. On the other hand, suppose the model flopped in all ten cases of the other datasets. In this latter scenario we could safely conclude that the statistical significance we discovered at first was most likely spurious; it was an illusion that we created by trying enough different specifications until we finally got lucky. Thus, the *reproducibility* of the test with *different data* will validate the model. In this discussion we have now found the interrelationships that exist among the concepts of reproducibility, truthfulness, scientific integrity, specification searching, the fallacy that association is causation, and the cult of statistical significance (a la Ziliak and McCloskey).

I have described this in rather simple terms, but it gets quite a bit more complicated for econometricians when they have limited resources and limited data available to sort out what appears to be causality and what appears to be just dumb luck. Along these lines, one of the most important citations in Christensen and Miguel's paper is to the pivotal work done by Professor Edward Leamer. In 1983, Leamer wrote one of the most famous articles in economics entitled, "Let's Take the Con out of Econometrics," in *American Economic Review.* (In this case, the AER *did actually provide the public with a highly valuable article!*) In short, Leamer's study offers various mathematical techniques, such as "extreme-bounds analysis" to enable the researcher to more positively determine whether the apparent causality, reflected in statistically significant coefficients, is genuine or merely coincidental.

In spite of its value, Leamer's 1983 study and subsequent work like it were within the subfield of econometrics, which examines precisely how econometrics should be used. The vast majority of economics professors are not econometricians (or even teachers of econometrics)—they only *use* econometrics as a tool for getting the empirical results they need to support their theoretical model—whatever that theoretical model might be. Consequently, as strange, and as irresponsible, as it may sound, many will actually view the issue of whether they properly used econometrics in their work as an issue that is outside their area of expertise! (Few would admit this however.)

Pre-Analysis Plans

In their discussion of the problems of excessive specification searches, Christensen and Miguel have offered, as a possible solution, the idea that researchers prepare and register "pre-analysis plans" of their intent to test a certain model prior to actually testing the data. [26] Then, when their model pans out, they might submit the paper and have evidence behind it that they only tested what they said they were going to test. At first glance, this may sound like a good idea, but in reality it has two major problems—one conceptual and the other logistical.

The conceptual problem reflects a point that I had already expressed—the idea that specification searches are actually a good thing in moderation—they can be the work horse of scientific discovery. I believe a lot of theoretical economists miss this point because they are oriented in a completely different way. To them, the really important part of the "discovering" is working out the complex mathematics of a new model, and making sure the impressive properties of the model do not have any flaws. From their perspective the next step is to get the model to effectively "pass inspection" to get published, by having it produce statistically significant statistics when tested against data. Scientific discovery *can* happen this way, but only if the researcher is sufficiently lucky to know enough about the phenomena they are studying to propose a model first.

In La-La Land they will always be this lucky, but in the real world they often need to run various tests on the data that will help them develop the true understanding they need of the phenomena they are studying. From there they may then develop a workable model.

In other words, researchers can scientifically and legitimately let the data tell them what model to use, rather than develop a model first and then hope the data obediently follow their orders. This other way of looking at it then flies in the face of idea that we should have preregistered "pre-analysis plans" as a condition for publication, as if the only thing we need to demonstrate is that the data were obedient!

As if this problem were not enough, there are two other significant logistical problems with regard to the pre-analysis idea. First of all, it would require resources on the part of the journals to keep track of these plans, and to share them with the public or examine them themselves to see if the researchers really did what they promised. The journals may simply not agree to it. The other logistical problem, more importantly, is that these pre-analysis conditions can be gamed in half-a-dozen ways. For example, what is to stop researchers from running a million specification tests anyway before coming up with a model and just not tell anyone? Then, once they created the model that works in cranking out significant coefficients, they can pretend this model was the one they had in mind all along. They could then register it with the journal and pretend to be waiting for a more current dataset that would add one more year of data to the dataset they already tested (which probably will not make much of a difference in the results), and when the new data comes in they will be poised to committing the perfect crime, with the only difference being that getting the work published cost them a little more time. I can think of other ways the new rule could be gamed as well, but I think the one just mentioned is sufficient.

THE ROAD TO THE UNDERWORLD THAT WAS PAVED WITH SUPPOSEDLY GOOD INTENTIONS

When BITSS burst on the scene in 2012, five years after I established AIRLEAP, my colleagues and I who were actively working on promoting professional ethics in economics initially viewed its arrival as a *godsend*. We all seemed to be fighting for the same cause, but unlike AIRLEAP, whose very existence might be seen as a flash in the pan, BITSS arrived as a *force* within the economics community, with all the necessary "heavy artillery" to make things happen. It was, first of all, backed by UC-Berkeley, a very high-ranking university, and likewise, it had prominent economists behind it. Most importantly, BITSS had three other ingredients that would surely guarantee its success: (1) a fantastic, and indeed, incredibly valid cause (at least on the surface, as will be discussed shortly), (2) volunteers who were both highly motived and highly educated, and, last but not least, (3) *Substantial funding!* Thus, it has an impressive website, a fantastic exhibitor's booth at the AEA economics conference, and a popular following with its offers of prizes and grants to research on transparency and reproducibility in the social sciences. It has, as a result, also generated considerable literature in its topic areas, in spite of its relatively brief existence.

We then approached some of their leading members to join us in presenting papers at economics conferences. In June 2016, I had organized an AIRLEAP session at the Western Economic Association International meetings on "Promoting Integrity and Transparency in Economics," and had invited Christensen and Miguel to present their paper on "Transparency and Reproducibility in Economic Research," which was simply an earlier version of their NBER paper that I have been describing above. In that session I was also the "discussant" of their paper, where I offered my comments on it before the session attendees (though few people attended). At that time, I only had one concern about their paper that I felt would be useful to express in the session, and Christensen (who was there presenting the paper) briefly responded to it, which I will discuss shortly. However, by then my concerns were already mounting about the kind of research that BITSS and its members (and grantees) were performing, and similarly I was developing broader concerns about where this, apparently blossoming subfield on reproducibility and transparency in economics, was heading.

From my own perspective, reality finally set in, and I came to realize that the subfield so far was actually *creating more harm than good*—doing more, though indirectly, to support the absence of reproducibility and transparency in economics than it was to encourage reproducibility and transparency. Nevertheless, colleagues of mine in AIRLEAP (three other members of the board of directors, including the chair) had organized a session on "Replication and Ethics in Economics," at the 2017 annual meetings of the AEA, which I attended.[27]

The irony of the situation is that all of the efforts that are being made in this area of research are very well intended. I believe the contributors truly believe they are trying to "make a difference" in a positive direction. I also believe that their energy, commitment, and fundamental understanding of the subject, can, in fact, make a very positive difference if they were correctly applied. Below I offer five interrelated reasons why I believe this blossoming subfield is, overall, doing more harm than good, in spite of the good intentions of its participants.

Victim to the Curse of Scholarship

I had devoted most of chapter 7 of this book to explaining how scholarly arguments to improve the academic economics profession generate nice publications and bring recognition to its authors, and basically "preach to the choir" to like-minded scholars. Beyond that, they fall on deaf ears to everyone else, including, especially the deaf ears of those who need to change the most from hearing the arguments. The fact that most economics professors cannot hear the arguments being made is not independent of the reasons why those professors need to change. What kills the effort the most, however, is not any malicious attitude among those who need to change, but simply a naïve perspective that the arguments being brought before them are simply outside their area of expertise, and thus they do not know what to make of them. They do not feel personally qualified even to think about the ideas being discussed, and so they do not think about them at all. Moreover, they often keep in the back of their mind a level of comfort in knowing that, whatever criticisms they might be hearing about their actions, such criticisms must also apply to many well-respected members of their community who are doing the same thing that they are doing, and so they might ask themselves, "How bad can any of this be?"

The curse of scholarship is not a curse that had been imposed upon scholarly researchers by some outside entity, but a curse that scholars have brought upon themselves. They address the issues of ethics and integrity as if they were trying to make a difference, but the bottom line is that they are not committed to the objective of *reaching out to the people who need to change and convincing them to change*; the agenda, unfortunately, is the expression of what they believe to be great ideas for which they should receive credit. They are, in short, working for their own credit and recognition, not for change. Consider, for example, the following passage from the introduction in Christensen and Miguel's NBER working paper (with my emphasis added):

> The *goal of this piece* is to *survey this emerging literature* on research transparency and reproducibility, and *synthesize the insights emerging in economics* as well as from other fields—awareness of these issues has also recently come to the fore in political science (Gerber, Green, and Nickerson 2001; Franco, Malhotra, and Simonovits 2014), psychology (Simmons, Nelson, and Simonsohn 2011; Open Science Collaboration 2015), sociology (Gerber and Malhotra 2008a), finance (Harvey, Liu, and Zhu 2015), and other research disciplines as well, including medicine (Ioannidis 2005). *We also discuss productive avenues for future work.*[28]

The goal is thus to produce a good scholarly work that will be recognized as such, and (as suggested in the last sentence) help other people join the same party by producing more of the same. The latter aspect of this goal may be particularly popular, since it may involve receiving research grants from BITSS, not to mention new opportunities for publications. What is also made clear from this one passage, and throughout most of the actual working paper, is the message that this topic is somehow incredibly complicated and interdisciplinary, suggesting that it is all "over the head" of a typical economist who might attempt to think about the topic.

Most importantly, however, the stated goal of the work includes nothing—not even a suggestion—that the authors are trying to change anything for the better. They are simply trying to understand the problem, apparently for the sake of satisfying an intellectual curiosity, and as an end in itself. If the goal were stated in a completely different way, such as "laying the groundwork for fixing a bad problem," then their work might possibly attract the attention of people who are not already scholars in this particular subfield. However, when the stated goal is simply the satisfaction of an intellectual curiosity, and not the correction of a wrong, then it provides an incredibly "easy way out" for anyone who simply is not interested in this body of scholarly research (or feels unqualified to study it).

The Delusion that the Concerns Are All Being Addressed

The above quotation from the Christensen and Miguel paper already suggests, with its long list of references, that none of this is new—that great minds have already been working on it. In turn, this subtly implies that there is nothing to worry about—the issue is already being handled in the context of "business as usual" for the economics profession. Similarly, the AEA conference session that I mentioned earlier was entitled, "Replication and Ethics in Economics: Thirty Years after Dewald, Thursby, and Anderson," suggesting that the homework has already been done, and begging the question of whether there is anything else we need to do.

Promoting a Passive, Nonjudgmental Perspective of the Problem

Related to the factor just mentioned, a very uncomfortable question needs to be identified and addressed here. It is uncomfortable because in identifying and addressing this question we will necessarily reduce the support that BITSS or the subfield more generally will receive from different groups. However, such a "reduction" will not be a true reduction, but what I would prefer to call a "correction" of the ambiguity that now exists with regard to the subfield's true goals. This uncomfortable question is this: (1) Is the subfield committed to identifying and addressing what is very wrong in the profession with regard to the absence of reproducibility and transparency, or (2) is the subfield just another scholarly discipline that is devoted primarily to scholarly pursuits, without "making waves" and without necessarily correcting anything in the system but at least understanding it better to satisfy an intellectual curiosity? Let us call the first of these a "progressive and critical agenda" and the second a "passive and nonjudgmental" agenda.

BITSS obviously hedges its bets between these two approaches, in an apparent attempt to appeal to as many people and institutions as possible, with each giving BITSS the benefit of the doubt that BITSS really has the particular agenda that they want to see it have. This is, of course, not an unusual strategy; in some respects it reflects exactly how politics generally work in terms of political entities taking multiple positions to appeal to a broad mixture of people with different viewpoints.

BITSS' mission, as it is stated on its website,[29] clearly has this ambiguity. The mission has five elements, which are quoted below, one at a time, with a discussion following each element:

"*1. Build consensus on key issues facing students, faculty, researchers, funders, journals, and other key partners to be more transparent in the social sciences.*" This element sets the tone for the leaders of BITSS to see their work as being "consensus building"—implying, in effect, that BITSS will only advocate changes that will "make everyone happy." While wanting to make everyone happy is an admirable desire at many levels, it also places an extreme limitation on any effort to make any real progress in this area. It will certainly be easy to get all the parties involved to "pay lip service" to more transparency and reproducibility, but requiring a consensus implies that it will be unlikely that any solution will impose new restrictions on authors, journals, or research institutes, or that any entities will be held more accountable to ensure transparency and reproducibility, with repercussions if they do not.

"*2. Improve our understanding of the problem and build evidence on solutions for increased transparency through long-term study of researcher practices.*" This element effectively expresses the hope that scholarship ("long-term study") will lead the way for change, which is highly questionable for the reasons recently mentioned. Another discomforting aspect of this element is its inclusion of the words "long-term," suggesting that there is no urgency to solving the problem—that we have all the time in the world to study it, while continually receiving more grants to do so and acquiring more publications to our credit along the way.

"*3. Increase supply of and access to tools and resources for research transparency, which is a necessary precursor for widespread adoption of best practices across the research community.*" This element further extends and emphasizes the argument that we need further study in order to figure out what to do—that research on transparency is a necessary precursor for improvement. This is highly debatable for two reasons: Transparency and reproducibility is rooted, primarily, in a commitment to honesty—for the most part, and as such, "it is not rocket science" and should then not be viewed as rocket science. As I have already implied, it is somewhat self-serving for those who are pushing for more advanced studies to claim that such studies are necessary before any decisions are made or any policies are established. It is also an indirect way of postponing any direct efforts that might be achieved through criticisms of any of the parties involved, especially criticisms of (or even stronger measures against) the researchers who claim findings that cannot be reproduced when others apply the same data to the same model. This kind of nonreproducibility problem may, in many cases, be best recognized as a consequence of simple irresponsibility or dishonesty on the part of the researchers involved. In such basic cases, the problem does not need "further study" as if we were planning to colonize the planet Mars but had not yet worked out the details.

The strategy of doing nothing until further studies are performed is a standard and well-known mechanism, in policy arenas, to ensure that nothing is done about a problem while at the same time appearing, to a naïve public, to be making an effort to address that problem.

"*4. Deliver coursework and change research practices at scale by harnessing the BITSS network of students, academic faculty, and researchers (a 'push' mechanism).*" In order to understand the wording of this element, I had to look up what is meant by "at scale" which I found is a term of art in information processing that means "at the required size to solve the problem."[30] The applicable meaning of the verb "to harness" in this case would be "to utilize." Most of this element is tautological (circular in logic), in that it is essentially saying that part of BITSS's mission is to put to use BITSS's resources, which any organization could state as its mission, since the only reason it had developed those resources was to accomplish its mission! "Deliver coursework" implies that the problem should be addressed in the education of researchers, displaying that BITSS is primarily an organization for academics, which is further demonstrated by BITSS' "Catalyst Program."[31] The words "change research practices" is remarkably vague and diplomatically soft, as if the more appropriate wording of "improve research practices" would be too accusatory of current practices. This begs the question of whether BITSS is even willing to make any criticisms at all. Beyond the circularity of the element, however, there is the organization's self-promotion, essentially saying that part of its mission is to ensure that its network is recognized.

"*5. Provide recognition and awards for the adoption of behaviors related to research transparency (a 'pull' mechanism).*" This element also appears to "sound nice" at a cursory level, especially to naïve readers and lay audiences. It reflects the "be nice" philosophy that one often sees in principles of management, where it said that people should be encouraged to do what is right "with a carrot rather than a stick," or with "sugar rather than vinegar," etc. If we go below the shallow surface of this sugary policy, however, and ask what is really being said here, we may find this element somewhat troubling.

I have great difficulty, in particular, with the concept that researchers should be rewarded for demonstrating behavior that is ethically correct and that meets basic standards of scientific integrity. Suggesting that they should be rewarded for such behavior implies that such behavior is above and beyond what they would normally be expected to do, which simultaneously implies that, if they did not demonstrate ethical behavior or scientific integrity they are in the norm. In my view, this perspective does as much to perpetuate the continued existence of unethical behavior and violations of scientific integrity as it does to try to solve these problems.

Overall, I find BITSS's approach to the topic of reproducibility and transparency to be highly passive, with absolutely no sense of urgency, and certainly no sense of outrage at the unethical behavior that is often evident when the published research findings in economics cannot be validated. To me this does more harm than good—ultimately it reflects and promotes a tolerance for something that should not be tolerated. Moreover, as already mentioned, studying a problem to death, is, in the end, simply another way of failing to address it.

Pacifying and Crowding-Out Resistance

I could see representatives from BITSS reacting to the criticism I expressed earlier about its stated mission by saying that I have simply been seeing them in wrong light in the first place—that their purpose was never to criticize, or identify any wrongdoing on anyone's part, but simply to study the issues and increase our knowledge about them, in the presumptuous hope that, as we get smarter about all of it, we will wind up doing the right thing. Yet, in spite of such a passive position, BITSS hedges its bets for more public recognition and support by also suggesting that it is, in fact, an *activist* organization that is pretending to be *fighting for social change*.

For example, shortly after presenting its mission, it describes itself as part of an "'open social science' *movement*" (my emphasis).[32] "Movement" is clearly a buzzword here that suggests an activist perspective. Similarly, BITSS lists having six partners in the "open social science *ecosystem*" (another loaded word): "The Berkeley Institute for Data Science," "The Center for Open Science," "*Innovations for Poverty Action,*" "Meta-Research Innovation Center at Stanford," "Mozilla Science Lab," and "Project TIER" [my emphasis].[33]

Those who want to see BITSS as a passive supporter of the status quo in the research practices can probably be satisfied with BITSS stated mission alone, as described above. Yet, those who are looking to join an activist organization, and who might, for example, mosey by the BITSS exhibitor's booth at an economics conference and ask what BITSS is doing to save the world (so to speak), they may also like what they are told. They could be told, in particular, that BITSS has partnered with the organization "Innovations for Poverty Action (IPA)." Of course, any organization with "Action" in its title is suggested to be an activist organization.[34] BITSS thus provides plenty of superficial evidence for those who want to see BITSS as being part of an activist, "eco-oriented," "movement" like Greenpeace. While IPA is rather timid (at least on paper) in comparison to other supposedly activist organizations, it is not too shy to describe the problem that it addresses as one in which existing policies to alleviate poverty are, in many cases, "ineffective" and involve "wasted money."[35]

In truth, IPA is playing the same kind of publicity game—it is not an activist organization in the least, as one might normally think from its title or from its initial description of itself in its brief "About" page on its website. In actuality, it is an organization that exists primarily (if not exclusively) to carry out and promote "randomized control trials" that essentially perform experiments with impoverished communities in developing countries by offering specific programs to some and not to others and seeing what differential effects occur as a result.[36]

There is an ongoing debate over whether randomized trials on impoverished communities have been ethical. Ziliak and Teather-Posadas make a strong case against them in a recent chapter in the *Oxford Handbook of Professional Economic Ethics*, entitled, "The Unprincipled Randomization Principle in Economics and Medicine," in which they conclude, "Randomized trials are neither necessary nor sufficient. And they're often unethical."[37] Obviously, there is *no consensus whatsoever* on this issue, in spite of BITSS's touting that consensus building is the first element of its mission.

Academic economists who might be inclined to support much more aggressive actions to address scientific integrity problems in the profession still face the problem of having to work within the confines of the subfield that has published in this area and that has already established its leading and recognized experts. Because of BITSS's strong funding, its recruitment and organization of prominent participants, its association with top-ranked institutions, and the precedence it has set in publishing in leading top-ranked outlets (like NBER Working Papers) BITSS is clearly the "500-pound gorilla in the room" with regard to this subfield. Anyone who might advocate more aggressive or critical approaches to the topic will thus appear to be in the minority—perhaps perceived as a "radical element" of the subfield by comparison to the "standard" that BITSS has set. Whether this situation was by design in the creation of BITSS or simply an unplanned circumstance is anyone's guess (though the people who created BITSS would surely know). What is important for now is that this situation does exist, and it is a major barrier to progress being made with regard to efforts to promote ethics and scientific integrity in economics.

Reproducibility Can Backfire by Validating Studies That Are Actually Invalid

As mentioned earlier, at the Western Economic Association International meetings, in 2016, I had discussed the BITSS-supported paper by Christensen and Miguel on "Transparency and Reproducibility in Economic Research." In my discussion I did not bring up any of the above-mentioned concerns about BITSS, mostly because many of them had not occurred to me at that time, and even if they had occurred to me, they would have been inappropriate for that venue in any case. Nevertheless, I did mention one concern that Christensen politely dismissed as being, in his view, peripheral to the ideas of his paper. I continue to believe it is relevant, however. The concern was related to my overall criticism about much of the published economic literature in technical journals, which I have written on extensively throughout this book. However, at the session my comment was rather simple and it did not go into the broad issues that I have raised in this book. The comment was as follows (though I expressed it much less formally in the conversation at the session):

Suppose there is a study that has potential flaws and that should therefore be scrutinized on the basis of the legitimacy of its underlying assumptions, the logical and mathematical validity of its model based on those assumptions, or the accuracy of the data that were used to test the model. Yet, regardless of these weak links in the chain, tests are made by other researchers confirming that, when the same data are used to test the same model, the same results are found, and in this sense alone the results have been validated. Such extra testing and validation to essentially prove that "the math applied to the data was done right" might then create a false validity with regard to the study overall, when the study might simply be based on arbitrary assumptions that are essentially "rediscovered" when data are used to test them. Or, the data may be equally arbitrary or erroneous, but those data do imply the results found in the study when the mathematics of the model is performed in the same way. If we therefore focus too much on reproducibility, we may find ourselves creating *a false sense of confirmation in findings that are still, inherently invalid.* Thus, before efforts are made to reproduce findings, efforts should be made to verify that such findings are *worth* reproducing!

Many have argued, for example, that one of the causes of the great recession of 2008–9 was a tendency for some economists to observe a continual, annual 10 percent (or so) rise in housing prices, in comparison to a 2 or 3 percent inflation rate, and assume (without much thought, of course) that this trend will continue on indefinitely. If research papers reporting such findings could boast that their estimated rate of increase in housing prices has been confirmed by several other, independent analyses, such superficial support could only increase the public's belief in such a trend, and deter the public's questioning the belief that housing prices rise by 10 percent each year.

While reproducibility of research findings is still an essential requirement for the validation of a study, it should not be misinterpreted as confirming all aspects of the study. An overemphasis on it could thus cause more harm than good by fostering such a misinterpretation. This also creates an additional bias toward support for studies that were well funded, or conducted by prominent economists, or published in top-ranked journals, where resources will be more easily found to supposedly "validate" the studies in terms of reproducibility. Studies that were not in top-ranked journals may not attract enough resources to demonstrate reproducibility, creating a situation where the profession could be inclined to value work in top-ranked journals even higher, relatively, by their now having an extra property of demonstrated reproducibility—as if the obsession with valuing top-ranked journal articles (as I have described in previous chapters) were not bad enough already!

Wasteful Discussions and Analyses

One might naïvely assume that studies on transparency and reproducibility in economics would be committed to investigating directly how ethics and scientific integrity in economic research might best be achieved. Along these lines one might then naively assume, as well, that such studies would be immune to getting lost in esoteric, mathematical exercises pretending to offer a higher understanding of the phenomena being studied. However, in reality such esoteric exercises are there often to impress and entertain a very unique audience that easily confuses these exercises with useful knowledge. Unfortunately, in this respect the study of transparency and reproducibility in economics hosts the same viral disease that is pervasive throughout theoretical economic literature.

In their 2016 working paper, Christiansen and Miguel review a great deal of literature that falls within this category. To understand what is going on here, we can start by recognizing that it is open season for anyone to create "a model" to explain topics like publication bias, as described earlier. You just need to make some simplifying assumptions about how randomness is generated in research findings, and from there derive how likely it is that publishable, statistically significant, results will occur by chance alone. This is essentially what I had done in the example I provided earlier in explaining publication bias, though it can be done at a much more mathematically complicated and abstract level. As an illustration, I provide a snippet of this type of discourse from the Christiansen and Miguel paper in Figure 9.2, where, again, I deliberately present this as a figure to emphasize that there is no expectation for readers to understand it—the figure only shows how it looks.

As demonstrated in chapter 6, a wealth of data on citations can be, and have been, used to support numerous studies of the factors that determine citation counts, where these studies are subject of course to whatever mathematical assumptions are made to the heart's desire of the researcher. Since each publication also provides statistical findings, and there might be some way of pinpointing the single most relevant level of statistical significance in each publication, there is also then a wealth of data that interrelate publications with their achieved levels of statistical significance. Thus, in much the same way that some researchers have studied citation counts, theoretical economists (and other scientists as well) can use, and have already used, such data to generate numerous studies that explore the distributions of reported significance levels among publications. These studies perform all kinds of analyses that compare these distributions to what some model might have predicted these distributions of significance levels to be according to certain assumptions, like the kinds of assumptions shown in Figure 9.2.

There is in all this an incredible delusion, among the people who produce and study this discourse, that there is actually something good being done. Overlaying the incredibly sophisticated, and deliberately impressive, mathematics involved is the incredibly simplistic logic that: (1) publication bias (and the like) is a very important issue, (2) I have a real lot of great data and really interesting mathematical models with which to study it, and (3) therefore, I am doing good by developing a sophisticated study that uses these models and data—I am one of the "good guys" who is trying to do something about publication bias by helping us understand it better. It is hard to count the vast number of flaws in this logic, so I will focus on only a few of them. First of all, it should be obvious that the models used to predict the

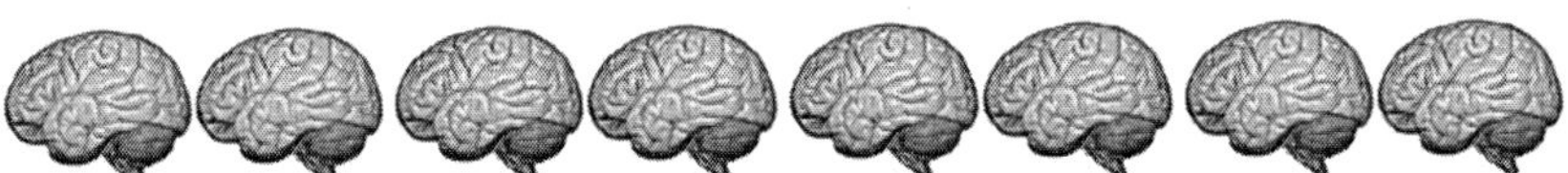

For simplicity, consider the case in which a relationship or hypothesis can be classified in a binary fashion as either a "true relationship" or "no relationship". Define R_i as the ratio of true relationships to no relationships commonly tested in a research field i (e.g., development economics). Prior to a study being undertaken, the probability that a true relationship exists is thus $R_i/(R_i+1)$. Using the usual notation for statistical power of the test $(1-\beta)$ and statistical significance level (α), the PPV in research field i is given by:

$$PPV_i = (1-\beta)\, R_i \,/\, ((1-\beta)R_i + \alpha)$$

Clearly, the better powered the study, and the stricter the statistical significance level, the closer the PPV is to one, in which case false positives are largely eliminated. At the usual significance level of $\alpha = 0.05$ and in the case of a well-powered study $(1-\beta=0.80)$ in a literature in which half of all hypotheses are thought to be true ex ante $(R_i = 0.5)$, the PPV is relatively high at 89%, a level that would not seem likely to threaten the validity of research in a particular economics subfield.

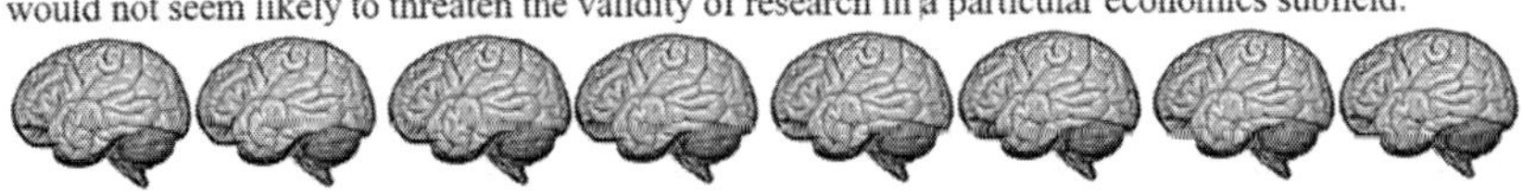

Figure 9.2 Excerpt Illustrating the Mathematics of Publication Bias. Created by the author with reference to: Christensen, Garret and Edward Miguel. "Transparency, Reproducibility, and Credibility of Economics Research." National Bureau of Economic Research Working Paper 22989, December 2016, 4-5. Brain Image by Wikimedia Commons, Shannan Muskopf (Own work), accessed May 6, 2017, http://tinyurl.com/lcx92ro.

distribution of statistically significance results are incredibly arbitrary, as evidenced by the mere fact that these models differ substantially among each other, owing to the different assumptions that they make. Secondly, statistical significance alone is not important, as already discussed extensively before, and yet it is deemed to be so important in these studies only because it provides a convenient common denominator to serve as fodder for these studies (in much the same way that citation and publication counts do for the studies conducted of them).

Thirdly, as mentioned in the Christiansen and Miguel paper, the mathematics involved would suggest that there are not that many publications that just make it above the threshold of achieving statistical significance, because that would be too coincidental. So these models say that there is a tendency, by chance alone, for there not to be that many studies that achieve just the minimum amount of statistical significance needed. By this logic, when there is, in fact, a disproportionally high number of studies that make it right above the threshold, it is suggesting, according to these models, that there is a lapse of scientific integrity—that researchers are tending to continue to data mine and explore "alternative specifications" until they can finally squeeze out from the data just enough of the minimal statistical significance they need to enable them to get the paper published. This analytical approach conversely implies that if the findings tend to be notably above the threshold in terms of their statistical significance, then they are more likely to have involved less data mining, excessive specification searching, and other shenanigans, and are more likely to be genuinely valid and reflective of scientific integrity.

Gee whiz, is there anything missing in this type of model? How about the fact that many researchers *already know that these kinds of models exist*, and that if they do report statistics that are right above the threshold, they know they are more likely to be suspected of beating up the data (whether they did or not), and so they have an extra incentive to beat up the data just a little more to see if they can raise their findings higher, above the threshold, to be less suspect. Perversely, those researchers who performed perfectly valid research with nothing at all to hide, but did happen to acquire results that were only slightly within the 5 percent threshold would be less inclined to start beating up the data or model for even better results—they had already captured the high ground of scientific integrity, so why would they want to descend from it only to avoid a suspicion that would be incorrect and unfair? (I am reminded of the sophisticated detective shows on television where the smart detective reasons that the primary suspect is not guilty, because if they were, they would have had an alibi!)

Hey! Let ME Play!

Please allow me to grab the ball in this modeling game, just for a minute—I would like to play too. Let us suppose that a researcher can acquire a large data set, where the data do not at first glance support a particular model, but there is enough randomness in the data, and enough options in the specification of the model, to enable the researcher to beat up the data until it finally gives up and supports the development of a publishable model (on whatever the particular topic is at hand) with statistically significant coefficients. Let us say it might take the researcher one month of work to do this. Suppose that, without achieving that statistical significance the paper has no chance of being published, but with it, it has a 10 percent chance.

Under this hypothetical situation, the question then becomes, is it worth beating up the data for a month for a 10 percent chance of publication, in addition to whatever personal cost there is of violating scientific integrity?

Well, as an economist, we might reason that this decision would be based on the expected inherent value of the extra publication to the author(s). Suppose in scenario #1 the author is not prominent, the theoretical model that they would present in the article is not mathematically impressive, and the article itself is not profound, so there is no way that it would ever be accepted to a top-ranked journal—only to a low-ranking journal which would do little or nothing for the author's career. Under this scenario, the extra month of work to play around with data and specifications, and to violate scientific integrity in doing so, is just not worth it.

Now consider an alternative scenario #2 where the situation is the same except that the author is, in fact, a rising star author from a prominent institution, and a fantastic writer and brilliant theoretician, who might then be facing a 10 percent chance of having the paper accepted by AER, if only that 5 percent significance level can be squeezed out of the model. In this case, since an AER article is so valuable (as discussed in chapter 6), it might well be worth the author's time to do whatever tricks are necessary, and live with the knowledge that they violated scientific integrity as well, for that 10 percent shot at an AER article.

We can now smell the scent of a new analytical model in the making! We can combine the "models" that weight the value of articles for career development (discussed in Chapter 6) with the models on randomness and publication bias (discussed in this chapter) to create one theoretical "unified model." With this unified model it would be easy to demonstrate, through basic economic theory, that *the higher the rank of the journal, the more likely it is that any one of its articles will be in violation of scientific integrity.* This would follow directly from economic principles, since only the most highly valued articles (in the highest ranked journals) would compensate the researcher for the opportunity cost of the additional time needed to crank out the mandatory statistical significance, using whatever data mining and specification experiments it requires, and the reward would also justify whatever discomfort might be felt by the author in compromising scientific integrity.

We could title the paper, "The Greater Likelihood for an Article in Top-Ranked Journals to Violate Scientific Integrity: A Game-Theoretic Analysis." While this synthesis would naturally follow quite easily from basic economic and statistical principles, it goes without saying that such an analysis would *never see the light of day*, since no top-ranking journal would ever publish it for obvious reasons. Whether a lesser journal might publish it is an open question, though a lesser journal might appear petty and jealous for doing so, and thus it might not for this reason alone. Nevertheless, the logic behind such a model offers yet another reason for why the profession needs to move away from its obsession with publication counts, and away from treating those who happen to get articles in leading journals as celebrity-like, jackpot winners.

CONTINUING THE DISCUSSION OF CROSS-CUTTING TOPICS

Fairness in the Hiring of Economics Professors

There is one thing that people should understand right off the bat about the job market for new economics professors: The vast majority of graduate-student applicants do not enjoy it in the least. There is often a great deal of frustration with it, anger, and legitimate complaints of unfairness. Also, although I have no empirical evidence to support the claim, I have heard from reliable sources who are deeply involved in the hiring process, not only for their own institutions but in discussions with others in other institutions, that there is a substantial degree of discrimination in the process. There is "reverse discrimination" in the hiring of underrepresented groups, which exists in many other fields, and I have heard, there is also discrimination against the hiring of Asians, who are overrepresented among graduate students in economics. I think that this issue should be studied rigorously and it should be addressed directly by the academic economics community, which certainly has the ability to address it.

In applying for a teaching position, the following eight factors (not in any particular order) will determine whether an applicant will be granted an interview: (1) the ranking of the school from which they graduated, (2) their grades (transcript), (3) their dissertation topic (and their adviser), (4) their publication record (and to a lesser extent their conference papers),

(5) their job market papers—how well they impress the prospective employer (and other written materials like a cover letter and personal statements) , (6) their teaching experience (including scores on student-teacher evaluations), (7) prior work experience (especially if it is impressive, such as experience working at the Federal Reserve Board of Governors, if they could get that kind of work), and, (8) their connections, of course, in terms of their recommendations and any personal communications that their adviser might have had with the prospective employer.

Many of the ethical issues that underlie the hiring process are essentially the same as the other ethical issues affecting the entire profession. In particular, because each academic department wants to maintain its reputation in publishing, they will hire those potential professors who they believe will be productive in publishing (and who are also, therefore, likely to be successful at acquiring grants for the university). Many departments also want effective teachers as well.

What is common knowledge today, and has been going on for several decades (including when I applied to teaching positions back in the late 1980s), may come as a surprise to those readers who are not familiar with the topic. It is that, during the job interview, very little time is ever devoted to discussing technical aspects of economics. There is, indeed, very little discussion of the details involved in the applicant's dissertation or job market papers, or details about the course material they used in their teaching experience, etc. So what *do* they talk about in job interviews for teaching positions in economics?

At an AIRLEAP training seminar on ethics in economics in Chicago in 2017, Professor W. Charles Sawyer delivered a presentation on "An Insider's View of the Academic Job Market: What Job-Market Applicants Should Know." In his presentation he mentioned what is the most important aspect of the job interview, and that is the "idle chitchat" that accounts for the "majority of the time" of the interview. As Sawyer put it in his presentation, "The most critical factor may well be whether the interviewer(s) 'like' you personally. Life isn't fair."

In all job interviews for all professions, the organization surely wants to hire someone who is personable, and who will develop a good working relationship with the people who work there. However, of all the jobs economists can acquire, academic jobs seem to have the strongest requirement for applicants to "hit it off, right off the bat," with the existing coworkers. Why is this so important, and what does it mean? Honestly, I do not think it means very much—it is simply a long-standing tradition. What caused the tradition in the first place might have been a combination of academic departments evolving out of former "gentlemen's clubs" when only rich men were professors. Perhaps it was maintained thereafter as an easygoing, intellectual refuge from the hard knocks of life that so many other professions must experience (as discussed in chapter 8), though the pressure to publish surely puts more than a dent into that perspective.

Having said all this, I think there still is something that is not right in a group of people deciding to hire someone based on that individual's social appeal. The decision to hire based largely on what one group of people happens to like about the individual's personality is superficial, and to some extent adolescent. It is also somewhat irresponsible if it ever involves a tradeoff (as it often must) between the people who are most liked and those who are best qualified and have the most potential to be great professors. As Sawyer mentioned when he said "Life isn't fair," there must be many instances in which one candidate for a teaching position is better qualified and does have greater potential than another to be a great professor, but did not display as good a rapport with the hiring officials as the less-qualified person, and so the less-qualified person was given the position. This is unethical in the sense that the professor being hired is there for the purpose of teaching students and sharing the university's quest of knowledge, and not for the purpose of befriending other faculty members in the department. Of course, once they are hired, and people get to know each other better, they may not like each other after all, which calls into question even more how relevant the idle chitchat is during the job interview for economics professors.

In addition, this great emphasis on applicants being likable to the hiring committee fosters a type of "inbreeding" where departments tend to evolve into clubs of like-minded people with similar personalities, thereby squelching a diversity of opinions and personalities in the work environment. In my view, such cliquishness is not healthy for the profession. It helps breed overconfidence in La-La Land escapism described earlier, and in some cases may help breed scapegoatism/ dehumanization.

The Need for Whistle-Blower Protection in Academic Economics

I was once attending a meeting of members of an organization that offered research grants to economics professors. I heard one of the leaders of the organization's grants program mention that a professor in one department had publicly criticized the organization's issuance of grants in certain areas, suggesting that the organization was not fair in its grants allocations. The leader proudly mentioned to the insiders at this meeting that he had contacted the dean of the university where the criticizing professor had a position. He said that he had a frank discussion with the dean in which he told him that his organization did not appreciate professors from the dean's university openly criticizing his organization's practices. He further explained that there would be negative consequences to any university that was the source of such criticisms.

Economics professors are, indeed, generally expected to toe the line and remain largely silent about ethical issues involving their work or the work of others in the same institution or subfield, for fear of adverse consequences that might affect their receipt of grants in the future, the precious acceptance of their papers by a journal, their promotion to tenure, etc. It is thus rare to see economics professors accuse one another of violating scientific integrity, etc., though all professors appear to have free license to bash people in other sectors, as demonstrated in Chapter 8. This absence of whistle-blowing protection, as might exist in many other professions, acts greatly to help perpetuate the problems of the profession that have been described throughout this book. When any profession is as "self-regulating" as academic economists, the situation fosters a culture that scares and punishes the profession's critics. This is a surely a formula for disaster, condemning the academic economics profession to be ridden with ethical problems, as it most certainly is.

NOTES

1. See, for example, David Colander, The Making of an Economist, Redux (Princeton, NJ: Princeton University Press, 2008).

2. These meetings are also called the annual meetings of the Allied Social Sciences Associations (ASSA) which is a group of associations that the AEA invites to attend, including the AEA itself as one of the associations, though the AEA is solely responsible for organizing and running the conference.

3. See National Association of Forensic Economics, "NAFE's Ethics Statement," accessed February 5, 2017, http://nafe.net/Ethics.

4. See The American Finance Association, "Code of Ethics & Guidelines,accessed February 5, 2017, http://tinyurl.com/hyvthbd.

5. George DeMartino, "Econ Ethical Codes of Conduct, accessed February 5, 2017, http://tinyurl.com/jxapaj4.

6. American Mathematical Society, "American Mathematical Society Policy Statement on Ethical Guidelines," accessed February 5, 2017, http://tinyurl.com/qdpe9pk.

7. American Physical Society, "Ethics and Values: 02.2 APS Guidelines for Professional Conduct," accessed February 5, 2017, http://tinyurl.com/j6cjjcw.

8. American Statistical Association, "Ethical Guidelines for Statistical Practice," accessed February 5, 2017, http://tinyurl.com/hv654rt.

9. David Colander, "Creating Humble Economists: A Code of Ethics for Economists," in The Oxford Handbook of Professional Economic Ethics, ed. George DeMartino and Deirdre McCloskey, (New York: Oxford University Press, 2015), 737–49.

10. Colander, "Creating Humble Economists," 742–43.

11. George DeMartino, "Harming Irreparably: On Neoliberalism, Kaldor-Hicks, and the Paretian Guarantee," (video presentation at the 15th annual Summer Institute

for the History of Economic Thought, University of Richmond), August 13, 2015, http://tinyurl.com/gp39ldw.

12. American Statistical Association, "Ethical Guidelines for Statistical Practice," last updated August 11, 2011. http://tinyurl.com/okfy87r.

13. See National Science Board, Science and Engineering Indicators—1996 (Washington, DC: U.S. Government Printing Office, 1996), http://tinyurl.com/zlkxjgp.

14. See Gary Hoover's four articles in his website on "Plagiarism in the Social Sciences," http://tinyurl.com/gllslxc.

15. Walter Enders and Gary Hoover, "Whose Line Is It? Plagiarism in Economics," Journal of Economic Literature, 42(3) (2004), 487–93.

16. Enders and Hoover, "Whose Line Is It?"

17. Daniel Arce, Walter Enders, and Gary Hoover, "Plagiarism and Its Impact on the Economics Profession," Bulletin of Economic Research 60(3) (2008): 234.

18. Arce et al., "Plagiarism and Its Impact on the Economics Profession," 235.

19. Arce et al., "Plagiarism and Its Impact on the Economics Profession," 232.

20. Arce et al., "Plagiarism and Its Impact on the Economics Profession," 239.

21. Arce et al., "Plagiarism and Its Impact on the Economics Profession," 234.

22. Enders and Hoover, "Whose Line Is It?" 487.

23. Christopher Pappas, "Top 10 Free Plagiarism Detection Tools," eLearning Industry, November 18, 2013, http://tinyurl.com/jf2ufzo.

24. In some cases, no one except the organization itself is listed as the author. This, in my view, is a completely different situation that is not at all exploitive. It is often done to protect individuals and the organization itself in various ways, depending on the type of study and type of organization.

25. Garret Christensen and Edward Miguel, "Transparency, Reproducibility, and Credibility of Economics Research," National Bureau of Economic Research Working Paper 22989, December 2016.

26. Christensen and Miguel, "Transparency, Reproducibility, and Credibility of Economics Research," 61.

27. It was listed as an AEA-organized session, not an AIRLEAP-organized session.

28. Christensen and Miguel, "Transparency, Reproducibility, and Credibility of Economics Research," 3. My emphasis in italics.

29. Berkeley Initiative for Transparency in the Social Sciences, "Mission and Objectives," accessed February 7, 2017, http://www.bitss.org/about/.

30. "At Scale—Computer Definition," Your Dictionary, accessed February 7, 2017, http://www.yourdictionary.com/at-scale.

31. Berkeley Initiative for Transparency in the Social Sciences, "The Catalyst Program," accessed February 9, 2017, http://www.bitss.org/catalysts/.

32. Berkeley Initiative for Transparency in the Social Sciences, "Mission and Objectives," accessed February 9, 2017, http://www.bitss.org/about/.

33. Berkeley Initiative for Transparency in the Social Sciences, "Partners," accessed February 9, 2017, http://www.bitss.org/about/partnerships/.

34. By the way, I do not mean to use this label in a demeaning manner—I myself founded AIRLEAP which I would regard as an activist organization to some extent,

and I would much rather BITSS be one as well, instead of pretending to be one as I am arguing here.

35. IPA: Innovations for Poverty Action, "What We Do" Accessed February 9, 2017,http://www.poverty-action.org/about/what-we-do.

36. "What We Do."

37. Stephen Ziliak and Edward Tether-Posadas, "The Unprincipled Randomization Principle in Economics and Medicine, in The Oxford Handbook of Professional Economic Ethics, ed. George DeMartino and Deirdre McCloskey, (New York: Oxford University Press, 2015), 448.

Chapter 10

Product Evolution and a Personal Story

HOW MUCH SOMETHING CAN CHANGE DEPENDS GREATLY ON *WHAT WE CALL IT*

Let us start this chapter with a riddle! Consider the following: There is one product that many households have today in their home (and which they may often use), which can be bought in certain stores, and which is based on technology that is over 2,000 years old. As another clue, if, unfortunately, their entire house burned down to the ground, this is the only thing in the house that can be pulled out from the remaining ashes, washed off, and be good as new. What is it?

The answer is a cast-iron skillet.

Now, here is another question: Can a Cast-Iron Skillet "Improve in Quality"? The answer is yes and no. Yes, because it can be "enameled" (to protect against rusting), but that is about it, and otherwise it cannot improve in quality. It cannot otherwise improve in quality for reasons involving its chemical makeup and its physical shape. Since we are calling it a "cast-iron skillet," it can only be made of cast iron, which by definition is a particular oxide of the element iron, so we cannot improve it by making it out of anything else, since then it would no longer be a "cast-iron skillet" (and that would be a replacement, not an improvement).

Suppose we were not restricted to quality change in the cast-iron skillet, and we broadened the object of our study to all frying pans. Would this give us more room for quality improvement? Yes, it certainly would. Cast-iron skillets will be replaced at first by stainless steel pans that are easier to handle and clean. Those stainless steel pans would then give rise to Teflon-coated pans, as still more quality improvement. But, after that we will be stuck again with regard to quality improvement.

Now, what if we started the analysis, not with a cast-iron skillet, nor a frying pan, but with a "cooking device." Well, now we can forget about frying from a pan and stove and replace them by a completely different, improved cooking device—a microwave oven. All of a sudden we can have much greater potential for quality improvement in food cooking devices than we had with frying pans, which was much greater than what we had with cast-iron skillets. So, how much quality improvement there can be is clearly a function of how broadly we define the product or service. In other words, quality improvement is a function of semantics.

As another example, when movies first came out, originally from the "moving picture show," they did not have any sound, but when they did incorporate sound, we still called them "movies" (or "talkies" at first). Thus, we could say that movies improved enormously in the 1920s as they acquired sound. However, now let us consider radios. In the 1940s, people used to gather around in their living rooms and sometimes do little more than sit there and listen to radio shows. Did radios improve substantially in the 1950s? No, we would say that they did not. But, imagine if the first televisions were not called televisions, but called, instead, "picture-radios," and seen as a new type of radio that has the additional special feature of providing a moving picture show. In this case, we would have said that radios improved enormously in the 1950s, and kept improving ever since. Now suppose that we called radios, and televisions, and the like, "home entertainment systems." We would see the continuous quality improvement in this broad category up to the present day, which would include the most modern, household virtual reality entertainment centers in which one could "suit-up" and walk around in their home while essentially experiencing a different reality, all around them, wherever they turned and looked.

I have now defined two household goods: (1) food preparation devices and (2) home entertainment systems. Needless to say, I could go on and on discussing all kinds of other goods and services, but these two will do just fine for my immediate purposes. To understand quality change from a scientific perspective, we need to ask ourselves first *what it is that we want to understand*–hopefully not arbitrary degrees of quality change based on arbitrary conventions in semantics, though this has actually been the constraint in how quality change has been measured traditionally in economics, as I have just suggested. As I have also just suggested, and will soon support with additional arguments, quality change makes the most sense to study when we define goods and services broadly in terms of the *functions that they serve*.

Our defining products in terms of the functions they serve have three very important benefits: First, they enable us to understand the physical factors that are associated with the technological change. Second, they allow us to process and understand new products as they enter into markets, where, essentially, *there are no longer any new products, but simply improved products*. Finally, and most importantly, when we define products by the purposes they serve, we can identify fundamental aspects of those *purposes* that may enable us to *predict which products will improve more over time, and account for larger shares of a growing economy.*

THE SAD AND DISAPPOINTING HISTORY OF ECONOMIC THEORIES ON TECHNOLOGICAL CHANGE

As many of us already know, in economics, and especially in the economics of growth theory, we are always asking ourselves, how do we acquire more goods and services (or more valuable goods and services) than what we had before? The total value of all final, consumed goods and services is what we generally refer to as economic output, and any increase in such economic output is economic growth. As economists know from their first introductory class, we can think of output as being based on a "production function," which is generally a function of labor, the use of capital equipment, and in some cases materials and energy. In this context, technological change occurs as a change in the production function, enabling us to get more output (or equivalently higher-quality output) with the same inputs of labor, capital, etc. When this occurs, we essentially get something for nothing (as we have not increased inputs)—it is, in this sense, humanity's "freebie" or "bonus" that enables each generation to be better off than the previous one (in general).

Now how would we think of this bonus in output in *econometric* terms? Quite simply, we think of it as the increase in output that *cannot be explained* by any increases in the inputs (since the extra output from technological change occurs without any increase in inputs). Or, in even simpler terms, we might just call it what it is—*economic growth that we cannot explain*. After all, this is precisely correct—economics has never explained it—only measured it.

Back in 1956 Professors Robert Solow and Trevor Swan noticed this economic growth that we cannot explain,[1] and they gave it a name based on a vague notion of what must be causing it. They called it "technological progress" or "technical change," which is what we often now call "technological change." *Putting the pieces together, we can now truly understand what "technological change" actually is in economic thought—it is economic growth that economics simply cannot explain.* Yet, I have never seen this expressed, or *admitted*, in this way in the economic literature or in textbooks. The academic economics community prefers to pretend that technological change is something that economists have actually analyzed and understand.

How much of observed economic growth is unexplained, and thus attributable, by definition, to technological change, is really anyone guess, because it would depend greatly on how carefully, and under what arbitrary (and philosophical) assumptions we use to measure output. Such ambiguity was analyzed in the literature with regard to how we measure capital services (since the more we can explain with physical capital, the less we have left that is unexplained, which we can attribute to technological change). However, the ambiguity is most apparent in instances in which extreme quality improvement has coincided with extreme cost reduction. Consider, for example, the discussion on cameras in cell phones in chapter 5.

In fact, the analysis could work backwards: Instead of our developing a methodology from scratch to figure out what percentage of economic growth is attributable to technological change, one could start with an assumption of what that percentage growth is, and from there construct the specific assumptions that it would take for a defensible methodology to derive that exact percent change. This might surely raise concerns about scientific integrity, but I have mentioned this just to emphasize how arbitrary, or fuzzy, the assumptions would be in this kind of analysis. In any case, just for the sake of argument, or as a prop for our further discussion, let us pretend, for the moment, that we have found that, on average in the course of a year, 50 percent of all observed economic growth is attributable to technological change and the other 50 percent attributable to increases in the quantities of inputs.

I have observed for thirty years many organizations that very much want to promote and publicize, through economic discourse, the importance of scientific research and technological change. These organizations have often hailed the Solow-Swan model as an incredible and wonderful "discovery" in economic theory. They loved this "discovery" because to them it implied that technological change, and by implication, scientific advancement (and by implication as well, increased budgets of science agencies and increased donations to other science-funding institutes) was wonderful for the economy. (By the way, I am not saying here that it is *not* wonderful for the economy, but that is not my point). I heard for decades arguments being made like "Thanks to the marvelous advancement of economic theory, we know that a huge percent of all economic growth is *because of technological change*."[2] But, what does this all *really mean*? Again, it was not a *discovery* upon which such economic theory had been built, but a *definition*—defining "technological change" as whatever causes the economic growth that we simply cannot understand.

Now let us fast-forward a little, into the 1960s and 1970s, to find some other people on the scene, like Professors Zvi Griliches (whom I mentioned in chapters 2 and 5, as you may recall) and Edwin Mansfield looking at technological change as a function of money spent on research and development, where they inserted R&D expenditures into the production function of the economy to see how much this addition helps us to understand economic growth.

Flash forward even more to the 1980s and we find economics professors like Richard Nelson and Nathan Rosenberg describing the unexplained economic growth in a slightly different way–calling it "a black box" and saying, we must make progress in this discourse by "looking *inside* the black box" and seeing how it works. So these professors, and many others, started looking at what firms do when they develop new products. They studied the "process of innovation," trying to figure out how some companies, and even countries, are so much better at innovation than others.

Integrated into these approaches—the R&D approach, and the innovation approach—were cross-sectional analyses of industries, over time, to compare how much different kinds of industries have grown. These seemingly infinite number of cross-sectional studies were facilitated by a wealth of data on industries (from Census Bureau surveys primarily), organized by industrial categories.[3] In these studies it was observed that some industries have, indeed, grown more than others. The industry of agriculture, for example, might not grow much, compared to the industry of electronic equipment. However, there were *no real explanations* offered for their difference in growth rates. It was as if all the different industries lined up to see the *technological-growth fairy* (like a photo-op line at Disney World to meet the Blue Fairy in Pinocchio) where the technological growth fairly would then sprinkle differing amounts of magical, technology fairy dust on them, and whichever industries received more fairy dust would experience more technological change (or unexplainable economic growth). These studies found that information technology (IT) industries luckily received a real lot of fairy dust, the automotive manufacturing got some, and the construction industry not so much, etc. From this, academic economists were saying that they were "studying technological change" (if we want to euphemistically call it "studying"). Moreover, they felt and claimed that they have gained knowledge of *how* technological change occurs, by essentially observing these patterns. Such research efforts received a great deal of financial support, generated numerous high-ranking publications in technical journals, and built the careers of many academic economists, especially at the top-ranked schools (like Harvard, MIT, Stanford, University of Pennsylvania, etc.).

In short, academic economists have never really *understood* economic growth that is not explained by increases in production inputs. They have instead simply danced around the statistics by continually introducing new terminology (defined in rather shallow ways) for what they cannot explain, and designing highly complex mathematical models using large datasets that do little more than either (1) *observe* patterns across various industries (or regional areas, or other variables that they could find) or (2) *rediscover* in these models the mathematical properties that were bestowed upon them by the models' initial assumptions.

As mentioned, such research, and the publications and career building that went with it, were always supported by plenty of research funding that essentially continued to flow to economics professors to basically promote arguments in support of R&D funding. These research efforts continued to find new terminology which did little more than circle around its own definitions with high-powered mathematics, as in the case of Helpman and Trajtenberg's "General Purpose Technology" term which was described in detail in chapter 3.

Similarly, Professor Paul Romer had enormous success peddling highly esoteric mathematical models that were built primarily around the notion that technological change occurs because of the development and accumulation of one special factor, which is . . . (imagine pausing for a drum roll here) . . . *ideas.*[4] For decades I have been in awe and disbelief at how academic economists have often described and interpreted Romer's work on the importance of *ideas* as a brilliant and pathbreaking discovery in economic thought and economic theory. To me it is analogous to a chemistry professor announcing that they too have come to understand technological change as it relates to chemistry. "You see," the chemistry professor revealed, "technological change in chemistry is all based on . . . {another drum roll please} . . . *molecules.*" Yes, technological progress has been based new molecules, new engineering designs, new scientific discoveries, and more broadly "new ideas." *Who knew?* (Other than every nine-year-old.)

PRODUCT EVOLUTION AND ITS CAUSES

The Difference between Observing Technological Change and Understanding It

Now, as I had promised a while back, let us get back to the previous discussion about the two household products I mentioned: cooking devices and home entertainment systems. Four hundred years ago, within the most technologically advanced societies of that time (though depending on how one defines that), people's food cooking devices included a fireplace and a cast-iron cauldron that together were probably the most expensive products inside their humble home, and perhaps the third most valuable products they owned, after the dwelling itself and their livestock.[5] (They probably did not own their own land.) Today, of course, the fireplace and cast-iron cauldron have been replaced by the stove, traditional oven, and microwave oven. Also 400 years ago, the home entertainment system was a window in the house to look out from. Today, the home entertainment system, if you are rich, would include your own media room (or small movie theater) in your house, or a virtual reality entertainment system. Moreover, whatever you have for your home entertainment system, it is *also* likely to be the third most expensive product you own, after your house and car, unless you've got an indoor swimming pool, or a very impressive jewelry collection, or wine cellar, etc.

Many years ago, many more people were employed in the production and distribution of cooking devices; now many more people are employed in the production and distribution of home entertainment systems. For example, just go to a Best Buy or Sears, where you can get both, and see how many people are working on selling ovens compared to products associated with home entertainment. By economic theory today, what do we have to explain this evolution in the value of output between the two products (or types of products)?

Was it because the technology fairy sprinkled more fairly dust on the home entertainment equipment industry and less fairy dust on the food appliances industry?

Was it because the firms that produce home entertainment systems decided to spend much more money on R&D than the firms that produce cooking equipment? Does that make any sense? Are we willing to believe that if the amounts each industry spent on R&D were reversed, then the growth pattern of these two industries would be reversed? Of course, we would know better than to believe that from basic intuition, even if we might have difficulty explaining it.

Was it because the firms that make home entertainment systems were designed to be much more innovative than those that make cooking equipment? Are we inclined to believe that if only the really clever inventors and managers in the home entertainment systems industry worked instead in the food appliance industry, then the food appliance industry would have grown just as much?

Was it because home entertainment systems involved a "general purpose technology" like "*electronics*"*?* The last time I checked, microwave ovens are also electronic and so are all stoves and ovens in the sense of having a great deal of electronic controls regardless of whether they happen to be fueled by electricity or gas. (In fact, what is *not* electronic these days? Perhaps this book itself in your hands now is being read electronically on an iPad!)

Was it because there were *great ideas* (a la Romer) that led to improved home entertainment systems, while not so many great ideas developed for cooking appliances? What would this even mean (if we tried to think about it) and what would it tell us?

In short, in the many decades of the development of the economics of technology, as reflected in the most prestigious technical journals and books written by the most prominent economics professors, there has been virtually no discoveries, nor useful theories, that could explain the difference in economic growth between, in this example, food preparation appliances and home entertainment systems. More generally, there has been virtually no economic theory that could explain how goods and services evolve over time and, in doing so, account for economic growth. Given how important economic growth is, and how such changes essentially fuel economic growth and explain how humanity's existence has improved over time, this situation is *simply horrible*, and, in my view, *inexcusable*. It is a void that has been allowed to exist for reasons that will be outlined shortly.

Now let us start from scratch, with an interdisciplinary approach. First of all, cooking is a physical process whose parameters with regard to quality are very constrained, because food preparation is simply the application of energy, of different forms and rates, to particular food materials.[6] It is the same kind of constraint as the one we originally saw in the cast-iron skillet. Well-defined, physical metrics generally cannot improve in quality, precisely *because* they are well-defined physical processes whose own definitions prevent their further improvement. These products *can* improve in the direction of cost reduction (microwave ovens getting a lot cheaper, for example), but they cannot improve so much in terms of quality, and when they get cheaper, they promote overall economic growth, but they themselves shrink as a share of the economy.

Home entertainment systems are not defined in terms of physical constraints but defined in terms of the sensory stimulation that they provide. Moreover, the senses to which they appeal—sight and sound for now, and moving to include touch in virtual reality systems—are generally insatiable. In contrast, the satisfaction of hunger is a very satiable human endeavor, which is precisely why people tend to stop purchasing more food, and stop purchasing even better-tasting food, when they already have all that they want. (They may even spend money to take classes, or join organizations, to induce them to reduce their consumption of it!)

It was not more R&D and better innovation in home entertainment, and less R&D and worse innovation in cooking equipment, that caused the differences. It was the properties of entertainment systems themselves that attracted more R&D and innovation to it, and the properties of cooking equipment that limited its R&D and innovation.

It is these properties of products, based on the characteristics of the functions they serve, that cause them to grow at different relative rates. By extension, nations that are more heavily invested in producing those products that grow in quality more are like ships finding the right currents to move them faster and easier, where the faster-growing products are like the faster currents that carry a nation's economy. *Economists need to study how technology has changed humanity and will continue to change humanity, where economists study this topic with a scientific commitment to understanding what is truly occurring in the physical world.* The habit of simply building esoteric mathematical models to dance around data sets of industrial statistics that we can only observe and cannot understand—models that do little more than mathematically reinterpret their initial assumptions—does virtually nothing. The only thing that it has done over the past five decades has been to help create propaganda in support of R&D expenditures, to the delight of the organizations that fund this economic research. At the same time, they draw resources away from potential research on technological change that could easily be more useful.

More than half my career in economics may be broadly described as interdisciplinary work between economics and the natural sciences. My initial interest in the area was, in part, a consequence of my having some background in the natural sciences, with undergraduate courses in biology, chemistry, and physics. I also had courses in psychology, in which I developed a particular interest in perception—a subfield of psychology that I believe is very useful in many areas of economics, including the study of technological change, as already suggested by the recent discussion of sensory perception and satiation.

There is widespread agreement among economic professors that advances in science and technology offer great promise for improvements in living standards, but as I have already argued, there appears to be no agreement whatsoever over whether advances in science and technology could ever be well understood within the field of economics. Those who do believe that scientific advances could be well understood, and who choose to study it as economists (though most economists do not), fall into two distinct camps: (1) those who believe the topic could be approached through an interdisciplinary framework, in which contributors to the subfield exercise some understanding of the natural sciences and engineering in addition to economics, and (2) those who, in effect, keep their minds strictly within the field of economics. This second group simply builds upon the existing economic literature associated with science and technology, without feeling a need to acquire knowledge within the fields of the natural sciences or engineering. In this latter group there is a much greater reliance on the assumptions that theoretical economists have used in explaining technological change.

As might already be obvious, I have always fallen under the first group, whose members preside primarily in industry or in government (in my case), as opposed to academia. Within academia, the second group is clearly dominant among those academic economists who study the economics of science and technology.

As a graduate student in the 1980s specializing in economic development I was particularly interested in development strategies, that is, what advice economists could offer to the leaders of developing nations to help them promote their nation's economic growth and to reduce their levels of poverty. At that time I was told of one particular "industrial strategy" (involving the strategic selection of industries for the government to support one way or another). Such theories of industrial strategies had come from famous earlier economists, such as H. Singer (1950), R. Prebish (1950), and W. Arthur Lewis (1952). In fact, Lewis had won the Nobel Prize in 1979 for this and various other analyses explaining the constraints on growth faced by developing countries.[7] I became fascinated with the industrial strategy topic for developing countries, but saw holes in it from an interdisciplinary perspective, and I felt I could contribute to fill those holes with a broader approach.

I had thus chosen my own dissertation topic in this area independently (without receiving suggestions from professors on the topic), and then sought to find a dissertation advisor to support it. I did find a professor to support it (Kelvin Lancaster), who, fortunately for me, found my approach interesting. I successfully defended the dissertation in 1991, and then developed it further into my first book, *Quality Measurement in Economics: New Perspectives on the Evolution of Goods and Services*.[8] I expanded the analysis again, in a few journal articles and then another book, *Economics, Science and Technology*.[9] In spite of these publications, and some endorsements I received from them, it might surprise noneconomists, but should not surprise economists in the least, that my contribution on the topic of product evolution was doomed to failure from the beginning, in terms of ever finding significant recognition or acceptance within the academic economics community. Except for my briefly mentioning it myself in the courses that I thought, as far as I know it never entered into anyone else's lectures in an economics class, nor had ever seen the light of day in any textbook. Likewise, my books never sold, and were thus rarely read.

As the vast majority of professional economists (academic or otherwise) already know, nearly all technical economics books, which are neither textbooks nor books written for the general public, are priced and published for the university library market only. In other words, a publisher will typically print about 500 copies of a 250-page book (or perhaps 1,000 copies if the author is lucky) and sell them to 500 libraries around the world at about $200 each, and less than 100 other people or companies in the world might purchase it. By three or four years later (or earlier if the author is not lucky), the same or a different publisher will come up with a new book on roughly the same topic, now advertised as a more current version of the same book, so the libraries will purchase it as well, and no one will have an incentive to purchase the earlier book thereafter.

As I have just indicated, these books exist primarily for the author's own benefit as a credential for their curriculum vitae in a similar way as a technical journal article that (with few exceptions) only the libraries will have in hard copy (if the journal even exists now in hard copy), and it will not be read seriously by more than a handful of people in the world. This begs the question, though, of what happens when someone advances economic thought and publishes their ideas in journals and books? If that is not enough for those ideas to be added to the body of economic thought being taught and learned, and those ideas simply fade away, then what else does it take for new ideas to be recognized and incorporated into the material that is taught to new economists and which becomes "economics proper"?

The naïve answer that I think any reasonable person might be expected to offer (especially if they are not very familiar with the academic economics profession) is simply that it must depend on the perceived value of those new ideas. The best ideas should of course "bubble-up" to become part of the newest widely recognized and accepted discourse in economics. If they do not, it must mean (in theory at least) that those ideas must not be such good ideas after all. This is a perfectly reasonable assumption, I think, but unfortunately it is not true. Many ideas do not get recognized in economics, even after they are published, because, unlike most literature in the natural sciences, economic literature is *not discovery-based*; it is based on all of the game-playing factors listed in previous chapters (such as the factors mentioned in the chess analogy at the end of chapter 4). The same factors come into play when it comes to the popularity and recognition of work *after* it had been published.

An Introduction to Product Evolution

As I had mentioned, back in the 1950s development economists like Singer, Prebish, and Lewis were trying to think of development strategies that the leaders of developing nations might consider to improve their economies. This is still somewhat true today, but to a much lesser extent. One of the problems for developing countries at the time, as these economists observed, was that manufactured goods kept getting better and better—"improving in quality"—while the primary products did not. As a result, as the world's economy was growing through the improvement of manufactured products, it appeared that only the industrialized countries were experiencing that growth and getting richer.

As a simple, hypothetical example (with small numbers to emphasize that this is hypothetical), suppose there were only three types of products: radios, televisions, and the metal ore, and metal ore is refined to make radios and televisions. Suppose that, at one time, the developing countries provided 10,000 tons of the metal ore each year to the industrialized countries, at $100 per ton, or $1 million per year. From this, the industrialized countries produced 100,000 radios at $20 per radio (and made other things like buildings with the rest of the metal which it did trade). Say the industrialized countries sold half of those radios it made (50,000) back to the developing countries for a total of $1 million. There was then a "balance"—10,000 tons of ore in exchange for 50,000 radios each year.

Now suppose, twenty years later, the industrialized country no longer produced 100,000 radios, but instead, 100,000 televisions, which it sells at $100 each to whoever will by it, and which is still made using the metal ore provided from the developing country. The metal ore still sells for $1 million, and so now the developing country can buy 10,000 televisions. The industrialized country, on the other hand, winds up with 90,000 televisions, valued at $9 million, when twenty years earlier it had only 50,000 radios, valued at $1 million. In short, in this little story, the industrialized country grew enormously, while the developing country did not grow at all. (While the developing country now has televisions, it has one-fifth as many televisions as the number of radios that it had before, while the industrialized country has nine televisions for every five radios that it had before.)

One broad "economic" interpretation of all this, which Singer, Prebish, Lewis, and others expressed, was that manufactured goods grow in quality while primary products do not. They reasoned, therefore, that, if industrialized countries produce only manufactured goods, and developing countries produce only primary products, then industrialized countries will get richer and richer, and developing countries will remain poor. Their proposed solution then to enabling developing countries to grow was for developing countries to engage more in manufacturing.

In learning about all this as a graduate student in economics I saw it as a useful framework, and one that, to me at least, was very interesting. However, I also found it to be limited. For instance, the literature on this included debates among economists over whether primary commodities could, in fact, improve in quality at all. Some of the discussions on the topic considered the purity of metal ores, where a ton of a particular ore, such as copper, might have a higher content of pure copper (or pure copper oxide to be precise) than a ton of copper ore used to have. Coffee, cotton, and other agricultural products could improve in quality, as well, as could just about every commodity in some way or another. In the simplest debate imaginable, these critics of the theory were essentially saying, "Some economists are saying that primary products do not improve in quality, but they do! Therefore, their theory is wrong, and so it may not be a bad strategy for developing countries to stay specialized in primary products."

One of the obvious disappointments that jumps out from such shallow considerations is the idea that these factors are, of course, all a matter of degree. If primary products on average improve in quality by, say, 1 percent per year, while manufactured goods improve in quality by 10 percent per year, then certainly it would not be a good strategy for developing countries to stick with primary products, but most of the discussion did not even go this far. Truthfully, I found at least three general aspects of this debate to be absurd, and still do some thirty years after I began to study it. To me, each of these aspects reflected an incredible myopia on the part of economics professors where they are simply unable to see what might be obvious to anyone who has studied the natural sciences.

First, consider the argument made that a ton of a metal ore may improve in quality by having a higher content of the metal oxide itself per unit weight (e.g., per ton). Of course, this is possible, but from a scientific perspective, what does this mean? One would hope that whoever might analyze this issue would have enough of an understanding of basic chemistry to know that metals are chemical elements, and that the chemical element itself has a constant, exact form. In other words, every single atom of any chemical element (at the same temperature and pressure) is exactly the same as every single other atom of that same chemical element (barring any unnecessary discussion of "isotopes" at this level). Similarly, every single molecule of the metal oxide is the same as every other single molecule. Therefore, the most that the "quality" of any ton of metal ore can have is 100 percent purity—it cannot improve in quality beyond that without becoming a different metal, but then that would change the definition of the product being measured. Hence, defining the product as the particular metal implies that it cannot improve in quality except to the extent that it could be more pure, that is, have less contaminants. Thus, to say that "primary products can improve in quality" and then to use an example metal of greater purity is essentially a trivial argument that may be "technically correct" but which otherwise basically misses the point entirely. If, for example, a ton of a metal ore is 3/4 pure, then it can only improve in quality by 1/3 (since 4/3 x 3/4 = 1), after which it cannot improve in quality whatsoever.

Surely this is extremely elementary, but what I found particularly amazing is that none of this clear limitation on the quality of metal ores was ever brought up in any of the literature that mentioned the quality of metal ores (as far as I could see from my research at the time), as if it had never crossed the minds of the authors who argued that ores could improve in quality. My guess, in reading this literature and in my experiences with academic economists, is that it never really did cross their minds to consider the physical properties of the product they were studying. This, in my view, is a reflection of the perspective of some academic economists, who feel there is no need for them to understand any science associated with the objects they are analyzing; for them, as sad as it sounds, economic theory alone provides them with all they need to understand.

Why Let Existing Names and Categories Constrain Our Understanding?

What I also found even more troubling about this debate over whether manufactured products and primary goods undergo different rates of quality change is the question of why, to begin with, the discussion was even based on the distinction between these two types of products. That is, what is so special about primary versus manufactured products? The only possible answer is that this dichotomy already had precedence in the literature and in people's minds (in terms of categories of products), which I believe is an incredibly weak reason, especially given our presumed purpose here, which is to understand whether products are increasing in quality or not (or more broadly to understand their relative rates of quality improvement). Along these lines, I simply asked, why not create our own categories of products based on an understanding of which products will likely improve in quality and which will not? In fact, why not take this further, and instead of finding some "all-or-nothing" category, or even categories at all, why not consider some new variables that could explain and enable us to predict how much quality change we expect to occur for any particular product?

For example, instead of primary versus manufactured goods, why not define one of these categories as "metal ores" and for this category define "percent purity" as a variable of interest. In this way we will then know, from the beginning, what its true limits are in terms of quality improvement per unit weight. Or, to make things even easier (in a scientific sense at least), why not adjust the unit of measure to be the quantity of the relevant molecule itself (e.g., one ton of ore at 75 percent purity, is 0.75 equivalent tons of the metal oxide, end of story). This is analogous to buying a can of food at the grocery store which lists its "net weight"—its weight without the water it contains.

When I have made this and similar arguments to economists over the years, many would offer the extremely simplistic and disappointing response, "Oh, but we cannot change the units of measure—the prices we are analyzing are in those units—metal ore is sold by the ton, not by its quantity of the specific molecules of the metal oxide." However, the constraint here would only be that of "comfort levels" as opposed to any genuine analytical constraint, and such dependence on comfort levels flies in the face of standard principles of scientific reasoning and of the responsibility of any analyst (who might be analyzing *anything*) to define the variables for their analysis based on what makes the most sense in the exercise. Specifically, there would be two levels of discomfort for most academic economists in converting the price of any chemical (including metals) to a price per quantity of molecules such as a price per mole or per thousand moles.[10] The first level of discomfort is the high school-level chemistry that it involves, and the second is the fact that the vast majority of academic economists do not make "price adjustments." Even though making such adjustments would be conceptually no more difficult than converting a price per pound to a price per kilogram, it would still generally be outside their comfort level.

If academic economists did take such a bold step to take into account high school-level chemistry and math to convert quantities of chemical materials to these scientific measures, then their understanding of quality change, especially for primary commodities, would become so much clearer. Of course, the situation is made a bit more complex (but only a bit) in the sense that the raw material, which contains contaminants, requires additional processing costs to separate those contaminants from the material. Nevertheless, this could be better understood as a variation in the processing cost associated with certain quantities of the chemical of interest.[11]

By this latter measure, there can never be any improvement in quantity, given the precise chemical definition of what we are measuring. A chemical engineer might view this entire discussion with amazement—how could something so simple and basic within their own profession's knowledge base not be studied in this way by the economists who are supposedly analyzing the product?

To add to the complexity now, let us consider that quality improvement is only one tendency that products may experience that would raise their price over time, while the other is "cost reduction"—the ability, through technological advances, to produce the same product cheaper. So, for example, through the use of more efficient machinery, it might become cheaper to extract or to move a ton of a particular metal ore, and so (through a "downward shift in the supply curve") its price will fall in a competitive market. Cost-reducing technological change might then harm developing countries by reducing the revenue they receive for those products. On the other hand, any trained economist will realize that it is more complicated than that, because the lower production costs might translate to a freeing up of resources that can be used to produce something else as well. (For example, if the cost reduction is due to machinery replacing labor, this would create a new labor supply to produce other things that the nation had not produced before.) In this way, cost reduction in production processes might be beneficial to developing countries in the long run especially, and in the long run it should generally be beneficial to all nations in the world economy in allowing more to be produced with the same resources.

We can now analyze two factors that need to be considered in a nation's potential industrial strategy: producing those products that are expected to improve in quality (and thus sell for higher prices) over time (without increasing as much in their costs of production) thus yielding higher returns per unit, and those products that will become cheaper to produce over time, thus increasing efficiency that can free up resources, enabling the expansion of economic growth elsewhere.[12] There are, then, essentially two winners when it comes to industrial strategy: quality-improving winners and cost-reducing winners. Furthermore, nothing says that these two effects cannot be combined, so that some products might be winners in both directions, while others might be losers in both directions.

Examples of double winners are not hard to find, with the epitomic example being computers. An example of a quality-only winner (in general) might be medical services; and an example of a cost-reducing winner might be industrial pipes. Examples of double losers in general are *not* easy to find, since technological change is oriented toward making things better and cheaper, not worse and more expensive, but such examples can be found as well. An example of a double loser might be wilderness camping areas. Because of air, water, and noise pollution, loss of wildlife species, etc., wilderness camping areas may tend to decrease in quality over time, and because of pressures to develop land for urban and suburban use, they may become more expensive from an "opportunity cost" standpoint.

At this point, I would expect many readers to be skeptical about the idea I just mentioned regarding the prospect of establishing new categories of products from which we might observe predicable patterns of quality improvement or cost reduction. After all, the only products I have been describing, thus far, are pure chemicals, and the vast majority of products are not, by any means, pure chemicals. Also, many should have caught the fact that I have only been discussing goods thus far—not services—when in reality, most of the economy, these days, is attributable to services, with this book essentially being all about one of these services—the service provided by economics professors. Such skepticism is warranted, and I would continue to ask for the readers' indulgence—we have only "just started" the discussion of product evolution.

Before going further to other categories, it might be useful to revisit how pointless the distinction is between primary versus manufactured goods. To demonstrate how pointless it is, I will give a counterexample of how a *primary good* could indeed undergo *enormous quality* improvement, while a *manufactured good* may undergo *no quality improvement*. Suppose, for instance, that a new diamond mine is established in a country which is found to contain diamonds that are much larger than diamonds from other diamond mines in the world. As a result, the diamonds from that mine per unit weight (whatever unit one prefers) will be more valuable than diamonds from previous mines, and thus the quality of this primary product has greatly improved. As an example of manufactured goods that do not improve in quality, consider basic building materials like steel girders used in construction, where the item is essentially a pure chemical shaped in a precisely defined structure, but it is still called a "manufactured product," since it is made in a production plant.

A Little Bit of Science Can Go a Long Way

In the late 1990s, many economists seemed to be fascinated with the rapid rate at which quality improvement was occurring in IT, but did not seem to offer much of an explanation for it, other than to watch the change occurring and present summary statistics on it (again, as if fairy dust were the explanation). At that time, one might find published comments similar to the following: "If the automobile industry underwent the same rate of technological change as the computer industry, then we would be able to buy a car today that could take us to the moon and back in ten seconds." While many articles analyzing the statistics of the computer industry were published in economics, often in very sophisticated ways, it was rare to see any discussion of the causality involved, or how it can actually come to be that computers might increase in quality by 100 percent each year, while cars might only do so by 5 percent per year (with half of those improvements probably attributable to the placement of better computers into those cars).[13] Of course, IT has continued to grow rapidly in both quality improvement and cost reduction up until the present day, but by around 2000, as people became accustomed to the Internet, the euphoria and amazement wore off.

One useful distinction that can be made regarding any product, whether that product is a good or service, is whether it involves any significant physical requirement *beyond the processing of information*. We can think of "information" as an "ingredient" within any product or service. More precisely, there are two aspects of information—the physical manipulation of it, that is, what hardware does, and the information itself, including information about how other information should be processed, that is, data and software. While this is all quite obvious, the economic significance of these constructs, and how they explain why IT has undergone such rapid, simultaneous quality improvement and cost reduction, in comparison to nearly all other products in the economy, is, amazingly, very poorly understood by economists, especially academic economists.

Looking as both an economist and a scientist, I would argue that the first most important concept that academic economists should be recognizing and teaching about the growth of the IT industry is that it is primarily a function of the unique and inherent economic properties of information and information processing. Consider, for the moment, what products are made of, or more precisely, what they need to be made of, in order for them to serve their purpose and to be demanded and consumed. Food products, for example, must have nutritional components, and must taste good—both of which are primarily chemical and physical requirements. Structures, of course, must have physical properties—a house must be able to hold up to all sorts of weather conditions, must have functioning plumbing, etc., which requires a great deal of physical materials that are properly assembled. Transportation, of course, has the physical requirements of having to move objects across space at certain speeds, against whatever physical constraints are imposed by the medium through which the objects are traveling (and surface if on land or water), with an ability to change direction as needed, and to maintain and protect the passengers and cargo within the particular environment that is inside the vehicle. There is no physical way around the amount of energy that is required to accelerate and deaccelerate the movement of any mass, regardless of how efficiently it could be done. (For any mass, m, and velocity v, the energy needed to move it will always be equal to $0.5mv^2$ even if all other factors, like the mass of the vehicle itself or the friction it might encounter, are assumed to be zero).

Now, forgetting about hardware for the moment, let us ask a similar question about information itself: What are the inherent physical requirements of storing information? Unlike food, units (or bits) of information do not require minimal amounts of chemical nutrients; unlike structures, they do not require a specific physical amount of building materials; unlike transportation (as a service or a vehicle) they do not require minimum levels of energy to move physical objects of significant mass. Information, in other words, has no physical requirements, except at *the smallest level possible that could allow the information to exist*, as in the placement of individual atoms in a particular array (as in a DNA molecule), or the wave pattern of a particular electromagnet transmission (as in a radio signal). Consider, for example, the use of Wi-Fi in a public library somewhere, in which billions of bits of information are being instantly transmitted to many computers in the room in an environment in which there is no apparent physical indication (at least to our human senses) that there is anything even there to make that transfer possible, except, perhaps, for the visual appearance of a few routers on the ceiling.

If economists were to categorize products by aspects of their physical requirements, such as whether they in fact even have physical requirements beyond a negligible degree, then this will enable economists to better understand Product Evolution. For example, IT services have become an enormous growth industry for India. Why is this the case, as opposed to automobile manufacturing becoming a growth industry for India? Much of the answer lies easily within the framework of product evolution as just described.

As another example, let us consider two electronic household appliances that entered into the US market substantially at about the same time in the 1960s and early 1970s—air conditioners and color televisions—and compare how these products evolved. Around 1967 only relatively rich households had them both, and a decade or so after that only the poorest households did not have them both (not counting those living in very cold climates). Surely, since they were first introduced, air conditioners improved considerably in quality and experienced cost reductions as well. However, their quality improvement was at quite a lower scale than that experienced by color televisions. Indeed, one might imagine traveling with a time machine from today back to a typical household's living room in the mid-1970s during a hot summer's day, and not notice a single difference in the coolness of the room than in an air conditioned living room in a typical house today. Imagine, on the other hand, the difference one would see in the color television (whose screen would be much smaller, and inside a rather large and heavy wooden or plastic box).

From the above discussion about IT we now may better understand how color televisions could have undergone much greater cost reduction than air conditioners. That is, if we were to keep the same screen size and resolution of the color TV in 1967 and sold the item today, they would be dirt cheap in comparison to what it cost then (adjusting for inflation, relative to the costs of other goods). Also, part of the full, effective cost of the air conditioner is what must be paid for its energy consumption, which must always be a physical amount—the energy required to cool a room of a certain size, which is an inescapable level of energy dictated by the physical laws of thermodynamics.[14] The TV also produces light energy, which is also inescapable, but it is much less than the energy needed to change substantially a room's temperature.

One question, however, is why TVs kept offering larger and better screens, while air conditioners hardly underwent any quality improvements by comparison. To me, the answer lies in the function these different appliances serve, and the answer is closely tied to human perception. When it comes to our wanting to have air conditioning in our homes, we have an extremely simple physical requirement, which is that the temperature in the room be at a certain level, such as 70 degrees Fahrenheit. Once that 70 degrees in the room is achieved, there is virtually nothing more that the air conditioner can do for us (assuming air purification is a different service, but even then the physical requirements would be rather limited as well). Our sense of touch with regard to the air in the room has been satiated as soon as any air conditioner can effect that temperature change that we desire. In sharp contrast, as argued earlier, the TV appeals to our two most widely used senses—vision and hearing—which, when combined, provide entertainment, whose quality, and our appreciation of it, is largely unlimited (at least in humanity's current state). This is precisely why people are willing to pay more to have wall-size TVs with surround sound, or even 3-D features. As a product, TVs can grow in quality to meet the unlimited human desire to be better entertained with larger visual fields, richer sounds, etc. Strategically, then, TVs offer much more "fertile ground" for economic growth than air conditioners, because this product is meeting a larger human desire in terms of the senses involved in the product's consumption. The nation that commits to, and is successful at, producing the world's best-quality TVs will therefore have a brighter future than the nation that commits to, and is successful at, producing the world's best-quality air conditioners, by this basic principle.

On the other hand, technological change and human perception are indeed quite complex, and this quality of TVs may, in fact, no longer exist if eventually virtual-reality headsets replace TV watching (as already suggested as well). Virtual reality would offer even greater sensory input, involving touch in addition to interactive visual and auditory input. It would also, at least in principle, require much less energy consumption, because light would only need to pass from the apparatus to the eyes of the person who wears the headset, as opposed to being broadcast to be seen by anyone looking at the TV from across the room, although there would be some additional, minimal energy consumption in the information processing involved.[15]

But What Does This Have to Do with Economics?

The approach here is entirely consistent with one of the very best, and one most important economic theories ever developed. It is a theory that has already given rise to invaluable contributions to price estimation (through "hedonic price indices"), which was already discussed briefly in chapter 2. Yet, in my view, economists have barely reaped the benefits of the theory; because so much more could be accomplished in economics if this theory were much better recognized and studied. As I have already suggested, it is Lancaster's theory on the Characteristics of Goods, which had been published in *The Journal of Political Economy* in 1966, under the title, "A New Approach to Consumer Theory." The conclusion that Lancaster wrote in his article can be seen as having a direct connection to the ideas underlying Product Evolution. That conclusion reads as follows (with my own emphasis in italics):

> In this model we have extended into consumption theory activity analysis, which has proved so penetrating in its application to production theory. The crucial assumption in making this application has been the assumption that goods possess, or give rise to, multiple characteristics in fixed proportions and that *it is these characteristics, not goods themselves, on which the consumer's preferences are exercised.* The result, as this brief survey of the possibilities has shown, is a model very many times richer *in heuristic explanatory and predictive power than the conventional model of consumer behavior and one that deals easily with those many common-sense characteristics of actual behavior that have found no place in traditional exposition.*
>
> This paper is nothing more than a condensed presentation of some of the great number of possible ways in which the model can be used. *It is hoped that*

> *a door has been opened to a new, rich treasure house of ideas for the future development of the most refined and least powerful branch of economic theory, the theory of the consumer himself.*[16]

As I have argued in the books and articles I have written on Product Evolution, there is a "flip-side" to product evolution which I believe is quite useful. When one categorizes products by the broad functions that they serve, these broad categories themselves have inclinations towards certain relative degrees of quality improvement and cost reduction. That is, the broad categories are, to some extent, *predetermined by their nature*, to undergo quality improvement and cost reduction regardless of the particular path such quality improvement or cost reduction takes by way of specific products, or producers, or even nations.

The industrial categories, and the product categories, that we use now to understand the economy continue to be useful for a variety of reasons, many of which are obvious. However, imagine a different taxonomy where we separate out the economy into the broad purposes that products serve, such as Food and Nutrition, Shelter and Living Space, Transportation, Entertainment, Social Interaction, Information Storage and Processing, Communication, Health Maintenance and Improvement, Law Enforcement and Military, Legal Services and Maintenance of Justice, and Government and Public Policy. Within each of these broader purposes, there are subpurposes, and there are also overlaps, as when a fine restaurant, for example, may be seen as providing food, shelter, and entertainment, all at once.

Imagine further that the entire economy, in terms of everything that is produced and distributed, may be seen as growing in each of these sectors, with subsectors within those sectors growing at their own rates as well. This is essentially how we look at the economy already with regard to existing industrial or product sectors, but now with "purpose-served" sectors we can have a stronger ability to make predictions on long-run trends in their growth. For example, transportation and shelter tend to have similar technological challenges at basic levels of engineering, and where improvements are fairly linear or one-dimensional in nature: getting from one place to another faster in the case of transportation, and producing the same indoor space in a building cheaper in the case of shelter, neither of which, in itself, ties into sensory perception to any significant degree. Food and nutrition also have basic limits, though their link to an appeal to the senses and the enormous range of production possibilities imply that both cost reduction and quality improvement may continue to a moderate degree. The most open-ended, especially with regard to quality improvement, are entertainment and health, and in some futuristic way these two sectors may be more closely interconnected in various ways that might be too imaginative for this particular discussion.

As cost reduction works its way through all of the products in the economy, research into extending our life expectancy, and improving our health, physical capabilities, and knowledge, will always remain open-ended areas for limitless quality improvement, and will likely continue to capture a larger and larger share of the economy as technology advances.

Those who might be unfamiliar with the topic of quality measurement might be wondering how "quality" could be objectively measured, and might then be skeptical about how such theories could be tested, or even understood in a rigorous sense. Actually, "quality" is defined here in strictly an economic sense in terms of a degree of opportunity cost, and is directly translatable to monetary terms. This is the same general meaning of quality used throughout economics. As the simplest possible example, suppose there is only one kind of car in period 1, model-A; two kinds of cars in period 2, models A and B (when model B was introduced), each representing 50 percent of the market; and only one kind of car again in period 3, model B, after model A had become obsolete. Suppose that, in period 2 when both cars were available, model B, being of higher quality, sold at twice the price as model A. Yet further suppose that, because of cost-reducing technology, model B in period 3 sold at exactly the same price as model A in period 1. We would then say that model B had twice the quality of model A, on the basis of their relative prices in period 2, and thus between period 1 and period 3 cars had undergone a 100 percent increase in quality. Likewise, cars experienced a cost reduction of 50 percent between period 1 and 3, since the cost, per unit of quality, declined by 50 percent. As any price index economist who might work for the Bureau of Economic Analysis (as I had) or the Bureau of Labor Statistics will say, there is indeed plenty of mathematics that could be used to test these hypotheses (or similar ones), if one is provided with data on quantities, prices, and the descriptive characteristics of products mentioned in the hypotheses.

WILL PRODUCT EVOLUTION AND SIMILAR TYPES OF EXPANSIONS IN THOUGHT EVER BE RECOGNIZED?

Product evolution is but one of many examples of how economic research can be conducted to expand economists' understanding of the world without that research having to build on already-established, highly advanced and complex, theoretical models. Economics professors can, and should, make their own new models to fit new ways of understanding the world. When they do, however, they may be isolated, as I have been for the last three decades, in trying to promote my ideas on product evolution. As far as I know, there has been no other published research on product evolution that has taken off from where I left it, or has, for that matter, recognized and utilized my findings, in research or in teaching. In my view, there were five reasons for this.

The first reason, as I mentioned earlier, is that my dissertation had been supported by a professor who happened to have been quite prominent, but who was at a stage in his career where he was no longer regularly publishing articles in top-ranked journals. If he were, then the way the game is played might have involved my coauthoring an article with him on the topic early on in my career, thereby helping to enable my research to find a home in the ivory tower of recognized economic theory.

The second reason is that, while my research did involve math, it never involved a level of advanced and impressive mathematical formulations that would be considered worthy of an article in a top-ranked journal. Indeed, if that were my goal, I could have imposed esoteric mathematical models into the research. In fact, it was occasionally suggested to me that I do that, even at my dissertation defense for example, for the very purpose of making the work more publishable in top-ranked journals. (The suggestion was based entirely on "helping me with my career," as opposed to improving the science of what I was exploring.) If I did, it would only be for show and would not be warranted by the basic, interdisciplinary ideas that I was presenting. In other words, in my view, imposing the unnecessary math would have only detracted from the main ideas I was trying to present, and would have compromised and confused my main thesis. Furthermore, I simply did not want to waste my time doing that, and the Economics Department at Columbia (including four of the five professors on the dissertation committee) saw no need for it either, since they believed the dissertation, itself, had enough developed ideas in it without my needing to provide more impressive mathematics.

Third, my work had a quality to it that prevented its recognition by economists who were studying technological change and publishing in the area. Namely, it was simply too interdisciplinary, in spite of the fact that my references to biology, psychology, chemistry, and physics were quite elementary, at the undergraduate level at best, though mostly at a high school level. Yet, the discomfort level among economics studying technical change with even high school chemistry was there, and similarly, if reviewers did not feel qualified to verify some of my statements involving psychology or the natural sciences, the easiest way out is to take the position that my research is too different from standard economic research to warrant their (or others') recognition.

Fourth, a huge problem that I encountered was due to the interdisciplinary nature of the work across *subfields of economics itself.* In particular, while I had barely scratched the surface of this aspect of the research in this chapter, as I mentioned, the empirical study of evolutionary quality measurement and cost reduction had to be based on the analysis of prices. Prices were, in fact, wonderful for my research—they provided plentiful data that I was able to use to measure the separate effects of quality improvement and cost reduction. However, the problem was that the research then involved the utilization of "price index theory" and empirical testing of time trends in relative prices. Price index theory had grown into a subfield of its own, not at all for the study of technological change, but primarily for the study of best practices for national accounting statistics, that is, for measuring inflation, cost-of-living indices, etc. Within the profession, those interested in price index theory have no interest in the study of technological change, and vice versa. What this means is that, when my research was presented to academic economists for review, for a journal article or simply a seminar presentation, I usually encountered a response from "technological change" economists that my analysis "was about price indexation" which was outside their purview—and so they would say that my findings would need to be aired by price-index economists (who were generally well versed in microeconomic theory). However, the research was not, by any means, a "contribution" to price index theory—I was simply using price indexation as a tool for studying technological change. Nevertheless, because my use of price indexation was not *impressive to price index economists* (which was never its intention) it was not seen by them as useful or interesting research. Hence, my work could proceed no further from there, having been dismissed by technological change economists because it involved price theory, and then dismissed by price index economists because it did not have anything mathematically sexy about price index theory.

Similarly, the research was interdisciplinary across other subfields of economics in which academic economists had become highly specialized in their own particular stovepipes. For instance, as I mentioned earlier, some of the research might be viewed as an extension of the history of economic thought related to the development economics literature associated with the "gains from trade" (e.g., work by Prebish, Singer, and Lewis). That literature never went into any discussion of technological change itself, even though I found it to be implicit within the ideas that were being expressed. In any case, to the vast majority of academic economists who develop macroeconomic models of the effects of technological change, any references to such literature on the gains from trade by economists in the 1950 and 1960s would easily be met by the knee-jerk reaction of "What does any of this have to do with technological change? This is about the history of economic thought as it relates to international trade."

A fifth reason was that the research involved something which economists, and especially academic economists, rarely do, which is look very hard at what the data actually are, and consider reinterpreting and reclassifying those data on the basis of new concepts. Part of building a solid foundation on quality measurement and on product evolution is to develop a means of scientifically measuring the quantities of products, thereby connecting such measures to the sciences to which they relate. As examples, I offered the measurement of food in units of calories, as a biologist or even a nutritionist would measure food quantity, and the quality per unit calorie (or thousand calories) would be reflected in the nutrients received per calorie.[17] This was nothing new of course, and Lancaster used the same example when he first introduced his characteristics of good approach. Similarly, for measuring information processing as a service (or a service provided by a unit of capital equipment) the relevant measure of quantity would be the number of calculations per second (or millisecond). Such "natural" measures of quantity can serve as the "numeraire" as it is termed in economics, and prices can simply be translated per unit of quantity based on existing data on prices.

The problem was that these kinds of methods are generally too alien to academic economists. On issues such as units of measure, academic economists are generally extremely conservative, passive, and set in their ways. They are unwilling to consider new approaches to measurement, unless the approaches are recognized as coming from a prominent economist who is already famous for having developed advanced theory (like William Nordhaus, who wrote a paper that measured quantities of light in "lumens").[18] Likewise, academic economics, when approached with novel ideas about measurement techniques, are often unable to think beyond the surface of these ideas, and are quick to dismiss them if they are outside the little boxes in which they are accustomed to considering economic ideas.

For example, the concept of a calorie as a scientific measure of food quantity is fairly standard across several disciplines, including development economics where it is often an indicator of well-being. I recall, for instance, a brilliant lecture delivered by an excellent economist (Henry Bahn) who worked for USDA, which was about the living conditions in Haiti shortly after the horrible earthquake that occurred there in 2010. He mentioned that the daily per capita calorie intake in Haiti was about 1,300, which to me (and I believe to most of the audience witnessing the presentation) said more about the conditions in the country than any other statistics that he could have provided. In any case, though I had been an economist at USDA myself for over four years, with a large part of my time there analyzing and authoring studies involving agricultural prices, the reaction that I had received, from academic economists, to my idea of measuring quantities of food in calories in the economic study of technological change was that my work reflected a severe ignorance of the field. That is, in response to my posing the idea in a couple articles, I received no positive feedback on the idea (other than the articles being accepted for publication), but I received consistent negative feedback from academic economists that the idea was ill-conceived and unrealistic—that I should have never posed it, because I should have known that *food is priced per pound, not by calorie, and that consumers buy food on the basis of price per pound.* Thus, according to these reviewers, my research lacked a basic knowledge and understanding of the topic that I was investigating.

NOTES

1. Robert M. Solow, "A Contribution to the Theory of Economic Growth," Quarterly Journal of Economics, 70(1) (1956): 65–94. Trevor W. Swan, "Economic Growth and Capital Accumulation," *Economic Record*, 32(2) (1956): 334–61.
2. This all goes back to that article in *Science* magazine where I was cited, discussed in Chapter 6: David Malakoff, "Does Science Drive the Productivity Train."
3. Industrial categories in those days were organized by "Standard Industrial Classification" Codes, or SIC codes; now we use NAICS codes (for North American Industry Classification System).
4. See, for example, Bernard Wysocki, Jr., "For Economist Paul Romer, Prosperity Depends on Ideas," *Wall Street Journal*, January 21, 1997.
5. Or their slaves, if one calls that ownership.
6. I am not including here the development of the recipes for food, which is entirely different, in terms of the industry involved and its appeal to the senses.
7. See, for example, "W. Arthur Lewis," Library of Economics and Liberty, accessed February 10, 2017, http://tinyurl.com/h5tyjzu.
8. Payson, Quality Measurement in Economics.
9. Payson, Economics, Science and Technology.
10. A mole of molecules or atoms is only a specific number of those molecules or atoms; that number is called "Avogardo's constant," which is approximately 6.022×10^{23}.
11. Those who know more about mining might also be quick to point out that my discussion is overly simplistic, since some of what I am calling "contaminants" would, in fact, be other minerals that would be extracted besides the main mineral that is being discussed.
12. Some might be quick to point out that competition in the production of higher-quality products will lead to a long-term equilibrium in which the profitability of the higher-quality products is lost, which is also taught in standard microeconomics. However, in products that are continually evolving in quality, that tendency never catches up—there is always profits to the new, higher-quality product, because new products keep entering before they can be fully mass produced by all potential suppliers.
13. Those familiar with *this* topic may ask, "Wait a minute, what about all the talk about Moore's Law?" Moore's Law did receive quite a bit of attention—I lectured on it myself—but in truth, it too was just a simple observation (that the number of transistors per square inch on an integrated circuit doubles every year).

14. One could ultimately say that this is not necessarily the case—that people could wear suits whose internal temperature was cool, and that the room would not have to be cooled, though this would be a different product.

15. For those with broader vision, this need not end here—virtually reality equipment could conceivably be replaced by neutrally implanted devices, if humanity ventures that far, and one can speculate beyond that as well, but I will not do that here.

16. Kelvin J. Lancaster, "A New Approach to Consumer Theory," *Journal of Political Economy* 74(2) (1966), 154–55.

17. Of course, this could be made more complex, where quality is not a "scalar" but a vector, in terms of the characteristics of goods, such as the food's provision of protein, fiber, various vitamins, etc., per unit calorie. The analysis could indeed be as complex as needed depending on the questions the researcher is trying to answer. I have simplified this discussion for ease of understanding and exposition.

18. See William Nordhaus, "Do Real Output and Real Wage Measures Capture Reality? The History of Lighting Suggests Not," Cowles Foundation Discussion Paper No. 1078, September 1994.

Chapter 11

Conclusion

What Must Be Done in Academic Economics

As suggested throughout this book, there are many aspects of the academic economics profession that I believe can induce any reasonable person into outrage, especially if they truly care about, believe in, and devoted their lives to, the field of economics. Some good examples of these aspects, which I have already discussed in this book, include: (1) How people can spend many months of work on a paper, and pay $200 to apply to have their paper considered by *American Economic Review*, while the journal expressly reserves the right to reject their paper out of hand, "without review." (2) How prominent professors may be paid millions of dollars to promote an advocacy position on a policy issue, but keep that funding a secret and pretend to present their research on the topic as if they were simply objective researchers pursuing their own independent interest in the topic. (3) How the only thing that many academic economists seem to care about is whatever they need to do to get their next publication, regardless of whether it contributes to anything useful. (4) How scapegoatism/dehumanization of federal officials is tolerated and sometimes even encouraged. (5) How, for the sake of publications, the profession focuses on highly advanced, esoteric, mathematical models of a separate reality, motivated more by mental self-gratification than by any real commitment to advance useful knowledge. (6) How the profession easily ignores interdisciplinary studies that offer better ways of understanding the economy, only because economics professors are generally disinterested in other fields. (7) How theorists in the profession often arbitrarily contradict the profession's own established theories. (8) How the profession finds itself scrambling around in data manipulations for the sake of acquiring "statistically significant" relationships that are, in actuality, neither important nor significant. (9) How foreign graduate students are exploited in their need to accumulate publications in order to acquire a teaching position so they can remain in the United States.

A STORY ABOUT "JUSTIFICATION"

In 2008–2010, I was organizing conferences and conference sessions for the Society of Government Economists (SGE), as a member of their board of directors, and where, in 2009–2010, I served as their president. During this time I managed the "selection process" by which papers were accepted or rejected to our own SGE conference, and to several sessions we had that were allotted to us by the American Economic Association (AEA) to fill during the AEA annual meetings (also called the "annual meetings of the Allied Social Sciences Association"). In spite of the name of our society, we had (and the SGE still has today) a great many members who are not government employees, nor even former government employees. That is, the SGE was always open to accepting members from all sectors who might have an interest in the economics done by government, and thus we had many members who were economics professors, private consultants and other private-sector economists, and economists from NGOs like the World Bank. We would even have members occasionally from libertarian organizations where these members had a career writing papers that often criticized the work of government economists.

Like most economic associations, we were not very selective in our acceptance of papers to our own conference, so that we could have a larger conference. However, the sessions we controlled for the AEA meetings involved an entirely different situation. First of all, the demand to be in one of those sessions was extremely high—it was prestigious to be in one, and so the fact that our association was allotted seven or eight of them (depending on the year), we had a valuable asset in this sense which legitimized us as a well-recognized, economics association. Since we only had seven sessions for the AEA meetings in 2009–10, but so many economists (including those from all sectors, not just government) with papers to present wanted to "get into the AEA meetings through us," we were forced to be fairly selective, accepting less than half of papers that people proposed to us.

The most contentious feature of our selection process, to some of the board members and to many of the paper applicants, was a particular requirement that I imposed (and the board approved) for the applications. Like most other economics associations with sessions at the AEA meetings, we did not require for the application a draft manuscript of the proposed paper, but only a proposed title and an abstract with a word limitation. In my view, for something as important to people's careers as an AEA conference paper (especially for junior economists in any sector), a title and short abstract, in a double-blind peer review process, is pretty thin and would make the selection process somewhat arbitrary. For example, someone who is a great writer, but not so good an economist, might be able to write an impressive abstract that could sound better than one written by an economist whose paper would probably be much better. Therefore, with the board's approval at that time, I imposed another requirement for the application—a brief *justification statement* (of 250 words or less)—to explain why the paper being proposed is a paper that we should accept to the AEA meetings. (The abstract, in contrast to the justification statement, only describes the paper in most cases but does not explain what makes the paper worth accepting.) To me, the justification statement with a 250-word maximum was not much to ask, and was important for several reasons at several levels. In association with explaining why the paper should be accepted, we suggested that the abstract explain how the paper contributes to a better understanding of economics.

Among the many reasons for our requiring the justification statement, perhaps the simplest and shallowest one was that the abstract alone did not provide enough information for the paper's selection. That is, many of the abstracts of papers waste no time in getting down to the technical weeds of the particular model the paper presents, which were simply not well understood by the economists in our selection committee who did not have specific and advanced knowledge of the particular topic of the paper. Thus, a justification statement would simply remove much of the guesswork in the selection process. At other levels, it seems that at justification statement is warranted by the simple concept that we should have a legitimate *justification* for accepting the paper, and in this regard, we are offering an opportunity to the proposer to *make their case*.

At an even broader level, we might recognize that a justification statement seems to be appropriate for *just about anything that involves important human decision making*. If one is applying for a research grant, some statement is surely needed as to why the funder should back the research in question—how is it beneficial to the funder, or how is it beneficial to society (if benefiting society is the funder's objective)? When one applies for a new job, it is common for the perspective employer to ask the applicant, "Why do you want this job? . . . How will our organization benefit from your coming on board?" Indeed, in my receiving a contract from my publisher to write this very book, it was surely necessary for me to provide an explanation of why this book should be written, sold, and read—this book, itself, needed a justification statement.

Unfortunately, it was quite sobering to me to learn that, in spite of how logical and sensible it was to me that we should require a justification statement for proposed presentations at AEA conference sessions, the idea was met with incredible difficulty from many of the economists who were proposing their papers to us. Many were perplexed by it, apparently never having had to write a justification statement for any research they had ever performed, or perhaps for anything else they have ever done in their lives.

We thus received many email messages from highly educated people raising questions like, "*What do you mean* when you ask for an explanation of why our paper is important, or contributes to valuable knowledge, or is beneficial for economics?" Although I would never respond to them with this thought, the thought that would automatically enter into my mind when hearing such questions was, "Wow! If you do not even know *why* your research is valuable and important, then why the heck are you doing it?" We received many protests and complaints about our justification requirement, and those board members who were originally opposed to it (but were outvoted at the time) recycled their stance on the issue, mentioning to me and the other SGE Board members, "A lot of people are complaining and asking why they are supposed to provide a justification statement to support their proposed paper! Now, what do you suggest we tell them?"

Over the next couple years, I found that I could not win the war of attrition that had developed over this issue within the SGE Board of Directors—eventually I had just become too tired to fight for it. After serving my time as the SGE president and as the manager of our selection process (which are positions that should be rotated in any case, for obvious reasons), the SGE fell back into removing any justification requirement in its applications for conference papers, and as far as I know, has never looked back. I wonder if some people were deeply opposed to it because there was an element of truth embedded in our request for a justification statement, which is a truth that some people may not want to admit to themselves—that their research, in fact, *did not have* much justification behind it, or at least whatever justification it did have was minor in comparison to all the other circumstances that determined why that research was being conducted. Such circumstances were just that—circumstances—like the authors simply having a particular background in the topic of their paper, perhaps from their dissertation work, and so it is much easier for them to pile new mathematical theory on top of mathematical theory that they already knew, than to start from scratch learning new theories about topics that might be more important or more relevant to current issues.

As I have also repeated incessantly throughout this book, the frame of mind of many of the paper proposers (even those who were not academics) was that the real *justification* for their research was the mantra that it will *contribute to the literature* when it gets published. That was their final goal, and to them, their obvious goal, other than having the conference presentation itself to add to their curriculum vitae, and to justify their organization providing the funding of their trip to the AEA meetings.

So what can we take from all this? The *punchline* is simple: *Many* (not all–but many) economists who present conference papers, and who, in a broader sense, perform economic research, *cannot even explain why they are doing it!* All they can utter is the pathetic explanation: "We wanted to do this *to contribute to the literature*." Likewise, they cannot tell you why anyone should *read* their paper, or what anyone should get out of their paper (besides its technical conclusions) other than the equally worthless words, "because they might find it interesting." *In their supposedly advanced minds, they essentially have no justification, or defensible reason, for what they are doing, and for that matter, think it is strange that they should be expected to have such a justification or defensible reason for what they are doing.*

If we take a minute to think about all this, as fellow colleagues living the life of the mind, there is only one conclusion that we can make from it, which is that *this situation is absolutely absurd*—how can this be happening in a field as incredibly important as economics? It is true because economists in general—and especially academic economists who have led and promoted this perspective—believe that publication, without other justification, is a perfectly fine end in itself. This is a profession that has become lost in its own simple, little, nonsensical world—a profession without self-reflection—without a sense of purpose—without a worthwhile cause—without a will, or a commitment, to do anything that is useful and important.

MY FAVORITE LOST-IN-SPACE EPISODE

In the same vein, I am reminded of an old television series that I used to watch in my childhood called *Lost in Space*. In 1966, episode 22 of the first season was called the "Magic Mirror" (which was in black and white in those days). The main character in that episode was a preteenage girl named Penny Robinson, played by the actress Angela Cartwright, who would later be seen as one of the children in the motion picture *The Sound of Music*. In the middle of the episode Penny winds up going through a mirror, into another world on the other side of the looking glass. (Of course, this was obviously not a very original idea by the writers of the show!) Once there, on the other side of the looking glass, Penny met a new companion—a boy who had a character similar to Peter Pan. He too, much earlier, had fallen into that alternative universe, and had never been able to escape from it.

While Penny was there, she struggled to find a way out, in order to get back to her home and family, and she finally did. She escaped by standing near a pool of water, seeing her reflection in the water, and shooting her reflection with a gun that she had found. This act of "shooting her own reflection" (as it was also termed in the episode itself) instantaneously transported her back to the real world on the other side of the mirror. Once there, she then waited for her new companion in that other world to join her by doing the same.

The boy wanted to follow her, and tried, but he could not perform the same task. While looking at the pool of water and pointing the gun to it, he sadly and quite emotionally said, "I can't do it. . . . I have no reflection." (And in the episode we are shown the pool of water without his reflection in it.) The basic idea was that he had been on the other side of the looking glass for so long that his reflection had completely faded away over time, and so, with nothing for him to shoot at—with no reflection for him to see—he was condemned to remain in that alternative universe for eternity.

Economics professors who perform unscientific, literature-only, theoretical work (of no value to anyone outside a small circle of other theoretical economists working on the same models) had been selected among those who are most inclined to believe in the value of their work. Alternatively, we might say that they have been selected and trained to be the *least concerned* about the true value of their work to society, in contrast to their seeing their work as justifiable by providing a living for them, along with a shallow list of superficial accomplishments in their curriculum vitas or in whatever they see from a RePEc search on their names. Like Penny's friend in the above-mentioned *Lost in Space* episode, they too may be unable to see their own reflection. They may thus be unable to *shoot* at their reflection (to critically evaluate what they are ultimately doing, and not doing). They may then be incapable of joining their colleagues on the other side of the looking glass, back in the real world.

ALL IS NOT LOST, EVEN IF YOU JUST LOVE MATHEMATICAL GAMES

Admittedly just about any type of analysis conducted to advance knowledge could be called a "game," and those involving mathematics could thus be called a "mathematical game." In this regard, economics itself is one big mathematical game. What a firm does to stay in business, for example, and to maximize its profits, is a mathematical game. It is a very important game that economists are expected to know how to play. It is mathematical games like this, in fact, that make economics, *economics*. There is nothing wrong with this, *per se*, but that does not mean that *any* mathematical game is justified in economics. The mathematical (and sociological) game of developing esoteric theories that can be published but have no value in any other sense is *not wrong because it is a game*! It is *wrong* because it is the *wrong game*, which economics professors should not be playing.

So what is the *right* game? It is one that rewards work that benefits society, and does not reward mental self-gratification as an end in itself, or cronyism and elitism. Economics professors need to sit down, roll up their sleeves, and figure out how to create, promote, and maintain this new game. It is an economics game; so economics professors have the ability to design it—they just need the will.

I am reminded again of Sandman's quip, discussed in chapter 2, about how, if technical people do not like the expression, "Risk = Hazard + Outrage," he has the answer: Write Risk = "a *function* of hazard and outrage." If nontechnical people ask what this actually means, he answers, it means "'Risk = Hazard + Outrage' in 'techy talk'".

Along the same lines, I have a solution to those readers, and perhaps those leaders of the academic economics community, who may scoff at my conclusion that all economics professors need is *a new game*. The solution to such scoffing is to forget I ever mentioned the word "game." Instead, pretend I said: "Economics professors need to develop a *new paradigm* for integrating what is socially beneficial about their work with the profession's system of incentives." For those who ask, "But what does 'a new paradigm' really mean?" No problem—I will tell you: It means "a new game," in techy talk.

MY FULLY EXPECTED COUNTERATTACK TO THIS BOOK

Some theoretical economists will personally not like hearing much of what this book has discussed, to say the least! There is a large body of prominent theoretical economists who are actively involved in publicizing theoretical economic literature, and that body is well organized and well funded, analogous, perhaps, to the National Rifle Association in its promotion of firearms in the United States. I have interacted with this group (of prominent theoretical economists I mean) myself at various times. If indeed this book were to begin to receive some attention, the first "line of defense" that would be implemented by the organized defenders of all theoretical economic literature, as it exists today, would be, of course, to downplay this book's existence. One possible strategy, then, by those who want to discredit this book for such political reasons might be to say publically that they know nothing about it, and to devise quips to fend off any questions that might come to them about it, such as in the following type of conversation:

Someone might ask a senior member of the profession, "Have you ever heard about the book, *How Economics Professors Can Stop Failing Us?*"

That person's reaction might then be, "No, I can't say that I have, but I must say, it sure sounds *pretty silly*! I'm sorry . . . but I only read serious books in economics. . . . I don't have time to read silly books that sound like '*witch hunts*'!"

"Really?" the first person might ask.

And, to this, the senior member might reply, "Oh, yes, our profession has always faced these kinds of *grandiose condemnations* by people who just don't like us, or who have an axe to grind against us, and we always will. No worries though—we have learned quite well how to ignore them, and we will certainly ignore this one as well!"

Like hikers in the woods who stop when they see, at a distance, a bear walking on the trail ahead of them, and wait until the bear has safely gone away, many leaders in the academic economics profession who do not like this book will ignore its existence and simply wait for it to go away. At least that will be their initial strategy. My hope, of course, is that enough attention will be raised about the arguments in this book that such a strategy will not be viable. (Readers who would also like this attention to be received can certainly help the profession in this regard!) After that, the possibilities for improvements to the profession are seemingly endless.

In any case, once leaders of the profession will find themselves needing to respond, they are most likely to claim that this book is highly distorted, prejudicial, and unfairly hostile. The tone of the reactions will change from a humorous dismissal of the book to the profession's leaders now claiming to be *unfairly victimized*. Oh, those poor people were picked on by a schoolyard bully!

Thus, after ignoring this book's existence does not work, the next measure by those who do not want the public to hear what it says would be to denigrate and diminish it as much as they possibly can, which might best be done by a peripheral attack on both its style and its author. The attack would probably involve accusations that it is highly unprofessional, immature, and clearly shows that, in spite of the author's claims to the contrary, he has "an axe to grind."

Similarly, accusations will undoubtedly be made that this book simply reflects *a complete lack of understanding* of what theoretical economic literature is all about. It will be said that the author simply does not realize that the objective of top-ranked literature is to extract only a part of what is going on in the world so that we could see how the individual parts work. To the contrary, I am fully aware of that principle, and have raised it myself in the economics classes that I have taught. And, I have presented extensive arguments as to why that principle is completely peripheral to my critiques of the profession. Nonetheless, I am confident that this accusation will come regardless. (I know this from my experience with some of the very people who will be likely to espouse it.)

Likewise, this book will most certainly be accused by some of the elite members of the profession as adopting an "amateurish," "unintellectual," and "unprofessional" posture on economic scholarship. In particular, they may comment that my continued use of the term "the *curse* of scholarship" reflects some kind of childish escapism that proves that I am unworthy of contributing to any reasonable discussion of the epistemology of economics.

The tiny fraction of academic economists who have contributed to literature on the relationship between economics and the philosophy of science, which, to me, is another publication game in its own right, may also join in and say that I was plebian and unimpressive in my discussion of the how theoretical economics is "unscientific." They will say that I have failed to read, understood, and summarize in this book the most advanced scholarly discourse on the topic (as if, in some alternative La-La Land, that was this book's purpose). As I have argued, scholarly discourse to explain the points that I make in this book, at the highest level of the art, would hardly be understood by most people, and would certainly never be read by anyone outside that tiny circle of academic economists who just happen to love the stuff. It would thus serve no useful purpose; it could only tell the members of this tiny group what they already know and believe. By my citing them profusely and studying their work they might happily welcome me to their club—a self-serving club that has done little to improve the profession. They may thus be insulted for how I have described them, as I have just described them now (I cannot blame them for that!), and they may then be inclined to retaliate in kind with criticisms of the book. But if they do it in a publication, they are giving the book points in the citation game (which is positive feedback in their world), so they are faced with a dilemma!

Others, especially some of those whom I have described in chapter 8 (on "Academic Economics at Its Dumbest and Ugliest") might be inclined to return the favor as well with sharp critiques of this book. But then again, they may remain quiet about it, so as not to draw attention to the book and its accusations. I hope that they do counterattack—let us hear what they have to say for themselves about the issues I have raised!

One of the other, completely different critiques that will surely be made of this book will be, "It says what is already known about academic economics, and what has already been said in much better ways." Such a statement will serve as a convenient device for those in the profession to discourage others, especially the public, to take any interest in these arguments under the pretense, "Yeah, yeah . . . we've heard it all before . . . there's nothing *new* to see here!"

Actually, this would be true, in part. It is, indeed, common knowledge among the vast majority of academic economists that most of the theoretical research performed by academic economists is simply a game—an intellectual game like chess or bridge, serving only two main purposes: the accumulation of credentials (and any pride that may come with it), and (for some) the self-amusement and gratification that comes with it.

Note that I said "most" in the above sentence, not "all," and that in this book I have mentioned and praised some extremely valuable theoretical work in economics. Nevertheless, those who are bent on criticizing this book will surely have trouble remembering this part of the book, and claim that I have *trashed ALL academic economics*, thereby intentionally suggesting that the book is delusional and written by an ignorant maniac.

As for the idea that the arguments in this book have been "better said" by other books, I would say that we should think carefully about what might be meant by "better said." Or, in broader terms, we should think about how the observations in the book would best be said. To this, I would argue that the answer depends greatly on the audience, and it is fair to assume that the audience in this case is quite varied—again I am not writing to the hundred people in the world who might regularly write articles for the journal *Economics and Philosophy* (though some of the criticism the book will receive will be based on such an assumption).

In spite of all this, I am, in fact, very hopeful for positive change in the profession. I also believe that the truth, that *most* (not all!) theoretical literature published in top-ranked journals is essentially worthless, would eventually be recognized by the public, with or without this book. And, I am hopeful that positive actions will be taken to address this horrific problem. I obviously wrote this book to serve as a catalyst for this eventual and desperately needed change in the profession.

FUNDAMENTAL FLAWS IN THINKING AND CULTURE

As this book has shown, the profession suffers enormously from fundamental flaws in perspectives, or in ways of thinking, and in its culture. One of the most fundamental of these flaws is that economics professors simply *do not know what to think about!* Most do not know *what to question*, or even why they should question *anything*. Their only interests are to knock out more journal articles as best they can, while still keeping up with all their teaching responsibilities. As this book has discussed, this perspective is something that they simply inherited, often without question, from the generations of economics professors before them; it is a perspective in which many economics professors have been thoroughly indoctrinated.

Some economics professors have actually escaped from this shallow (or worse) mind-set, by questioning whether the economics they do is correctly serving a useful function (in applications or in promoting a better understanding of the world), and by thinking seriously about fixing what they see is wrong. However, some of these individuals have unfortunately jumped out of the frying pan and into the fire in the new approaches they have taken to fix the problems that they have identified. In particular, it is not enough to criticize the profession validly, but then offer as a solution some alternative, esoteric theory on how things are wrong. Such efforts suffer from the same problem of being self-serving intellectualizations with the ultimate purpose of impressing and publishing, and remaining esoteric to avoid making waves, but with no hope of fixing any real problem.

In particular, BITSS appears to have identified some real problems, and appears to be addressing some of them, but remains motived to "contributing to the literature" as an ultimate end. Likewise, BITSS happily funnels money to professors to think deep thoughts and publish clever papers with sophisticated mathematical models on the lack of scientific integrity in the profession, and from there these professors walk away with pride that they have supposedly "done what they could."

BITTS is not alone. Like BITTS, the heavily funded Institute for New Economic Thinking, acts in the same way, at even a larger scale. The research they fund, and the papers they publish, often look great—*but is anyone asking what effect they have actually had?* (That is, what have these well-funded projects actually accomplished in terms of effecting real change in the profession, as opposed to simply creating another source of research grants, leading to publications that will barely be read and will do nothing to reduce the professions problems?

At the beginning of this book I joked about my not being an old hippie from the 1960s. However, there was one expression that was popularized in the 1960s by hippies, which will ring true for all human endeavors for eternity. It is the simple expression, "If you are not part of the solution, then you are part of problem." And, I do *not* see BITTS, or the Institute for New Economic Thinking, or any of the other relatively new grant programs that are supposedly addressing the problems identified in this book, as *being part of the solution*. What they and other similarly minded organizations have done is to absorb (if not to simply "pay-off"!) the critics of the profession, who might have otherwise approached the problem more aggressively and effectively, and perhaps might have otherwise been a *part of the solution*.

IS THERE AN ECONOMIST IN THE HOUSE?

Here is an undoubtedly facetious question, though I will ask it anyway: Are there any *economists* in the house? As I have argued elsewhere in this book, if we want to stop academic economists from producing *garbage*, the answer is not to produce more and more journal articles, explaining by way of an esoteric mathematical model, supported by globs of new data, how academic economists are simply producing garbage. As economists, we, of all people, should see the futility in this. An *economist* (if any of us happen to know any!) would state the following: To stop academic economists from producing waste at society's expense, *we need to stop paying them to do it!* We must end their research grants for producing waste, and more generally end the incentive system that supports it. As economists, how could we not realize this? Those who have the power and authority to end these incentives should do it, *now*!

At this writing I see three provocative articles advertised on the main webpage of the Institute for New Economic Thinking: "How Money Drives U.S. Congressional Elections," "The Value-Extracting CEO: How Executive Stock-Based Pay Undermines Investment in Productive Capabilities," and "Why Economists Should Think of Themselves as Plumbers." These look like good articles (though the second one I have seen recycled over and over again for about a decade by its author). In the same vein, The Institute for New Economic Thinking should support a study, containing guidance for actual *action*, regarding how most support for highly theoretical, self-serving, and for the most part *worthless*, economic literature should be eliminated, or drastically reduced, by a change in incentives, including a *defunding of such research*. This would cause the Institute to drift away from the happy, and at times incestuous, family of institutes and foundations (both governmental and private) that fund theoretical economic research. Sometimes it is worth losing friends if it is a necessary consequence of doing what is right, or as they say, one cannot make an omelet without breaking some eggs.

It is incumbent upon all governments, all influential government-like NGOs like the World Bank and the IMF, and all educational/charitable foundations like the Pew Charities and Rockefeller Foundation, to identify, and cease to support, worthless, literature-only discourse. The process of identifying research that should not be funded is not so hard—criteria have already been established in this book, and organizations can of course revise those criteria, make them their own, and operationalize them in any way they see fit.

At the simplest level, funding organizations could broaden the people they use to peer review grant proposals, to include experts who have expressed the same kind of criticisms of the profession that have been expressed in this book. These funding organizations should not rely entirely on peer reviewers who happen to be the most published experts on the particular topic of the proposal, as those reviewers would represent an extremely biased sample of economists who would be in favor of the provision of financial support for that topic area. By using, instead, more diverse and critical or skeptical peer reviewers, these funding organizations would be much better positioned to adequately scrutinize the grant proposals, and as a result, they may well reduce the waste that would otherwise be spent on worthless, literature-only theoretical research.

The addition of any new filter against literature-only theoretical research by these funding organizations would remove the misguided, blind faith these organizations currently have in the literature-producing system, and replace that misguided faith with a much more realistic, and much less naïve, perspective. Moreover, these organizations should, of course, *want* to do this, because they should easily recognize that they will continue to waste enormous amounts of money, and disserve the public, if they do not.

When *good scholarship* (that is committed to a useful purpose) and good activism (also committed to a useful purpose) are combined, along with a healthy dose of good entrepreneurial support to provide the resources—*this* is when successful, societal change can take place. The problem, unfortunately, is that great scholars are generally horrible at being activists or entrepreneurs; great activists are often horrible at being scholars or entrepreneurs; and great entrepreneurs are often horrible at being scholars or activists. It is not hard to find people who would get "an A" in any one of these three "classes," but those who do get an A in any one of them usually do no better than a D in the other two. It is this very problem, one could argue, that has kept the academic economics profession from moving past its obsession with playing the theory-publishing game, in spite of the common knowledge, even among the players, that the game is very wrong and extremely wasteful at best, and extremely harmful at worst.

If change for the better is going to happen, scholars who are interested in helping need to better acquaint themselves with activism and entrepreneurship, activists who are interested in helping need to be more scholarly and entrepreneurial, and entrepreneurs who are interested in helping need to be more scholarly and more supportive of activism.

WHAT LEADING ECONOMICS PROFESSORS NEED TO DO

As already mentioned, the first thing that leaders (senior faculty) must do, if they are at all capable, is to reevaluate and greatly reconsider where their loyalties lie. At present, their loyalties are divided across all of the following entities:

1. Their department (and by extension their university): its reputation (including especially its ranking), the money it receives from grants, and, if applicable, the prestige it enjoys from it having prominent professors.
2. The students: enabling them to enjoy their college experience, feel it was a valuable experience to them, and have an ability when they graduate to secure careers as a result of that experience.
3. The faculty in their department: making them feel good about being there so they do not leave.
4. The various other organizations to which they belong and may serve as an officer or board member, such as economic journals, and associations and societies.

5. Friends and collaborators: the colleagues with whom they have coauthored, people they have been friends with over the years, etc.
6. Economic science: the role they play in disseminating and advancing useful knowledge about economics, and their commitment to the world as leaders in the field.

As demonstrated throughout this book, item #6, commitment to the pursuit of useful knowledge, often directly contradicts item #1, upholding the department's reputation. These loyalties contradict each other especially with regard to assessing the value of the department's faculty on the basis of how many high-ranking publications they produce. Item #1 also effectively contradicts item #2, caring about the students, when the students wind up being taught by faculty who are focused much more on their research papers than on preparing for their classes (or faculty whom had been selected, at the start, with the skills to publish but not to teach). Likewise, depending on the faculty, item #1 may contradict item #3 (keeping the faculty happy) when those faculty members are pressured to produce high-ranking publications, while they would otherwise choose to pursue research that is more meaningful to them and more useful to society. Item #6 can also be contradicted by item #4 (serving journals, societies, and associations) and by #5 (staying close with friends and collaborators) when senior faculty encourage their friends and other members of their department to feed papers to those journals with which those senior faculty are affiliated, at the cost of having more research that would genuinely promote useful knowledge (though not get published in those particular journals).

The senior faculty need to rethink these loyalties and eliminate these contradictions. They could start by focusing on the only two ultimate loyalties that they should have: loyalty to the students (#2) and loyalty to economic science (#6). The other loyalties should then fall into place in turn. That is, their commitment to both will then, ultimately, promote the reputation of the department and university (#1), and make the faculty in their department happier in knowing that they are doing more meaningful work for their students and for society (#3). Such benefits should also rub off on their journals and associations (#4) and on their friends and colleagues (#5). However, in the short term, the journals (i.e., their editors) may not be happy about the loss of papers being sent to them for possible publication, and the loss of credit those journals may be receiving for making-and-breaking the careers of academic economists. As argued throughout this book, such a loss of influence by the journals would, for the most part, be a wonderful thing!

In terms of the specific actions that this reevaluation of loyalties will entail, here are suggestions for senior faculty based on arguments I have presented. Admittedly, these may be a bitter pill for senior faculty to swallow:

1. *Eliminate all publication-count scoring games in the hiring and promotion decision processes.*
2. If this does involve a change in the department's policy then stand by it, and take pride in it; if it is already a policy for the department not to use such a scoring game then take pride in that as well.
3. As a substitute for the publication-count scoring game institute a much better method of assessing the quality of candidates' work.
4. Announce to all potential candidates that the change is coming so that many can comfortably replace their current work to create top-ranked journal publications with preferred work for other (not necessarily top-ranked) journals or for books. Or, they may now simply choose to spend more time preparing their lectures for the benefit of their students.

Many economics departments appear, at least officially, to avoid playing the scoring game for publications. As an example, in my view the Department of Economics of the University of Minnesota has rather admirable "Standards for Promotion and Tenure" which include the following statements:

> Faculty research is expected to make a significant contribution to the body of economic science and/or offer important insights into significant policy issues. It is expected that members of the department will be leading researchers and may be directly influential in the formulation of economic policy. . . . The department has a national and international reputation for leadership in research and teaching, as evidenced, for example, by repeated high rankings in surveys of faculty quality and effectiveness of graduate programs. Accordingly, the Department values distinguished disciplinary and interdisciplinary research and teaching, and publicly engaged scholarship that disseminates knowledge about Economics and its practical application to widely diverse audiences. . . . "Scholarly research" must include significant publications and, as appropriate, the development and dissemination by other means of new knowledge, technology, or scientific procedures resulting in innovative products, practices, and ideas of significance and value to society. "Other creative work" refers to all forms of creative production across a wide range of disciplines. (p. 1–3)[1]

As the above quotation implies, the University of Minnesota's Economics Department produces high-quality economic research with the deliberate intention of making a significant contribution to the "body of economic science." All indications are that it does so without a publication-point scoring game in place. If this is true, then other economics departments at other universities should follow the University of Minnesota's lead.

What would greatly help the profession redefine itself in the right direction would be the infusion of *new required courses*, for all degrees in economics, on *professional ethics, scientific integrity, and responsible leadership in economics*. Such courses cannot be taught by just any of the existing professors, since they are largely unqualified to teach it, as this book has largely demonstrated! But, as this book has also demonstrated, there are exceptional economics professors who have already done much to lead the way in developing what such courses should teach, and some have already taught such courses that can be used as examples for other economics departments to adopt. These courses, in any case, need to focus on how economists should address practical issues and how we should commit ourselves to the development and dissemination of valuable knowledge.

FINALLY, THE NEED FOR COURAGE AND COMMITMENT

Virtually all of the arguments I have made in this book are simply not encountered among the vast majority of economic professors, or at least not encountered by them to any significant degree. These professors do not include the small minority who actually do take a genuine interest in whether their daily lives as economics professors are managed responsibly for both themselves and for society. "Defenders of the faith" (defenders of the status quo, that is) who feel a responsibility to fend off any criticisms at all of the economics profession, will be, as usual, very quick to throw up their hands and lament. "But what can we do? Just look at us measly little, nerdy, economics professors! We have no basis for ensuring that other measly little, nerdy, economics professors like us will produce valuable research. And besides, who are *we* to tell *them* what to do?"

It is indeed ironic how the most prominent members of the economics profession will proudly, confidently, and often arrogantly advise the leaders of entire nations on economic policy, telling them at times to lay off hundreds of thousands of government workers, or end wars, or stop climate change, etc., but when it comes to an effort to make any change in their own profession, they cry that they are powerless!

As discussed earlier in chapter 8, the AEA, acting much like a labor union, though led by many people who staunchly oppose labor unions, used its clout in 1981 to organize eight Nobel laureates in economics to write a letter to the Reagan administration in the White House to save the National Science Foundation's grant program in economics, which was providing plenty of funding to academic economists (especially at the top-ranked schools) to support their research and even to help financially support their enrolled graduate students. It is amazing to see how organized, powerful, and influential certain groups like the AEA can be when money is involved—a principle, I believe, that is quite consistent with well-established economic theory!

Yet, the same prominent economists, who could bring issues to the attention of the highest leaders of the nation, and get substantial, successful results from these efforts, turn into *shy little kittens* when it comes to acknowledging their capability to straighten out what they, themselves, have already identified as being wrong with their own profession. Part of this inability to act or to acknowledge the legitimacy of such criticisms comes from a pathetically shallow pseudo-loyalty to the *image* of the profession as if that image were a dear friend, and criticizing her would appear disloyal and ungrateful for "everything that she has done for us!" To many of them, they may also become *frightened little kittens*—afraid that any negative publicity against economic theory might damage the *gravy train* of research funding that they have enjoyed so much for decades (and which their deans continue to expect from them).

In short, there is a conflict of interest in which many prominent leaders in academic economics feel they should defend the profession against any negative publicity, even if that negative publicity is true, and even if it will lead, in the end, to a much-improved profession. As already suggested, they may even confuse such behavior as a reflection of *loyalty* on their part. Yet, as I mentioned in the first chapter, in my view, such beliefs would most certainly reflect *disloyalty!* Economics professors should be most loyal, not to themselves (which, in itself, contradicts the definition of loyalty), but to the people they purport to serve—to their students, and more generally, to society overall which depends entirely on good economics for its infinitely important policy decisions (and ultimately for its survival).

Economics professors who have the most recognition and authority in the profession have certainly accomplished great things, individually. I believe that many of them could not have risen to their prominence merely by contributing to literature-only discourse—many have probably also advanced valuable knowledge in economic thought. At the same time, let us not kid ourselves; they most likely also, either directly or indirectly, have promoted and supported literature-only discourse during their careers and are probably doing now at this very moment.

I realize that professors often feel a responsibility to make decisions that are in the best interests of their university and department. Therefore, even if they know that it would be "doing the right thing," how many of economics professors would suddenly advocate a policy that would ultimately cause the other professors in their department to receive fewer grants, or cause their department to fall in status from having fewer publications? How many would want to do that unilaterally, even if other professors in their department, and outside their department, stood firm to the status quo acceptance of literature-only discourse? How many would maintain such a stance of opposing literature-only discourse when they are then being accused of betrayal by their colleagues and their superiors? There is, indeed, a "prisoner's dilemma" implicit in this situation. Because of this prisoner's dilemma problem and other problems mentioned throughout this book, prominent professors are simply not able to support this change, and if they do not, the more junior members of the profession will be even less capable of supporting it.

At the beginning of this book I argued that there is no good reason why economic thought should defer from the purpose of advancing valuable knowledge. Indeed, complacency, laziness, and cowardice are not good reasons. However, I believe that the pathetic dysfunctionality of the academic economics profession has finally reached the point of being widely recognized by both the members of the profession, and by the public. Thus, the show is over; it is time for economics professors to close the curtain and walk off the stage. At the close of the show, economics professors can now begin to consider taking up a new occupation—one involving a commitment to teach students about economics in the best way possible, and to contributing to valuable knowledge in the field of economics.

NOTE

1. Department of Economics, University of Minnesota, "Standards for Promotion and Tenure," November 6, 2009, accessed February 10, 2017, http://tinyurl.com/hgpnnwf.

Bibliography

"1993 Jack in the Box E. Coli Outbreak." Wikipedia. Accessed February 5, 2017. http://tinyurl.com/pgaoxvs.

"AEACGR: Contact the Committee: Government Relations Office." American Economic Association. Accessed February 5, 2017. http://tinyurl.com/zmuefh3.

American Economic Association. "American Economic Review." Report of the Editor. American Economic Review, Papers and Proceedings, 104(5) (2014) 621–31.

American Economic Association. "Disclosure Policy." Accessed February 4, 2017. http://tinyurl.com/hm5tzgc.

American Economic Association. "The American Economic Review: Submission Guidelines." Accessed April 7, 2015. https://www.aeaweb.org/aer/submissions.php.

American Finance Association. "Code of Ethics & Guidelines." Accessed February 5, 2017. http://tinyurl.com/hyvthbd.

American Indian Higher Education Consortium. "TCU Roster and Profiles Profiles." Accessed February 5, 2017. http://tinyurl.com/zs6bmek.

American Mathematical Society. "American Mathematical Society Policy Statement on Ethical Guidelines." Accessed February 5, 2017. http://tinyurl.com/qdpe9pk.

American Physical Society. "Ethics and Values: 02.2 APS Guidelines for Professional Conduct." accessed February 5, 2017. http://tinyurl.com/j6cjjcw.

American Statistical Association. "Ethical Guidelines for Statistical Practice." Accessed February 5, 2017. http://tinyurl.com/hv654rt.

Andersen, Hans Christian. "The Emperor's New Clothes" in Hans Christian Andersen, Fairy Tales Told for Children. Copenhagen, Denmark: C.A. Reitzel, 1837.

"Andrei Shleifer." Wikipedia. Accessed June 24, 2016, http://tinyurl.com/z757fu5.

Anton S. Troianovski. "Shleifer to Resume Teaching." The Harvard Crimson, April 24, 2006.

Arce, Daniel, Walter Enders, and Gary Hoover. "Plagiarism and Its Impact on the Economics Profession." Bulletin of Economic Research 60(3) (2008): 231–43.

"At Scale – Computer Definition." Your Dictionary. Accessed February 7, 2017. http://www.yourdictionary.com/at-scale.

Berkeley Initiative for Transparency in the Social Sciences. "Mission and Objectives." Accessed February 7, 2017. http://www.bitss.org/about/.

Berkeley Initiative for Transparency in the Social Sciences. "Mission and Objectives." Accessed February 9, 2017. http://www.bitss.org/about/.

Berkeley Initiative for Transparency in the Social Sciences. "Partners." Accessed February 9, 2017. http://www.bitss.org/about/partnerships/.

Berkeley Initiative for Transparency in the Social Sciences. "The Catalyst Program." Accessed February 9, 2017. http://www.bitss.org/catalysts/.

"Bernt P. Stigum." The MIT Press. Accessed February 4, 2017. http://tinyurl.com/zolsv8l.

Blaug, Mark. The Methodology of Economics or How Economists Explain. New York: Cambridge University Press, 1992.

Bureau of Labor Statistics. "American Time Use Survey User's Guide: Understanding ATUS 2003 to 2013." June 2014, http://www.bls.gov/tus/atususersguide.pdf.

Bureau of Labor Statistics. "American Time Use Survey." Accessed October 25, 2014. http://www.bls.gov/tus/home.htm.

Bureau of Labor Statistics. "American Time Use Survey: Table A-1. Time spent in detailed primary activities and percent of the civilian population engaging in each detailed primary activity category, averages per day by sex, 2013 annual averages." Accessed October 25, 2014. http://www.bls.gov/tus/tables/a1_2013.pdf.

Burwell, Sylvia Mathews. "Impacts of the Cost of the Government Shutdown." White House Report, November 7, 2013. Accessed February 5, 2017. http://tinyurl.com/zgtaq9b.

Caputo, Michael R. "The Intrinsic Refutable Implications of Rational Addiction Theory Are Not Observable, while the Comparative Dynamics that Are, Are Not Refutable," Accessed April 3, 2015. http://tinyurl.com/zw9ud2f.

Card, David and Stefano DellaVigna. "Nine Facts about Top Journals in Economics." National Bureau of Economic Research, Working Paper 18665, January 2013.

"Cengage." Accessed February 5, 2017. http://tinyurl.com/za3m6k8.

Christensen, Garret and Edward Miguel. "Transparency, Reproducibility, and Credibility of Economics Research." National Bureau of Economic Research Working Paper 22989, December 2016.

Ciarelli, Nicholas M. and Anton S. Troianovski. "'Tawdry Shleifer Affair' Stokes Faculty Anger Toward Summers." The Harvard Crimson, February 10, 2006.

Clarke, Harry. "Professional Ethics for Economists: Notes on DeMartino." August 12, 2013. Accessed February 4, 2017. http://tinyurl.com/gv7ab93.

Colander, David. "Creating Humble Economists: A Code of Ethics for Economists." In The Oxford Handbook of Professional Economic Ethics, edited by George DeMartino and Deirdre McCloskey, 737–38. New York: Oxford University Press, 2015.

Colander, David. "The Ethical Quandary of Positive Versus Normative Economics." Paper presented at the seminar of the Association for Integrity and Responsible Leadership in Economics and Associated Professions, entitled "Principles of Ethics, Scientific Integrity, and Responsible Leadership: A One-Day Training Seminar for Economists." Chicago, January 8, 2017.

Colander, David. The Making of an Economist, Redux. Princeton, NJ: Princeton University Press, 2008.

Collins English Dictionary, "Scapegoat." Accessed March 4, 2007, http://tinyurl.com/j72yuyr.

Collins English Dictionary. "Scapegoatism." Accessed March 4, 2007. http://tinyurl.com/j99t9gs.

Conley, John P. and Ali Sina Önder. "The Research Productivity of New PhDs in Economics: The Surprisingly High Non-Success of the Successful." Journal of Economic Perspectives, 28(3) (2014): 205–16.

Copeland, Larry. "Life Expectancy in the USA Hits a Record High." USA Today, October 9, 2014.

DaVinci Instititute. "Niels Bohr and Albert Einstein." February 28, 2016. Accessed February 2, 2017. http://tinyurl.com/jaofd8u.

Dekker, Erwin and Arjo Klamer. "About Doing the Right Thing as an Academic Economist." In The Oxford Handbook of Professional Economic Ethics, edited by George DeMartino and Deirdre McCloskey, 101–15. New York: Oxford University Press, 2015.

DiLorenzo, Thomas. Organized Crime: The Unvarnished Truth about Government. Auburn, Alabama: Mises Institute, 2012.

DeMartino, George. "Econ Ethical Codes of Conduct." Accessed February 5, 2017. http://tinyurl.com/jxapaj4.

DeMartino, George. "Harming Irreparably: On Neoliberalism, Kaldor-Hicks, and the Paretian Guarantee," Video of presentation at the 15th annual Summer Institute for the History of Economic Thought, University of Richmond, August 13, 2015. http://tinyurl.com/gp39ldw.

DeMartino, George. The Economist's Oath: On the Need for and Content of Professional Economic Ethics. New York: Oxford University Press 2011.

Department of Economics, University of Minnesota. "Standards for Promotion and Tenure." November 6, 2009. Accessed February 10, 2017. http://tinyurl.com/hgpnnwf.

Dictionary.com. "Scapegoat." Accessed March 4, 2007. http://tinyurl.com/zqro5g3.

Dictionary.com. "Scapegoatism." Accessed March 4, 2007. http://tinyurl.com/hyjjpqc.

Eckel, Catherine. "Economic Games for Social Scientists." In Laboratory Experiments in the Social Sciences, edited by Murray Webster, Jr. and Jane Shell, 497–516. Burlington, MA: Elsevier, 2007.

"Econ Journal Watch, *Watch*." Ethical Economics Support. December 22, 2015. http://tinyurl.com/j2hqnwo.

"Economic Science Association." Accessed February 5, 2017. http://tinyurl.com/zwapz88.

"Economics and Ethics." Accessed February 5, 2017. http://tinyurl.com/h4h5kny.

eMarketer. "Social Usage Involves More Platforms, More Often; Growing Interest in More In-Person Connectedness." July 2, 2013. http://tinyurl.com/p3hf46a.

Enders, Walter and Gary Hoover. "Whose Line Is It? Plagiarism in Economics." Journal of Economic Literature, 42(3) (2004): 487–93.

Engemann, Kristie and Howard Wall. "A Journal Ranking for the Ambitious Economist." Federal Reserve Bank of St. Louis Review 90(3) (2009): 127–39.

European University Institute. "Salaries in Economics in US Academia 2010–11." Last updated April 23, 2012. Accessed on February 12, 2017. http://tinyurl.com/n6ux7d9.

Ferguson, Charles H., Audrey Marrs, Chad Beck, Adam Bolt, Matt Damon, Paul A. Volcker, George Soros, et al. The film Inside Job. 2011.

Figlio, David, Morton Schapiro, and Kevin Soter. "Are Tenure Track Professors Better Teachers?" National Bureau of Economic Research Working Paper # 19406. September 2013.

Fisher, Franklin M. and Karl Shell. The Economic Theory of Price Indices: Two Essays on the Effects of Taste, Quality, and Technological Change. New York: Academic Press, 1972.

Friedman, Daniel and Shyam Sunder. Experimental Methods: A Primer for Economists. New York: Cambridge University Press, 1994.

Friedman, Milton. Essays in Positive Economics. Chicago: University of Chicago Press, 1953.

Fuchs, Stephen. "A Sociological Theory of Scientific Change." Social Forces 71(4) (1993): 933–53.

Galbraith, John Kenneth. Economics and the Public Purpose. New York: New American Library, 1975.

George, Donald A.R. "Quality Measurement in Economics: New Perspectives on the Evolution of Goods and Services. By Payson. Steven." Book Review. Economic Journal, 105(428) (1995): 233–35.

Goolsbee, Austan. "Does Government R&D Policy Mainly Benefit Scientists and Engineers?" American Economic Review 88(2) (1998): 298–302.

Griliches, Zvi. "Productivity, R&D, and the Data Constraint." Presidential Address to the American Economic Association. American Economic Review 84(1): (1994): 1–23.

Helpman, Elhanan and Manuel Trajtenberg. "A Time to Sow and a Time to Reap: Growth Based on General Purpose Technologies." In General Purpose Technologies and Economic Growth, edited by Elhanan Helpman, 55–84. Cambridge, MA: MIT University Press, 1998.

Hitler, Adolf and Ralph Manheim. Mein Kampf. Boston: Houghton Mifflin, 1972.

Hodson, Derek. "Re-thinking Old Ways: Towards a More Critical Approach to Practical Work in School Science." Studies in Science Education, 22 (1993): 85–142.

Hoover, Gary. "Plagiarism in the Social Sciences." Accessed February 10, 2017. http://tinyurl.com/gllslxc.

"Ideals of the Ku Klux Klan." Jackson Sun. October 1960. Accessed May 7, 2017, http://tinyurl.com/l9zyqaa.

IDEAS/RePEc. "Economics, Science and Technology." Accessed June 16, 2016, http://tinyurl.com/znca9kr.

IDEAS/RePEc. "Recursive Impact Factors for Journals." Accessed November 27, 2016. http://tinyurl.com/jnf2ybg.

IDEAS/RePEc. "Simple Impact Factors for Journals." Accessed February 4, 2017. http://tinyurl.com/z3pvmf5.

IDEAS/RePEc. "Top 10% Authors, as of December 2016, with Details." Accessed June 20, 2016. http://tinyurl.com/hgnxbc8.

Internal Revenue Service. "SOI Tax Stats - Individual Statistical Tables by Filing Status." Table 1.3 All Returns: Sources of Income, Adjustments, Deductions, Credits, and Tax Items. August 12, 2013. Accessed July 17, 2014. http://tinyurl.com/pmqv35q.

IPA: Innovations for Poverty Action. "What We Do" Accessed February 9, 2017. http://www.poverty-action.org/about/what-we-do.

James Madison University, Department of Economics. "Criteria for Promotion and Tenure Decisions." Amended July 2010. Accessed February 4, 2017. http://tinyurl.com/hkzp568.

Kalaitzidakis, Pantelis, Theofanis Mamuneas, and Thanasis Stengos. "An Updated Ranking of Academic Journals in Economics." The Rimini Centre for Economic Analysis, WP 15_10, April 2010. Accessed February 4, 2017. http://tinyurl.com/jcxq2k8.

Keen, Steve. Debunking Economics-Revised, Expanded and Integrated Edition: The Naked Emperor Dethroned. London, Zed Books, 2011.

Keeports, David and Dean Morier. "Teaching the Scientific Method." Journal of College Science and Teaching, September/October 1994: 45–50.

Kelman, Steven. "Cost-Benefit Analysis: An Ethical Critique," AEI Journal on Government and Society Regulation, January/February 1981, 33–40.

"Kelvin John Lancaster." Columbia|Economics. Accessed February 5, 2017. http://tinyurl.com/hlgroux.

Klein, Daniel. "The People's Romance: Why People Love Government (as Much as They Do)." The Independent Review, 10(1) (2005): 5–37.

Klein, Daniel. "If Government is so Villainous, How Come Government Officials Don't Seem Like Villains? With a New Postscript." In The Dynamics of Intervention: Regulation and Redistribution in the Mixed Economy (Advances in Austrian Economics, Volume 8), edited by Peter Kurrild-Klitgaard, 223–44. Bingly, UK: Emerald Group Publishing Limited, 2004.

Kodrzycki, Yolanda and Pingkang Yu. "New Approaches to Ranking Economics Journals." Federal Reserve Bank of Boston Working Paper 05–12, 2005. Accessed February 4, 2017. http://tinyurl.com/zaoht8d.

Koob, George F. "The Potential of Neuroscience to Inform Treatment." National Institute on Alcohol Abuse and Alcoholism. Accessed May 5, 2017. http://tinyurl.com/mc6edo4.

Krugman, Paul. "How Did Economists Get It So Wrong?" New York Times, September 2, 2009.

Lancaster, Kelvin J. "A New Approach to Consumer Theory." Journal of Political Economy 74(2) (1966), 132–57.

Leontief, Wassily. "Theoretical Assumptions and Nonobserved Facts." Presidential Address to the American Economic Association. American Economic Review, 61 (1971): 1–7.

Lipsey, R.G. and Kelvin J. Lancaster. "The General Theory of the Second Best." The Review of Economic Studies 24(1) (1956): 11–32.

Livingston, Gretchen. "The Odds that You Will Give Birth to a Boy or Girl Depend on Where in the World You Live." Fact Tank, September 24, 2013, Pew Research Center. Accessed February 4, 2017. http://tinyurl.com/mjmwfgc.

Maiese, Michelle. "Dehumanization." Beyond Intractability, July 2003. Accessed February 5, 2017. http://tinyurl.com/2nhpaz.

Malakoff, David. "Does Science Drive the Productivity Train?" Science Magazine, August 25, 2000, 1274–5.

Mata, Tiago and Tom Scheiding. "National Science Foundation Patronage of Social Science, 1970s and 1980s: Congressional Scrutiny, Advocacy Network, and the Prestige of Economics." Minerva 50(4) (2012): 423–49.

Marx, Karl, Friedrich Engles, Samuel Moore, and David McLellan. The Communist Manifesto. Oxford: Oxford University Press, 1992.

Mayer, Thomas. Truth Versus Precision in Economics. Hants; UK: Edward Elgar, 1993.

McCloskey, Deirdre. "Mr. Max and the Substantial Errors of Manly Economics." Econ Journal Watch 5(2) (2008):199–203.

McCloskey, Deirdre. "Rhetoric Matters: The Case for Standards of Ethical Conduct in Economics." Paper presented at a session on "Examining the Practice of Ethical Economics" organized by the Association for Integrity and Responsible Leadership in Economics and Associated Professions, San Francisco, January 4, 2009.

McCloskey, Deirdre. "The A-Prime C-Prime Theorem." Eastern Economic Journal. 19(2) (1993): 235–38.

McPherson, Michael A., Myungsup Kim , Megan Dorman, and Nishelli Perera. "Research Output at U.S. Economics Departments." Applied Economics Letters 20(9) (2013): 889–92.

National Association of Forensic Economics. "NAFE's Ethics Statement." Accessed February 5, 2017. http://nafe.net/Ethics.

National Science Board. Science and Engineering Indicators—1996. Washington, DC: U.S. Government Printing Office, 1996. http://tinyurl.com/zlkxjgp.

National Science Foundation. "Economics." Accessed February 11, 2017. http://tinyurl.com/ju7r2dl.

National Science Foundation. "Division of Physics: Investigator-Initiated Research Projects (PHY)." Accessed February 11, 2017. http://tinyurl.com/jho45a8.

Noerpel, Tony. "The Con in Economics." Blue Ridge Leader, March 5, 2013. Accessed February 4, 2017. http://brleader.com/?p=10734.

Nordhaus, William. "Do Real Output and Real Wage Measures Capture Reality? The History of Lighting Suggests Not." Cowles Foundation Discussion Paper No. 1078, September 1994.

Ormerod, Paul. The Death of Economics. New York: John Wiley & Sons, 1997.

Oxford Online Dictionary. "whimsy." Accessed February 5, 2017. http://tinyurl.com/zfmsg8c.

Pappas, Christopher. "Top 10 Free Plagiarism Detection Tools." eLearning Industry, November 18, 2013. http://tinyurl.com/jf2ufzo.

Payson, Steven. "Regardless of Philosophy, Economics Will Not Be a Science Until it is Based on Science." Journal of Post Keynesian Economics 19(2) (1996): 257–74.

Payson, Steven. Economics, Science and Technology. Northampton, MA: Edward Elgar, 2000.

Payson, Steven. Public Economics in the United States: How the Federal Government Analyzes and Influences the Economy. Santa Barbara, CA: ABC-Clio, 2014.

Payson, Steven. Quality Measurement in Economics: New Perspectives on the Evolution of Goods and Services. Brookfield, VT: Edward Elgar Publishing Company, 1994.

Pearl, Judea. Causality: Models, Reasoning, and Inference. New York: Cambridge University Press. 2000.

Puzo, Mario and Francis Ford Coppola. Screenplay for the film The Godfather. 1972.

Reinberg, Steven. "Americans Living Longer Than Ever: CDC." HealthDay, January 6, 2014.

Rosenberg, Alexander. Economics—Mathematical Politics or Science of Diminishing Returns? Chicago: University of Chicago Press, 1992.

Rothstein, Jesse. "Teacher Quality Policy When Supply Matters." American Economic Review 105(1) (2015): 100–30.

Rothstein, Jesse. Curriculum Vitae. Accessed February 4, 2017. http://tinyurl.com/zhopeba.

Sailer, Steve. "Economist Andrei Shleifer Demoted by Harvard." The Unz Review: An Alternative Media Selection, October 15, 2006. Accessed February 4, 2017. http://tinyurl.com/gobf4qn.

Samuelson, Paul. "Discussion." American Economic Review 53(2) (1963): 232–236.

Samuelson, Paul. Foundations of Economic Analysis. Cambridge, MA: Department of Economics, Harvard University, 1947.

Sandman, Peter. "Introduction to Risk Communication. 2016". Video recorded lecture. Accessed February 3, 2017. https://vimeo.com/166620414.

Schneider, Andrea and Klaus W. Zimmerman. "Fairness and Its Price" Review of Social Philosophy 70(2) (2012): 181–199.

Scott, Charles S. and John J. Siegfried: "American Economic Association Universal Academic Questionnaire Summary Statistics", American Economic Review: Papers & Proceedings 101(3) (2011): 664–67.

Shogren, Jason F., Seung Y. Shin, Dermot J. Hayes and James B. Kliebenstein. "Resolving Differences in Willingness to Pay and Willingness to Accept." American Economic Review, 84(1) (1994): 255–70.

"Significance." Oxford Dictionary. Accessed February 4, 2017. http://tinyurl.com/zlcmegg.

Smith, Adam. "An Inquiry into the Nature and Causes of the Wealth of Nations. Cannan edited by Vol. 2 [1776]." Accessed February 5, 2017. http://tinyurl.com/gszbea2.

Smith, Adam. An Inquiry into the Nature and Causes of the Wealth of Nations. London: William Strahan, 1776.

Smith, Herman. "Real Smart Folks, But No Wheel." Accessed October 25, 2014. http://ambergriscaye.com/museum/digit4.html.

Smolin, Lee. The Trouble with Physics: The Rise of String Theory, the Fall of Science, and What Comes Next. New York: Houghton Mifflin, 2006.

Social Capital Gateway. "Ranking of Economics journals based on the Impact Factor." Accessed February 4, 2017. http://tinyurl.com/jkpodms.

Solow, Robert. "A Contribution to the Theory of Economic Growth." Quarterly Journal of Economics, 70(1) (1956): 65–94.

Solow, Robert. "Building a Science of Economics for the Real World." Prepared Statement to the House of Representatives, Committee on Science and Technology, Subcommittee on Investigation and Oversight, Washington, DC, July 20, 2010, 2–3. http://tinyurl.com/j7tpxfo.

Springer. "Scientometrics." Accessed February 4, 2017. http://tinyurl.com/hjxapuz.

Staiger, Douglas and Jonah Rockoff. "Searching for Effective Teachers with Imperfect Information." Journal of Economic Perspectives 24(3) (2010): 97–118.

Stern, David. "Uncertainty Measures for Economics Journal Impact Factors." Journal of Economic Literature 51(1) (2013): 173–89.

Stiglitz, Joseph. "Needed: A New Economic Paradigm." Financial Times, August 19, 2010.

Stiglitz, Joseph E., Amartya Sen, and Jean-Paul Fitoussi. "Report by the Commission on the Measurement of Economic Performance and Social Progress." Report to the President of the France, September 14, 2009. Accessed February 5, 2017. http://tinyurl.com/jafwpoq.

Swan, Trevor. "Economic Growth and Capital Accumulation." Economic Record, 32(2) (1956): 334–361.

"The Death of Economics." Amazon. Accessed December 8, 2016. http://tinyurl.com/jnb2qw6.

Thurow, Lester. Dangerous Currents: The State of Economics. New York: Random House, 1983.

U.S. News and World Report. "Higher Education: Search Online Colleges." Accessed September 30, 2016. http://tinyurl.com/674epbp.

U.S. News and World Report. "National Universities Rankings." Accessed September 30, 2016. http://tinyurl.com/3kf92xy.

Varian, Hal R. Microeconomic Analysis: Second Edition. New York, NY: W.W. Norton & Company, 1984.

Virginia Tech. "2014–15 Tuition and Fees." Accessed July 17, 2014. http://tinyurl.com/jaq27t6.

"W. Arthur Lewis." Library of Economics and Liberty. Accessed February 10, 2017. http://tinyurl.com/h5tyjzu.

White, Robert W. and Norman F. Watt. The Abnormal Personality. New York: The Ronald Press Company, 1973.

Wong, Stanley. "The 'F-Twist' and the Methodology of Paul Samuelson." American Economic Review 63(3) (1973): 312–25.

World Health Organization. "Metrics: Disability-Adjusted Life Year. DALY." Accessed October 27, 2014. http://tinyurl.com/3rt842h.

Wysocki, Bernard Jr. "For Economist Paul Romer, Prosperity Depends on Ideas." Wall Street Journal, January 21, 1997.

Ziliak, Stephen and Deirdre McCloskey. "Lady Justice Versus Cult of Statistical Significance: Oomph-less Science and the New Rule of Law." In The Oxford

Handbook of Professional Economic Ethics, edited by George DeMartino and Deirdre McCloskey, 352–366. New York: Oxford University Press, 2015.

Ziliak, Stephen and Deirdre McCloskey. The Cult of Statistical Significance: How the Standard Error Costs Us Jobs, Justice, and Lives. Ann Arbor: University of Michigan Press, 2008.

Ziliak, Stephen and Edward Tether-Posadas. "The Unprincipled Randomization Principle in Economics and Medicine, in The Oxford Handbook of Professional Economic Ethics, edited by George DeMartino and Deirdre McCloskey, 423–52. New York: Oxford University Press, 2015.

Index

About the Author

Steven Payson has over thirty-two years of professional experience in economics, having worked as an economic consultant for over three years at ICF Incorporated (starting in 1979), as an associate at the Inter-American Development Bank (from 1987 to 1991), and as federal government economist for the next twenty-five years at the National Science Foundation and the Departments of Agriculture, Commerce, and Interior. He has also taught economics, as an adjunct faculty member, at Columbia University, Trinity College (in Washington, DC), American University, Marymount University (in Virginia), Virginia Tech, and most recently Georgetown University where he taught classes on the "Economics of Technology, Innovation, and Growth." In the Commerce Department, Dr. Payson served as chief of the Special Studies Branch, and then chief of research, in the Government Division of the Bureau of Economic Analysis. In the past six years he has been a senior economic advisor in the Department of the Interior, first under the assistant secretary for Indian affairs, and then in the Bureau of Safety and Environmental Enforcement. In 2006, Dr. Payson founded the Association for Integrity and Responsible Leadership in Economics and Associated Professions (AIRLEAP®)—a 501(c)3 nonprofit organization whose board of directors is chaired by Distinguished Professor Deirdre McCloskey. For the past eleven years he has been the executive director of AIRLEAP, where he has organized many conference sessions and training seminars for economists on professional ethics, scientific integrity, and leadership responsibility, featuring many of the world's most leading experts on these topics. In 2009–2010, he also served as the president of the Society of Government Economists. Dr. Payson wrote his first book in 1994, which was based on his dissertation three years earlier: *Quality Measurement in Economics: New Perspectives on the Evolution of Goods and Services*. He then wrote, in 2000, *Economics,*

Science and Technology, and in 2014 he edited a three-volume set, containing forty-four chapters written by sixty authors, entitled *Public Economics in the United States: How the Government Analyzes and Influences the Economy*. In addition to his new book on *How Economics Professors Can Stop Failing Us: The Profession at a Crossroads*, Dr. Payson is now completing another book with Lexington Books, entitled *The Downsizing of Economics Professors: How It Will Happen, and Why It Will Succeed.* Dr. Payson received a bachelor of arts degree in 1979 from Wesleyan University in Connecticut, a master's of science degree in economics from the London School of Economics in 1982, and a PhD in economics from Columbia University in 1991. For work he has performed in the government, Dr. Payson received a bronze medal from the Bureau of Economic Analysis, and a gold medal from the Department of the Interior.